OXFORD QUICK REFERENCE

The Oxford Dictionary of **Musical Terms**

Alison Latham has edited several music reference books, including the *Cambridge Music Guide*, the *Oxford Companion to Music*, and the *Oxford Dictionary of Musical Works*, as well as books on Giuseppe Verdi and Alexander Goehr.

VISIT ONLINE
OXFORD
QUICK
REFERENCE

The Oxford Dictionary of

Musical Terms

EDITED BY
ALISON LATHAM

UNIVERSITY PRESS

OXFORD
UNIVERSITY PRESS

Great Clarendon Street, Oxford OX2 6DP

Oxford University Press is a department of the University of Oxford. It furthers the University's objective of excellence in research, scholarship, and education by publishing worldwide in

Oxford New York

Auckland Bangkok Buenos Aires Cape Town Chennai
Dar es Salaam Delhi Hong Kong Istanbul Karachi Kolkata
Kuala Lumpur Madrid Melbourne Mexico City Mumbai
Nairobi Shanghai São Paulo Taipei Tokyo Toronto

Oxford is a registered trade mark of Oxford University Press
in the UK and certain other countries

Published in the United States
by Oxford University Press Inc., New York

First published 2004

British Library Cataloguing in Publication Data
Data available

Library of Congress Cataloging-in-Publication Data
The dictionary of musical terms / edited by Alison Latham.
p. cm. — (Oxford paperback reference)
ISBN 0-19-860698-2
1. Music—Dictionaries. 2. Music—Terminology. I. Latham, Alison. II. Series.
ML108.D576 2004
780'.14-dc22

2004021958

ISBN 978-0-19-860698-7

Typeset in Swift and Frutiger by SPI, Pondicherry, India
Printed in Great Britain by Clays Ltd, Elcograf S.p.A

Preface

Anyone who is interested in or involved with music—the collector of recordings, the concert-goer, the teacher, the student, the performer—will encounter numerous terms in several languages, whether in CD booklets or programme notes, in scores or parts, in reviews, or in specialist musical literature. Such terminology is complex, and can represent a formidable barrier. This dictionary is designed to be a ready reference to musical terms, conceived with the intention of enhancing the user's understanding and enjoyment of this great art form.

The present book focuses on the constituent elements of Western art music: pitch, modality/tonality, scales, intervals, chords, rhythm, metre, analysis, melody, harmony, counterpoint, notational systems, signs, tempo and expression marks; it also covers terms used in compositional procedures (e.g. canon, fugue), performance practice, and tuning systems. Forms (e.g. rondo) are described, as are genres (e.g. symphony), musico-liturgical subjects, and elements of dance where they impinge on the musical canon. Aesthetic terms which have been applied to music (e.g. Impressionism) and those used to define historical eras (e.g. Baroque), now part of musico-historical vocabulary, are elucidated. Numerous musical abbreviations are explained.

It is impossible to define certain complex musical genres without reference to their history and evolution; 'sonata', for example, has denoted different forms at different periods. But such historical background has been kept to a minimum, in favour of succinct definition. Readers who would like historical surveys of genres and their composers (and indeed much else) are referred to *The Oxford Companion to Music* (Oxford University Press, 2002; ed. Alison Latham), from which many of the entries in this dictionary are drawn.

The proportion of articles' length, one to another, is a subject for which lexicographers are often taken to task. It may seem odd, for instance, that in the present dictionary the definition of sonata form is longer than that of the sonata as a genre. That is deliberate editorial policy: the purpose of this book is to clarify the terminology associated with the way music is constructed and notated rather than to provide a survey of its history and exponents.

Pam Coote, of Oxford University Press, initiated this dictionary. I am most grateful to her, and to her colleagues Joanna Harris and Lisa Begley, for their help with its production. Polly Fallows contributed invaluable advice and expert copy-editing, for which I thank her.

Alison Latham
Pinkneys Green
July 2004

How to use this dictionary

Translations of terms and their commonly used foreign-language equivalents are given in round brackets at the beginning of relevant entries. Alternative names or spellings are given in square brackets. Abbreviations in common usage (e.g., i.e., etc.) are not explicated in a separate list. Languages are abbreviated as follows: Amer., Cz., Dan., Eng., Fr., Ger., Gk., Heb., Hung., It., Lat., Pol., Port., Rom., Rus., Sp., Sw. Musical abbreviations are defined in the appropriate alphabetical place.

Terms included in this dictionary to which useful further reference may be made are marked with an *asterisk if they occur in the text of an entry; otherwise the reader is directed to 'see also' one or more entries listed at the end.

Pitches are notated *C*, *c*, *c''*, *c'''* etc, where *c'* is 'middle' C.

How to use this dictionary

A. 1. The sixth degree (submediant) of the scale of C major (*see* SCALE, 1). It is commonly used as a standard in the tuning of instruments, and orchestras tune to 'concert A'. *See* PITCH. **2.** Abbreviation for *alto or *altus. **3.** Abbreviation for *antiphon.

a (It.), **à** (Fr.). 'With', 'for', 'to', 'at'. Terms beginning with this preposition or its compounds are normally given under the word or first noun immediately following, e.g. *a *battuta, a bene *placito, a *cappella, à la *pointe d'archet*. In early music, the Italian form refers to the number of voices in a polyphonic work ('*a* 2' means in two voices); in music after *c*.1700 it indicates that two instruments should play the same line.

ab (Ger., 'off'). A term indicating the removal of a mute or an organ stop.

ABA, ABACA. Symbolization for, respectively, *ternary and *rondo form, in which the different letters represent the various thematic or structural sections.

abandonné (Fr.), **abbandonatamente, con abbandono** (It.). 'Free', 'relaxed'.

abbassare (It., 'to lower'). A specific type of *scordatura in which the string of an instrument of the violin family is tuned to a lower pitch than usual so that a note outside its normal compass may be obtained.

abbellimenti (It.). 'Embellishments'; *see* ORNAMENTS AND ORNAMENTATION.

abdämpfen (Ger.). 'To damp down', 'to muffle'—i.e. to mute, especially in connection with timpani.

Abendmusik [Abendlied] (Ger., 'evening music', 'evening song'). The series of concerts held at the Marienkirche in Lübeck, Germany, during the 17th and 18th centuries.

Abgesang (Ger.). The final, contrasting strophe of **Bar* form.

abgestossen (Ger., 'separated'). An 18th-century violin *staccato.

abnehmend (Ger., 'decreasing', 'subsiding'). **Diminuendo*.

abridged sonata form. A form closely related to *sonata form. Its 'abridgment' lies in the fact that, in the development section, new thematic material is presented rather than a development of the themes of the exposition.

absetzen (Ger.). **1.** 'Remove', 'take off'. **2.** In 16th-century music *absetzen in die Tabulatur* means 'to transcribe into tablature'.

absolute music. Instrumental music that exists, and is to be appreciated, simply as such, in contradistinction to *programme music.

absolute pitch. The ability to identify any note heard, or sing any note on demand, without a pitch reference; this faculty is also known as 'perfect pitch'.

abstract music. 1. Another term for *absolute music. **2.** A term used by some German writers (*abstrakte Musik*) to mean music lacking in sensitivity, 'dry' or 'academic' in style.

Abstrich (Ger.). In string playing, 'down-bow'.

abwechseln (Ger.). 'To exchange', i.e. to alternate instruments in the hands of the same player.

Abzug. 1 (Ger., 'a drawing down'). A term used in the 16th and 17th centuries in connection with a lute tuning where the lowest string is lowered a whole tone (*im Abzug*) or, by extension, for an extra, open string, added below the stopped courses (*mit Abzügen*). *See* SCORDATURA. **2** (Ger., 'departure', 'withdrawal'). An *appoggiatura that makes a decrescendo onto the principal note, or a trill with only one repercussion, i.e. the equivalent of the inverted *mordent.

a cappella (It.). 'In the church style'; *see* CAPPELLA.

accarezzevole, accarezzevolmente (It.). 'Caressing', 'caressingly'.

accelerando, accelerato (It.). 'Becoming faster'; it is usually abbreviated to *accel.*

accent. 1. Emphasis given to a particular musical event by a sudden increase (or, occasionally, decrease) in volume (dynamic accent), a lengthening of duration (expressive lengthening), a slight anticipatory silence (articulation), or a combination of these. The dynamic accent is the most common type and may be indicated by any one of a number of signs or markings, for example >, –, *fz*, *sf*, *sfz*, *fp*, or the short slur. Expressive lengthening may also be indicated by the sign '–'. Certain notes may be 'self-accenting' because of their relatively high or low position. 'Metrical accentuation' can be used to give extra emphasis to strong beats in a bar, or to throw the listener off balance by emphasizing weak beats (*see* BEAT, 1; SYNCOPATION). *See also* DYNAMIC MARKS. **2** (Fr.). The *springer. **3** (Fr.). An *appoggiatura that inserts a grace note between two notes a 3rd apart, or that repeats the first of two notes a 2nd apart.

acciaccatura (It., 'crushed note'; Fr.: *pincé étouffé*; Ger.: *Zusammenschlag*). A late Baroque keyboard *ornament. It consists in the simultaneous striking of the main note with a dissonant auxiliary note (usually one step below), the latter being released immediately. The acciaccatura was used for emphasis in arpeggiated chord-playing. The term 'acciaccatura' is incorrectly used for the short *appoggiatura, represented by the sign 𝆔.

accidental. A sign used in musical notation either for a note outside the given key of a piece of music or to cancel such a note. The sharp raises the note before which it is placed by one semitone; the flat lowers it by one semitone; the double sharp and double flat respectively raise and lower it by a whole tone; the natural cancels any other accidental. These signs and their names in English, French, German, and Italian are shown in Table 1 (their early shapes are given in parentheses where applicable). A sign is valid for the note that it precedes (but not for the same note in octaves above or below) throughout the rest of the bar, unless expressly contradicted by another sign. Some composers frequently add bracketed accidentals in order to clarify complicated passages or chords. However, in music before 1700 (and even some later) an accidental is not valid for the entire bar but only for the note before which it occurs and for immediate repetitions of the same note. Where an accidental affects a note which is tied over a bar-line, it remains valid for the tied note in the following bar. In modern scholarly editions, accidentals recommended by the editor are usually placed

Accidental, TABLE 1

	♯	♭	× (✱, ⧣)	♭♭	♮
English	sharp	flat	double sharp	double flat	natural
French	dièse	bémol	double dièse	double bémol	bécarre
German	Kreuz	Be	Doppelkreuz	Doppel-Be	Auflösungszeichen, Quadrat
Italian	diesis	bemolle	doppio diesis	doppio bemolle	bequadro

in small type above the relevant notes, to distinguish them from those that appear in the original sources.

accolade (Fr.). *Brace.

accompagnato (It.). 'Accompanied': hence *recitativo accompagnato*, a *recitative accompanied by instrumental ensemble rather than by continuo alone. The gerund *accompagnando* designates a subsidiary part.

accompaniment. The musical background for a principal part or parts. The accompaniment is usually instrumental; the relation between it and the principal part varies from the subordinate to an essential part of the texture or musical idea, notably in the 19th-century song.

accoppiare (It.). *See* ACCOUPLER.

accord (Fr.; It.: *accordo*). **1.** *'Chord'. **2.** The 'tuning' of an instrument. *See* ACCORDATURA.

accordatura (It.). 'Tuning'. A term used both generally and for the normal tuning of stringed instruments, in contrast with special tunings (e.g. *scordatura).

accorder (Fr.). 'To tune'; *accordé, accordée*, 'tuned'.

accordo (It.). *'Chord'.

accoupler (Fr.; It.: *accoppiare*). 'To couple'. The term is used in connection with organ stops, hence *accouplé* (Fr.), *accoppiato* (It.), 'coupled'; *accouplement* (Fr.), *accoppiamento* (It.), 'coupling', 'coupler'; *accouplez* (Fr.), an instruction to couple.

accusé, accusée (Fr.). 'With emphasis'.

acht (Ger.). 'Eight'; *Achtel, Achtelnote*, 'eighth', 'eighth-note', i.e. the *quaver; *Achtelpause*, 'quaver rest'; *achtstimmig*, in eight voices or parts; *Achtfuss*, an 8′ organ stop.

acoustic. Related to the sense of hearing or the science of sound (acoustics). The term is often applied to the quality of a building with regard to the way music or speech is transmitted within it. It is sometimes applied to instruments relying on an air-filled resonator or soundbox to transmit their sound, to distinguish them from those amplified electronically.

act tune. The instrumental music played between the acts of a play or *semi-opera in the English theatre of the late 17th and early 18th centuries. *See also* INCIDENTAL MUSIC.

actus musicus (Lat., 'musical action'). In German Protestant music of the 17th and 18th centuries, a semi-dramatic vocal composition based on a biblical story. It is similar in form and function to the contemporary Lutheran *historia*, but more elaborate, and was a forerunner of the German *oratorio.

adagietto (It., dim. of *adagio*). Slow, but less so than *adagio; it is also used as a movement title.

adagio (It.). A tempo indication which, when it first appeared in the early 17th century, and from the 19th century onwards, generally meant 'very slow', the equivalent of *lento* or *largo*; in the 18th century it sometimes implied that ornamentation was necessary. In some earlier music it probably meant 'leisurely' (between *largo* and *andante*). It has occasionally been qualified as *adagissimo* (still slower). The term 'adagio' is often also used for the slow movement of a multi-movement work, irrespective of whether it is so marked.

added sixth chord. A triad, usually the subdominant, with an extra note, the 6th (in the key of C major: F–A–C–D); this chord can be thought of as the supertonic 7th chord in first inversion. In strict harmony, the chord should resolve onto the dominant or tonic chord, but many composers have used it purely for effect. It is a popular final chord in jazz.

addolcendo (It.). Becoming **dolce*.

addolorato (It., 'pained'). Sadly.

a

à deux (Fr.), **a due** (It.), **a 2.** A term with two opposite meanings, depending on the context. Applied to two orchestral instruments notated on the same staff (e.g. flutes 1 and 2), it indicates that they should play in unison. Applied to a group of instruments that usually play in unison (e.g. first or second violins), it means that they are to divide into two bodies, each taking one of the two lines notated on the staff (*see* DIVISI). Similarly, in vocal or instrumental music *a* 2, *a* 3, and so on, indicate division into that number of parts. *À deux mains* (Fr.) and *a due mani* (It.) mean 'for two hands'; *à deux voix (choeurs)* (Fr.) and *a due voci (cori)* (It.), 'for two voices (choirs)'. The terms *à deux cordes* (Fr.) and *a due corde* (It.), 'on two strings', are used to indicate that the same note should be played on two strings together, in order to increase the tone power.

adiastematic neumes. Neumes (*see* NOTATION) that give an idea of melodic movement without recording exact pitch, and that give less information on relative pitch than *heighted neumes or *diastematic neumes.

adjunct. A term applied to notes inessential to the harmony, such as accented or unaccented *passing notes.

adoración (Sp.). A Latin American religious folksong, synonymous with *aguinaldo* and *villancico.

a due (It.). *See* À DEUX, A DUE, A 2.

Aeolian mode. The authentic *mode on A.

affabile (It.). 'Affable', i.e. in a gentle, pleasing manner.

affannato, affannoso (It.). 'Breathless', 'agitated'.

affections, doctrine of (Ger.: *Affektenlehre*). A term formulated in the early 20th century to describe an aesthetic theory of the Baroque period relating to musical expression. Following Ancient Greek and Latin orators who believed that the use of certain modes of *rhetoric influenced the emotions, or affections, of their listeners, the theorist-musicians of the late 17th and early 18th centuries argued that the 'affection' of a text should be reflected in its musical setting through an appropriate key and qualities of melody, thus arousing a suitable affection in the listener. *See also* FIGURES, DOCTRINE OF.

Affekt (Ger.). 'Fervour'; *affektvoll*, 'full of fervour'; *mit Affekt*, 'with warmth', 'with passion'. In Germany in the Baroque era the term was used to describe the expressive character of a piece. *See also* AFFECTIONS, DOCTRINE OF.

Affektenlehre (Ger.). *See* AFFECTIONS, DOCTRINE OF.

affetto, affetti (It., 'affection', 'affections'). **1.** A term that appears in the title of various late 16th- and early 17th-century publications, probably to emphasize the 'affective', 'emotional', character of the music. *See* AFFECTIONS, DOCTRINE OF. **2.** In early violin sonatas, a type of ornament (*tremolo or *arpeggio).

affettuoso, affettuosa (It.). 'Affectionate', 'tender'; *con affetto* (It.), *affectueusement* (Fr.), 'with affection', i.e. warmly. The term was used in the 17th and 18th centuries for slow movements; as an independent tempo indication, it falls between *adagio* and *andante*.

affrettando (It.). 'Hurrying'.

agevole (It., 'comfortable'). Lightly and freely.

aggiustamente, aggiustatamente (It.). 'Exact' (in rhythm).

aggradevole (It.). 'Pleasing'.

aggregate. A term used to denote a passage in which each note of the chromatic scale is present once. It is commonly used in the analysis of atonal music, usually in the '12-note aggregate'.

agiatamente (It., 'comfortable'). Freely; not to be confused with *agitatamente* (*see* AGITATO).

a

agile, agilement (Fr.). 'Agile', 'with agility'.

agitato (It.). 'Agitated', 'restless'; *agitatamente*, 'in an agitated manner'.

Agnus Dei (Lat., 'Lamb of God'). Part of the Ordinary of the *Mass, sung during the Breaking of the Bread.

agogic (from Gk. *agōgē*, 'leading'). **1.** A term used to describe accentuation demanded by the nature of a particular musical phrase rather than by the regular metric pulse of the music (metrical accentuation). The following, for example, may be given prominence by a slight expressive lingering conferring the effect of an *accent: the first note, highest note, or final cadence of a phrase; a note significantly higher or lower than the preceding notes and reached by a leap; or a pungent discord about to resolve to a concord. **2.** In a wider sense, 'agogic' refers to aspects of expression in performance created by rhythmic modification, e.g. *rallentando*, *accelerando*, rubato, or pause.

agréments (Fr.). A generic term for the 'small ornaments' found in 17th- and 18th-century French music. *See* ORNAMENTS AND ORNAMENTATION.

aguinaldo (Sp.). *See* ADORACIÓN.

ähnlich (Ger.). 'Similar', 'like'.

air. 1. A term used in England from the 16th century to the 19th to mean a song or melody. *See also* AYRE. **2.** In France in the 16th century, *air* denoted a solo song with lute accompaniment. There were several types, including the **air de cour* and the **air à boire*. The term could be applied to instrumental as well as vocal music in 17th- and 18th-century stage works, the *airs* providing interludes between passages of accompanied recitative. There were four main types of operatic *air*: the 'dialogue' *air*, with continuo accompaniment, used as an alternative to recitative; the 'monologue' *air*, usually an extended piece on the scale of the Italian aria, reserved for moments of emotional crisis or reflection; the 'maxim' *air*, a lighthearted reflection on the trials of life, often sung by secondary characters; and dance-songs. **3.** As in France, in England in the early 17th century the instrumental air formed part of such stage entertainments as the *masque. **4.** The air became an optional movement in the Baroque and Classical *suite, generally lyrical rather than dance-like.

air à boire (Fr.). 'Drinking-song'. A simple type of *air* (*see* AIR, 2) which enjoyed great popularity in France in the late 17th and the 18th centuries.

air and variations. *See* VARIATION FORM.

air de cour (Fr., 'court *air*'). A type of short strophic song cultivated in France during the late 16th century and the first half of the 17th. It was usually for four or five unaccompanied voices or for solo voice with lute or keyboard.

Ais (Ger.). The note A♯; *Aisis*, the note A𝄪.

aisé (Fr.). 'With ease', i.e. unhurried.

ajouter (Fr.). 'To add' (e.g. an organ stop).

Akkord (Ger.). 'Chord'.

Akzent (Ger.). 'Accent', 'stress'; *akzentuieren*, 'to accentuate', 'to stress'.

alba (Provençal). A 'dawn song' that describes lovers parting, usually including a dialogue with a watchman who warns them of approaching danger. It was absorbed into the Minnesinger repertory as the *Tagelied*.

Alberti bass. A type of accompaniment to a melody, most commonly found in keyboard music, which consists of a series of 'broken chords' treated as shown in Ex. 1 (see overleaf). It takes its name from the 18th-century Italian composer Domenico Alberti, in whose harpsichord sonatas it occurs frequently.

alborada (Sp.). 'Morning song'. The word is applied to a type of instrumental music, sometimes played on bagpipes

Alberti bass, Ex. 1

and small drum, in which rhythmic freedom is a striking characteristic. *See also* ALBA; AUBADE.

album-leaf (Fr.: *feuille d'album*; Ger.: *Albumblatt*, pl. *Albumblätter*). A 19th-century title for a short instrumental piece (generally for piano), usually of an intimate character and dedicated to a friend or patron.

aleatory music. Music in which chance or indeterminacy are compositional elements. The term (from the Latin *alea*, 'game of dice') gained currency during the second half of the 20th century. Aleatory music was a reaction against the strict notational conventions of postwar avant-garde composition, in favour of allowing interpreters an element of freedom of choice. This might involve varying the order of precisely notated events, or determining the contents of events themselves in the light of new notational practices which avoided specifying every detail of pitch, rhythm, and dynamic. *See* INDETERMINATE MUSIC.

all', alla (It.). 'To the', 'at the', i.e. in the manner of, e.g. **alla zingarese*.

alla breve (It.). An indication meaning 'double the speed', so that, for example, 4/4 is given the effect of 2/2 (i.e. the basic time unit becomes the minim, rather than the crotchet shown in the time signature).

alla marcia (It.). 'In the style of a march'.

alla mente (It., 'according to inclination'). An improvised passage.

allant (Fr.). **1.** 'Going', i.e. **andante*; *un peu plus allant*, 'a little more quickly'. **2.** 'Continuing', e.g. *allant grandissant*, 'continuing to grow', i.e. getting louder.

alla Palestrina (It.). 'In the style of Palestrina', i.e. of 16th-century *a cappella* polyphony. By the 17th century this was termed the *stile antico* or *stile osservato*. It was revived in the 19th century by the Cecilian Movement, which advocated a return to polyphony in Roman Catholic church music.

allargando (It.). 'Broadening', i.e. becoming slower, often with an accompanying crescendo.

alla turca (It., 'in the Turkish style'). A term applied to music of the Classical period composed in a supposedly Turkish style, often involving percussion instruments, derived from the traditions of *janissary music.

alla zingarese (It.). 'In the Gypsy style'.

alla zoppa (It., 'lame', 'limping'). **1.** A term used in the 17th century to describe dance movements in syncopated rhythm. **2.** A term used more specifically to describe a rhythm where the second quaver of a 2/4 bar is accentuated. *See also* SCOTCH SNAP.

alle (Ger.). 'All', i.e. tutti (*see* TUTTO).

allegramente (It.), **allégrement** (Fr.). 'Brightly'; *see* ALLEGRO.

allegretto (It., dim. of *allegro*). A tempo faster than *andante* but slower than *allegro* and in a lighter style. The term is also used for a short piece or movement with the tempo marked *allegretto* or *allegro*.

allegro (It.). 'Bright', 'lively'. The term was originally used as an expression mark rather than a tempo indication, e.g. *allegro e presto*, *andante allegro*, but it now simply means 'quick'. It is also used for a fast piece or movement, particularly the first movement, in sonata form, of a sonata, symphony, or similar multi-movement work.

allein (Ger.). 'Alone'; e.g. *eine Violine allein*, 'one solo violin'.

alleluia. The Latin form of the Hebrew exclamation 'hallelujah' ('praise the Lord'). It became traditional as a part of the Proper of the Roman Mass, sung between the gradual and the Gospel.

allemande (Fr., 'German'; It.: *alemana, allemanda*) [alman, almaine]. A couple dance popular from the early 16th century to the late 18th; as an instrumental form it was one of the four standard movements of the Baroque *suite. Music for the allemande was in moderate duple time and was frequently followed by a more lively afterdance in triple time (the 'tripla'). The instrumental allemande developed from the 17th century onwards; there are examples for ensembles and solo instruments such as the lute, guitar, and keyboard. In the Baroque suite, the allemande, in binary form, was generally in quadruple time, and with a flowing, imitative character; it was often followed by a courante using the same thematic material. By the beginning of the 19th century, 'à l'allemande' meant simply any dance 'in the German style', for example the ländler.

allentando, allentamente (It.). 'Slowing down'; *see also* RALLENTANDO.

allmählich (Ger.). 'Gradually'.

allo. Abbreviation of **allegro*.

all'ongarese (It., 'in Hungarian style'). Music in the 'Hungarian' style, i.e. based on Gypsy dances, became popular in the early 19th century.

alman [almain]. *See* ALLEMANDE.

al segno (It., 'to the sign'). An indication to go to the sign (𝄋), meaning either 'return to the sign' (i.e. the same as *dal segno*), or 'continue until you reach the sign'. *See also* DA CAPO.

alt. 1 (It.). 'High'; term for the notes of the octave in the range *g'* to *f''*, which are said to be *in alt* (those in the octave above are said to be *in altissimo*). It is usually used with reference to the voice. **2** (Ger.). 'Alto' (contralto) voice. As a prefix to the names of instruments, it signifies the alto voice of a family.

alta (It.). **1.** 'High'. **2.** A 15th-century dance form, the equivalent of the *saltarello. **3.** A standard loud music (*alta musica*) ensemble in the 15th century, consisting of two (sometimes three) shawms and a slide trumpet or, later, a sackbut. *See also* HAUT, BAS.

altered chord. A chord which has one or more of its notes chromatically altered by accidentals foreign to the key. The most common altered chords are the *Neapolitan 6th and the three kinds of *augmented 6th.

alternatim (Lat., 'alternately'). The term describing performance by two (occasionally more) performers or groups of performers in alternation. It is most commonly found in the singing of psalms and canticles, where alternate groups of singers have performed alternate verses since the late 4th century, a manner of performance that survives as *antiphonal psalmody. The more ancient practice of responsorial psalmody contrasted a soloist with congregation or choir; the soloist sang the verses of the psalm and the others responded with a refrain. From the 15th century, the organ was increasingly used as a substitute for vocal polyphony (*see* VERSET). The most notable repertory of *alternatim* organ music is from 17th- and 18th-century France.

alternativo (It.), **alternativement** (Fr.). A term often used in 18th-century dance music for a contrasting middle section, later known as 'trio'. Sometimes the term is applied to the entire piece, in which case it implies that the two contrasting sections may be 'alternated' at the performer's discretion.

altiste (Fr.). **1.** 'Viola player'. **2.** Alto (contralto) singer.

alto (It., 'high'). **1.** For the male alto, *see* ALTO VOICE. **2.** A low-register female voice, properly referred to as *contralto. (In the standard choir grouping SATB, the A usually refers to the contralto part but can also denote the male-voice part.) **3.** The middle-pitched member of a family of instruments, with a range lower than treble or soprano and higher than tenor. (Fr.). **4.** 'Viola'.

alto clef. *See* CLEF.

alto voice. The male alto has a range of some two octaves, from about F below middle C to the soprano *e''* or even *f''*, although it is rare to find a singer who can sing throughout this range with ease, some concentrating on the upper registers, others on the lower. The male alto is sometimes distinguished from the *countertenor on the grounds that the former is a 'natural' high tenor, using the head voice with a powerful, even heroic sound, while the latter is produced as a *falsetto, tending towards the lower part of the range and having a comparatively weak sound; but usually the two terms are interchangeable.

altro, altri; altra, altre (It.). 'Another'; 'others'.

altus (Lat., 'high'). In early vocal music, the abbreviated form of *contratenor altus* ('high [part] against the tenor'), the voice part immediately above the tenor in a vocal ensemble. *See* CONTRATENOR.

alzato [alzati] (It., from *alzare*, 'to raise', 'to lift off'). A direction to remove, for example, a mute in instrumental playing.

amabile (It.). 'Amiable', 'lovable'.

amarevole, amarezza (It.). 'Bitterly', 'bitterness'.

ambitus (Lat., 'circuit'). The range of a melody in Gregorian chant.

Amen (Heb., 'so be it'). The terminal word of prayer in Jewish, Christian, and Muslim worship. It has been extended many times by composers into a lengthy composition. Shorter settings have been made for liturgical use.

Amen cadence. *See* CADENCE.

amener (Fr., 'to lead'). A 17th-century dance in triple time, usually with dotted notes on the second beat, a type of *branle.

amore (It., 'love'; Fr.: *amour*). **1.** A term found in expression marks, e.g. *amorevole*, *amoroso* (It.), 'loving'; *amorevolmente*, *amorosamente* (It.), 'lovingly', 'tenderly'. **2.** When attached to instrument names (e.g. viola d'amore, flûte d'amour), the term implies a richer and rounder tone than that of the normal instrument and probably a lower pitch.

amoroso (It.). 'Loving', 'affectionate'. *See also* AMORE, 1.

anacrusis (from Gk. *anakrousis*, 'a striking up'). An unstressed note or group of notes at the beginning of a phrase of music, forming an *upbeat. The term is also used of poetic metre.

analysis. The study of musical structure without reference to any factors beyond the music itself. The analytical process generally involves breaking the structure down into its component parts and investigating the way in which they combine to make a coherent whole. There are many methods and types of analysis, including by theme, by form (D. F. Tovey), by fundamental structure (Heinrich Schenker), by phrase structure (Hugo Riemann), set theory and computer technology (Allen Forte), and information theory.

anche (Fr.). 'Reed' on a wind instrument.

ancora (It.). **1.** 'Again', an indication to repeat a section. **2.** 'Still', 'yet', e.g. *ancora più forte*, 'still louder'.

andächtig (Ger.). 'Devoutly'; *mit Andacht*, 'with devotion'.

andamento (It., 'walking'). An 18th-century term for 'sequence' (*see* SEQUENCE, 1), or for a fugal subject which is longer than usual.

andante (It., 'walking'). Moderately slow; since the late 18th century it is taken to indicate a speed between *adagio and *allegro. *Più andante* or *molto andante* generally means slower than *andante*. The term is also used for a piece or movement in a moderately slow tempo and of a less solemn nature than an Adagio.

andantino (It.). The diminutive of *andante*, now taken to indicate a tempo slightly less slow than *andante*, though in the 18th century it implied a tempo slower than *andante*. The term is also used for a piece or movement at such a tempo.

Anfang (Ger.). 'Beginning'; *vom Anfang*, 'from the beginning', is thus equivalent to **da capo*.

angenehm (Ger.). 'Pleasant'.

anglaise (Fr., 'English'). **1.** A 17th- and 18th-century country dance, usually in quick duple time. **2.** Any dance thought to be connected with England (e.g. the *hornpipe).

Anglican chant. A simple harmonized melody for singing the unmetrical texts, chiefly the psalms and the canticles, of Anglican services. The main principle of 'single' chants is that of the Gregorian tones: a short two-part melody is repeated to each verse of the text, the varying numbers of syllables in the different lines being accommodated by the flexible device of a reciting note at the opening of each line, while the succeeding notes are sung in time and (normally) take one syllable each. Chants accommodating two verses are called double chants. There are a few triple and quadruple chants but they are rarely used. Early Anglican chants were adapted directly from Gregorian tones and resemble continental **falsobordone*. The number of chants sung in cathedrals and colleges proliferated after 1660, when the melody was moved from the tenor to the soprano.

angosciosamente (It.). 'With anguish'.

ängstlich (Ger.). 'Anxiously', 'uneasily'.

anhalten, anhaltend (Ger.). 'To hold on', 'continuing'.

Anhang (Ger.). 'Appendix', 'supplement'. A term used in scholarly editions of music to denote the appendices which may contain alternative readings or variants of certain portions of the music or text. It can also be used for appendices to catalogues, listing additional works.

anhemitonic scale [tonal scale]. A *scale with no semitones, i.e. one of the four pentatonic scales or a whole-tone scale.

animando (It.). 'Animating'; *animandosi*, 'becoming animated'; *animato* (It.), 'animated'. Often used to qualify *allegro*, it implies (increasingly) rapid tempo.

animant (Fr.). 'Lively'; *en animant*, 'becoming more lively'.

animé (Fr.). 'Animated', i.e. at a moderately quick tempo.

animo, animoso (It.). 'Spirit', 'spirited'.

anmutig (Ger.). 'Graceful'.

anreissen (Ger., 'to tear at'). In string playing, an exceptionally forceful pizzicato.

Ansatz (Ger.). **1.** On wind instruments, *'embouchure'. **2.** On stringed instruments, 'attack'. **3.** In singing, the arrangement of the vocal apparatus. **4.** In piano playing, 'touch'.

Anschlag (Ger.). **1.** In keyboard playing, 'touch'. **2.** A double *appoggiatura, in the sense of ornament. **3.** 'Attack'.

anschwellend (Ger.). 'Swelling', i.e. getting louder.

answer. A term used, particularly in fugal writing, to denote the second (and fourth) statements of the subject, or theme, usually at the interval of a perfect 4th or 5th. *See* FUGUE.

antecedent and consequent. A pair of musical phrases that complement each other in length, rhythmic symmetry, and harmony.

anthem. An English-language choral piece of moderate length for use in worship, typically on a prose text selected from the Bible or the liturgy. The term is not used for settings of unvarying liturgical texts, such as the *canticles (*see also* SERVICE). The word

a

'anthem' (an Anglicization of *'antiphon') meant a short Latin plainchant used before a psalm, or a longer one at the end of the daily offices of Lauds, Compline, and Vespers, especially sung in praise of the Virgin Mary, or other saint. The texts of such antiphons could also be set polyphonically. The golden age of the anthem was the first half of the 17th century. Solo voices were contrasted with full choirs in the *verse anthem, sometimes with the accompaniment of viols. Choral anthems were described as 'full' (as opposed to 'verse'). The word has been extended beyond church use in the term *'national anthem' and to denote a solemn, hymn-like song.

anthems, national. *See* NATIONAL ANTHEMS.

anticipation. A note that occurs immediately before the chord to which it belongs.

antienne (Fr.). *'Antiphon'.

antimasque. One of the entries in a *masque.

antiphon. A liturgical chant sung as the refrain to the verses of a psalm. The word *antiphonon* is Greek, sometimes used to mean 'octave'. Antiphons were most often used in the Roman rite for the psalms of the Office (the largest groups being for Matins, Lauds, and Vespers). They were also used at Mass, for the introit, offertory, and communion chants. There are two special categories of antiphons, not connected to a psalm and not usually simple in style: the antiphons of the Blessed Virgin Mary, sung daily at Compline from the 13th century; and processional antiphons, sung during religious processions, or at a place where a procession paused (a 'station').

antiphonal psalmody. The chanting of psalmodic texts by alternating choirs or soloists with the addition of one or more refrains (*antiphona*) after each verse. Following the disappearance of the refrains in the Roman rite, the term also came to be applied to the *alternatim* performance of psalms and canticles.

antiphony. A term, derived from Christian chant, that refers to the singing of sections of a chant by two choirs in alternation. 'Antiphony' is also used of alternation between forces in polyphonic choral music (*see* CORI SPEZZATI) or instrumental music, and is often encountered in ethnomusicological descriptions of similar practices ('call and response') in non-Western music.

Antwort (Ger.). 'Answer', in *fugues.

anwachsend (Ger.). 'Growing', 'swelling'.

apaisé (Fr.). 'Calmed'.

aperto (It., 'open'). **1.** 'Clear', 'distinct'. **2.** A term used in horn playing to indicate unstopped notes. **3.** An indication in 14th-century music of alternative endings to sections (*see also* OUVERT AND CLOS). **4.** A term used by Mozart in some of his early works as a qualification to *allegro*, its precise meaning now unclear.

apothéose (Fr.). A work written in honour of a dead person, especially in 18th-century France. *See also* TOMBEAU.

appassionato, appassionata (It.). 'Impassioned'.

appena (It.). 'Scarcely', 'slightly'; *see* PEINE, À.

applied music. The American term for the study of performance as opposed to theory.

appoggiando (It., 'leaning'). A style of playing in which succeeding notes are closely connected and stressed.

appoggiatura (It., from *appoggiare*, 'to lean'; Fr.: *appoggiature*; Ger.: *Vorschlag*). A dissonant note that 'leans' on a harmony note, taking part of its time value. Typically the dissonance is a step above or below the main note. The term generally denotes a harmonic resource where a note in one chord is held over as a momentary, discordant part of the combination which follows; more specifically, it is an *ornament. The ornament has had a variety of names (forefall, backfall; Fr.: *appuyé*, *coulé*, *port de voix*) and has been indicated and performed in many ways. The most common representation has been by a small note, but its notated value need not correspond to its length when played.

In the mid-18th century, appoggiatura performance was codified into two main categories: the first type, the (normal) long appoggiatura, takes half the value of the main note, or, if placed before a dotted note, two thirds of its value (in compound time, an appoggiatura onto a dotted note tied to another note takes the full length of the dotted note). The second type is the short appoggiatura (Ex. 1*a*); in certain circumstances (for example when the main note is one of a series of reiterated notes, or when the main note is a short one and is followed by others of the same value) the appoggiatura should be played much shorter (but still on the beat), as in Ex. 1*b* and *c*. In either case the two notes will typically be slurred and played with a diminuendo. There was also a 'passing appoggiatura', used only to fill in gaps between notes a 3rd apart and (exceptionally for an appoggiatura) taken before the beat instead of on it. The standard long and occasional short appoggiaturas are the norm for the Classical period. During the 19th century, composers began to write long appoggiaturas in full notation. The short appoggiatura was then notated by the new sign 𝅘𝅥𝅮. The expression 'double appoggiatura' has been used for three different effects: two simultaneous appoggiaturas, the figure shown in Ex. 2, and the slide (*see* SLIDE, 2).

appuyé (Fr., 'leant on'). Emphasized; *see* APPOGGIATURA.

aquarelle (Fr., 'water-colour'). A title sometimes given to a piece of music of delicate texture.

arabesque (Fr.; Ger.: *Arabeske*). A term originally used to describe the ornamental style of Arabic art and architecture. In music it is used for a florid, delicate composition. (The term is also used for a ballet posture.)

arcata (It.). In string playing, the 'bow-stroke'; often followed by *in giù* (down-bow), or *in su* (up-bow); *arcato*, 'bowed', indicates a return to use of the bow after a pizzicato passage.

archet (Fr.). 'Bow'.

archetto (It.). 'Bow'.

arch form. At its simplest, arch form is synonymous with *ternary form, comprising three sections, ABA, where the first is repeated after a contrasting middle section. It may be extended to create a larger 'arch', for example ABCBA, where the first two sections are repeated in reverse order after the contrasting middle section, thereby creating a mirror symmetry.

arco (It.). 'Bow'; *coll'arco* ('with the bow'), an instruction to stop playing pizzicato.

Appoggiatura, Ex. 1

Ex. 2

a

ardito (It.). 'Bold'; *arditamente*, 'boldly'.

aria (It., 'air'; Fr.: *air*; Ger.: *Arie*). A self-contained song for solo voice, usually forming part of an opera or other large work; it is a lyrical air, unlike the speech-imitating *recitative. The earliest type of aria was the strophic song, often in triple time. By the end of the 17th century the *da capo* aria (so called because the repetition of the A section could be indicated by writing the words *da capo* after the B section) prevailed. During the 19th century arias became more elaborate and complex, but by the end of the century they were generally part of the dramatic structure rather than self-contained numbers. *See also* ARIETTE; CABALETTA; CAVATINA; DA CAPO; SCENA.

arietta (It., dim. of *aria*). An operatic song, but shorter and less developed than an *aria. The term was first used in the mid-17th century.

ariette (Fr.). In 18th-century French opera, a **da capo* aria in the Italian style; in **opéra comique* it was a short, simple song.

arioso (It.). **1.** In vocal music, a term indicating a lyrical, as opposed to declamatory, manner of performance. **2.** By extension, a short passage of accompanied *recitative that has a regular metre and a melodic character. **3.** A short aria in the operas of, for example, Handel. **4.** Rarely, an instrumental piece or passage of a lyrical character.

arlecchinesco (It.). Music in the spirit of a harlequinade.

armonia (It.). **1.** *'Harmony'. **2.** *'Chord'.

armonioso, armoniosamente (It.). 'Harmonious', 'harmoniously'.

armure (Fr.). *'Key signature'.

arpa (It.). 'Harp'.

arpège (Fr.). *'Arpeggio'; *arpéger*, to spread a chord; *arpègement*, the spreading of a chord.

arpeggiando, arpeggiato (It.). Terms used in string playing to denote a bouncing bowstroke played on broken chords, so that each bounce is on a different string.

arpeggiare (It., 'to play the harp'). An instruction to spread the notes of a chord, usually from the bottom upwards, in harp-like fashion. *See* ARPEGGIO.

arpeggio (It.; Fr.: *arpège*). The notes of a chord 'spread', i.e. played one after the other from the bottom upwards, or from the top downwards. The effect is chiefly used in keyboard and harp music (chords of three or four notes may be spread on a stringed instrument, but not in the same way). To develop their technique, instrumentalists (especially pianists) practise arpeggios formed out of triads.

arraché (Fr.). 'Torn': a forceful pizzicato.

arrangement (Ger.: *Bearbeitung*). The adaptation of music for a medium different from that for which it was originally composed, for example the recasting of a song or a symphony as a piano piece, or of an orchestral overture as an organ piece. Such a process involves more than that of simple *transcription since many effective passages in the original would sound much less so in another medium.

Ars Antiqua (Lat., 'ancient art'). A term used in French theoretical writings of the early 14th century to describe earlier notational systems that had been superseded by the technical advances of the *Ars Nova. Some historians have used the term to embrace all polyphonic music of the late 12th and the 13th centuries.

arsis and thesis (from Gk.). Terms that originally referred to the 'raising' and 'lowering', respectively, of the foot in Ancient Greek dance. When applied to music they refer to the *upbeat and *downbeat. In the 16th and 17th centuries, the phrase 'per arsin et thesin' meant 'inversion' (*see* INVERSION, 3); the same phrase was used in the 18th century to describe a fugue in which the answer is in inverted rhythm, i.e. with strong beats in the subject becoming weak beats in the answer, and vice versa.

Ars Nova. The title (meaning 'new art') of a treatise (*c.*1322) transmitting the teachings of Philippe de Vitry, which has come to be used to describe a period of musical composition (and the music written during that period), beginning *c.*1315 and ending *c.*1375. Music of this time is distinguished from earlier music (*Ars Antiqua) because of advances in musical notation that allowed for a far greater range of measured rhythmic note divisions than had been possible before: from long to breve, breve to semibreve, and semibreve to minim (a newly defined note-value). In each division the upper value could be worth two or three of the lower value, so that a wide range of subdivisions was possible. The term 'Ars Nova' also implies a breaking of musical boundaries beyond the merely technical; the concept of 'new art' arose at a time when the polyphonic art song was emerging as an important genre.

ars subtilior (Lat., 'the more subtle art'). A term used to describe French vocal music of the late 14th century. Composers after Machaut developed a sophisticated and complex musical style using the new note-values introduced in the *Ars Nova period and developing their potential for complex rhythmic schemes.

articulation. A term denoting the degree to which each of a succession of notes is separated in performance; it may lie at either of the extremes of **staccato* and **legato*, or anywhere between the two. Articulation may be expressive or structural; if the latter, it is analogous to the use of punctuation in language. The shaping of phrases, particularly on keyboard instruments, is largely dependent on articulation. Articulation in singing is produced by such techniques as *portamento or the taking of breaths, and by the treatment of vowels and consonants.

art music, art song. Terms used to describe music that is written down and that takes a more or less established form to transmit some sort of artistic expression. The term is often used in contradistinction to folk and popular music, as well as some forms of liturgical music (especially plainchant) and dance music, but the distinctions have become blurred.

As (Ger.). The note A♭.

a.s. Abbreviation for **al segno*.

assai (It.). 'Very', e.g. *allegro assai*, 'very fast'. It was sometimes used in the 18th century to mean 'rather', like the French *assez*.

assez (Fr.). 'Rather', e.g. *assez vite*, 'rather fast'.

Atempause (Ger., 'breathing pause'). A tiny pause on a weak beat, often indicated by an apostrophe, to emphasize the following strong beat, a guide to phrasing rather than an indication that a wind player or singer should take a breath; it is used effectively in Viennese waltzes.

atonality. The antonym of *tonality; atonal music (the term 'post-tonal' is preferred by some theorists) is that which does not adhere to any system of *key or *mode. *See also* SERIALISM; TWELVE-NOTE MUSIC.

attacca (It.). 'Attack'; often given as *attacca subito* ('attack quickly'), it is used at the end of a movement to indicate that the next should follow without a break.

attacco (It., 'attack'). A very short fugue subject of perhaps three or four notes, used as material for imitation.

attack (Fr.: *attaque*; Ger.: *Anschlag*, *Einsatz*). The prompt and decisive beginning of a note or passage by either vocal or instrumental performers. Good 'attack' is a vital element in rhythm. The principal first violin in an orchestra (leader; Amer.: concertmaster) is in French called the *chef d'attaque*, 'leader of the attack'.

aubade (Fr., from *aube*, 'dawn'; Ger.: *Morgenlied*). Early morning music. The repertory of the troubadours included the *alba, and in 17th- and 18th-century courts aubades were played in honour of royalty. The Spanish equivalent is the *alborada.

aube (Fr.). *See* ALBA.

auf (Ger.). 'On'; e.g. *auf der G*, 'on the G (string)'.

aufgeregt (Ger.). 'Excited'.

Auflage (Ger.). 'Edition'.

auflösen (Ger., 'to loosen', 'to untie'). In harp playing, to lower again a string which has been raised in pitch.

Auflösung (Ger.). **1.** The resolution of a discord. **2.** The cancellation of an accidental; *Auflösungszeichen*, the natural sign (♮).

Aufstrich (Ger.). 'Up-bow' in string playing; 'down-bow' is *Niederstrich*.

Auftakt (Ger.). 'Upbeat'.

Auftritt (Ger.). 'Scene' (of an opera or other stage work).

Aufzug (Ger., 'pulling up'). The raising of a curtain; hence an 'act' of an opera, etc.

Augenmusik (Ger.). *'Eye music'.

augmentation. A compositional procedure in which the note-values of a musical statement are lengthened (usually doubled), as in the climactic presentation of certain fugue subjects.

augmented fourth. *See* TRITONE.

augmented interval. A major or perfect *interval increased by a semitone.

augmented sixth chord. The chords of the augmented 6th are *altered chords, built on the flattened submediant. The three common forms, with typical resolutions in the key of C, are given in Ex. 1. The so-called 'Italian' and 'French' 6ths usually resolve onto the dominant chord, and the 'German' 6th onto the dominant or the second inversion of the tonic; the 'German' 6th may also, by an enharmonic change, be transformed into a *dominant 7th of the flattened supertonic (in C major, D♭ major or minor).

augmented triad. *See* TRIAD.

aural training. *See* EAR-TRAINING.

Ausdruck (Ger.). 'Expression'; *mit Ausdruck, ausdrucksvoll*, 'expressively'.

Ausfüllgeiger (Ger., 'filling-out-fiddler'). A *ripieno part.

Ausgabe (Ger.). 'Edition'.

aushalten (Ger.). 'To sustain'; *ausgehalten*, 'sustained'.

äusserst (Ger.). 'Extremely', e.g. *äusserst schnell*, 'extremely fast'.

Auszug (Ger.). **1.** An arrangement, usually for piano (*Klavier-Auszug*), of an opera, orchestral work, etc. **2.** 'Extract'.

authentic. 1. A description of a work that can be positively attributed, in all its essential details, to a given composer. **2.** In the context of ethnomusicology, the term refers to an uninterrupted folk tradition, unaffected by outside influences, and not the revival of that tradition. **3.** Authentic performance (a somewhat discredited term) implies the use of instruments (or replicas of them), and of *performance practice, that are believed to have been familiar to the composer.

authentic cadence. *See* CADENCE.

Augmented sixth chord, Ex. 1

'Italian' 6th 'French' 6th 'German' 6th

authentic mode. Any of the church *modes whose range includes the octave lying above that mode's *final.

autograph. A manuscript written in the hand of its author or composer. The term 'holograph' is now frequently used to mean a manuscript wholly in the hand of its composer or author.

auxiliary note. A variety of *passing note which, instead of proceeding to another note, returns to the one it has just left. Such a note may be either diatonic or chromatic. Shakes, mordents, and turns provide examples of the auxiliary note applied as ornamentation.

avant-garde (Fr.). Originally a military designation for an advance party of soldiers (a 'vanguard'), the term has come to signify a group of composers or other artists who assume the role of pioneers on behalf of their generation, rejecting established practice in their striving to pave the way for the future. The term came into use after World War II and was applied particularly to those composers who used total *serialism or electronics, or who wrote *aleatory music.

ayre. The old English spelling of *air. It came to denote the *lute-song of the period 1597–1622.

azione sacra (It., 'sacred action'). A term used to describe the Italian *sepolcro* (a musical enactment of the Passion set at the holy sepulchre, usually presented within a single act) as cultivated by the Habsburg court in Vienna during the second half of the 17th century. As the term spread from Vienna to Italy it became synonymous with 'oratorio' in general, as it did also in Vienna during the 18th century.

azione teatrale (It., 'theatrical action'). A genre of music theatre popular in the 18th century, especially at the courts of Vienna. Similar to the **festa teatrale*, but usually on a smaller scale, the *azione teatrale* generally had a plot with a mythological or allegorical theme and was presented in a single act with up to five characters and a small orchestra.

B. 1. The seventh degree (leading note) of the scale of C major (*see* SCALE, 1). **2.** In German, the note B♭ (B♮ is called H). **3.** Abbreviation for *bass (e.g. SATB: soprano, alto, tenor, bass) or for *bassus.

Bacchanalia (Fr.: *bacchanale*). An orgy of riotous dancing or singing in honour of Bacchus, the Greek and Roman god of wine.

Bach-Werke-Verzeichnis. *See* BWV.

backfall. A 17th-century English term for a descending *appoggiatura. *See also* FOREFALL.

badinage, badinerie (Fr., 'playfulness', 'trifling'; Ger.: *Tändelei*). An optional movement occasionally found in the 18th-century *suite; it is in a frivolous style but of no particular form.

bagatelle (Fr., Ger.). A short and unpretentious instrumental piece, usually for keyboard.

balancement (Fr., 'wavering'). An 18th-century term for tremolo, used mainly to denote the **Bebung* in clavichord music or a *vibrato in vocal and string music.

ballabile (It.). 'Suitable for dancing', i.e. in a dance style. A movement in 19th-century opera intended for dancing.

ballad (from Lat. *ballare*, 'to dance'). The origin of the term 'ballad' is in medieval dance-song, but the word had lost this connotation by the late Middle Ages. By the 14th century it referred to a strophic solo song with a narrative text (not to be confused with a **ballade*). Though primarily products of oral tradition, from the 16th century onwards ballads were also published in 'broadsides' (broadsheets). Ballad tunes were used in *ballad opera. The English 'sentimental' ballad appeared towards the end of the 18th century.

ballade (Fr.). **1.** One of three standard poetic forms used for 14th- and 15th-century chansons (*see also* RONDEAU; VIRELAI). It consists of three structurally identical stanzas each concluding with the same refrain line and each sung to the same music, in the form aab. The *ballade* remained the dominant poetic form for late 14th-century composers, who often set texts in which the standard theme of courtly love is combined with classical or mythological allusions. **2.** The name given by Chopin to a long, dramatic type of piano piece, the musical equivalent of a poetic *ballad of the heroic type. The title was used by later composers.

ballad opera. An English form of theatrical entertainment, related to the French *vaudeville of the end of the 17th century and beginning of the 18th, and to the German **Singspiel*, on which it had an influence. It consists of a spoken play (usually comic) with many interpolated short songs, the music for which was borrowed from popular songs of the day (*see* BALLAD). The inventor of ballad opera was the poet John Gay, who launched *The Beggar's Opera* in 1728.

ballata (It.). One of the three poetic forms used in Italian secular songs from the late 13th century to the early 15th (the others being the *madrigal and the **caccia*). Its musical form is AbbaA: A (*ripresa*, or refrain), bb (two *piedi*), a (*volta*, together with the *piedi* forming a stanza), A (*ripresa*). The *ballata* resembles the *virelai* in form. Early *ballate* are monophonic; polyphonic works were first written down *c.*1360, the form attaining a popularity among Italian composers equivalent to that enjoyed by the *ballade* north of the Alps.

ballet de cour (Fr., 'court ballet'). A French courtly entertainment of the late 16th and the 17th centuries. It borrowed elements from the French *entremets* and the Italian *intermedio* and was the ancestor of both modern ballet and French opera. A *ballet de cour* normally consisted of up to five *entrées* (dances and choruses) with corresponding *vers* (librettos distributed to the spectators), each introduced by spoken or sung *récits*; it opened with an *ouverture* and concluded with a *grand ballet* in which, at least once a year, the king danced.

balletto (It.; Fr.: *ballet*) [ballett]. **1.** An Italian dance popular in the 16th and 17th centuries. **2.** An Italian dance-song deriving, in the work of Giovanni Giacomo Gastoldi, from the original dance and from the *canzonetta (especially in its form: two repeated sections, each ending with a refrain of such nonsense syllables as 'fa-la' or 'lirum-lirum'). Gastoldi used strong, regular rhythms, homophonic textures, and simple melodies and harmonies. Some composers included balletti in their madrigal comedies. Balletti were extremely popular and the style was taken up by composers in Germany and, particularly, in England.

ballo (It.; Fr.: *bal*; Ger.: *Ball*; Sp.: *baile*). **1.** A ball, i.e. a social dance; *tempo di ballo*, 'at dancing speed'. **2.** A formal court dance of the 15th to the 17th centuries. Unlike simpler social dances, the *ballo* could have up to four changes of metre and was choreographed by a dancing master. **3.** The music for a ball. The term *ballo* occurs in this context mainly in the 16th century, when it denoted a collection of dances, such as branles, pavans and galliards, and saltarellos. It was also used in connection with stage music.

band. A group of instruments. The term was originally used for any group, but today there is a distinction between orchestras and bands. Brass bands use only cup-mouthpiece instruments (as well as percussion). Concert or wind bands, often now called wind orchestras, include all the winds and percussion and are derived from *military bands. Opera orchestras are usually identical with contemporary symphony orchestras but pit bands for stage musicals vary in size and constituents. On-stage bands (*banda*, pl. *bande*, in Italian opera scores) are most commonly wind and percussion.

bar. A line drawn vertically through a staff or staves of musical notation, normally indicating division into metrical units (of two, three, four beats, etc.); now also the name for the metrical unit itself, the line being commonly called a 'bar-line'. American usage, however, normally reserves the term 'bar' for the line itself, describing the metrical unit as a 'measure'. *See also* DOUBLE BAR; NOTATION; RHYTHM.

barber-shop singing. A style of singing, usually for male-voice quartet, characterized by close harmony, with prominent use of 7th chords, and chromatic melody; its present form developed in the USA in the late 19th century. Its ancestry is in the madrigal, the round, the glee, and the partsong.

barcarolle (Fr.; It.: *barcarola*) [barcarole]. A song in 6/8 or 12/8 time sung by Venetian gondoliers, with an accompaniment suggesting the rocking of a boat. Barcarolles are found in several 19th-century operas. The genre was transferred to instrumental media, particularly the piano.

Bar form. A musical design originally associated with the poetic forms of the German *Minnesinger and *Meistersinger. It takes its name from the medieval German term for 'strophe'—*Bar*. The form can be represented by the letter scheme AAB, where the first strophe, or *Stollen*, is repeated, and the last strophe, or *Abgesang*, provides a contrast.

bariolage (Fr.). In string playing, a special effect used to produce a contrast in tone-colour. It is achieved by playing the same note alternately on two different strings, one stopped and the other open; the term is also used for a repeated passage played on different strings.

baritone. A male voice with a range between those of the bass and the tenor: roughly *A* to *g′*, going up to *a♭′* or even *a′* in Italian and French opera. Until the early 19th century the term was little used, and there was no formal distinction between the baritone and bass voices. The quality of a baritone voice may vary from dramatic, as required for Verdi and Wagner roles, to light and almost tenor-like, sometimes called 'baryton Martin' after the French opera singer Jean-Blaise Martin (1767–1837). For the bass-baritone, *see* BASS, 1. (There is a valved brass instrument called a 'baritone'.)

baritone clef. *See* CLEF.

bar-line. *See* BAR.

Baroque. A term derived from the Portuguese *barroco*, meaning an irregularly shaped pearl, used to imply strangeness and extravagance. It was first applied, in French, to art and architecture, but since the early 20th century it has been used to designate music of the period *c*.1600–*c*.1750. The aesthetic principle of the Baroque era was that music should express affective states and move the listener's passions, a development with roots in the rise of humanism. During the 17th century theorists developed parallels between *rhetoric and music (*see* AFFECTIONS, DOCTRINE OF; FIGURES, DOCTRINE OF). The introduction of the *basso continuo gave rise to a different relationship between melody and bass, with opportunity for musical contrasts (of texture, tempo, and dynamics) and therefore heightened expression. In dramatic music this led to the development of the aria, and in instrumental music to the emergence of the *sonata, *suite, and *concerto grosso. *See also* STILE CONCITATO.

barré (Fr.). A term used in lute and guitar playing for the simultaneous shortening of the length of all or several strings by placing the forefinger across them at some particular fret. The same effect may be produced artificially by use of a *capo tasto* (a bar clamped over the fret).

barzelletta (It., 'little jest'). An Italian poetic form used *c*.1500, especially for the *frottola.

bas (Fr.). *See* HAUT, BAS.

bass. 1. The lowest male voice, with a range of roughly *E* to *f′*. The quality of a bass voice can vary widely, from the *Bass-buffo*, or *komischer Bass*, to the majestic. In the 19th century the bass voice was used either for villains or for kings and other figures of authority. Slavonic basses are able to achieve great depth, sometimes reaching *G′*. The 'bass-baritone' has a range that extends higher, but it retains the bass quality on the lower notes. **2.** The lowest note in a chord. For the distinction between 'root' and 'bass', *see* ROOT, ROOT POSITION. **3.** The lowest regions of musical pitch. **4.** A low-pitched member of a family of instruments, with a range lower than tenor and higher than contrabass or double bass.

bassadanza (It.). *See* BASSE DANSE.

bass clef. *See* CLEF.

basse (Fr.). 'Bass', i.e. the lowest male voice.

basse chantante (Fr.), **basso cantante** (It.). 'Singing bass'; a lyric bass voice, sometimes of baritone quality.

basse chiffrée (Fr.). *'Figured bass'; *see also* CONTINUO.

basse continue (Fr.). 'Continuo bass'; *see* FIGURED BASS; CONTINUO.

basse danse (Fr., 'low dance' [i.e. close to the ground]; It.: *bassadanza*). The principal court dance of the 15th and early 16th centuries. It was performed by couples with a stately gliding motion; the afterdance (e.g. the *tordion* or *recoupe*) was characterized by livelier movements and leaps. The earliest known music for the basse danse dates from the 15th century. The melodic material is centred on a kind of cantus firmus (frequently derived from a pre-existing source), round which the other parts improvised; each note of this tenor corresponded to one step of the dance.

basse fondamentale (Fr.). *'Fundamental bass'.

basso (It.). 'Low', 'bass'.

basso buffo (It., 'comic bass'). A term used to describe a bass who specializes in comic roles. Such parts, usually resourceful servants or elderly, gullible men, became important in Italian *opera buffa* from the mid-18th century.

basso continuo (It., 'continuous bass'). Another name for the *figured bass, one of the principal features of Baroque compositional and performance practice style. *See also* CONTINUO.

basso ostinato (It., 'obstinate bass'). A form of *ground bass in which a short bass pattern is repeated many times unchanged and above which melodic variations occur.

basso profondo (It., 'deep bass'). A bass voice of exceptionally low range.

basso ripieno (It.). A bass part for only the tutti sections of 18th-century orchestral works. *See* RIPIENO.

basso seguente (It., 'following bass'). *See* CONTINUO.

bassus (Lat.). In early vocal music, the abbreviated form of *contratenor bassus* ('low [part] against the tenor'), the voice part immediately below the tenor and the lowest in the ensemble. *See* CONTRATENOR.

bataille (Fr., 'battle'). *See* BATTLE PIECE.

battaglia (It., 'battle'). *See* BATTLE PIECE.

battement (Fr., 'beating'). A 17th-century term for any ornament consisting of two adjacent notes, such as a *mordent or *trill.

batterie (Fr.). **1.** Percussion instruments in general. **2.** A drumroll. **3.** An 18th-century term for arpeggio, broken-chord figuration, etc. **4.** **Rasgueado*.

battle piece (Fr.: *bataille*; It.: *battaglia*). A composition in which the sounds of battle are realistically imitated, a type of 'programme music' especially popular from the 16th century to the 18th. Battle pieces were a feature of 19th-century opera.

battre (Fr.: 'to beat'). A term applied both to conducting and to playing percussion instruments.

battuta (It.). 'Beat', 'bar', 'measure'; *a battuta* indicates a return to strict time after, for example, a passage *ad libitum* or *a piacere* or an *accelerando* or *rallentando*. It can also mean the strong beat at the beginning of each bar.

b.c. Abbreviation for *basso continuo.

Be (Ger.). The flat sign (*see* FLAT, 1).

beam. A horizontal line linking two or more notes into a group.

bearbeiten (Ger.). 'To work over', 'to arrange'; *bearbeitet*, 'arranged'; *Bearbeitung*, 'arrangement'.

beat (Fr.: *temps*; Ger.: *Zahlzeit*, *Schlag*; It.: *battuta*). **1.** The basic unit of time in mensural music, i.e. that chosen by the conductor when he or she 'beats' time. The beats are usually categorized according to where they fall in the bar: as 'weak' beats (the second and fourth in a four-beat bar, the second and third in a three-beat bar, or the second in a two-beat bar), or 'strong' beats (the first and, to a lesser degree, the third in a four-beat bar, and the first in a three-beat or a two-beat bar). For other terms used to describe different kinds of beat, *see* ANACRUSIS; DOWNBEAT; UPBEAT. **2.** A 17th-century English term for an ornament, describing either an ascending *appoggiatura, or an ascending appoggiatura repeated several times, so that it is virtually an inverted *trill. In the 18th century, 'beat' denoted a *mordent.

Bebung (Ger., from *beben*, 'to tremble'; Fr.: *balancement*; It.: *tremolo*). A *vibrato effect unique to the clavichord; gentle variation of finger pressure on a key causes an undulation of pitch similar to violin vibrato, helping to 'reinforce the tone'. An important expressive device in 18th-century clavichord playing, *Bebung* was nevertheless used sparingly and was only exceptionally notated, by dots over the note beneath a slur.

bécarre (Fr., 'square b'). **1.** The natural sign (*see* NATURAL, 2). The term derives from one of the two forms of the letter 'b' used in medieval notation; *see* DURUM AND MOLLIS. **2.** In 17th-century usage, 'major', e.g. *fa bécarre*, F major.

bedächtig (Ger.). 'Cautious', 'deliberate', i.e. slow.

bedrohlich (Ger.). 'Threatening'.

Begleitung (Ger.). 'Accompaniment'; *begleitend*, 'accompanying'.

behend [behende] (Ger.). 'Agile', 'nimble'; *behendig*, 'nimbly'.

Beisser (Ger., 'biter'). An 18th-century name for the *mordent.

beklemmt (Ger.). 'Anguished', 'oppressed'.

bel canto (It., 'beautiful singing'). A term applied to an elegant Italian style of singing. It is particularly used for the arias in Italian operas of the late 18th and early 19th centuries, which were lyrical and fluid. Bel canto singing is characterized by beautiful tone and effortless technique in executing highly ornate and florid passages.

belebend, belebt (Ger.). 'Lively', 'animated'; *belebter*, 'more animated'.

bell-ringing. *See* CHANGE-RINGING.

bémol (Fr., 'soft [i.e. rounded] b'; It.: *bemolle*). **1.** The flat sign (*see* FLAT, 1). The term derives from one of the two forms of the letter 'b' used in medieval notation; *see* DURUM AND MOLLIS. **2.** In 17th-century usage, 'minor', e.g. *mi bémol*, E minor.

ben, bene (It.). 'Well', 'much'; e.g. *ben marcato*, 'well marked'; *ben bene*, 'really well'.

beneplacito, a. *See* PLACITO.

bequadro (It., 'square b'). The natural sign (*see* NATURAL, 2).

berceuse (Fr.; Ger.: *Wiegenlied*, *Schlummerlied*). A lullaby, or cradle-song, usually in 6/8 time with a rocking accompaniment. It was taken over into art music from the folk repertory not only as a song but also as a short instrumental piece, often for piano.

bergamasca (It.; Fr.: *bergamasque*). A term originally used to describe peasant dances and songs from the district around Bergamo in northern Italy. In the late 16th century the dance had a fixed harmonic scheme for the accompanying guitar: I–IV–V–I. Many 17th-century guitar pieces were written on this pattern. Bergamo is also associated with the *commedia dell'arte*, so the title 'bergamasca' has been used for pieces associated with Harlequin, particularly in France in the 18th and late 19th centuries.

bergerette (Fr., 'shepherd maid'). **1.** In the 15th century, a French poetic and musical form, identical in structure with the **virelai*, but with only one stanza. **2.** A title occasionally used for 16th-century instrumental dances in quick triple time, similar to the *saltarello. **3.** An 18th-century *air*, setting pastoral or amorous verse, very similar to the **brunette*.

beruhigend (Ger.). 'Becoming calmer'.

Bes (Ger.). B𝄫.

beschleunigend (Ger.). 'Getting faster', i.e. **accelerando*.

Besetzung (Ger.). Setting, scoring, orchestration.

bestimmt (Ger.). 'Decisively'; it is sometimes used for a line in a score which is to be given prominence.

betont (Ger.). 'Stressed', 'emphasized'.

beweglich (Ger.). 'Agile', 'sprightly'.

bewegt (Ger.). 'Agitated', 'moved' (in the sense of both motion and emotion); *bewegter*, 'quicker'.

bezifferter Bass (Ger.). 'Figured bass'.

Bg. (Ger.). Abbreviation for *Bogen*, 'bow'; *Bogenstrich*, 'bowstroke'.

bicinium (Lat.). An unaccompanied composition for two voices or instruments. The term was also used more specifically for the teaching pieces composed by 16th-century Germans.

bien nourri (Fr.). 'Well nourished', i.e. with a rich, full sound.

bimusicality. A facility to participate fully in the musical systems of two different cultures, e.g. Western and Japanese, akin to bilingualism.

binary form. A musical structure consisting of two parts or sections. The first modulates from the tonic key and concludes with a cadence in a related key, usually the dominant for pieces in the major, the relative major for pieces in the minor. The second starts in the new key and works back to the tonic. For example, if the piece is in C major the first section will end with a cadence on G major; the second will then begin in G major but modulate back to C major, the key in which the piece will end. It is usual to repeat each of the two sections of the structure. Sometimes the second section of a binary piece is considerably longer than the first because other related keys are often explored on the way back to the tonic key, to give the piece more interest.

Although many late Renaissance dances comprised three strains, binary form came to be used in nearly all dance movements (allemandes, courantes, sarabandes, gigues, etc.) in 17th- and 18th-century dance suites. Whereas early Baroque dances often remained in one key throughout, by the mid-Baroque period the tonal scheme as described above had become the norm. Some of the finest examples of binary form are found in Bach's suites. The expansion of binary form and its combination with *ternary form led eventually to the development of Classical *sonata form. Binary-form pieces continued to be written in the 19th century, usually cast as a 'theme and variations'. In the 20th century, binary form was used as the basis for complex structural devices.

bind. Another name for the *tie.

bis (Fr.). 'Twice', i.e. again, a second time. **1.** An instruction that a passage so marked should be repeated. **2.** A term used by French and Italian audiences to demand an encore.

bisbigliando (It., 'whispering'). In harp playing, a special effect resembling a tremolo, obtained by moving the finger quickly against the string.

bitonality. The combination of two keys simultaneously. The harmonic clashes of bitonality are especially associated with the music of Ives and Milhaud.

Bkl. (Ger.). Abbreviation for *Bassklarinette*, 'bass clarinet'.

Blasmusik (Ger.). 'Wind music', i.e. music for wind instruments.

Blechmusik (Ger.). 'Brass band music'.

blind octaves [interrupted octaves]. A device found in virtuoso piano writing in which the rapid alternation between each hand of octaves, or of octaves with single notes, produces an effect approximating to continuous triple octaves.

block harmony. A succession of similar or identical chords.

B moll (Ger.). The key of B♭ minor (not B minor).

bocca chiusa (It.). '[With the] mouth closed', i.e. humming.

boceto (Sp.). 'Sketch'; the word was used as a title by Granados and other Spanish composers.

b

Bockstriller (Ger.). *'Goat's trill'.

Bogen (Ger.). 'Bow'.

bois (Fr., 'wood'). *Avec le bois*, 'with the wood' (of the bow, i.e. *col legno*); *les bois*, 'the woodwind'; *baguette de bois*, 'wooden-headed drumstick'.

borea (It.). *See* BOURRÉE.

borre, borree. Old English spellings of *bourrée.

bouche fermée (Fr.). '[With the] mouth closed', i.e. humming.

bouchés, sons. *See* SONS BOUCHÉS.

bourdon (Fr.). 'Drone', 'drone pipe', or 'drone string'. The term also sometimes denotes the lowest pipe, string, voice, or register whether used for a drone or for a low, often repetitive accompaniment. Depending on the nature of the instrument or music, bourdons can be incessant or intermittent and may, for example when humming while blowing a flute, change from one pitch to another. The word is also used for the lowest bell in a ring without implying a drone.

bourrée (Fr.; It.: *borea*) [borre, borree]. A couple dance fashionable in France during the 17th and 18th centuries, in quick duple metre with a characteristic single upbeat. It was not used as an instrumental form until the second half of the 17th century. The bourrée occurs frequently in operas and ballets by French court composers. Like the gavotte, it later found its way into the *suite as an optional movement, where it often followed the sarabande.

boutade (Fr.). An improvised composition, usually a dance.

Br. (Ger.). Abbreviation for *Bratschen*, 'violas'.

brace (Fr.: *accolade*). The perpendicular line and bracket connecting two or more staves in piano or orchestral scores; also a name for the staves thus connected.

branle (Fr., also *bransle*; It.: *brando*) [brawl, brangill]. Originally a sideways step in the *basse danse, it became established as a popular circle dance by the 16th century. There were four main forms: the *branle simple* and *double* in duple time; the *branle gai* in triple time; and the *branle de Bourgogne* in a mixture of metres. There are many regional versions, such as the *branle d'Écosse* (Scottish branle) and the *branle de Malte* (Maltese branle). The branle was absorbed into the repertory of court dances and became popular in England.

Bratsche (Ger.). 'Viola'.

Brautlied (Ger.). 'Bridal song'.

bravura (It., 'skill'; Fr.: *bravoure*). A term used to describe showmanship in performance; *aria di bravura*, a brilliant virtuoso aria making great demands on a singer's vocal technique.

break. 1. The point of change between vocal and instrumental registers, especially important on clarinets. **2.** A momentary silence after a musical phrase, normally indicated by a comma above the staff. No loss of time must occur, the break being made by slightly shortening the last note of the phrase.

breathing, circular. *See* CIRCULAR BREATHING.

breit (Ger.). 'Broad', i.e. *largo. In string playing, *breit gestrichen* means 'broadly bowed'.

breve (from Lat. *brevis*, 'short'; 𝅜 or 𝅜). Formerly, as its name suggests, the shortest time-value in musical notation, but now (the longer note-values having gradually fallen into disuse) the longest—twice the length of the semibreve. The breve is now rarely encountered, except in church music.

breve, alla. *See* ALLA BREVE.

bridge. 1. A 'bridge passage' serves as a link between two other passages of greater prominence in the piece as a whole. Thus in *sonata form a transition may be described as a bridge passage, as its function is to link the first group to the second, often modulating from the first tonal centre to the next. **2.** (Fr.: *chevalet*; Ger.: *Steg*; It.: *ponticello*). On stringed instruments, the piece of carved wood which supports the strings and transmits their vibrations to the belly.

brillant, brillante (Fr.). 'Brilliant', 'sparkling'. Many 19th-century concert pieces have 'brillant' or 'brillante' in their titles.

Brindisi (It., 'toast'). A term, perhaps connected with the Italian town of that name, applied to a drinking-song. Such pieces are often found in 19th-century opera.

brio (It.). 'Vivacity', 'liveliness'; *con brio*, *brioso*, 'with fire', 'with spirit'.

brisé (Fr.). 'Broken'; it is used of a chord played in *arpeggio fashion or of string music played with short, detached bow-strokes; *see also* STYLE BRISÉ.

broadside ballad. *See* BALLAD.

broken cadence. *See* CADENCE.

broken chord. The playing of a chord as individual notes rather than simultaneously—usually as an accompanying figure, as in the *Alberti bass.

broken consort. *See* CONSORT.

broken octave. The playing of octaves as single notes, sounded separately rather than simultaneously.

bruitism (from Fr. *bruit*, 'noise'). The use in music of sounds taken from an extra-musical source or context. The term is used most often of percussion or of electronic music that suggests the sounds of machinery. *See also* FUTURISM.

brummen, Brummstimme (Ger.). 'To hum', 'humming'; *see* BOUCHE FERMÉE.

brunette (Fr.). A French popular song on an idyllic, pastoral, or amorous text. The genre flourished in the 17th and 18th centuries, and some of the tunes were later used in harpsichord suites and comic operas. The songs frequently featured a 'jolie brunette', hence the title.

brusque (Fr.). A 17th-century French dance; Chambonnières wrote two, for harpsichord.

Bruststimme (Ger.). *'Chest voice'.

buffo, buffa (It., 'comic'). *See* OPERA BUFFA.

Bühnenmusik (Ger., 'stage music'). *Incidental music for a play; also any music played on stage as part of the drama or opera.

Bund (Ger.). On stringed instruments, 'fret'.

burden [burthen]. **1.** A term for a refrain repeated after the verses (or at other points) of a song, carol, etc. **2.** A drone; *see* BOURDON. **3.** The lowest of three voices singing together; *see* FABURDEN.

burla (It.). 'Jest'; *burlando*, 'jestingly'.

burlesque (Fr.; It.: *burlesca*; Ger.: *Burleske*). An entertainment with music that was briefly in vogue before *operetta and *musical comedy were developed in the mid-19th century. It was generally a parody or skit on more serious opera, a forerunner of the satirical *revue. Burlesque flourished in England. In America, burlesque (or 'burlycue') had a similar vogue in the same period.

burletta (It.). A name used in England from the late 18th century for Italian comic operas, then for English imitations of them.

burrasca (It., 'storm'). Music that illustrates a storm.

burthen. *See* BURDEN.

BWV. Abbreviation for Bach-Werke-Verzeichnis, an informal title given to the *thematic catalogue of J. S. Bach's works drawn up by the German music librarian Wolfgang Schmieder (1901–90). Bach's works are usually referred to by BWV number, though 'Schmieder' (sometimes abbreviated to S) is still occasionally used.

C. The first degree (tonic) of the scale of C major (*see* SCALE, 1).

c.a. Abbreviation for **coll'arco*.

cabaletta (It.). A term usually applied to a short aria of simple reiterated rhythm, with repeats; the first statement was to be sung as written, but thereafter the singer could embellish freely. In the 18th century the term grew to mean the final section only of an aria in several parts, usually quick and brilliant but now written down. It has also been used to describe the first section of an aria; this would, on its reappearance, be varied and often with triplets in the accompaniment (suggesting a possible derivation from *cavallo*, 'horse', from the galloping movement).

cabaret song. A genre of song that originated in the cabarets of Paris and Berlin at the beginning of the 20th century. It is a strophic ballad in which the text—usually satirical, erotic, or sentimental—is as important as its musical content, and is frequently delivered in a style poised between speech and song. In Germany a strong political element was added.

caccia (It., 'chase', 'hunt'). **1.** A 14th- and 15th-century Italian vocal genre. The text describes the hunt in vivid, programmatic terms, including the cries of the huntsmen, the barking of the dogs, etc. The music sets the text as a two-part canon, to which is added a third part—with longer note-values, apparently intended for an instrument—in the tenor. **2.** The term is also applied to the hunting horn (corno da caccia or cor de chasse) and to Bach's tenor oboe (oboe da caccia).

cadence [close] (Fr.: *cadence*; Ger.: *Kadenz, Schluss*; It.: *cadenza*). A melodic or harmonic motion conventionally associated with the ending of a phrase, section, movement, or composition. A cadence emphasizes arrival on the interval or chord most fundamental to the tonality of a passage. There are four basic types.

A cadence is normally called 'perfect' if it consists of a tonic chord preceded by a dominant chord (Ex. 1*a*). This may also be known as a final, full, or complete cadence, or a full close, and it is considered to have the greatest degree of finality of all the cadences. Some theorists claim that for the cadence to be perfect the final chord must have the tonic in the top part and that both chords must be in root position (Ex. 1*b*).

Ex. 1

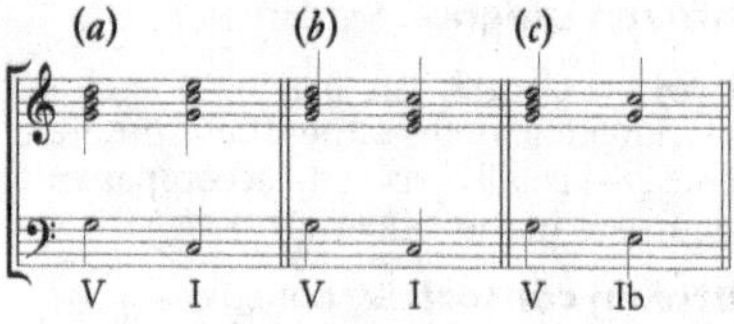

(*a*) (*b*) (*c*)

V I V I V Ib

An 'imperfect' cadence normally consists of the dominant chord preceded by any other chord (most commonly I or IV; Ex. 2). This lacks the finality of the perfect and plagal cadences and is therefore often used in the course of a composition, at the end of a phrase, and more particularly half-way through a section or period, whence it has acquired conventional musical settings of the word 'Amen'. Some American theorists view this cadence only as a variation of the perfect cadence, distinguishing the dominant-tonic cadence described above by the term 'authentic'; by extension, they term the closing harmonic progression IV-V-I or IV-Ib-V-I, with its mixture of subdominant and dominant elements, a 'mixed' cadence (Ex. 3).

Ex. 2

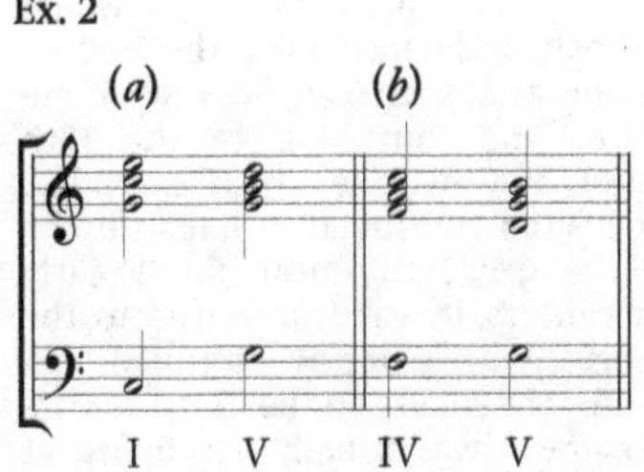

A cadence is normally called 'plagal' if it consists of a tonic chord preceded by a subdominant chord (Ex. 4). This is traditionally known as an 'Amen' (less commonly 'church' or 'Greek') cadence, from its association with the additional names 'half', 'semi-', or 'demi-cadence', or 'half close'. Again, American usage differs, reserving the name 'imperfect' for any cadence in which the final chord either does not have the root in the top part (also called 'semi-perfect'; Ex. 1*a*) or is not in root position (also called 'inverted'; see Ex. 1*c*), and describing a cadence ending with a dominant chord as a half-cadence or semi-cadence.

A cadence is called 'interrupted', 'deceptive', or 'false' where the penultimate, dominant chord is followed not by the expected tonic but by another chord, often the submediant (Ex. 5). Other, less common names for this cadence are 'abrupt', 'avoided', 'broken', 'evaded', irregular', or 'surprise'.

The Phrygian cadence, common in modal polyphony, has survived in later music in various forms (Ex. 6). In a tonal context, however, its Phrygian-mode connotations (corresponding to the scale on the white notes of the piano beginning on E) are less obvious, and in a major key it is often regarded as a variety of imperfect cadence resolving on the dominant of the relative minor. The Landini cadence (named after Francesco Landini) is characterized by the insertion in the top voice of the sixth degree of the scale between the leading note and the tonic. In the 16th century the third degree of the scale was included in the final chord (*see* TIERCE DE PICARDIE).

Any of the four main types of cadence—perfect, plagal, imperfect, and interrupted—can be decorated or extended in a variety of ways, for

Ex. 3

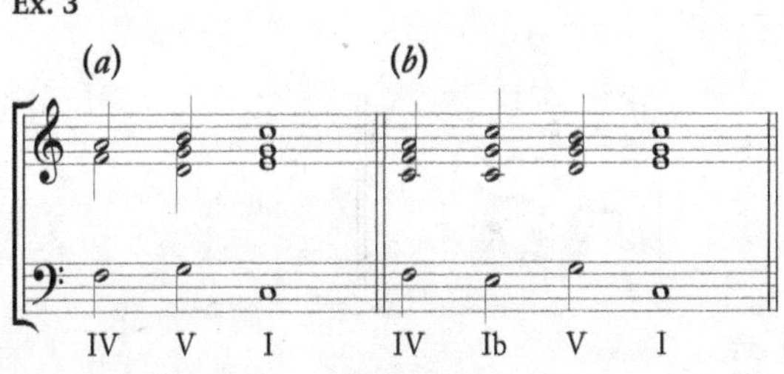

Ex. 4

Cadence, Ex. 5

example by adding a 7th (or other interval) to the dominant or by inverting either chord, which has the effect of reducing the cadence's finality. Terms sometimes used to qualify a cadence in terms of its chord positions include 'radical' (both chords in root position), 'medial' (the penultimate chord inverted), and 'inverted' (the final chord or both chords inverted). A 'suspended' cadence is one involving a delay (often on the second inversion of the tonic chord) before the two main cadential chords, such as may occur immediately before a soloist's cadenza or other elaborative passage (Ex. 7).

cadenza. A virtuoso passage near the end of a concerto movement or an aria. During the Baroque era a singer would embellish a cadence near the end of a *da capo* aria; such 'cadences' were improvised and short, but by the 18th century they became much extended. This custom continued in Italian opera until the early 19th century. In the early 18th century it was transferred to the concerto, with extensive brilliant passages for the soloist. In the Classical concerto, there was usually a cadenza at the end of the recapitulation and before the concluding tutti of the first movement, indicated by a *fermata over a 6–4 chord. This was quite long and consisted not only of brilliant passage-work but also of a 'working out' of the themes of the movement. Cadenzas were sometimes played in movements other than the first, notably in rondo finales where the restatement of the main theme is intended to be preceded by a flourish, although this is more properly called a 'reprise' or 'fermata'. The 'concerted cadenza' (written out) was also found, where several instruments took part. The improvised cadenza largely disappeared in the 19th century, when such flourishes were notated as part of the composition.

Ex. 6

Ex. 7

cadenzato (It.). 'Rhythmical'.

caesura. A term sometimes used interchangeably with 'pause' to indicate a note that is held for longer than its written value. More specifically it was used in the Viennese Classical tradition in its German form, *Cäsur* or *Zäsur*, to indicate where a singer or wind player should take a breath (shown by a comma or a 'v' above the staff); it is also used to denote the holding up of the metre, often heard in the Viennese waltz.

calando (It.). 'Lowering', 'dropping', i.e. gradually dying away in volume and sometimes also tempo.

calata (It.). A 16th-century Italian dance, resembling the *basse danse.

calcando (It.). 'Trampling', i.e. gradually quickening.

calmando, calmato (It.). 'Becoming calm'.

calore, con (It.). 'With warmth', 'with passion'; *caloroso*, 'passionately'.

cambiare (It.). 'To change'; an instruction in an instrumental part for a woodwind player to change to another instrument, a brass player to change crook, or a timpanist to alter the tuning.

cambiata. 1. *See* ÉCHAPPÉE. **2.** *See* NOTA CAMBIATA.

camera (It., 'chamber'; Fr.: *chambre*; Ger.: *Kammer*). In the early Baroque era, a designation often attached to music to be performed in a setting other than a church (*chiesa*) or theatre, usually a domestic room. A musical distinction was drawn between pieces considered appropriate to a sacred place and those intended for a secular context. A *sonata da camera* usually consisted of a slow prelude and a sequence of dance movements (as in the later *suite), whereas a *sonata da chiesa* alternated slow and fast movements with no connection to dancing and generally used the organ as continuo.

camerata (It., 'club', 'society'). A term used in 16th-century Italy for a small, informal academy or group of intellectuals who met to discuss particular aspects of a subject. In music the term refers in particular to the Florentine Camerata, a group made up chiefly of literary figures who met in the 1570s and 80s to discuss the music of the Ancient Greeks. Two members of the group, Jacopo Corsi and Jacopo Peri, set to music Rinuccini's *Dafne* (performed 1598), which was effectively the first opera. The Camerata was important mainly for the development of *monody and of the **stile rappresentativo*.

Cammerton (Ger., 'chamber pitch'). The concert pitch standard prevailing in Germany from *c*.1740 to 1820; *see* PITCH.

camminando (It.). 'Walking', i.e. moving on.

canarie (Fr.). A 17th-century French dance derived from rituals indigenous to the Canary Islands; it is in a fast, often dotted, triple metre and occurs in harpsichord suites and operas.

can-can. A lively dance, developed from the quadrille, usually performed by a troupe of women. It became popular in the music halls of mid-19th-century Paris, and was used by French operetta composers.

canción (Sp.). 'Song'. A term referring particularly to a 15th-century type of serious song, in contrast to the popular *villancico; *canción danza*, 'dance-song'.

cancionero (Sp.). A 'songbook' or, in modern usage, a collection of poetry. The word is used for the monophonic songbooks of the Iberian Middle Ages, for poetry collections, for the Spanish polyphonic songbooks of the years after *c*.1490 and, particularly from the 19th century, for collections of Spanish folksongs.

cancrizans (Lat., 'crab-like'). *See* RETROGRADE.

canon. A device in *counterpoint whereby a melody in one voice (or part) is imitated throughout, note for note, by one or more other voices, which normally begin after the first voice and overlap it. The word 'canon' (from the Greek *kanōn*) means 'rule' or 'precept', and was first used in the 15th century in connection with any piece of music which was intentionally written out in an obscure or enigmatic way and required resolution before it could be performed. At that time a piece that was strictly canonic in the present-day sense was more commonly called a *rota*, chace, *fuga* (whence the term *fugue, which now has a distinct meaning), *rondellus*, or **caccia* (whence the more familiar English *catch, or *round, e.g. *Three Blind Mice*). Contrapuntal writing that is not strictly canonic is usually termed *imitation; the composition of a true canon, however, has traditionally been regarded as among the most highly skilled compositional techniques.

The first voice to enter with the melody is the *dux* ('leader') or antecedent, and any imitating voice is the *comes* ('companion') or consequent. Canons may be described in terms of the distance (in bars or fractions of bars) between the imitating parts; for example, 'canon of two bars' means that the second voice enters with the melody two bars after the first, the third voice two bars after the second, and so on. They may also be described in terms of the interval between the voices: the commonest is the canon in unison or at the octave, but canons at the 4th and 5th are also common. Rounds and catches are canons in unison, and they also exemplify the principle of perpetual or infinite canon: when each voice reaches the end it immediately begins again, so that the piece is self-perpetuating and can be repeated as many times as desired. A canon with a separately composed ending may be termed a finite canon.

A canon for two voices using one line of melody is called a canon two in one, three voices with one melody a canon three in one, and so on. Sometimes two canons are carried on simultaneously (e.g. first and third voice in canon with one melody, second and fourth in canon with another): such group canons are defined as canon four in two, as appropriate to the number of voices and melodies involved.

A canon in which the imitating voice or voices gives out the melody in notes of longer rhythmic value than the original is called a canon by augmentation; one in which it imitates in shorter note-values is a canon by diminution. A canon in which the imitating voice gives out the melody backwards (both voices usually starting together) is called variously a retrograde canon, *canon recte et retro*, *canon rectus et invertus*, or *canon cancrizans* ('crab canon'). A canon by inversion is one in which any ascending interval in the first voice becomes a descending one in the second. These last two devices may be combined to form a mirror canon or canon in retrograde inversion, where the second voice has the melody backwards and with the intervals inverted.

A canon described as *per arsin et thesin* ('raising and lowering') may be a canon by inversion or, more usually, one in which notes on naturally accented (strong) downbeats in the first voice are displaced to unaccented (weak) upbeats in the second voice. A canon that includes 'free' parts (e.g. a four-voice piece that combines a canon two in one with two freely moving voices) is called a mixed or accompanied canon.

Canons are described as strict or free according to whether or not each pitch interval is imitated exactly. All canons at the unison and octave are necessarily strict, but at any other interval the relative position of tones and semitones in the scale used by the imitating voice is different from that in the original. In order to reproduce strictly the intervals of the melody, some notes in the imitating voice must be adjusted by accidentals; in tonal canons these will imply modulations that the continuing first voice cannot fulfil without itself modulating, which may lead to still further difficulties. Hence free canon, which allows the imitating voice to alter some intervals so as to avoid unwanted modulation, is commoner than strict. In the 20th century there was a renewed interest in canon as a means of connecting with tradition. Post-tonal composers have written rhythmic canons in which the pitch materials are not constrained by melodic correspondence,

canon cancrizans. *See* CANON.

canonic imitation. Strict *imitation, as in a *canon.

canso. Troubadour name for a strophic song taking courtly love as its theme.

cantabile (It.). 'Singable', 'in a singing style'. Beethoven often used the term to qualify a slow or moderate tempo indication, such as *adagio* or *andante*.

cantando (It.). 'Singing', **cantabile*.

cantata (It.; Fr.: *cantate*; Ger.: *Kantate*). Literally a piece to be sung, as opposed to a 'sonata', an instrumental work to be played. The term applies to a variety of genres, usually to those featuring a solo voice, with instrumental accompaniment and quite often of a quasi-dramatic character. The Baroque cantata was the most important vocal chamber genre of the era; the 18th-century church cantata was the main musical contribution to the Lutheran service.

The earliest examples, which appeared in the 1620s, used strophic variation; but a division soon began to appear (as also in operas of the period) between sections in which the text was set syllabically without much repetition (anticipating recitative) and ones where repeated and balanced phrases provided a more tuneful, aria-like character. A second generation produced longer and more sectionalized settings with frequent alternation between the incipient recitative and aria of the period, and using an intermediate stage similar to arioso. These cantatas were usually for soprano and continuo, later orchestra. In France and England, the cantata was essentially the same as the Italian type.

In parallel with the development of the secular cantata there arose that of the solo motet to a sacred text. Most influential on the Protestant cantata was the concertato chorale, a form derived from the early 17th-century practice of setting hymns with a different combination of voices, solo and choral, for each verse. It was on this basis, and that of the secular cantata with recitatives and arias, that the church cantata of the first 30 years of the 18th century developed, eventually attaining its climax with the large-scale works of Bach. The grand church cantata typically involved an orchestral prelude, a chorus (on a chorale or biblical text), two pairs of recitatives and arias, separated by a further chorus (often using the same chorale), and a final chordal setting, again of the basic chorale, for congregational use. Bach is known to have composed over 300 church cantatas, many of which have been lost, as well as a number of secular works including the well-known 'Peasant' and 'Coffee' cantatas. The genre fell from use in the 18th century, but during the 20th 'cantata' was an umbrella term for diverse choral and orchestral works.

cante flamenco. *See* FLAMENCO, CANTE FLAMENCO.

canti carnascialeschi (It., pl. of *canto carnascialesco*). *'Carnival songs'.

canticle (from Lat. *canticulum*, dim. of *canticum*, 'song'). A song or prayer (other than a psalm) derived from the Bible and used in the liturgical worship of Eastern and Western Christian Churches. The three canticles drawn from the New Testament used daily in the medieval and modern offices of the Roman rite are the *Benedictus* (for which the **Jubilate* is sometimes substituted), the **Magnificat*, and the **Nunc dimittis*, at Lauds, Vespers, and Compline respectively. The Book of Canticles is another name for the Song of Solomon.

cantiga (Sp., Port.). 'Song'. A term usually taken to refer to the 13th-century Spanish monophonic song in honour of the Virgin Mary.

C

cantilena (It.; Fr.: *cantilène*). **1.** A lyrical vocal melody or instrumental passage performed in a smooth style, particularly in the 18th century. **2.** A short song or, in medieval times, any secular piece, such as a *ballade*, *virelai*, or *rondeau*. **3.** In choral music, the part that carries the main tune. **4.** A type of *solfeggio, or vocal exercise, using the whole scale.

cantillation. The chanting of a text in a plainchant style. The term is used primarily in connection with the performance of Jewish liturgical music.

cantio (Lat.). 'Song', especially the medieval, monophonic song; *cantio sacra*, 'sacred song' or *motet.

cantique (Fr.). *'Canticle', *'hymn'.

canto (It., Sp.). 'Song', 'melody'; *col canto*, 'with the melody', i.e. the accompanist should follow closely any fluctuations in tempo etc. made by the performer of the melodic line.

canto carnascialesco (It.). *'Carnival song'.

canto de órgano (Sp.). Spanish term for polyphony in the Renaissance and Baroque periods (as opposed to *canto llano*, 'plainchant').

cantor. 1. In modern Anglican and Roman Catholic usage, the singer who is charged with the duty of intoning the first words of psalms, antiphons, and hymns. Cantors, especially on feast days, often work in pairs at the desk in the middle of the choir. *See also* KANTOR. **2.** The leading singer in a synagogue.

cantoris (Lat., 'of the singer'). The side of the choir on which the *precentor sits, now normally the north side. Choral music sometimes has passages marked *cantoris*, indicating that the singers on that side should take the passage. *See also* DECANI.

cantus (Lat.). 'Song', 'melody'. The term has been used more specifically to denote the highest voice-part in a polyphonic work; *see* PART, 1.

cantus coronatus (Lat., 'crowned song'). A medieval term for a type of embellished trouvère song, perhaps so called because it or its composer had won a prize.

cantus firmus (Lat., 'fixed melody' or 'firm melody', pl. cantus firmi; It.: *canto fermo*). A pre-existing melody taken as the basis of a new polyphonic composition. Such melodies can be plainchant, secular, or invented themes. The cantus firmus was usually 'held' in long notes in the lower voice, the tenor. Plainchant melodies, or sections of them, were taken as cantus firmi in the earliest forms of polyphony (e.g. *organum, *clausula) and in the 13th- and 14th-century *motet and some early mass movements. Secular melodies were used occasionally in the 13th- and 14th-century motet, and frequently in the mass from at least the mid-15th century. Invented themes are those originally derived from the *hexachord or from the vowels of a group of words (usually a name) by applying *solmization syllables; the latter is sometimes described as a *soggetto cavato* (It., 'extracted subject').

From *c*.1480 there was a decline in the use of a cantus firmus as an important structural component, and by the 16th century strict cantus-firmus masses and motets were seen as old-fashioned, and were composed only rarely. A late flowering of the cantus firmus was in the use of chorale melodies as the basis of such forms as the *chorale cantata and the *chorale prelude.

cantus fractus (Lat., 'broken song'). A rhythmicized form of plainchant used in the 15th century, particularly for new melodies for the Credo and certain antiphon, sequence, and hymn texts.

cantus planus (Lat.). *'Plainchant'.

canzo. *See* CANSO.

canzona (It., 'song') [canzona francese, canzona da sonar]. The most important instrumental form of the late 16th and early 17th centuries. The earliest canzonas, for lute or keyboard instruments, were arrangements of such vocal works as French chansons from the first half of the 16th century. These chansons, with their lively rhythms and melodies, often imitative openings (typically beginning with a minim and two crotchets or similar motif), and their simple, distinctive structure (with repeated sections at the beginning or end to give an AABC, ABCC, or even ABCA pattern), translated well from a vocal to an instrumental idiom. Later composers embellished their models elaborately, transforming their nature. This led to the composition of pieces conceived wholly in instrumental terms.

By the end of the 18th century such works had become extremely popular, especially among composers in Venice. Giovanni Gabrieli's canzonas were written for the large instrumental ensemble at St Mark's, adapting the idiom of **cori spezzati* to bring a grand scale into instrumental music. The sectional nature of the canzona conveyed the contrasts of emotion that were to the taste of Baroque composers. Different sections came to be contrasted so that they either brought new counterpoints or harmonies to a single unifying theme—in effect, sets of free variations—or were essentially diverse in texture and musical material. This second manner ('patch canzona' or *'quilt canzona') led to individual sections becoming almost independent units or movements. By *c.*1650 most such pieces were called, more logically, 'sonata'. Fugal movements in sonatas, however, were sometimes entitled 'canzona'.

canzone (It.). 'Song'. **1.** The canzoni of Dante and Petrarch, lyric poems written in such a way as to be apt for musical setting, were used by several composers in the 15th and 16th centuries. **2.** In the 16th century, 'canzone' was frequently used as a title, or as part of a title (*see*, e.g., VILLANELLA), for a popular or folk-like secular song.

canzonetta (It., dim. of *canzone). 'Canzonet'. From the late 16th century to the 18th, a term applied to short vocal pieces in a light, often dance-like style. The term appeared in England mainly through the collections of Italian canzonettas made by Thomas Morley, whose canzonets tended to match the seriousness and the form (single-stanza, through-composed) of the madrigal. Germans also used the term. In the 18th century, 'canzonetta' was used as a title for a light, lyrical kind of solo song; it has also occasionally been borrowed for instrumental pieces.

capella. A common misspelling of **cappella*.

capo (It.). *See* DA CAPO.

cappella (It.). 'Chapel'; *a cappella, alla cappella*, 'in the church style', meaning that a piece of choral music is to be sung unaccompanied (or, if accompanied, that the instrument—probably an organ—should simply double the voice parts). A rare application of the term makes it a synonym for **alla breve*.

capriccio (It., 'whim', 'fancy'; Fr.: *caprice*). **1.** A term applied to a piece of music, vocal or instrumental, of a fantastical or capricious nature. In the 16th century it was sometimes given to madrigals, but in the early 17th it was used more for keyboard pieces using fugal imitation, though not necessarily following the rules of strict counterpoint. The Baroque capriccio closely resembles the keyboard *canzona, *toccata, or *ricercar; other examples are related to dance forms. Programmatic elements are common in many capriccios, with pieces imitating such sounds as birdsong or horn calls. Other keyboard capriccios were often in the style of free fantasias. In the 19th century, the term was used both for short, humorous pieces and for colourful orchestral works. **2.** In the 18th century the direction *a capriccio* was sometimes used to indicate a *cadenza. Often written out in full, such passages were sometimes published separately as virtuoso technical studies. Paganini called his violin studies capriccios.

C

capriccioso (It.), **capricieux** (Fr.). 'Capricious'; *capricciosamente*, in a lively, informal style.

caprice. *See* CAPRICCIO.

carezzando, carezzevole (It.). 'Caressingly', 'soothingly'.

carmen (Lat.). 'Song', 'poem'. The word was used during the Middle Ages and the Renaissance to refer to various kinds of vocal music; it has also been used in connection with instrumental music derived from vocal chansons.

Carnival song (It.: *canto carnascialesco*, pl. *canti carnascialeschi*). A secular song performed in late 15th- and early 16th-century Florence as part of the festivals of Carnival (before Lent) and Calendimaggio (from 1 May). One of the most common types was the *mascherata, performed by masked singers. More serious texts were set as *carri* and *trionfi*.

carol. A term associated with Christmas song but which has been used to denote various different genres. In the Middle Ages it referred to a song, in a musical form peculiar to England, which began with a refrain (a 'burden') and was followed by verses (stanzas) of uniform structure; the burden is repeated after each verse. Beginning as a monophonic dance-song (Fr.: *carole*), the carol evolved in the 15th century into a vigorous polyphonic song in triple metre. After the Reformation the carol declined, but the term was applied to Christmas folk *ballads or strophic hymns with Christmas words, some with a refrain. In the later 19th century Victorian Christmas hymns in square, four-part harmony were introduced; these remain in current use.

carole (Fr.). A medieval French name for a round dance (*see* ROUND).

carré (Fr.). A double semibreve or breve.

cassation (Ger.: *Kassation*; It.: *cassazione*). An 18th-century instrumental form, especially popular in Vienna and elsewhere in Austria. It is related to the *divertimento and *serenade, and consists of a variable series of movements for strings and wind in sonata or dance form, each shorter but more numerous than the corresponding movements of a symphony. Cassations were light in character; unlike the serenade, their performances were not restricted to the evenings, though they were usually performed in the open air.

castrato (It.). A male singer who kept the soprano or alto range of his voice into adulthood as a result of having been castrated before puberty. This practice originated in Italy and Spain in the 16th century. Castratos sang in the Sistine Chapel choir until the late 19th century; in opera they reached the summit of their popularity in 18th-century *opera seria* and survived into the mid-19th century. They were famed for their brilliant, penetrating timbre and extraordinary breath control.

catalogue, thematic. *See* THEMATIC CATALOGUE.

catch. A variety of English *round, with the additional feature that the words are so treated as to introduce some point of humour (often a pun); they celebrate the joys of drink, male conviviality, hunting, or lechery. The origin of the term is unknown. Catches were popular between the late 16th century and the 19th and were usually performed by three or more men. *See also* GLEE.

cavata (It., 'epigram'). In musical usage, a short *arioso at the end of a passage of recitative.

cavatina (It., dim. of *cavata*). In 18th- and 19th-century opera, a short solo song, simple in style and lacking the *da capo*, often consisting of a short instrumental introduction to a single sentence or statement set to music. In 19th-century Italian opera the music frequently demanded elaborate virtuosity. The term is sometimes applied to a song-like air included as part of a long scena or accompanied recitative, or to a songlike piece of music.

cb. (It.). Abbreviation for *contrabasso* ('double bass') or *col basso* ('with the bass').

C clef. *See* CLEF.

c.d. (It.). Abbreviation for **colla destra*.

cebell [cibell]. A type of gavotte, found mainly in late 17th-century English harpsichord music. The name comes from an *air* in gavotte style from Lully's opera *Atys* (1676) that accompanies the descent to earth of the goddess Cybele. In England the title 'Cebell' or 'Cibell' was used for keyboard pieces (the first English example, however, is a lute piece).

cedendo (It.). 'Becoming slower'.

cédez (Fr.). 'Yield', i.e. slow down; *cédant*, 'slowing down'.

celere (It.). 'Quickly', 'swiftly'; *celeramente*, 'with speed'.

cembalo (It.). 'Harpsichord'.

centonization. Composing by patchwork (Lat.: *cento*), using pre-existing material. The term *cento* has been used in literature since classical times to describe a poem built of received matter, particularly from Homer and Virgil. It was imported to the study of music to explain the recurrence of certain melodic shapes in different Gregorian chants.

cercar la nota (It., 'look for the note'). In vocal technique, a slight anticipation of the following note.

Ces (Ger.). The note C♭; *Ceses*, the note C𝄫.

chace (Fr.). A type of French 14th-century canon, usually for two or three voices; *see* CACCIA.

chaconne (Fr.; It.: *ciaccona*; Sp.: *chacona*) [chacony]. A form of continuous variation, similar to the *passacaglia, which became popular during the Baroque era as a dance and instrumental form. It originated in Latin America in the late 16th century as a lively dance in triple metre which had both instrumental and vocal accompaniment. The name derives from the appearance of the word *chacona* (of uncertain meaning) in the refrain. The first notated examples were Italian guitar tablatures that present only a series of harmonic schemes (e.g. I–V–VI–V; I–VI–IV–V; I–V–V–V) over which variations were composed. These were soon followed by fully notated pieces, almost always in triple metre and of a dance-like character, for violin, voice, chitarrone, or keyboard. Some Italian composers used the same melody throughout the piece, repeating it continually in the manner of a *ground bass.

In France, the chaconne became slower and more stately (as did the *sarabande on its removal to France from Spain). It was often in rondeau form with the repeated chaconne melodies restricted to the refrain sections, as in the passacaglia. In Germany the chaconne flourished particularly in the later 17th century and the first half of the 18th. Several were for solo organ: these were often highly contrapuntal and used newly composed bass patterns. The form was less popular in England, though there are some fine examples of 'chacony', notably by Purcell. The chaconne fell from favour in the Classical period but appeared occasionally in the late 19th century and during the 20th.

chacony. Old English term for *chaconne.

chaleur (Fr.). 'Warmth', 'passion'; *chaleureux*, *chaleureusement*, 'with warmth'.

chamber music. Music written for a small ensemble, either for private (domestic) performance or, if in the presence of an audience, for a relatively small hall. The usual combinations are those for from two to ten instruments, which may include the piano, all stringed instruments, woodwind, and, occasionally, brass instruments. *See also* CANZONA; CASSATION; DIVERTIMENTO; FANTASIA; OCTET; PIANO QUARTET; PIANO QUINTET; PIANO TRIO; QUARTET; QUINTET; SEPTET; SERENADE; SEXTET; TRIO, 1; TRIO SONATA; WIND QUINTET.

chamber opera. An opera written for small forces, especially instrumental ones. The genre proved particularly appealing to 20th-century composers. 18th-century operas for small forces, such as Pergolesi's *La serva padrona*, which is strictly speaking an *intermezzo, have retrospectively attracted the description 'chamber opera'. More radical musical and dramatic ideas combined with the instrumental forces of chamber opera to produce *music theatre in the 1960s and 70s.

chamber orchestra. A small orchestra, usually with the forces that predominated in the second half of the 18th century: pairs of oboes, bassoons, and horns with a small body of strings (six to eight first and second violins, four violas, four cellos, and one or two basses). Flutes, clarinets, trumpets, and timpani are added as required. Such orchestras play music of the Baroque and Classical eras on modern instruments (as distinct from 'early music orchestras' or 'period instrument ensembles') and have a considerable modern repertory.

champêtre (Fr., 'rural', 'rustic'). A *danse champêtre* is a peasant dance performed in the open air. There are examples of the 'fête champêtre' in French Baroque opera.

chance operations. A term introduced by John Cage for techniques that open the compositional process to chance, for example the tossing of a coin to determine pitches. *See also* INDETERMINATE MUSIC.

change-ringing. A style of ringing church bells or handbells, organized into a musical structure, which originated in the Church of England in the 17th century. The number of bells in a peal varies from three to 12, usually tuned to a diatonic major scale, or part of one. Each member of the bell-ringing team pulls the rope controlling one bell. The bells are rung in a number of pre-arranged sequences, or 'changes'.

changing note. *See* NOTA CAMBIATA.

chanson (Fr., from Lat. *cantio* via Provençal *canso* and It. *canzon*, 'song'). A song setting French words. The term is used chiefly of French polyphonic songs of the Middle Ages and Renaissance. From the 12th century survive such narrative genres as the *chanson de geste* (epic song) and such shorter lyrical forms as the *chanson de toile* (spinning song), divided into strophes sometimes including a refrain. Between the 13th and 15th centuries most of the shorter lyric forms, derived from the round dance (*carole*), were designated by their fixed rhyme form—*rondet*, *rondel*, **rondeau* (ABaAabAB), **ballade* (ababbcCC), or **virelai/bergerette* (ABccabAB)—and were set to music for two, three, or four voices.

During the 14th century there was increasing melismatic elaboration, rhythmic complexity, and independence of part-writing in the chanson, but in the 15th century a reaction to the mannered complexity of Ars Nova or *ars subtilior* composers is found in the chansons of English composers, who wrote mostly fixed-form poems for three parts. Although the lower parts were frequently conceived for and played on instruments, these chansons achieve greater clarity of melody and counterpoint—based generally on *fauxbourdon (6-3) rather than root-position (5-3) harmony. The highpoint of the polyphonic chanson as an international form was reached in the 16th century, when an enormous repertory of three-, four-, and five-part pieces appeared in print. With French supplanting Latin as the leading European language of the late Middle Ages, the chanson became the main type of secular music of Renaissance Europe. Chansons were also frequently arranged for instrumental solo or ensemble, inspiring such new forms as the *canzona, *fantasia, and *variations. They also provided the melodic and even harmonic substance for much new sacred music, notably 'imitation' or 'parody' masses and *Magnificat* settings. *See also* AIR, 2; AIR À BOIRE; AIR DE COUR; CHANSON DE CROISADE; CHANSON DE GESTE; CHANSON SPIRITUELLE; LIED; MÉLODIE; MONODY, 2; ROMANCE; SONG.

chanson de croisade (Fr., 'crusade song'). A type of song written by medieval singer-performers in the expectation of, or in reaction to, going on crusade. Most frequently associated with troubadours, such songs are also found among the works of Minnesinger, in which case they are known as *Kreuzlieder*.

chanson de geste. A French medieval epic poem, often of considerable length and divided into sections. The poem was sung to short musical phrases, probably involving a certain amount of repetition, of a simple nature so as not to distract the listener from the narrative.

chansonnier. A book (either manuscript or printed) whose principal content is chansons (French lyric poetry), either in their text form or set to music. In these terms the earliest chansonniers are the manuscripts transmitting the works of the troubadours and trouvères, but the word is more normally used with reference to polyphonic song manuscripts of the 15th and 16th centuries.

chanson sans paroles (Fr.). *'Song without words'.

chanson spirituelle (Fr., 'spiritual song'). A type of French secular *chanson of the second half of the 16th century, the texts of which are spiritual or moralistic in tone. Most examples were written by Protestants, though similar chansons by Catholics also exist. In many cases existing chansons were simply given new words.

chant. *See* ANGLICAN CHANT; PLAINCHANT.

chantant, chanté (Fr.). 'Singing', 'in a singing style'.

chanty. *See* SHANTY.

character piece (Ger.: *Characterstück*). A piece designed to convey a specific allusion, atmosphere, mood, or scene (such as pastoral serenity, agitation, or rustic ceremony), without a text, programme, or stage action. Such pieces held a unique place in the piano music of the 19th century, when abstract forms lost much of their appeal, *Romanticism encouraged literary influences on music, and *nationalism led composers to evoke the folk music of nations or ethnic groups. Character pieces are typically in a single movement and involve the return of the opening theme after a digression. *See also* BAGATELLE; BALLADE; CAPRICCIO; IMPROMPTU; INTERMEZZO; LYRIC, 2 (lyric piece); NOCTURNE; NOVELETTE; PRELUDE; RHAPSODY; SONG WITHOUT WORDS.

charivari (Fr.). A noisy and violent ceremony involving improvised music performed with household utensils. It was originally given as a public expression of disapproval but later took the form of a mock serenade performed beneath the windows of newly married couples. In Germany it is known as *Katzenmusik* ('cats' music'), in England 'rough music', and in Italy *chiasso* ('hubbub').

chef d'attaque (Fr.). *'Leader'.

chef d'orchestre (Fr.) *'Conductor'.

chest of viols. A term used in 16th- and 17th-century England for a matched set of viols, typically comprising two trebles, two or three tenors, and one or two basses, so called because they were kept in a specially built chest or press.

chest voice. A term used to denote the lower part of the male and female voice, in contradistinction to the head voice.

chevalet (Fr.). *'Bridge'.

chevrotement (Fr.). *'Goat's trill'.

chiamata (It., 'call', 'summons'; Fr.: *chamade*). In early Venetian opera, a fanfare-like piece written in imitation of hunting horns.

C

chiaro, chiaramente (It.). 'Clear', 'clearly'.

chiasso (It.). *See* CHARIVARI.

chiave (It.). *'Clef'; *chiavette*, 'little clef'.

chiesa (It., 'church'). For *concerto da chiesa see* CONCERTO; for *sonata da chiesa see* SONATA.

chironomy (from Gk. *kheir*, 'hand', *nomos*, 'law'). The practice of indicating the changing pitches of a melody by regulated movements of the hand, or (less commonly) by pointing to various positions on the hand (for the latter, *see* GUIDONIAN HAND).

chiuso (It., 'closed'). **1.** In horn playing, the same as *stopped. **2.** *See* OUVERT AND CLOS.

choeur (Fr.). 'Chorus' or 'choir'. The term *grand choeur* is also used to denote a group of stops added to the *fonds d'orgue* on French post-classical organs.

choir, chorus (Fr.: *choeur*; Ger.: *Chor*; It.: *coro*). Both terms denote a body of singers performing as a group, normally, though not necessarily, in parts. The English language appears to be alone in perpetuating a useful distinction between 'choir' and 'chorus'. The latter is commonly used to denote larger groups of singers—especially amateur enthusiasts, but also professionals in the theatre and opera house. 'Choir' is applied mostly to smaller bodies of singers: to ecclesiastical groups, and to small, expert groups such as are often composed of professionals and called 'chamber choirs'. A mixed-voice choir (or chorus) is one of women and men; a male-voice choir is of men or boys and men; a double choir is one arranged in two groups.

choirbook. A term generally used to denote a book from the 14th–17th centuries in which all the voices of a polyphonic composition are written separately. The upper voice is always on the top of the left-hand page, the lowest is usually at the bottom of the right-hand page, and so on. From *c*.1500, as choirs grew larger, individual partbooks gradually took over.

Chor (Ger.). 'Chorus' or *'choir'.

Choralbearbeitung (Ger., 'chorale reworking'). Specifically, a work—vocal or instrumental—based on a Protestant chorale melody (e.g. *chorale cantata, *chorale prelude). However, the term has also been applied more widely to pieces based on any kind of pre-existing sacred melody, particularly plainchant, and therefore embraces Notre Dame *organum as well as many late medieval and Renaissance motets.

chorale (from Ger. *Choral*). The strophic congregational hymn of the Protestant Church in Germany. The German term originally signified a plainchant melody sung chorally, but from the late 16th century its meaning was widened to include vernacular hymns. Strictly, the word 'chorale' implies both the text and the melody, but it is often used to describe the music alone—either a single-line melody or a fully harmonized version as in the four-part settings of J. S. Bach. Two main types of chorale book were published during the 16th century, one containing polyphonic settings for trained choirs, with the melody normally placed in the tenor voice, and the other with single-line melodies only, for congregations. The Thirty Years War fostered the composition of subjective, devotional chorales. During the 18th century harmonizations consisting of a melodic line with figured-bass accompaniment became standard. Chorale texts and melodies were the basis of many other genres; see the entries that follow this one.

chorale cantata (Ger.: *Choralkantate*). A cantata with two or more movements based on chorale texts (and usually also melodies). There are three main types: those in which one chorale is used for all the movements; those in which some movements use texts from other sources; and those in which some chorale verses are paraphrased as free poetry, in the form of recitatives and arias. The last type was devised by J. S. Bach.

chorale concerto. A 17th-century sacred vocal piece based on a chorale.

chorale fantasia. An organ work in the free style of a fantasia based on a chorale melody (*see* ORGAN CHORALE). Chorale fantasias, often large-scale works, were composed by many north German 17th- and 18th-century composers, and the genre was revived in the late 19th century.

chorale fugue (Ger.: *Choralfuge*). An organ fugue taking as its subject the first line (or two lines) of a chorale melody (*see* ORGAN CHORALE). Chorale fugues were composed in Germany from the late 17th century.

chorale mass. A mass based on the German chorales appropriate to the items of the Lutheran liturgy.

chorale motet (Ger.: *Choralmotette*). A polyphonic composition based on a chorale melody. At first the melody was treated as a *cantus firmus, but from the end of the 16th century it became more usual to use each line as a subject for fugal imitation. Sometimes the organ may replace one or more of the voice parts.

chorale partita. *See* CHORALE VARIATIONS.

chorale prelude (Ger.: *Choralvorspiel*). A setting of a chorale melody, usually for organ, and originally having the function in the Lutheran service of introducing congregational singing of that same melody. It could, however, particularly by the 18th century, take on an independent role. *See also* ORGAN CHORALE.

chorale trio. A type of *organ chorale devised by J. S. Bach.

chorale variations. A set of variations, usually for keyboard, on a chorale melody (*see* ORGAN CHORALE). The genre developed during the 17th century, modelled on secular variation sets.

Choralfuge (Ger.). *'Chorale fugue'.

Choralmotette (Ger.). *'Chorale motet'.

Choralvorspiel (Ger.). *'Chorale prelude'.

chord (Fr.: *accord*; Ger.: *Akkord*, *Klang*; It.: *accordo*). Two or more notes sounded together. The different types are named according to the *intervals they span: the *triad, for example—the fundamental chord in Western harmony—is built from a 'root' note with two superposed 3rds; the *dominant 7th consists of a triad on the dominant of the diatonic major scale with the addition of the note a 7th above the dominant. *See also* INVERSION, 1; ROOT, ROOT POSITION.

choreographic poem. A piece of music originally designed as a ballet, but which can also stand as an orchestral work in its own right.

Chorlied (Ger.). A choral song, especially one without accompaniment.

Chorton (Ger., 'choir pitch'). The term used by 18th-century German theorists to denote a *pitch standard higher than normal in Italy and in organs.

chorus. *See* CHOIR.

chromaticism (from Gk. *khroma*, 'colour'). The use of a scale that divides the octave into 12 equal intervals of a semitone (*see* SCALE).

church modes. *See* MODE.

ciaccona (It.). *See* CHACONNE.

cibell. *See* CEBELL.

circle of fifths. A graphic representation, in the shape of a circle, of key notes with their signatures (Fig. 1). C is at the top of the circle, from where the notes progress clockwise in ascending 5ths (C–G–D, etc.). At the bottom of the circle, the note F♯ is called also by its *enharmonic name, G♭, and the same happens with the next note, C♯/D♭; the notes on the return to C are then called by their flat names (A♭, E♭, etc.). The return to C can be made only in *equal temperament; if Pythagorean 5ths were used, the series would be infinite. The key signatures are placed against their respective key notes, the major keys being shown in the outer circle, the minor ones (in lower-case letters) in the inner one. The circle of 5ths shows the relative 'closeness' and 'distance' of one key from another: for example, C major and F♯ major, at opposite ends of the circle, have not one triad in common.

circular breathing. A technique by which a continuous tone is sustained on a wind instrument.

Cis (Ger.). The note C♯; *Cisis*, the note C𝄪.

cl. Abbreviation for clarinet.

class. A theoretical term, most common in writings about post-tonal music. The pitch class C is used to refer to Cs in general, with no particular C implied. 'Interval class' refers to the number of semitones between the constituent pitches, with the first pitch as 0: interval class 2 is C–D, or the equivalent; interval class 6 is C–F♯, C♯–G, and so on. The intention is to provide an alternative to terms from tonal theory, e.g. major 2nd, which have functional implications.

Classical. In a general sense, 'classical', when applied to music, refers to Western art music, as opposed to folk, light, or popular music. More specifically, the term 'Classical' was adopted in the 19th century to describe music from the period *c*.1750–1830, principally that of Haydn, Mozart, and Beethoven (the 'Viennese Classical School'); it is used also in contradistinction to the Romantic movement that followed. Characteristics of Classical music include symmetrical phrase structure, static bass lines, the use of dynamics and orchestral colour, and the use of modulation for structural purposes. *Sonata form permeates virtually all the music of the Classical period, which saw the development of the symphony, concerto, and string quartet. *See also* NEO-CLASSICISM; STURM UND DRANG.

Circle of fifths, Fig. 1

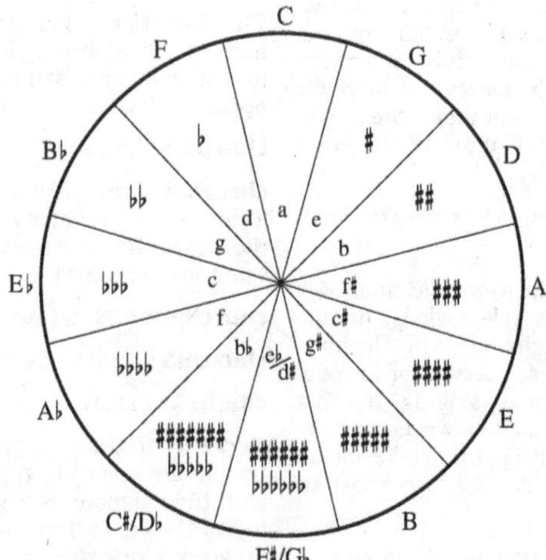

clausula (Lat.). **1.** A term usually related to medieval music, particularly that of the Notre Dame period, denoting either the concluding of a passage or the passage itself so concluded. It is often thought to mean 'cadence', but differs from the modern definition of that term in that it refers to the melodic formulas of the individual voices, with no implication of typical harmonic progressions. In the 18th century this distinction was lost, and 'clausula' became synonymous with 'cadence'; the *clausula vera* came to be seen as the equivalent of the perfect cadence, *clausula falsa* the interrupted cadence, *clausula plagalis* the plagal cadence, and so on. **2.** A polyphonic composition based not on an entire chant, as was the case with organum, but on a short portion of one. Clausulae may originally have been composed as passages for substitution in organum compositions, but they soon acquired their own position as self-sufficient pieces to be sung at appropriate points in the liturgy. The clausula developed into the 13th-century *motet.

clavecin (Fr.). 'Harpsichord'.

clavicembalo (It.). 'Harpsichord'.

clef (Fr., 'key'; Ger.: *Schlüssel*; It.: *chiave*). A sign written at the beginning of the staff to indicate the pitch of the notes. There are three signs in present-day usage (Fig. 1). The G (or treble) clef marks the second line up on the staff, and indicates that the pitch of that note is *g'* the F (or bass) clef marks the fourth line up on the staff, and indicates that the pitch of that note is *f*. The C clef is movable, and may be found marking either the middle line of the staff (alto or viola clef), or the fourth line up (tenor clef); in each case it indicates that that particular note is *c'*.

Fig. 1

The G clef is used for the upper staff of keyboard music, the soprano voice, and the high instruments (e.g. violin or flute). When the G clef appears with a figure '8' attached to its tail the pitch of the note is g (an octave below that of the ordinary G clef); this is the tenor G clef, and it is often used in vocal music. The F clef is used for the lower staff of keyboard music and for all bass voices or instruments. The alto clef is used for the viola and similar instruments, and the tenor for the high notes of the cello, bassoon, tenor trombone, etc. *See also* NOTATION.

clos (Fr.). *See* OUVERT AND CLOS.

close. *See* CADENCE.

close harmony. A passage of music is said to be in close harmony when the notes of the chords are all closely spaced, not extending beyond the interval of about a 12th. The technique appears in *barber-shop singing. When the notes are fairly widely spaced, a passage is said to be in open harmony. *See also* POSITION, 2.

cluster. A group of adjacent notes, usually on the piano, where clusters may be performed with the fist, palm, or forearm. Piano clusters were introduced in the early 20th century.

coda (It., from Lat. *cauda*, 'tail'). An addition to a standard form or design, occurring after the main structure of a piece or melody has been completed with a cadence in the home key. In *strophic form the coda would occur after the last verse, in *variation form after the last variation, in *binary form after the second section has ended (generally with a repeat mark), and in *sonata form after all the material of the exposition has been recapitulated.

codetta (It., dim. of 'coda'). **1.** A brief *coda or conclusion. **2.** In *fugue, any passage in the exposition that links two entries of the theme, provided that the theme ends with a definite cadence, giving the impression that what follows is in the nature of a link. **3.** A short cadential passage at the end of a *sonata-form exposition.

col, coll', colla, coi, colle (It.). 'With', 'with the'.

colenda. *See* KOLĘDA.

C

colla destra, colla sinistra (It.). 'With the right (hand)', 'with the left (hand)'.

colla parte, colla voce (It.). 'With the part', 'with the voice'. An indication to play another, written-out part, or to an accompanist to look to the main part for guidance on tempo, etc.

colla punta dell'arco (It.). In string playing, an instruction to play 'at the point of the bow'.

coll'arco (It., 'with the bow'; sometimes abbreviated *c.a.*). A direction to string players to resume playing with the bow after a pizzicato passage.

colla sinistra. *See* COLLA DESTRA, COLLA SINISTRA.

colla voce. *See* COLLA PARTE, COLLA VOCE.

collection. A term used in the discussion of atonal music to denote a group of different notes without making any implication about that group. Thus a *set is a collection, but a collection is not necessarily a set.

collegium musicum. An organization of professional musicians and amateurs who met regularly to sing and play music privately, either in such informal settings as coffee houses or public gardens, or in the homes of noble patrons. The *collegium musicum* originated in 16th-century Germany and spread to other German-speaking Protestant regions and to the Netherlands.

col legno (It., 'with the wood'). A direction to string players to strike the strings with the stick of the bow, rather than with the hair.

coll'ottava (It.). 'With the octave', a direction to a keyboard player to double notes an octave higher, or lower if 'basso' is added.

coloration. A device used in early music notation to reduce the normal value of a note by a third. Before about 1450 'colored' (*sic*) notes were usually red. Later, the note-heads of colored notes were normally filled in black. Coloration produced two slightly different rhythmic effects: in music in duple time (modern 2/4, 4/4) it was used to write down triplets; but, for music with triple-time elements (3/4, 6/8), colored notes produced a *hemiola effect of three against two, equivalent either to three straight crotchets in a modern 6/8 bar, or to three undotted minims across two bars of 3/4.

coloratura (It., 'colouring'). A term applied to elaborate decoration, either extemporized or notated, of a vocal melody (by figuration, ornamentation, etc.). A coloratura soprano is one with a high, light, agile voice capable of singing virtuoso arias.

colpo d'arco (It.). 'Bowstroke'.

combinatoriality. In *twelve-note music, that property of a set which makes one part of it complementary to another under the serial procedures of transposition, inversion, or retrograding (*see* SERIALISM). The term, a mathematical one, was first used in a musical context in the 1950s, although earlier 12-note compositions use the principle in a straightforward way. In the most common case, each hexachord of a 12-note set is combinatorial with the same hexachords of a transposed inversion: that is, each pair of hexachords combines to give all 12 notes.

come (It.). 'As', 'like'; *come prima*, 'as at first', i.e. to be performed as it was the first time; *come stà*, 'as it stands'; *come sopra*, 'as above'.

comédie-ballet (Fr.). A genre of music theatre cultivated at the French court during the late 17th century. Devised by Molière and Lully, it attempted to link the content of the ballet and song presented in the **intermèdes* to the plot of the principal (spoken) drama.

comes. *See* CANON.

comic opera. *See* OPERA; OPERA BUFFA.

comma. A minute interval (generally taken to be a ninth of a whole tone) which results when a succession of untempered 5ths and a similar succession of octaves arrive at what is ostensibly the same note, but is not really quite such. *See* EQUAL TEMPERAMENT; TEMPERAMENT.

commedia dell'arte. A form of semi-improvised Italian comic theatre popular in the 16th and 17th centuries. It made use of stock scenes (*lazzi*), characters, and masks. The plots usually concerned customs surrounding marriage and procreation, while mocking the earthier aspects of love and sex, and punning on gender reversals. The entertainment often had a musical performance as its climax, and dances and songs were usually performed both within the plays (often villanellas and scherzos) and between acts (madrigals). The episodic form influenced 17th-century Venetian opera and the madrigal comedy, and its conventions and characters—Arlecchino, Scaramuccia, Pantalone—informed a range of comic operas.

commedia per musica (It., 'comedy through music'). A term used in the 18th century, particularly in Naples, to refer to **opera buffa*.

commodo. *See* COMODO, COMODAMENTE.

common chord. A triad in which the 5th is perfect, i.e. the major or minor triad. In American usage, only the major triad is so described.

common time. Another name for 4/4 time. It is sometimes denoted by the letter **C**, which does not stand for 'common' but dates back to the period of mensural notation when triple (or perfect) time was indicated by a full circle, and duple or quadruple (imperfect) time by a semicircle (C).

commosso (It.). 'Moved', 'excited'.

comodo, comodamente (It.). 'Comfortable', 'convenient'; *tempo comodo*, 'at a comfortable, moderate speed'.

compass (Fr.: *étendue*; Ger.: *Umfang*). The range of pitches obtainable from an instrument or voice.

complete cadence. *See* CADENCE.

composition. The activity of composing and the result of that activity. It is not an exclusively musical term—applications to prose, poetry, painting, architecture, etc. are common—and in all cases it describes a process of construction, a creative putting together, a working out and carrying through of an initial conception or inspiration.

compound interval. An *interval larger than an octave.

compound time [compound metre]. A time signature having a triple pulse within each beat, such as 6/8, 6/4 (respectively, two beats of three quavers each, and two beats of three crotchets each; both called compound duple time), 9/8 (three beats of three quavers each; compound triple time), or 12/8 (four beats of three quavers each; compound quadruple time).

comprimario (It.). In opera, a role of secondary importance, or a singer taking such a part.

con (It.). 'With'. Phrases beginning with 'con' are given under the word following.

concert. A musical performance given for an audience, generally by relatively large numbers of players or singers; for performances by small groups or soloists, the term *'recital' is preferred.

concertante (It., from *concertare*, 'to agree', 'to act together'). A term used to describe music that has a solo element or is in some other way concerto-like. In common with *concertato, it was used in the Baroque period to describe a group of soloists, instrumental or vocal, in works such as the concerto grosso or in a motet where one (usually smaller) body of performers is contrasted with another. In the 18th century, 'concertante' was linked with the symphony in such titles as **symphonie concertante* (indicating a symphonic work with a number of parts for soloists), and with the string quartet to form the 'concertante quartet' (more usually found in the French form *quatuor concertant*), denoting that all four parts should be regarded as equal in status (not, as in the 19th-century use of the same title, indicating special brilliance in the first violin). In the context of accompanied keyboard sonatas, the label 'concertante' distinguishes an obbligato violin accompaniment from an optional one. In 20th-century instrumental works the term implies a soloistic element that falls short of what would be expected in a full concerto.

concertato (It., from *concertare*, 'to agree', 'to act together'). A term, related to 'concerto', used in the 17th century to describe music that involves some element of contrast in its performance. In instrumental music, a number of concertato soloists might be required to play in contrast to, as well as in combination with, a larger body of *ripieno players. In vocal works, a small *coro concertato* might be set against the full complement of singers (called ripieno or *cappella*).

concert band. An offshoot of the *military band, developed for concert tours by such bandmasters as John Philip Sousa.

concertino. 1. The group of soloists in a *concerto grosso. **2.** In the first half of the 18th century, a term denoting an orchestral work in the form of a small-scale symphony, having several movements but no soloists (*see* SYMPHONIE CONCERTANTE). Since the 19th century the word 'concertino' (Ger.: *Konzertstück*) has been applied to orchestral compositions in the style of a small concerto. Such works are usually in one movement but may contain sections of contrasting speed and character; they are sometimes for chamber ensemble rather than orchestra.

concert master. *See* LEADER.

concerto. A piece for one or more soloists and orchestra. The term has been applied to a wide variety of music, however, some of it not fulfilling this basic criterion. 'Concerto' is probably derived from the Latin *concertare*, which can mean 'to dispute' or 'to work together'; in Italian the same word means 'to agree' or 'to get together'. These dual concepts of competition and collaboration have underpinned the genre from its earliest history, though at different periods the emphasis has changed from one to the other.

At the end of the 16th century the term 'concerto' was most often used to denote music for vocal ensembles or for mixed vocal and instrumental forces. Throughout the 17th century it was used for works for smaller ensembles not only in Italy but also in Germany, where the *geistliches Konzert* became an important genre in Protestant church music. The purely instrumental concerto has its origins in the last two decades of the 17th century, when Italian composers began to exploit technical and textural contrasts between solo and tutti in sonatas performed by string orchestras. Particularly influential were orchestral trumpet sonatas, in which abrupt textural contrasts, brilliant passage-work, and thematic dialogue replaced the contrapuntal idiom of the solo sonata. These characteristics were soon transferred to solo violin writing in concertos for strings alone, and became a hallmark of the later Baroque concerto.

Two distinct types of instrumental concerto soon evolved in Italy. In the north the basic four-part string orchestra was complemented by a soloist drawn from its ranks (usually the principal violin); but in Rome the core of the orchestra was a concertino ensemble of two violins, cello, and continuo which could be strengthened by a larger group of strings (the ripieno). From this Roman practice the concerto grosso emerged, notably in the works of Corelli. As with the sonata, a distinction was maintained between 'chamber' concertos and 'church' concertos (respectively with and without dance movements), but in neither type is there a fixed number and order of movements.

A more far-reaching development of the concerto was achieved by a group of Venetian composers at the start of the 18th century. Their solo violin concertos reflected the mannerisms of the contemporary operatic sinfonia and are mostly cast in three movements (fast–slow–fast). Vivaldi's 600 concertos exploit a vivid orchestral language of simple effects and memorable ideas, coupled with new standards of virtuosity in his solo parts. His set of 12 string concertos *L'estro armonico* (op. 3, 1711) was the first to make regular and sophisticated use of the ritornello principle. The ritornello—a refrain of one or more ideas played by the orchestra—is stated in full at the start of the movement and returns at various times, in whole or in part, to punctuate the solo sections and underline the various tonal centres through which the music passes. The attraction of this principle lay in its power to dramatize the 'competition' between solo and tutti in connection with a movement's tonal plan, and in its flexibility as a means of organizing musical ideas. The pattern could be used for any combination of instruments (and voices): while the violin was the solo instrument in most concertos at the start of the century, repertories quickly developed for almost all other orchestral instruments.

Although the symphony replaced the concerto during the Classical period as the pre-eminent orchestral genre, the concerto continued to flourish in different guises. The elegance and melodic fluency of the *galant* style did not lend themselves to displays of virtuosity, and many composers wrote concertos for domestic consumption. In contrast, concertos written for professional virtuosos made greater technical demands and were often musically more ambitious. The concept of a dialogue was enhanced by a growing distinction in 'public' concertos between the grand symphonic manner of orchestral tuttis and the more intimate sonata style of solo passages. The mixture of symphony and sonata was most perfectly realized in Mozart's concertos. In the 19th century the concerto was increasingly affected by the pre-eminence of the virtuoso composer-performer and the symphony. The key figure in violin music was Paganini, whose three violin concertos stand at the peak of the 'display' repertory.

In the 20th century the repertory expanded to include concertos for instruments that had previously been neglected (e.g. the trombone and the saxophone).

concerto form. At each stage of its development the *concerto has adopted the forms characteristic of the epoch. However, it is the late 18th-century pattern, most commonly found in the opening movements of concertos, that has become known as concerto form.

A typical first movement might have the sections shown in Table 1.

Classical concerto form shared the clear tonal plan of symphony and sonata movements. The first, second, and fourth ritornellos (R) emphasize the main tonal centres of the tonic and dominant, while the first and second solo sections (S) modulate between these key areas. Some composers omitted the modulating R^3 and linked the second and third solos with a brief confirmatory tutti in the tonic. This was Mozart's usual procedure. Concerto form may be viewed as a reinterpretation of the Baroque ritornello principle within a Classical stylistic framework.

concerto for orchestra. In the 20th century, a name given to large-scale works in which the orchestra itself and

Concerto form, TABLE 1

R^1	S^1	R^2	S^2	R^3	S^3	cadenza	R^4
I	I–V	V	V–vi	vi–V–	I		I

various instruments or sections within it are given a prominent virtuoso role.

concerto grosso (It., 'large concerto'). In Baroque music, a *concerto in which a small ensemble of soloists (concertino) is contrasted with a larger group (ripieno).

concert overture. *See* OVERTURE, 2.

concert pitch. The internationally accepted pitch standard, according to which $a' = 440$ vibrations per second.

Concertstück (Ger.). 'Concert piece'. *See* CONCERTINO, 2.

concitato (It.). *See* STILE CONCITATO.

concord. A consonant chord or interval; *see* CONSONANCE AND DISSONANCE.

concrete music. *See* MUSIQUE CONCRÈTE.

condensed score. *See* SHORT SCORE.

conductor. The director of an ensemble, responsible for all aspects of performance.

conductus (Lat., pl. conductus). Latin medieval song. The earliest examples are Latin songs on sacred topics (principally Christmas), with several stanzas (quite often with a refrain) in regular, strongly accented, rhyming poetry. The melodies are simple and direct. The songs appear to have been used for processional and recessional purposes. Some of the early conductus are set for two voices, and this development was followed up with great energy and brilliance by the late 12th- and early 13th-century Parisian composers of the so-called Notre Dame School. Their compositions are for from one to four voices, and great variety of textual genre and musical style is displayed. Some are written with only one note (or chord) to each syllable of text; others are much more ornate, containing long melismas to certain syllables. Conductus were superseded by the motet.

conjunct motion. *See* MOTION.

consecutive interval. An interval which occurs between the same two parts in two consecutive chords, for example A and C between tenor and soprano in one chord followed by B and D in the same parts in the next chord, this being an instance of consecutive minor 3rds. In traditional harmonic teaching there are two 'forbidden' consecutive intervals: the 5th and the octave. In practice, the term 'consecutives' is used pejoratively, implying consecutive 5ths or octaves. American usage prefers 'parallel' to 'consecutive'.

consequent. *See* ANTECEDENT AND CONSEQUENT.

consonance and dissonance. Consonance (or concord) is the quality inherent in an interval or chord which, in a traditional tonal or modal context, seems satisfactorily complete and stable in itself. In traditional contrapuntal and harmonic theory, consonant intervals comprise all perfect intervals (including the octave) and all major and minor 3rds and 6ths, but what constitutes a consonant sonority has varied over time. Since the early 20th century many composers have accepted the Schoenbergian concept of the 'emancipated' dissonance, in which traditionally dissonant intervals and chords could be treated as relatively stable harmonic entities, functioning in effect as 'higher' or more remote consonances.

The opposite of consonance is dissonance (or discord): the quality of tension inherent in an interval or chord which, in a traditional tonal or modal context, involves a clash between adjacent notes of the scale and creates the expectation of resolution onto consonance by conjunct motion, as when the 7th in a *dominant 7th chord (in C major, the F, which is dissonant with the G) moves to a note within the consonant tonic major triad (E, in the case of C major). The term is ambiguous to the extent that one chord held to demand resolution onto consonance, the diminished 7th (e.g. D, F, A♭, B), is not strictly dissonant, since it contains no pitches a major or minor 2nd apart. *See also* INTERVAL.

consort. A group of players or singers, their music, or their performance. The word was in common use from the late 16th century to the early 18th in English musical life. One of the commonest consorts in the Elizabethan period was the combination of treble viol or violin, flute or recorder, bass viol, lute, cittern, and bandora. This is usually referred to as a 'broken consort', in contrast to the 'whole consort' of like instruments—of viols or a violin band, for instance—but it is now thought more likely that 'broken consort' referred to music that was broken into divisions or variations. 'Consort' was also used in much the same sense as the Italian term 'concerto': a piece of music for a group of players.

consort song. A song for solo voice and a *consort of some kind, usually of viols, that flourished in England from the mid-16th century to shortly before the mid-17th. The texture is polyphonic, usually in five parts (including the voice), so that the consort cannot be described as an 'accompanying' body; the instrumental parts were sometimes underlaid with words, so that entirely vocal performance was a possibility.

conte (Fr., 'tale'). A title sometimes given to an instrumental piece. *See* MÄRCHEN.

continuo (It., abbreviation of *basso continuo*, 'continuous bass'; Ger.: *Generalbass*) [thoroughbass]. A term meaning either the group of instruments (or single instrument) used to provide the bass line in a musical work or the notated bass line from which those instruments play, in which case it is more accurately called the basso continuo. The continuo is one of most important defining characteristics of the Baroque era. The bass line, properly speaking when it is 'figured' (i.e. with sets of numerals appended), was also known as thoroughbass or *bassus generalis*, indicating both its 'continuity' and pervading presence. This bass, when 'realized', completes the harmonic part of the polyphonic whole by supplying chords and contrapuntal extras notated only in shorthand in the score.

The continuo evolved because of the increasing tendency in the early 17th century towards bass-upwards harmony, and the contrapuntal orientation of treble melody and bass. During the late 16th century, instruments came increasingly to be used to accompany polyphonic choral works, mainly doubling the voice parts. Continuo-accompanied *monody (influenced by the Florentine *Camerata), in which the solo voice with its word-expressive capability was harmonically supported by the continuo, was developed. These monodies, when transferred to opera, gave rise to the declamatory aria for solo voice and continuo alone. This texture was also crucial to what became known as *recitativo secco* (*see* RECITATIVE), in which the unmetred vocal line accompanied only by the basso continuo advanced the dramatic content.

A continuo featured in the sonata notated for one, two, or sometimes three solo voices or melody instruments (e.g. violins, recorders), or both, with bass. This evolved into the solo *sonata and *trio sonata of the later Baroque. The continuo became an important feature of both the concerto grosso and the solo concerto. By the 1650s it was integral to virtually all Baroque ensemble music, whether sacred or secular. The decline in importance of the basso continuo is evident in the increasing number of pieces with notated four-part texture or with non-harmonic accompanying bass from the earlier part of the 18th century.

The realization of the continuo by various, originally mainly unspecified, instruments affects not only the sound but the entire interpretation of a musical work. Instruments capable of playing polyphonically, namely harpsichord, organ, and plucked strings (lute, guitar, lyra viol, etc.), would realize the figures (the harmony), while others (e.g. cello, bassoon, violone) would reinforce the bass line.

The general principle of the figured bass is for the numerals to indicate the essential intervals above the bass, giving a clue as to the chord required. In early 17th-century basses, intervals are sometimes specified literally, e.g. as '11', which later became '4' when compounds were not indicated and numbers above 9 not used. In general the 5th and 3rd were to be assumed when not indicated. No numbers meant a chord in root position (a 5-3 chord), while the figure 6 (or 6/3) indicated a first inversion. An accidental by itself referred to the (major or minor) 3rd of the chord; when linked with other figures it indicated the inflection of that interval. An occasional horizontal line under a series of notes directed the player not to change the harmony. 'Tasto solo' is an instruction to play only the bass line without realizing the harmony.

continuo lied (Ger.: *Generalbasslied*). A type of strophic song with continuo accompaniment that became popular in Germany during the Baroque period, especially in the mid-17th century. It was usually simple in style with a limited vocal range, regular phrase lengths, and subservience to the text; many examples are based on dance tunes. They were customarily for solo voice with continuo, but pieces for up to five voices were also composed and obbligato parts sometimes included.

contrafactum (from medieval Lat. *contrafacere*, 'to counterfeit'). A vocal piece in which the original text is replaced by a new one. In Latin plainchant, texts for new feasts were frequently adapted to the melodies of existing chants. Contrafacta are common in the songs of the troubadours, trouvères, and Minnesinger. The motet and other genres of medieval polyphony also include many adaptations of sacred compositions to secular texts and vice versa. After the mid-15th century contrafacta tended to replace a secular text with a sacred one.

contralto (from It. *contra alto*, 'against the alto', i.e. contrasting with the high voice; Ger.: *Alt*). The lowest female voice, with a range of roughly g to g″. It is characterized by a dark, rich tone-quality. In the 19th and early 20th centuries most female singers were described as either soprano or contralto, but from the mid-20th century *'mezzo-soprano' was increasingly used for lower female voices as the true, deep contralto became ever rarer.

contrapunctus (Lat.). 'Counterpoint'. The term was used in the Baroque period either in this general sense or more specifically to denote a fugal movement.

contrapuntal. Adjective formed from *'counterpoint'.

contrary motion. *See* MOTION.

contratenor (Lat., 'against the tenor'). In early vocal music, the name for a voice part with roughly the same range as the tenor, but composed after, or 'against', that part (*see* TENOR, 2). When four-part writing became common around the mid-15th century, the contratenor was divided into the *contratenor altus* ('high [part] against the tenor') and *contratenor bassus* ('low [part] against the tenor'), which in turn eventually became the alto and bass parts in the standard four-part (SATB) choir.

contredanse (Fr.), **contradanza** (It.). *See* COUNTRY DANCE.

Conzertstück (Ger., 'concert piece'). *See* CONCERTINO, 2.

coperto (It.). 'Covered'; e.g. drums muffled by being covered with a cloth, in funeral music.

coranto (It.). *See* COURANTE.

corda (It., 'string'; Fr.: *corde*). In piano music *una corda* denotes the 'soft' pedal, which shifts the action on grand pianos so that the hammer strikes only one of the three strings. Similarly, *due corde* indicated two strings on early pianos. Each is cancelled by the instruction *tre corde* or *tutte le corde* (It., 'three strings' or 'all the strings').

corde, à la (Fr., 'on the string'). In string playing, a direction to keep the bow on the string, to produce a *legato* effect.

Corelli clash. A type of *cadence involving a striking dissonance.

cori spezzati (It., 'broken choirs'). A term used to describe the division of musical forces into musically, and sometimes also spatially, distinct groups. It dates from the 16th century, when music for multiple choirs became popular, particularly at St Mark's, Venice. Such compositions exploit contrasts of register between vocal and instrumental groups and between full choir and a solo voice (or group of soloists) and make use of echo effects.

corrente (It.). *See* COURANTE.

cortège (Fr., 'procession'). A title given to a piece of music suitable for accompanying, or illustrative of, a procession.

cotillon [cotillion]. A ballroom dance in triple time, akin to the quadrille, that originated in France at the beginning of the 18th century and reached Germany a little later.

coulé (Fr.). **1.** 'Flowing', i.e. slurred, **legato*. **2.** *See* SLIDE, 2. **3.** An 18th-century term for the *appoggiatura.

countermelody. A melodic line, more extended or expansive than a fugal countersubject, which is subordinate to, and combines contrapuntally with, a principal line.

counterpoint. The coherent combination of distinct melodic lines in music. The term derives from the Latin *contrapunctum* ('against note'). Counterpoint arises when the natural procedure of two or more voices or parts performing exactly the same melody an octave or some other interval apart is modified, so that the voices are no longer heard in rhythmic unison. The effect is likely to be most immediately perceptible when the distinct voices use the same material in close proximity. This is the case when a texture is *heterophonic, or when the form is that of *round, *canon, *fugue, or some other genre in which the imitation of a leading voice by others is fundamental. However, there might be a single, slow-moving line, a *tenor or *cantus firmus, round which other more florid lines are arranged in ways that make it clear to the ear that these lines are decorating or embellishing the framework provided by the principal line.

Counterpoint came to prominence in music as a means whereby composers could exploit the ability of singers to demonstrate their skills at carrying independent lines in combination. The sacred vocal polyphony of medieval and Renaissance times culminated in the masses and motets of Palestrina. In the 16th century the theorist Gioseffo Zarlino codified the principles of counterpoint: the subordination of dissonance to consonance, within clearly defined rhythmic and metrical contexts; the creation of an equable balance between difference and similarity of direction and melodic shape in all the independent voices; the use of specific modes to govern the harmonic, vertical relations between voices, and within which the main cadences of a work are placed; and control over rhythmic diversity by means of regular successions of strong and weak beats.

As new vocal genres (opera, cantata) came into being *c.*1600, and instruments gained new prominence, laws relevant to purely vocal polyphony were deemed archaic and needlessly restrictive. In 1725 Johann Joseph Fux redefined contrapuntal practice in terms of elementary yet fundamental principles involving mode, cantus firmus, and contrapuntal voices, governed, in the simplest rhythmic and formal contexts, by the laws of part-writing; this became known as *species counterpoint. Double (triple, etc.) counterpoint is counterpoint in which two (three, etc.) parts may be heard inverted, i.e. with either (any) as the upper part; this is known as *invertible counterpoint.

countersubject. *See* FUGUE.

countertenor. The adult male voice with a range corresponding roughly to that of the female *mezzo-soprano or *contralto. It is usually produced by developing the *falsetto register, though occasionally it is a naturally very high, light tenor. Sometimes the term 'male alto' is used for the latter (*see* ALTO VOICE), but the terms are usually interchangeable. *See also* CONTRATENOR.

country dance (Fr.: *contredanse*; Ger.: *Kontretanz*; It.: *contradanza*). A dance that originated in English folk tradition but that found its way into more refined circles by the 16th and 17th centuries. The music was in binary form, with repeats, and generally in 2/4 or 6/8 time. In France, where it was very popular, the *contredanse* became increasingly formalized during the 18th century, giving rise to *contredanse* suites. The dance survived into the 19th century, when it gave way to the waltz, polka, and quadrille.

coup d'archet (Fr.). 'Bowstroke', 'bowing'.

coup de glotte (Fr., 'stroke of the glottis'). In singing, a vocal attack in which the glottis is closed and abruptly reopened.

couplet. 1 (Fr.). A term used to describe the stanza of a poem (not necessarily two rhyming lines). In 17th-century **rondeaux*, the term was used for the various sections connected by a repeated refrain. **2** (Fr.). In 18th- and 19th-century light opera, a *couplet* is a strophic song of a humorous character. **3.** A term for *duplet. **4.** The 'two-note slur', i.e. two notes of equal value slurred together. The second note is often slightly shortened to accentuate the phrasing.

courante (Fr., 'running'; It.: *corrente*, *coranto*) [corant]. A dance type that first appeared in 16th-century French sources. Its popularity lasted until the mid-18th century, and as an instrumental form it was one of the standard movements of the Baroque *suite. In the 17th century the dance took two distinct national forms: the Italian *corrente* and the French courante. The Italian version was a fast, lively dance in triple metre (3/4 or 3/8), in binary form, basically homophonic in style, and moving continuously in short note-values, especially in the upper part. The French courante was more elegant and stately. It also consisted of two repeated halves in triple time (usually 3/2), but the pace was much slower (it was described as the slowest of all the court dances) and there was greater rhythmic variety than in the evenly flowing *corrente*. Typical features of the courante were the use of hemiola, especially at cadence points, and a contrapuntal and imitative texture. In the *suite the courante was generally placed between the allemande (to which it was often thematically related) and the sarabande.

crab canon. *See* CANON.

cracovienne (Fr.). *See* KRAKOWIAK.

cradle-song. *See* BERCEUSE.

Credo (Lat., 'I believe'). Part of the Ordinary of the Roman *Mass, sung between the gospel and the offertory.

crescendo (It.). 'Growing', 'increasing', i.e. gradually getting louder. The term is often represented by the 'hairpin' sign (*see* DYNAMIC MARKS, Table 1) or by the abbreviation *cresc*. The opposite is **decrescendo*.

croche (Fr., 'hook'). *Quaver. (The French for 'crotchet' is *noire*.)

croiser (Fr.). 'To cross'; *croiser les mains*, in keyboard playing, a direction to cross the hands.

cromatico, cromatica (It.). 'Chromatic'.

cross-accent. A way of varying the expected accentuation of notes by placing stresses on the 'weak' beats of the bar, and detracting from the 'strong' beats by substituting rests for them or by holding over a note from the previous beat. *See also* SYNCOPATION.

cross-fingering. A technique that enables keyless woodwind instruments to play certain chromatic notes, since a note may be flattened by covering the sound-hole two below the one sounding.

crossover. A term used to describe either work by a performer or composer in a musical genre different from that with which he or she is usually associated, or the merging or hybridization of different musical genres.

cross-relation. *See* FALSE RELATION.

cross-rhythm. The regular use of conflicting rhythmic groupings, for example of three notes against four.

crotchet (♩). The note having a quarter of the value of the semibreve, or whole note; hence the American usage 'quarter-note'.

csárdás [czárdás] (Hung., from *csárda*, 'tavern'). A 19th-century Hungarian ballroom dance; it was especially fashionable from the 1850s to the 1880s. Musically, the csárdás is very similar to the fast (*friss*) section of the **verbunkos* and is characteristically in duple time with many syncopations. A slow (*lassú*) version appeared during the second half of the 19th century.

cue. 1. In an orchestral or vocal part, an extract from another, prominent part (usually printed in small notes), to warn a performer of an approaching entry, usually after a long rest. **2.** A gesture from a conductor to signal the entrance of a player or a section.

cuivre (Fr.). 'Copper', 'brass'. *Les cuivres*, the brass instruments; *cuivré*, 'brassy', playing with a forced, strident tone, especially on the horn, often combined with hand-muting.

cupo (It.). 'Dark', 'sombre'.

custos. *See* DIRECT.

cyclic form. The word 'cyclic' applies to any work in several movements, for example a suite, symphony, sonata, or string quartet. More particularly it is used to describe any such work in which the movements are connected by some musical theme or themes common to all, e.g. an **idée fixe*. There are many examples by 19th- and 20th-century composers. A related use of the term is found in sacred music (*see* CYCLIC MASS).

cyclic mass. A setting of the Mass Ordinary that links its movements through the use of common musical material, for instance a *motto theme or a *cantus firmus. Such masses eventually gave way to *parody masses, in which movements were linked by their derivation from a common polyphonic model.

czárdás. *See* CSÁRDÁS.

D. 1. The second degree (supertonic) of the scale of C major (*see* SCALE, 1). **2.** Abbreviation for *Deutsch, used as a prefix to the numbers of Schubert's works as given in the standard *thematic catalogue of O. E. Deutsch.

da capo (It., 'from the head'). An instruction to go back to the beginning of a piece, sometimes abbreviated *d.c.* The indication of where to stop is usually provided by the word *fine*, or a pause mark (𝄐). Sometimes the expression used is *da capo al segno*, 'from the beginning to the sign' (𝄋), or *da capo al fine*, 'from the beginning to the end'. Sometimes, also, to one of these expressions is added *poi segue la coda*, 'then follows the coda'—meaning that, the point indicated having been reached, a jump is made to the final section of the piece, usually marked 'coda'. The term was commonly used in Baroque instrumental music, such as concertos, and regularly in minuet-and-trio structures, to indicate the repeat of the minuet. A '*da capo* aria' is an *aria that has two sections, followed by a repetition of the first, thus making a tripartite structure ABA.

dada-mama. A rudimentary side-drum technique in which the hands produce a bouncing stroke in alternation (LLRR or RRLL).

dal segno (It., 'from the sign'). An indication that a passage is to be repeated not from the beginning but from the place marked by the sign 𝄋, then continued to the end, to the word *fine*, or to a double bar with a pause sign over it; it is often abbreviated *d.s.*

Dämpfer (Ger.). 'Mute'; *mit Dämpfern*, 'with mutes'; *Dämpfung*, 'muting' or (on the piano) 'soft-pedalling'.

danza tedesca (It., 'German dance'). The Austrian *ländler, or an early type of waltz.

dauernd (Ger.). 'Enduring', i.e. continuing, lasting.

d.c. Abbreviation for **da capo*.

decani (Lat., 'of the dean'). The side of the choir on which the dean sits, now normally the south side. Choral music sometimes has passages marked *decani*, indicating that the singers on that side should take the passage. *See also* CANTORIS.

deceptive cadence. *See* CADENCE.

décidé (Fr.), **deciso, decisamente** (It.). 'Decided', i.e. resolutely.

decoration. *See* ORNAMENTS AND ORNAMENTATION.

decrescendo (It.). 'Decreasing', i.e. gradually getting quieter. The term is often represented by the 'hairpin' sign (*see* DYNAMIC MARKS, Table 1) or by the abbreviation *decr.* or *decresc.* The opposite is **crescendo*.

degree. A term indicating a particular note of the musical scale (first degree, second degree, etc.). In music analysis there are special terms for these degrees of the scale which convey their harmonic functions when they are used as the bottom notes of chords: tonic (first degree); supertonic (second); mediant (third); subdominant (fourth); dominant (fifth); submediant (sixth), and leading note (seventh).

dehors, en (Fr.). 'Outside', i.e. emphasized or prominent.

delicato (It.). 'Delicate'; *delicatissimo*, as delicate as possible.

délié (Fr.). 'Untied', i.e. detached, or *staccato*; it also implies 'free'.

démancher (Fr.). In string playing, a direction to the player to move along the neck (Fr.: *manche*) of the instrument into a higher position.

demi-pause (Fr.). 'Half-rest', i.e. the minim or half-note rest.

demisemiquaver (𝅘𝅥𝅰). The note having 1/32 of the value of the semibreve, or whole note; hence the American usage '32nd-note'.

demi-ton (Fr.). *'Semitone'.

demi-voix (Fr., 'half-voice'). In vocal music, a direction to sing at half the vocal power; *see also* MEZZO, MEZZA.

density. An informal measure of polyphonic complexity, chord content, or general sound, chiefly used of 20th-century music where a more precise vocabulary does not exist. One may thus speak of 'dense textures', 'dense harmonies', etc.

déploration (Fr.). A mourning poem. In music, the term generally refers to a song composed on the death of a celebrated musician by one of his pupils or fellow composers.

derb (Ger.). 'Robust', 'rough'.

Des (Ger.). The note D♭; *Deses*, the note D𝄫.

descant. *See* DISCANT.

descort. The Provençal word for **lai*. It was also used for French works and (as *discordio*) for some Italian pieces.

desiderio (It.). 'Desire'; *con desiderio*, 'longingly'.

dessous (Fr.). 'Below', 'under'. A term used in 17th- and 18th-century French instrumental music for the lower part (the equivalent of a modern viola part).

dessus (Fr., 'above', 'over'). Treble, i.e. the highest part in an ensemble. In 17th- and 18th-century French instrumental music it meant the violin; a *dessus de viole* is a treble viol.

destro, destra (It.). 'Right'; *mano destra*, 'right hand'.

détaché (Fr.). 'Detached'; in string playing it is almost the equivalent of **staccato*.

deuterus. *See* MODE.

deutlich (Ger.). 'Distinct'.

Deutsch. Abbreviation for the standard *thematic catalogue of the works of Franz Schubert drawn up by the Austrian biographer and bibliographer Otto Erich Deutsch (1883–1967). Schubert's works, especially those without distinguishing title or opus number, are often referred to by Deutsch number (usually further abbreviated to D).

deux (Fr.). 'Two'; *à deux*, either an abbreviation for *à deux temps* (*see* DEUX TEMPS, 2) or 'for two (voices or instruments)'. *See also* À DEUX, A DUE, A 2.

deux temps (Fr., 'two time'). **1.** In 2/2 time. **2.** A *valse à deux temps* is either a quick waltz in which there are only two steps, falling on the first and last of the three beats of each bar; or, as the word *temps* can also mean 'beat', a waltz in two simultaneous time-values.

development. A process by which musical materials, generally melodic themes, are changed and extended; or a section of a piece in which this process takes place. Among the many ways of developing a theme are (1) sequence (*see* SEQUENCE, 1), either diatonically within a key or through a succession of keys; (2) rhythmic displacement, so that the metrical stress occurs at a different point in the otherwise unchanged theme; (3) alteration of pitch *intervals while retaining the original rhythm (a special case of this is inversion); (4) alteration of rhythm while retaining the original pitches (this is often called transformation of themes). (5) Treating a theme in contrapuntal *imitation can also be a feature of development. Perhaps the most powerful and varied technique, however, is (6) the division of a theme into parts, each of which can be developed in any of the above ways or recombined in a new way. Similarly, (7) two or more themes can be developed in combination; in some cases, themes are composed with this possibility in mind.

A 'development section' follows the close of the exposition in a piece in *sonata form, and typically develops one or more themes from the exposition through neighbouring or remote keys before returning to the home key for the recapitulation. The same term can be used appropriately for sections of sonata rondos or concerto movements.

devoto (It.). 'Devoutly'.

diabolus in musica (Lat., 'the devil in music'). A late medieval nickname for the disruptive interval of the *tritone, or diminished 5th.

dialogue. 1. Spoken dialogue is used in place of recitative in certain types of opera, for example the French **opéra comique*, the German **Singspiel*, the Spanish *zarzuela, and the English *ballad opera. **2.** A vocal work that contrasts or alternates two sung parts in a way that resembles spoken dialogue. Examples range from the dialogues for different singers found in medieval church dramas to simple songs in which a single voice takes both parts.

diapason (from Gk., 'through all'). **1.** The whole octave. **2.** The entire compass of an instrument. **3.** The foundation or unison stops of the organ. **4.** The diatonically tuned bass strings of a lute, theorbo, or archlute, etc. **5.** (Fr.). 'Pitch': the concert *pitch (*diapason normal*) of the note *a'* is 435 Hz; *diapason à bouche*, 'pitchpipe'; *diapason à branches* or simply *diapason*, 'tuning-fork'.

diapente (Gk.). Ancient Greek and medieval name for the interval of the 5th.

diaphonia, diaphony. 1. In Greek theory, 'dissonance', as opposed to *symphonia*, 'consonance'. **2.** From the 9th century to the 12th the word was commonly used by theorists to mean two-part polyphony.

diastematic neumes (from Gk. *dia-*, 'through', 'across', *stema*, an 'interval', 'gap'). A type of early plainchant notation used before the invention of the staff. The dots and squiggles ('neumes'; *see* NOTATION) were arranged in relation to each other so as to show their relative pitch. Occasionally the pitches were further clarified by the addition of a faintly scratched line representing the final note of the modal scale in which the chant was written. Neumes written without any attempt to show relative pitch are known as 'adiastematic'.

diatonic (from Gk. *dia tonikos*, 'at intervals of a tone'). In the major–minor tonal system, a diatonic feature—which may be a single note, an interval, a chord, or an extended passage of music—is one that uses exclusively notes belonging to one key. In practice, it can be said to use a particular scale, but only with the proviso that the alternative submediants and leading notes of harmonic and melodic minor allow up to nine diatonic notes, compared with the seven available in a major scale. Few pieces of tonal music are without tonal elaboration, the suggestion of different keys in the course of the music: thus a piece in C major that appears to modulate to its dominant, G major, and return to the tonic may be called diatonic if it uses only the eight notes—C, D, E, F, F♯, G, A, and B—belonging to the two keys. *See also* PANDIATONICISM.

diatonic scale. *See* SCALE.

Dichtung (Ger., 'poem'). A term found in such compounds as *symphonische Dichtung*, *'symphonic poem', or *Tondichtung*, 'tone-poem'.

dièse (Fr.). **1.** The sharp sign (*see* SHARP, 1). **2.** In 17th-century, usage, 'major', e.g. *mi dièse*, E major.

Dies irae (Lat., 'Day of wrath'). The sequence of the *Requiem Mass. It is normally included in choral and orchestral requiems, and the plainchant melody has been used in instrumental music for its inherent symbolism.

diesis (It.). The sharp sign (*see* SHARP, 1).

diferencia (Sp.). **1.** A term used for a kind of ornamentation in which a melody is broken up by fast figuration. **2.** 16th-century name given to variations. *Diferencias* are longer and more elaborate than *glosas.

diluendo (It.). 'Dissolving', i.e. dying away.

dilungando (It.). 'Lengthening'.

diminished interval. A major or perfect *interval decreased by a semitone.

diminished seventh chord. The chord of the diminished 7th usually appears on the seventh degree of the scale. It spans the interval of a diminished 7th and is made up of a succession of minor 3rds (thus in C major the chord is B–D–F–A♭). The diminished 7th usually resolves onto the tonic chord (Ex. 1*a*), but because the intervals of the chord are all the same, any one of its notes may be treated as the root, and modulation to other keys is easily effected (Ex. 1*b*; the modulation can be to either major or minor). The chord of the diminished 7th is often thought of as a dominant 9th chord with its root missing (*see* DOMINANT SEVENTH CHORD).

diminished triad. *See* TRIAD.

diminuendo (It.). 'Diminishing', i.e. gradually getting quieter. The term is often represented by the 'hairpin' sign (*see* DYNAMIC MARKS, Table 1) or by the abbreviation *dim.* or *dimin.* It is the equivalent of *decrescendo* but seems to have been in use earlier than the corresponding *crescendo*.

diminution. A melodic device, often found in fugal compositions, in which the time-values of the melody notes are proportionally shortened. For example, a melody moving in minims, crotchets, and quavers could undergo diminution to move in crotchets, quavers, and semiquavers (each value diminishing by half).

diminutions. *See* ORNAMENTS AND ORNAMENTATION.

di molto (It.). 'Very'; *allegro di molto*, 'very fast'.

di nuovo (It.). 'Again'.

direct (Fr.: *guidon*; Ger.: *Wachte*; It.: *guida*; Lat.: *custos*). The sign (~) occasionally used at the end of a page or line of music to give an indication of the pitch of the next note. It is most often found in early music.

dirge (Lat.: *naenia*; It.: *nenia*). A vocal or instrumental composition performed at a funeral or memorial service.

Dirigent, dirigieren (Ger.). 'Conductor', 'to conduct'.

Dis (Ger.). The note D♯; *Disis*, the note D𝄪. In earlier music *Dis* sometimes meant the enharmonic equivalent E♭, and as late as 1805 Beethoven's 'Eroica' Symphony (in E♭) was described as being 'in Dis'.

discant [descant] (from medieval Lat. *discantus*, 'sounding apart'). A medieval technique of composition in which one voice is added to a plainchant part, usually note against note and usually in contrary motion. The large 12th-century repertory of settings of Latin sacred songs from France (customarily called *conductus or versus), though not settings of plainchant, are examples of discant, at least in harmonic style. In the polyphony of the so-called Notre Dame

Diminished seventh chord, Ex. 1

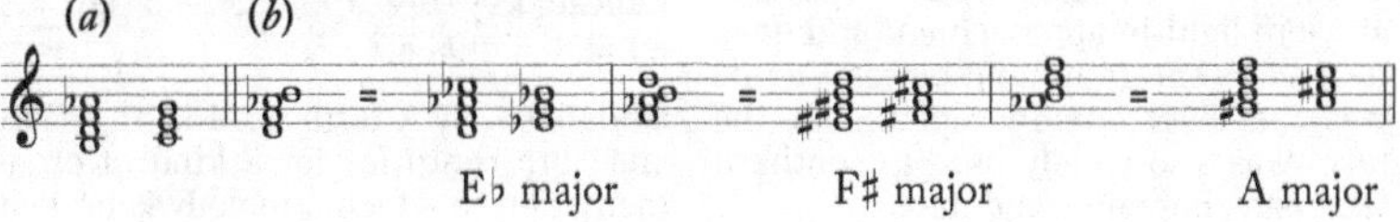

School, composed in 12th- and 13th-century Paris, discant technique was used in conductus and for setting phrases of plainchant. Parisian chant settings of this time alternate passages of discant (such passages are also known as *clausulae) with passages where the original chant is heard in long held notes, beneath an onward-moving upper part or parts (*see* ORGANUM, 4). By the second half of the 13th century, discant was the chief style of polyphony, and therefore the most common term for polyphony itself; the long-held-note style was more or less obsolete.

discord. A dissonant chord or interval; *see* CONSONANCE AND DISSONANCE.

disinvolto (It.). 'Free', 'jaunty'.

disjunct motion. *See* MOTION.

dissonance. *See* CONSONANCE AND DISSONANCE.

dithyramb (from Gk. *dithyrambos*; Fr.: *dithyrambe*; It.: *ditirambo*). An ancient Greek song in honour of Dionysus, the god of wine and good living. Originally a choral strophic song, it gradually became more elaborate, combining instrumental accompaniment, soloists, and groups of dancers. By the end of the 4th century BC it had become virtually a theatrical performance. The name is sometimes given to modern compositions of a free and passionate character.

ditonus (Lat.). Medieval name given to the major 3rd (i.e. equal to two whole tones).

div. Abbreviation for **divisi*.

divertimento (It.). 'Diversion', 'recreation'. The 18th-century divertimento, which was usually scored for a combination of solo instruments, was related to such genres as the *cassation, **Nachtmusik*, **notturno*, and *serenade, in that all were light in approach and intended to serve as entertainment pieces. Vienna was the divertimento capital, but the term was also widely used in southern Germany, Bohemia, and Italy.

The keyboard divertimento resembled the sonata, and was composed mainly by Austrians. There were also divertimentos for wind ensemble (often pairs of oboes, horns, and bassoons), or for strings (trio, quartet, quintet), sometimes with added wind instruments. Divertimentos could have up to nine movements, but more commonly only five or so were used (opening and closing Allegro movements in sonata form, two minuets, and a central slow movement). The genre proper died out at the beginning of the 19th century, but the term was occasionally used in the 20th for works of a light, brilliant character.

divertissement (Fr., 'diversion', 'entertainment'). **1.** In opera, a portion of a *tragédie lyrique* or *opéra-ballet* composed mainly of songs and dances and accompanied by spectacular stage effects, often having little connection with the main plot. In French *opéra-ballet* of the early 18th century each act (or *entrée*) had its own divertissement of dances. The divertissement persisted in France far into the 19th century and was also an important feature of Russian ballet. **2.** An all-purpose entertainment lasting an entire evening or even for several days or weeks. At the height of the *grand siècle* spectacular divertissements were arranged at court to celebrate royal births, marriages, and victories. **3.** In the early 19th century, a light *character piece, generally in several sections. The term was occasionally revived in the 20th century.

divisi (It.). 'Divided'. An indication in ensemble and orchestral scores that players who normally have the same part should divide into groups to play that part, often notated on the same staff; for string players, this is a practical alternative to using double or triple stopping, the number of 'divisions' required indicated by 'div. a 2', 'div. a 3' etc. *See* À DEUX, A DUE, A 2.

divisions. **1.** A term used in the 17th and 18th centuries for a kind of ornamentation in which a melody is broken up by fast figuration. **2.** More specifically, the performance of 'divisions upon a ground' was a characteristic English practice in the 17th century. Over a recurrent *ground bass, provided by a harpsichord or another instrument, a viol player would improvise variations or 'divisions'—splitting up the notes of the ground into shorter notes or providing a countermelody to it.

doctrine of affections. *See* AFFECTIONS, DOCTRINE OF.

doctrine of figures. *See* FIGURES, DOCTRINE OF.

dodecaphonic (from Gk., literally 'twelve-sound'). A term used to describe *twelve-note music. For the dodecaphonic scale, *see* TWELVE-NOTE SCALE.

dodecuple. An alternative word for *dodecaphonic.

doglioso (It.). 'Sorrowful'; *doglioamente*, 'sorrowfully'.

doh [do]. The first degree of the scale in the *Tonic Sol-fa system. Two methods of applying these *solmization syllables are in use: the *fixed-*doh* principle, in which they are applied to fixed notes of the C major scale—thus *doh* is always the note C; and the movable-*doh* principle, in which *doh* may be the tonic of any major scale.

dolce (It.). 'Sweet', sometimes 'soft'; *dolcemente*, 'sweetly', *dolcissimo*, 'very sweet'.

dolente (It.). 'Doleful', 'sad'; *dolentamente*, 'dolefully'.

doloroso (It.). 'Sorrowful', 'painful'.

dominant. The fifth degree of the major or minor scale.

dominant seventh chord. The dominant chord with the note a 7th from its root added (thus in C major the chord is G–B–D–F). The dominant 7th normally resolves onto the tonic chord, or the submediant chord, the added 7th note falling a semitone (Ex. 1*a*); it can be used in root position or in any one of its three inversions (Ex. 1*b*). Further additions can be made to the chord to produce the dominant 9th, 11th, and even 13th.

dompe. *See* DUMP.

dopo (It.). 'After'.

Doppel (Ger.). 'Double'; *doppeln*, 'to double'.

Doppelfagott (Ger.). 'Contrabassoon'.

Doppelfuge (Ger.). *'Double fugue'.

Doppelhorn (Ger.). 'Double horn'.

Doppelschlag (Ger., 'double stroke'). *Turn.

doppelt so schnell (Ger.). 'Twice as fast', i.e. at double speed.

Doppelzunge (Ger., 'double tongue'). Double *tonguing.

doppio (It.). 'Double'; *doppio movimento*, 'double the speed'.

Dorian mode. The *mode represented by the white notes of the piano beginning on D.

dot (Fr.: *point*; Ger.: *Punkt*; It.: *punto*). **1.** A dot placed above or below a note normally indicates that the note is to be played *staccato* or (in string music, when slurs are also present) **portato*; in some early keyboard music, however, it may instead signify chromatic alteration. **2.** In early mensural notation, a dot (or

Dominant seventh chord, Ex. 1

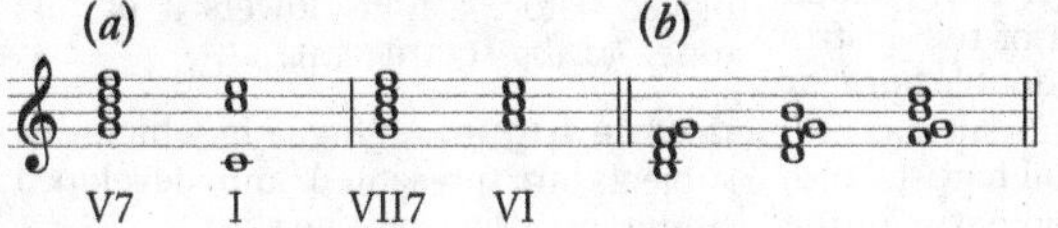

point; Lat.: *punctum*) placed between notes may be used to mark off groups of notes into rhythmic divisions. In such cases it acts rather like the modern bar-line. **3.** A dot placed immediately after a note normally makes the note half as long again (Ex. 1*a*); a second dot added after the first ('double-dotting') effectively adds half the value of the first dot (Ex. 1*b*). In modern notation dotted notes are used only when their value is contained within one bar, otherwise a *tie is used. The possible application by the performer of dotted or unequal rhythms to undotted notes (**notes inégales*) creates problems best approached through the history of *performance practice, since it is the lack of notational guidance that leads to difficulties in resurrecting this practice. **4.** Dots in vertical pairs beside a double bar or a bar-line indicate that a passage is to be repeated.

Ex. 1

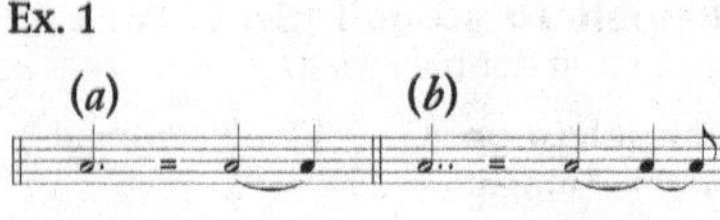

double. 1. To take more than one singing role or to play more than one instrument in the same work. Opera singers have 'doubles', or understudies, who are able to take over a role in case of the principal's absence. **2** (Fr.). In 17th- and 18th-century French music, a simple variation, usually consisting of an elaborated version of the melody, while the original harmony and rhythm are retained. A *double* often appears in keyboard suites as an ornamented reprise of the preceding dance. **3.** When applied to instruments, the English word 'double' indicates either low pitch (the double bass is the lowest member of the violin family) or a combination of two instruments in one, such as the double horn, or the duplication of elements such as keyboards (e.g. double-manual harpsichord) or ranks of strings (double harp). In the first case, the prefix 'contra' is sometimes used (e.g. contrabassoon).

doublé (Fr., 'doubled'). *See* TURN.

double appoggiatura. *See* APPOGGIATURA.

double bar. The double perpendicular line placed at the end of a complete work, or of a movement or section of one. Unless it coincides with a single bar-line, the double bar has no rhythmic value. When the double bar is preceded by two dots, placed one above the other, a repeat is indicated. If the repeat bar is marked 'prima volta' or simply '1' and is followed by a bar marked 'seconda volta' or '2', the repeat should be made, and at the end of it the player should take the second bar, which will lead into the next section of music. The two bars are sometimes called the first-time and the second-time bar.

double choir, double chorus. A choir arranged in two equal and complete bodies, usually with the aim of providing a spatial effect.

double concerto. A concerto for two solo instruments and orchestra or other instrumental ensemble.

double counterpoint. Alternative name for *invertible counterpoint.

doubled leading-note cadence. A three-voice progression in 14th-century vocal polyphony in which the outer voices move by step from leading notes (upper or lower) onto the octave (or 5th).

double dot. A pair of dots after a note, indicating that it should be prolonged by three quarters of its original length.

double flat. The sign (𝄫) that, when placed before a note, lowers it by one tone. *See also* ACCIDENTAL.

double fugue. A *fugue in which two subjects are presented and developed simultaneously from the start.

double mordent. A *mordent with two repercussions.

double pedal. *See* PEDAL POINT.

double phrasing. The addition of an extended slur over a group of notes which are already articulated by subsidiary slurs, staccato dots, or rests, to indicate that those notes still form part of a group in spite of their separation.

double sharp. The sign (𝄪) that, when placed before a note, raises it by one tone. *See also* ACCIDENTAL.

double stem. In notation, a note-head with two stems, one up and one down; it is used when two melodies written on one staff share the same note.

double stopping. In string playing, bowing two strings simultaneously to produce intervals or chords. In spite of the use of the word *'stopping', one or both of the strings may be open.

double tonguing. *See* TONGUING.

double trill. A trill performed simultaneously on two separate notes, usually a 3rd apart.

double whole-note (Amer.). *Breve.

douloureux (Fr.). 'Sorrowful', 'painful'.

doux, douce (Fr.). 'Sweet'; *doucement*, 'sweetly'.

downbeat (Fr.: *temps fort*; Ger.: *Niederschlag*). The first, 'strong', beat of the bar; *see* BEAT, 1.

drag. One of the ornamental rudiments of side-drum playing, consisting of two rapid strokes before the main one.

drame lyrique (Fr., 'lyric drama'; It.: *dramma lirico*). A modern name for a serious opera, generally implying a more intimate mode of expression than that of *grand opera or Wagnerian music drama.

dramma giocoso (It., 'jocular drama'). In the 18th century, a name often given to Italian comic operas. It commonly occurs in librettos in which standard character types from *opera seria* appear together with those from **opera buffa*.

dramma per musica (It., 'drama for music', 'drama in music'). *See* OPERA.

drängend (Ger.). 'Pressing on', 'hurrying'.

drawing-room ballad. A type of song designed primarily for domestic performance by amateurs. Drawing-room ballads are mainly strophic and generally of a romantic, sentimental nature; they were often originally composed as part of an opera.

drone (Fr.: *bourdon*). A steady or constantly reiterated note, usually on the keynote. It is the simplest of all accompaniments. Drones can be sounded through additional pipes (e.g. on bagpipes), by bowing or plucking strings (e.g. on a hurdy-gurdy), or by humming while playing.

d.s. Abbreviation for **dal segno*.

ductia. A medieval vocal (*cantilena ductia*) or instrumental dance form, related to the **estampie*.

due (It.). 'Two'; *a due, see* À DEUX, A DUE, A 2.

duet (Fr.: *duo*; Ger.: *Duett*; It.: *duo, duetto*). Any combination of two performers (with or without accompaniment), or a piece or passage written for such a combination. The most important forms are the vocal duet and the instrumental *duo; *see also* PIANO DUET.

dumka (from Cz. *dumat*, Pol. *dumać*, 'to ponder'; pl. *dumky*). A Slavonic folk ballad from Ukraine, with a lamenting quality. In the 19th century the name was also given to a type of instrumental music of a melancholy character.

dump [dompe, dumpe]. A 16th- and 17th-century English dance form, usually with a variation structure, over a tonic-dominant harmonic scheme, and slow and sad in character; dumps may have been composed as mourning pieces (their character is recalled in the expression 'down in the dumps').

duo. A piece of music for two performers. Although it is sometimes applied to early vocal duets, including the Renaissance *bicinium, and itself is French for 'duet', the word is now normally used exclusively for instrumental music. The numerous 18th- and 19th-century works for violin and keyboard can correctly be described as duos, but the term 'sonata' is generally preferred where appropriate. 'Duo' is more often used for music written for two equal or two melody instruments. The term is occasionally applied to performers who play such works: *piano duets ('duo' is rarely used for a work for two pianos or piano duet) might be played by a 'piano duo', and a pair of performers might be described as a 'violin and piano duo'.

duodecuple. An alternative word for *dodecaphonic.

duodrama. A *melodrama for two speakers.

duplet. A term for two notes that are to be performed in the time of three; they are indicated by the figure '2' placed above or below the two notes (see Ex. 1).

Ex. 1

$\frac{3}{4}$ ♩ ♩ ♩ | ♩ ♩ ‖ (2)

duple time. *See* TIME SIGNATURE.

duplex long. A note-value (■) found in medieval music.

duplum (Lat.). **1.** In two parts; used in medieval polyphony to describe a composition for two voices, e.g. *organum duplum*. **2.** In the 13th and 14th centuries, the 'second' voice part in a polyphonic work—that is, the voice immediately above the tenor. In a motet this part was also called 'motetus'. *See also* PART, 1.

dur (Ger.). 'Major', in the sense of key (e.g. *A-dur*, 'A major', *dur Tonart*, 'major key'); however, 'major triad' is *harter* (not *dur*) *Dreiklang*. The French word *dur* means 'hard', *majeur* being used for 'major'. *See also* DURUM AND MOLLIS.

duramente (It.). 'Harshly'.

durch (Ger.). 'Through'; *durchaus*, 'throughout'.

durchdringend (Ger.). 'Piercing', 'shrill'.

Durchführung (Ger., 'through-leading'). The development in a sonata-form movement or the exposition of a fugue; *Durchimitation*, 'through-imitation', i.e. imitation systematically applied to all parts of a polyphonic piece, a technique developed at the end of the 15th century and a particular feature of the 'Palestrina style'.

durchkomponiert (Ger.). *'Through-composed'.

durezza (It.). 'Harshness'; *con durezza* is an indication to play in a severe and determined manner. In the 17th century *durezza* meant 'dissonance' and hence a style of keyboard writing that featured chromaticisms and dissonance.

durum and mollis. In the letter notation used in medieval times, 'b' was written in one of two ways. The square, 'hard' (Lat.: *durum*) form (♮) stood for B♮, and this letter type became the basis of the modern 'natural' and 'sharp' signs in music. The rounded, 'soft' (Lat.: *mollis*) form (♭) stood for B♭, and the modern flat sign is a version of this letter. Since music in minor keys was originally written using flat key signatures, while major keys tended to have sharp signatures, the Germans use *dur* to indicate a major key (*C-dur*, etc.) and *moll* to indicate the minor (*A-moll*, etc.).

dux. *See* CANON.

dyad. A pair of notes. The term is sometimes found in writings on serial music.

dynamic accent. An *accent produced by an increase in volume.

dynamic marks. The terms, abbreviations, and signs used in musical notation to indicate relative intensity (loudness) and degree of accentuation. The most common are listed in Table 1. Composers have occasionally expanded these, using *fff*, *ffff*, *ppp*, *pppp*.

Dynamic marks, TABLE 1

Dynamic marks

pp	*pianissimo*	very soft
p	*piano*	soft
mp	*mezzopiano*	moderately soft
mf	*mezzoforte*	moderately loud
f	*forte*	loud
ff	*fortissimo*	very loud
fp	*fortepiano*	loud, then immediately soft
fz	*forzato* }	forced
sf }	*sforzato* }	
sfz }		
	crescendo	getting louder
	decrescendo, *diminuendo*	getting softer
		attack
		agogic accent

dynamics. The aspect of musical expression concerned with the variation in the volume of sound.

E. The third degree (mediant) of the scale of C major (*see* SCALE, 1).

ear-training. The process of improving 'aural perception', i.e. communication between the ear and the brain. *See also* SIGHT-READING, SIGHT-SINGING.

ecclesiastical modes. Alternative name for church modes; *see* MODE.

échappée (Fr.). 'Escaped (note)'. A melodic progression in which an unaccented passing note (i.e. a note that intervenes between two chords but does not form part of the harmony of either of them) appears outside the interval formed by the notes on either side of it, approached in the opposite direction to the resolution. When such a passing note is approached in the same direction as the resolution, it is called a 'changing' note (It.: *cambiata*, not to be confused with **nota cambiata*).

échelle (Fr.). *'Scale' (but the more usual word for the musical scale is *gamme*).

echo. The imitation in music of a natural echo effect, often used in vocal music during the late 16th and the 17th centuries, and especially associated with the madrigal. It was assimilated into theatre music; examples occur in early Italian oratorios and in French operas. It also permeated instrumental music; it is found in English consort dances, and in Venice (*see* CORI SPEZZATI). The effect was used in keyboard music designed for two-manual harpsichords, and in organ music, where it was achieved by the use of contrasting stops. In French Baroque harpsichord music the 'petite reprise' was an echo device whereby a short phrase at the end of a binary-form movement was repeated.

éclatant (Fr.). 'Brilliant', 'dazzling'.

eclogue [eglogue]. A short pastoral poem involving shepherds' dialogue, written in the form of a play and performed with incidental music. Later composers gave the title 'Eclogue' or 'Eglogue' to works of an idyllic, pastoral nature.

écossaise (Fr., 'Scottish'). A quick dance in 2/4 time, popular in France and England in the early 19th century. Despite its name it seems to have no connection with Scotland. *See also* SCHOTTISCHE.

égale (Fr.). 'Equal'.

églogue (Fr.). *'Eclogue'.

eguale (It., 'equal'). *See* EQUALE.

E.H. Abbreviation for *englisches Horn* or English horn, i.e. cor anglais.

eighth-note (Amer.). *Quaver.

Eile, mit (Ger.). 'With haste'; *eilend*, 'hurrying'; *eilig*, 'quick'.

einfach (Ger.). 'Simple'.

Einklang (Ger.). *'Unison'.

Einleitung (Ger.). *'Introduction'.

Einsatz (Ger.). *'Attack', 'entrance' (of an orchestral part).

einstimmig (Ger.). 'One-voiced', i.e. monophonic (*see* MONOPHONY).

Eintritt (Ger.). 'Entrance', of a fugue subject or a soloist in a concerto.

Eis (Ger.). The note E♯; *Eisis*, the note E𝄪.

élargissant (Fr.). 'Broadening', i.e. **allargando*.

electroacoustic music. Music that involves the combination of instrumental or vocal sounds with the electronic (often computer-assisted) manipulation of those sounds, or with sounds prerecorded on tape.

electronic music. *See* ELECTROACOUSTIC MUSIC.

elegia, elegiaco (It.). *'Elegy', 'elegiac'.

elegy (Fr.: *élégie*; It.: *elegia*). A song of lament, or an instrumental composition of mournful character. In the Renaissance, composers often wrote an elegy or **déploration* on the death of a colleague or teacher.

elevation (Lat.: *elevatio*). The music played during the Elevation of the Host (the lifting up of the consecrated bread and wine) in the Roman Mass. It consists usually of a motet or an organ piece or improvisation.

Elfenreigen (Ger.). 'Elfin dance'. *See* REIGEN.

embellishments. *See* ORNAMENTS AND ORNAMENTATION.

embouchure (Fr.). The manner in which a player's mouth and lips are placed when playing flutes, reeds, or brass instruments; the word has been used in English in this sense since the 18th century.

Empfindsamkeit (Ger., 'sentiment', 'sensitivity'). A term applied to an aesthetic movement that flourished in Europe and especially north Germany in the mid-18th century. In music its most important exponent was C. P. E. Bach, who emphasized that the highest aim of music was to touch the heart and move the affections.

Empfindung (Ger.). 'Expression', 'feeling'; *empfindungsvoll*, 'with feeling'. *See* EMPFINDSAMKEIT.

emporté (Fr.). 'Fiery', 'impetuous'.

empressé (Fr.). 'Eager', 'hurrying'.

ému (Fr.). 'Moved', 'with emotion'.

enchaînez (Fr.). 'Chain up', 'join together', i.e. the next movement should start immediately without a break (the same as **attacca*).

en dehors. *See* DEHORS, EN.

energico (It.). 'Energetic'.

Engeführung (Ger.). The equivalent of *stretto in fugal writing.

engraving. The process of cutting music notation into copper plates, from which the music is printed.

enharmonic (from Gk. *en*, 'in', and *harmoniā*, 'harmony'). **1.** In the music theory of the Ancient Greeks, a scale containing intervals smaller than a semitone. **2.** In modern harmonic music theory, taking account of *equal temperament, notes that differ from each other in name but not in pitch (e.g. C♯/D♭); on a keyboard instrument these notes are genuinely identical in all but name, but on any other instrument an inflection can slightly sharpen or flatten the note so that there is a difference in pitch. Keys, intervals, and chords can also be described as enharmonic.

enigmatic scale. *See* SCALA ENIGMATICA.

ensalada (Sp., 'salad'). A type of 16th-century *quodlibet. Such pieces were often humorous or programmatic but some were longer, with religious subject matter.

ensemble (Fr., 'together'). **1.** A group of instrumentalists or singers, of any size from two players to an entire orchestra, though the term is most often applied to a chamber-music group or a small chamber orchestra. **2.** By extension, the degree of unanimity of timing, balance, and style between the members of such a group: the subordination of the preference of the individual to that of the group. **3.** In opera, an item for two or more soloists.

entfernt (Ger.). 'Distant'.

entr'acte (Fr.). A piece of music, usually instrumental, played 'between the acts' of a play or opera. Purcell's entr'actes were known as *'act tunes'. *See also* INTERLUDE.

entrada. *See* ENTRÉE; INTRADA.

entrata (It., 'entrance', 'beginning'). An *introduction or *prelude.

entrée (Fr.; Sp.: *entrada*). A 17th- and 18th-century term for an instrumental piece before a ballet or a march-like piece played to introduce an important character or group of dancers. It is also used for an act in an *opéra-ballet*, in which each act is self-contained and devoted to its own subject, or for the moment of commencement of any part of a work.

entremés (Sp.). Originally a comic musical interlude performed between the acts of a play (*see* INTERMEZZO, 2); the term came to be applied to a brief and independent musical entertainment of a humorous nature.

entry. 1. The point in a composition at which a particular part begins or begins again after a rest; also the musical material with which the part begins at that point. **2.** In a *fugue, a statement of the subject.

entschieden, entschlossen (Ger.). 'Decided', 'resolute', 'determined'.

epicedium (Lat., from Gk. *epikēdeion*). 'Funeral ode'.

epidiapente (Gk.). 'A fifth above', a direction to give a part or parts of a *canon a 5th above.

epilogue. Alternative name for *coda.

episode. 1. A section of a *fugue between subject entries. **2.** The thematically and tonally contrasting sections in *rondo form.

epithalamium (Lat., from Gk. *epithalamion*). 'Wedding song'. The name is sometimes used for a piece of organ music to be performed at a wedding.

equale [aequale] (Lat., 'equal'; It.: *eguale*). A work in which all the parts are played by instruments or voices of the same type (*see* EQUAL VOICES). In Austria during the 18th century and the early 19th the term denoted a type of short piece played, usually by four trombones, at a funeral service.

equal temperament. A system of tuning the scale whereby the octave is divided into 12 equal semitones. It is based on a cycle of 12 identical 5ths, each slightly smaller than 'pure', the reason being that a chain of 12 pure 5ths exceeds the equivalent of seven octaves by an interval known as the 'Pythagorean comma'. To compensate for this, and in order for the circle of 5ths to arrive at a perfect unison, in equal temperament each 5th is smaller than pure by 1/12 of a Pythagorean comma, and the 3rds are adjusted so that three major 3rds, or four minor 3rds, are equal to an octave. To achieve this, major 3rds must be tuned slightly larger than pure, minor 3rds smaller. Most Baroque keyboard musicians preferred such alternatives as *mean-tone temperament or other slightly irregular tunings. The system eventually became the standard tuning for keyboard instruments and is now the tuning of the Western 12-note chromatic scale. *See also* TEMPERAMENT.

equal voices (It.: *voci eguali*; Lat.: *voces aequales*; Ger.: *gleiche Stimmen*). A choral composition for voices of the same kind, such as two or three sopranos. The parts are normally arranged so that the top line is divided between the participating voices. Occasionally the term is used less correctly in contradistinction to 'mixed voices', meaning for children's voices alone, women's voices alone, or men's voices alone, rather than a combination of men's and women's voices.

ergriffen (Ger.). 'Deeply moved', 'stirred'.

erhaben (Ger.). 'Lofty', 'noble'; *Erhabenheit*, 'nobility', 'sublimity'.

Erhöhungszeichen (Ger.). The sharp sign (*see* SHARP, 1).

Erleichterung (Ger.). 'An easing', i.e. a simplified version.

erlöschend (Ger.). 'Dying out'.

ermattend (Ger.). 'Tiring', 'weakening'.

erniedrigen (Ger.). 'To lower', i.e. flatten in pitch.

ernst, ernsthaft (Ger.). 'Serious'.

erotikon (Gk.). A love song, or its instrumental equivalent.

Ersatz (Ger.). 'Substitute'.

ersterbend (Ger.). 'Dying away'.

erweitert (Ger.). 'Expanded', i.e. broadened (at a steadier pace).

Es (Ger.). The note E♭; *Eses*, the note E𝄫.

esercizio (It.). *'Exercise'.

espressivo (It.). 'Expressive', 'with expression'; it is abbreviated *espr.*

esquisse (Fr.). 'Sketch'.

essential note. A note belonging to the chord in question, as opposed to a passing note, a suspension, an appoggiatura, etc., which are all 'unessential notes'.

essercizio. An old spelling of *esercizio* (*'exercise').

estampie (Fr.; It.: *istampita*, *stampita*; Provençal: *estampida*). A type of textless melody popular during the 13th and 14th centuries; the name was also applied to poetry. *Estampies* may have been purely instrumental, in which case they are the earliest known instrumental music in the West, and they may have been intended for dancing. The form, similar to that of the *lai, consists of a series of phrases (*puncta*), each of which is repeated immediately using a first- (*ouvert) and a second-time (*clos*) ending. The two endings are usually the same throughout the piece (i.e. AxAy, BxBy, CxCy, etc.).

estinguendo (It.). 'Extinguishing', i.e. dying away.

estinto (It.). 'Extinguished', i.e. barely audible.

estompé (Fr.). 'Toned down'.

estribillo (Sp.). A 17th-century term for a refrain in a song (e.g. in the *villancico).

éteint (Fr.). 'Extinguished', i.e. barely audible.

ethnomusicology. The study of music in its cultural context; the anthropology of music. The term was first used by the Dutch scholar Jaap Kunst (1891–1960) in the subtitle of a book. The discipline's origins, however, date from the late 19th century. During the second half of the 20th century, scholars suggested that ethnomusicology should be distinguished by its methodology rather than its object of study, 'fieldwork' and 'ethnography' becoming essential methodological tools. Ethnomusicology has developed into a worldwide network of disciplines, with different nations and regions asserting their own histories, fields, methods, and terminologies.

ethos. In the theory of Ancient Greek music, 'ethos' refers to the character conveyed by an entire piece of music or by one of its component parts.

étouffer (Fr., 'to damp', 'to stifle'). Direction to mute a violin, to damp a kettledrum, or to apply the soft pedal on a piano; *étouffoir*, a piano damper.

étude (Fr.). 'Study'. A piece that generally concentrates on a particular aspect of instrumental or compositional technique, often by repetition of the same figure or feature at various pitches. Earlier examples had used other terms, such as 'esercizio' (It.), 'exercice' (Fr.), 'lesson' (Eng.), or 'Übung' (Ger.). Piano studies were published in the early 19th century and, as the century progressed, began to be written for professional concert use as well as for private practice, resulting in works of such virtuosity as Liszt's *études*. In the 20th century, the piano study was especially cultivated by eastern European composers.

etwas (Ger.). 'Somewhat'.

Evangelist. The *narrator in a *Passion, who recounts the Gospel story either in plainchant or, as in most Passion settings from the mid-17th century onwards, in continuo-accompanied recitative. In 17th- and 18th-century German Passions (e.g. those of J. S. Bach), the part of the Evangelist was traditionally taken by a tenor.

evirato (It., 'unmanned'). A synonym for *castrato.

exequiae (Lat.). Music for funeral rites (exequies).

exercise. 1. A passage specifically designed for the practice of vocal or instrumental technique and with no aesthetic intent. **2.** A piece of a technical character, often intended to improve the performer's ability, but which is also a fully worked-out composition. Such pieces are usually given a title other than 'exercise' (e.g. toccata or *étude*). **3.** A piece of work, usually a composition, submitted by a candidate for a university degree in music.

exit aria (It.: *aria di sortita*). In Italian 18th-century *opera seria*, the first aria sung by each leading character. It occurred at the end of a scene, after which the singer left the stage.

experimental. With regard to music, making some radical departure in technique. During the 1960s the word came to have a more specific meaning, being used to distinguish anti-traditional composers, such as Cage, from the established *avant-garde of Boulez and Stockhausen.

exposition. The opening portion of a fugue or sonata movement, in which the principal thematic material is introduced. **1.** In a *fugue, each voice enters in turn with a statement of the subject or answer, then continues with the countersubject or other contrapuntal material until the last voice has completed its statement. There the exposition ends. **2.** In a movement in *sonata form, the first subject (or theme group) is stated in the main key; then there is a modulation to the complementary key, usually the dominant or relative major, in which key the second subject (or theme group) follows. There may be a series of cadences in the new key, the last of which marks the end of the exposition. This is often followed by a double bar and repeat mark, sometimes with a first ending providing a link back to the opening.

expression. A term that may denote either the expressive qualities of a performance or those inherent in a piece of music. In performance, expression is created through a complex interaction of a variety of discrete technical devices and practices, such as dynamic variation, choice of tempo, rubato, phrasing, articulation, variations in the use of vibrato, changes of instrumental or vocal timbre, or body movement. By these means a performance may be invested with emotion, and hence 'playing expressively' may be synonymous with 'playing with emotion'. Expression may also be inherent in a musical work. A melody, a harmonic progression, a dissonance, or another device or combination of devices may be said to give a work expression. Indications concerning dynamics or tempo are sometimes known as 'expression marks'.

Expressionism. An artistic movement concerned with the ruthless expression of disturbing or distasteful emotions, often with a stylistic violence that may involve pushing ideas to their extremes or treating the subject matter with incisive parody. The term is especially associated with the 'Blaue Reiter' group of painters, including Wassily Kandinsky and Franz Marc, who worked in Munich in the years before World War I, but it has been extended to cover also, for example, the poetry of Georg Trakl and some of the music of Schoenberg, Berg, and Webern, particularly the atonal, non-serial works they composed from 1908 to *c.*1920. The portrayal of characters in extreme or psychotic states, a feature of Expressionist drama, is to be found in the stage works of Schoenberg and, particularly, of Berg.

extemporization. *See* IMPROVISATION.

extravaganza. A term often applied to musical works written in a spirit of caricature or parody.

eye music (Ger.: *Augenmusik*). A term used to describe musical notation that portrays an idea visually but has no aural effect. It was much used in 15th- and 16th-century madrigals and sacred music, such words as 'black', 'darkness', or 'night' being set to black notes, and 'day', 'light', 'white', etc. to white ones. Songs of mourning were often written in black notation.

F. 1. The fourth degree (subdominant) of the scale of C major (*see* SCALE, 1). **2.** Abbreviation for **forte*.

fa [fah]. The fourth degree of the scale in the *solmization system. In French and Italian usage it has become attached, on the fixed-*doh* principle, to the note F, in whichever scale it occurs. *See* TONIC SOL-FA.

faburden. A type of improvised polyphony, chiefly in parallel motion, in 6-3 chords with 8-5 chords at the beginnings and ends of phrases, popular in England from the 15th century to the Reformation. The origins and significance of the term have been much disputed. It has been mistakenly equated with English *discant, and it has also been seen as an offshoot of *fauxbourdon, again almost certainly incorrectly. The purpose of faburden is to add two voices to a plainchant. The 'faburden' part begins a 5th lower than the chant, moves up to a 3rd below it, and remains at that interval for succeeding notes until the final note of a phrase, where the interval of the 5th is regained. A top part, called a 'treble', sings in parallel 4ths above the chant throughout. Faburden was most popular for processional music: litanies, antiphons, psalms, and hymns. It was used for alternate verses of hymns and canticles, as a contrast to plainchant verses. The majority of the early 16th-century English polyphonic *Magnificat* settings are based on faburden parts, not on plainchant.

facile (Fr., It.). 'Easy'; *facilement* (Fr.), *facilmente* (It.), 'easily', i.e. fluently and effortlessly.

Fackeltanz (Ger., 'torch dance'). A torchlight procession with music and dancing, part of the celebrations at German royal weddings, scored for military band.

fa fictum. *See* MUSICA FICTA.

Fag. (Ger.). Abbreviation for *Fagott*, 'bassoon'.

fah. *See* FA.

falsa (Sp., Port.). 'Dissonance'.

false close. Alternative name for an interrupted *cadence.

false relation. The simultaneous or adjacent appearance in different voices of two modally conflicting notes with the same letter name, often the major and minor 3rds of the same triad. This effect was much exploited by the madrigal composers of the late 16th century and the 17th, and became prominent again in the 20th century.

falsetto. The vocal register used by adult male singers to sing in the alto and treble ranges. The highest register of the female voice is often also called falsetto. A falsetto is produced when the vocal folds vibrate only at their edges. Tenors who cannot, or choose not to, produce a full-blooded top note slip into falsetto. In opera falsetto is sometimes used for comic effects.

falsobordone (It., 'false bass'). A technique of singing psalms in harmony, following simple chord progressions. The earliest *falsobordoni* were harmonizations of Gregorian plainchant psalm tones and appeared in Italy and Spain in the 1480s; they were for four voices and used what are now called root-position chords. The name was probably derived from *'fauxbourdon': both fauxbourdon and *falsobordone* involved a type of choral, chordal declamation, though achieved by different means. The use of *falsobordone* gradually declined during the 17th century.

fancy. *See* FANTASIA.

fandango (Sp.). An energetic Spanish dance for a single couple, accompanied by guitars and castanets alternating with sung couplets (cf. **seguidilla*). It originated in the early 18th century and is in quick triple time; its performance is characterized by a steady acceleration and by abrupt pauses in the music, with the dancers freezing in position until it starts again.

fanfare. A flourish of brass instruments, usually trumpets, sometimes also with percussion. Originally improvised (as distinct from military signals), fanfares are used for ceremonial purposes (e.g. at coronations or to announce the entrance of a dignitary) and are characterized by reliance on the harmonic series. Fanfares are now often fully composed, not only for state (natural) trumpets, but also for various brass instruments in six or more parts. In French, a *fanfare* is a brass band.

fantasia (It.; Fr.: *fantaisie*; Ger.: *Fantasie*, *Phantasie*) [fantasy, fancy]. A title often given to pieces of no fixed form, implying that a composer wishes to follow the dictates of imagination. In the early 16th century, lutenists used it for pieces that were not simply transcriptions of vocal music but were conceived originally for the instrument. Such pieces vary from short studies of an improvisatory nature (not dissimilar to the *ricercar of the time) to extended works in which contrapuntal and chordal passages alternate, and sections of brilliant passage-work demonstrate the skill of the player. In this latter sense the word was also used by keyboard composers, whose works in this vein are the precursors of the *toccata.

About the middle of the 16th century, fantasias for instrumental ensemble were written, borrowing vocal idioms from the motet. Unlike the ricercar, the fantasia had no didactic purpose, so there was no attempt to display contrapuntal skill or proficiency of any other kind. There are many fine English examples for keyboard. In England fantasias were often known as 'fancies'. A number of fantasias have a sectional construction, and introduce dance rhythms and even popular tunes. Such works led to the fantasia-suite, in which a large-scale polyphonic movement in the quasi-madrigalian manner was followed by dances.

On the Continent the fashion for violin music and the use of continuo parts led to the demise of the polyphonic fantasia early in the 17th century. Polyphonic works for keyboard with this title were, however, still to be found, especially in Germany. In the 18th and 19th centuries the term was used for lengthy, improvisatory works, sometimes based on an existing piece in another medium (e.g. a song). In general, however, the fantasia became a potpourri of themes from operas compiled as display pieces by virtuoso pianists.

fantasia-suite. A suite of dances preceded by a large-scale polyphonic *fantasia.

fantasy. *See* FANTASIA.

Farbe (Ger., 'colour'). In musical terminology, tone-colour. *See* KLANGFARBENMELODIE.

farce (It.: *farsa*). An 18th-century term denoting a short comic play with music, generally in two (sometimes three) acts, and often consisting of spoken dialogue interspersed with arias. Such pieces were performed as intermezzos between the acts, or at the end, of a larger opera or play. In the late 18th and early 19th centuries the term embraced a lighter kind of *opera buffa*.

fasola. *See* SHAPE NOTE.

fastoso (It.). 'Pompous'; *fastosamente*, 'pompously'.

fausset (Fr.). *'Falsetto'.

fauxbourdon. A technique of singing improvised polyphony, associated particularly with 15th-century

Franco-Burgundian sacred music. It has many similarities to English *faburden, but the derivation of either from the other has not been established, and there are significant differences between them. Fauxbourdon involved improvising a supplementary voice in parallel 4ths below a given voice (often a decorated plainchant). A third, composed, part would complete the texture. Like faburden, the technique of fauxbourdon was used as the starting-point for more sophisticated compositions. Some fauxbourdon pieces survive side by side with alternative versions, where fully composed parts are provided in place of the improvised line. Other compositions are written-out decorations of fauxbourdon. There were two ways of creating fauxbourdon by improvisation: by adding two voices above a cantus firmus, in 8-5 chords at the beginnings and ends of phrases and in 6-3 chords elsewhere; and by adding two voices below.

F clef. *See* CLEF.

feierlich (Ger.). 'Solemn', 'festive'; a term associated with public celebrations, either 'solemn' religious festivals and holy days or 'festive' secular celebrations and holidays.

Feldmusik (Ger., 'field music'). The general name given to 17th- and 18th-century music for brass instruments (*Feldpartiten*, *Feldstücke*, etc.) designed for outdoor performance. The earliest types were simply fanfares in four parts, played by military trumpeters (*Feldtrompeter*); later compositions included the more sophisticated *partita or *divertimento.

felice (It.). 'Happy'.

feminine cadence, feminine ending. The conclusion to a musical phrase in which the second chord of the cadence is less strongly accented than the first.

fermata (It.). The *pause sign (𝄐).

Ferne (Ger.). 'Distance'; *wie aus der Ferne*, 'as if from a distance'.

feroce (It.). 'Fierce'.

Fes (Ger.). The note F♭; *Feses*, the note F𝄫.

festa teatrale (It., 'theatrical celebration'). A genre of 18th-century music theatre especially popular at Viennese courts. It was usually performed in celebration of an important occasion (e.g. a birthday or wedding) and generally treated a mythological or allegorical subject.

festivo, festoso (It.). 'Festive'; *festivamente*, 'in a festive manner'.

Festspiel (Ger., 'festival play'). A term sometimes applied to musical stage works or to plays with incidental music. Wagner called his *Ring* tetralogy a 'Bühnenfestspiel'.

Feuer (Ger.). 'Fire'; *mit Feuer*, *feurig*, 'with fire', 'passionate'.

feuille d'album (Fr.). *'Album-leaf'.

feurig (Ger.). *See* FEUER.

ff, fff. Abbreviations for **fortissimo*.

Fg. (Ger.). Abbreviation for *Fagott*, 'bassoon'.

fiati (It., 'breaths'). Wind instruments.

ficta. *See* MUSICA FICTA.

fiero, fieramente (It.). 'Proud', 'fierce', i.e. high-spirited.

figura (Lat.). In medieval musical theory, the generic term for notational symbols.

figural (Lat.: *figuratus*; Fr.: *figuré*; Ger.: *figuriert*). Literally, florid or elaborately conceived. The adjectives 'figural', 'figurate', and 'figured' have been used to draw a distinction between polyphony (*musica figurata*) and plainchant (*musica plana*) and hence to distinguish any florid style of writing from a simpler one or a single florid polyphonic voice from a less elaborate one.

figuration. A term used loosely to describe passage-work or accompaniment with a distinctive shape (e.g. scales, arpeggio patterns) often derived from the repetition of an easily identifiable figure or motif. It is particularly common in working out variations and in the elaboration of a chorale or hymn tune (sometimes called a 'figured chorale'). *See also* FIGURE, 1.

figure. 1. A brief, easily distinguishable melodic or rhythmic motif, which may be as long as a few bars or as short as two notes. It may form the basis for the construction of a piece or movement. A persistent use of figures in keyboard accompaniment for songs is particularly common and is sometimes termed *figuration. **2.** An arabic number placed beneath a line of music to indicate (in terms of intervals from the bass) all or part of the implied accompanying harmonies. *See* CONTINUO.

figured bass [thoroughbass, general bass] (Fr.: *basse chiffrée, basse continue*; Ger.: *Generalbass, bezifferter Bass*; It.: *basso continuo*). A bass line with figures indicating the required harmonies. The figured bass was a feature of the Baroque period. Usually a bass instrument, for example the bass viol or cello, would play the single bass line while a keyboard or plucked instrument filled in the harmonies. *See* CONTINUO.

figured chorale. An *organ chorale in which a single *figure or motif is used continuously in the accompaniment to the melody.

figures, doctrine of (Ger.: *Figurenlehre*). A term formulated in the early 20th century to describe a theory of composition of the late Baroque period in Germany which relates rhetorical figures of speech to musical figures (*see* RHETORIC). *See also* AFFECTIONS, DOCTRINE OF.

filar il suono [la voce] (It.), **filer le son** [la voix] (Fr.). 'To spin the sound (of the voice)': in singing, an instruction to sustain a note without taking a breath; it can be a similar instruction to wind players and to string players not to use a change of bow. In modern times the term has been taken to imply a constant level of sound, but it has also implied a gradual *crescendo* and *diminuendo*. The same effect is known as **messa di voce*.

fin (Fr.). 'End'.

final (Lat.: *finalis*). The concluding pitch of a modal melody, and effectively equivalent to the tonic of a tonal scale (even though the differences between modal and tonal composition are probably more important than their similarities).

final cadence. *See* CADENCE.

finale. The last movement of a multi-movement instrumental work (e.g. a symphony, concerto, or sonata), or the closing section of an act of an opera or other stage work. As used by early 18th-century composers, the term was usually associated with a lightweight, tuneful movement, often in rondo or sonata form and typically in a fast 6/8 tempo. Later in the century the finale increased in weight and seriousness, counterbalancing the first movement and providing a consummating conclusion. The operatic finale, developed in the 18th century, included extensive ensemble passages and was often divided into contrasting sections.

Finalmusik (Ger., 'end music'). A type of piece related to the *divertimento, *serenade, or *cassation, played as the last item in an outdoor concert.

fin'al segno (It.). 'As far as the sign', i.e. repeat a piece up to the sign 𝄋.

fine (It.). 'End'; *al fine*, an indication to repeat a passage, but only to the place marked *fine*.

fingering. Numerical notation recommending which fingers should be used in performance. It is found chiefly in music for keyboard and stringed instruments, whose technique allows some choice in such matters. *See also* KEYBOARD FINGERING.

finite canon. *See* CANON.

fioritura (It., 'flourish', 'flowering'). A term denoting embellishment of a melodic line (or a part of one), either notated by the composer or added at the discretion of the performer. It is commonly used to describe extended or complex embellishments rather than standard localized ornaments such as trills, mordents, or appoggiaturas. It featured prolifically in the composition and playing of many 19th-century virtuosos.

f

first inversion [6-3 chord]. A term describing the vertical presentation of a chord when the 3rd rather than the root is the lowest note, the other notes being a 3rd and a 6th above it (hence 6-3). *See also* INVERSION, 1.

first-movement form. *See* SONATA FORM.

first subject. The first or principal theme of the first group of a *sonata-form movement.

first-time bar. *See* DOUBLE BAR.

Fis (Ger.). The note F♯; *Fisis*, the note F𝄪.

five-three chord. A chord in *root position, so called because the largest interval is a 5th and the middle one a 3rd (in close position). *See* INVERSION, 1.

fixed doh. A term applied to the system of sight-singing in which C is called *doh* in whichever key it appears (and D is called *ray*, etc.). The opposite system is the movable-*doh* system, in which *doh* is the name applied to the key note of every major scale, *ray* to the second note, and so on. See TONIC SOL-FA.

fl. Abbreviation for 'flute'.

flag [tail]. In notation, a line at the end of a *stem indicating that the note-value is reduced; a single line denotes a quaver, a pair of lines a semiquaver, etc.

flagellant songs (Ger.: *Geisslerlieder*). Vernacular songs sung by flagellants of the 13th and 14th centuries during their acts of pilgrimage and penance.

flageolet notes [flageolet tones]. Harmonics produced on stringed instruments; *see* HARMONIC SERIES.

flam. A rudimentary side-drum technique consisting of a rapid stroke before the main one.

flamenco, cante flamenco (Sp.). The songs, dances, and guitar music of Andalusia. To the original Andalusian strains were added Gypsy elements derived from invading musicians of Flemish or Moorish origin, or both; there is much discussion whether the name 'flamenco' derives from one of these sources. Different songs and dances developed in different regions. There are two broad divisions: *cante hondo*, *jondo*, or *grande*, a deeper strain dealing with themes of love, sorrow, and death; and *cante chico* or *pequeño*, the lighter side which includes fandango, habanera, and tango. Flamenco became a theatrical entertainment with troupes of musicians, singers, and dancers, and a percussion chorus which introduced the characteristic heel-tapping, hand-clapping, and castanet-clacking. Flamenco song has Phrygian characteristics (especially in its use of the minor 2nd) and uses many metres and cross-rhythm.

flat (Fr.: *bémol*; Ger.: *Be*; It.: *bemolle*). **1.** The sign (♭) that, when placed before a note, lowers it in pitch by a semitone. In English terminology the verb is 'to flatten' and the adjective 'flattened'; in American usage the corresponding terms are 'to flat' and 'flatted'. *See* ACCIDENTAL; for the origins of the flat sign and its early use, *see* DURUM AND MOLLIS; NOTATION. **2.** An adjective applied to vocal or instrumental performance, denoting inexact intonation on the low side.

Flatterzunge (Ger.). *'Flutter-tongue'.

flautando, flautato (It.). 'Flute-like': an instruction to a violinist to produce flute-like tones by bowing very lightly over the end of the fingerboard or using harmonics.

flauto (It.). 'Flute'. Until the mid-18th century the unqualified term meant 'recorder'; the flute was specified as *flauto traverso* or 'German flute'.

flebile (It.). 'Mournful', 'plaintive'; *flebilmente*, 'mournfully', 'plaintively'.

flessibile (It.). 'Flexible', i.e. not in strict tempo.

fliessend (Ger.). 'Flowing'; *fliessender*, 'more flowing'.

florid. A term applied to highly embellished music. It is particularly used of 18th-century vocal music, with its passage-work ('divisions') and ornamentation, but is also applied to 15th-century polyphony.

flott (Ger.). 'Brisk', 'lively'.

flottant (Fr.). 'Floating': an instruction to a violinist to use a smooth, flowing bow movement.

flourish. A trumpet call of the *fanfare type. In Restoration England the term also denoted a brief improvisatory passage that preceded the work proper and consisted largely of scales and arpeggios. The word has come to mean any florid instrumental passage.

flüssig (Ger.). 'Flowing'.

flutter-tonguing. A variety of *tonguing, produced by rolling the letter 'R', used especially on the flute.

focoso (It.). 'Fiery'; *focosamente*, 'in a fiery manner'.

folia [follia, folies d'Espagne]. A dance, probably Portuguese in origin, the characteristic harmonic framework of which was adopted by several 17th- and 18th-century composers as the basis of sets of variations. During the early 17th century it was popular in Spain as a sung dance with guitar accompaniment; it spread to Italy, France, England, and elsewhere, scored for various instrumental combinations. The bass line of the *folia* became standardized as a sort of *ground bass, and, as with other Renaissance ground-bass dances such as the **romanesca*, a particular melodic outline was commonly attached to it; this outline (or a rhythmic or melodic variant of it) eventually earned equal status with the bass line and the chordal structure as an identifying feature of the *folia*. Numerous composers wrote variations on the *folia* tune.

folies d'Espagne. *See* FOLIA.

foot. 1. Applied to instruments, 8′ denotes the written pitch, 4′ an octave higher, 16′ an octave lower, etc. The usage derives from the nominal lengths of organ pipes sounding *c*′. **2.** The lowest joint on flutes and recorders.

forefall. A 17th-century English term for an ascending *appoggiatura. *See also* BACKFALL.

forlana [furlano] (It.; Fr.: *forlane*). An Italian dance dating from the 16th century. During the Baroque period it became a lively dance similar to the *gigue, in triple or compound duple time, with dotted rhythms and repeated motifs. It was particularly popular in Venice and in 18th-century *opéras-ballets*.

form. The shape or structure of a musical work; the way in which the various elements in a piece of music—its pitches, rhythms, dynamics, timbres—are organized in order to make it coherent to a listener. Since music is essentially a temporal art, in live performance there is no chance for the listener to rehear a detail or part of a work. This is not the case with painting or literature, where the eye can continue to study a whole work or a detail of it for any length of time. In music a substitute for that property is some kind of repetition: a short sequence of sounds may be repeated, or a long and complex section. The word 'form' is usually applied to the structure of a single movement, e.g. *binary form, *ternary form. Works may be classified as single or compound forms. Single forms are formally complete and tonally self-contained and are not divisible into smaller units. Compound forms include two or more single forms; they are usually multi-movement works (*sonata, *symphony, string quartet, *suite).

See also BAR FORM; BINARY FORM; CANON; CANTUS FIRMUS; CONCERTO

FORM; CYCLIC FORM; DA CAPO; FUGUE; GROUND, GROUND BASS; HETEROPHONY; ISORHYTHM; MOBILE FORM; MOMENT FORM; RITORNELLO; RONDO FORM; SONATA FORM; SONATA RONDO FORM; STROPHIC; STROPHIC VARIATIONS; TERNARY FORM; THROUGH-COMPOSED; TRIO, 2; VARIATION FORM.

formes fixes (Fr., 'fixed forms'). The three chief poetic forms used for the late medieval chanson: the **ballade*, **rondeau*, and **virelai*.

f

fort (Ger.). 'Onward', 'away': an instruction in organ music to silence a stop.

forte (It.). 'Strong', i.e. loud; it is abbreviated *f*.

fortepiano. Loud, then immediately soft; it is abbreviated *fp*.

fortissimo (It.). Very loud; it is abbreviated *ff*.

Fortspinnung (Ger.). The development, or 'spinning out', of a short melodic motif to form a complete phrase, often using sequences.

forza (It.). 'Force', 'strength'; *con tutta forza*, 'with all possible strength', *forzando*, *forzato*, 'forcing', 'forced', i.e. strongly accented.

française (Fr., 'French'). A round dance in triple or compound duple time, popular in the 1830s. It is a later development of the *contredanse* (*see* COUNTRY DANCE).

Franconian notation. A type of notation codified *c*.1260 by Franco of Cologne. It was the true precursor of modern notation in that the rhythm of a note could now be read solely from its shape, rather than construed from the pattern of the other notes in the vicinity.

fredonner (Fr.). 'To hum'.

frei (Ger.). 'Free'.

French overture. *See* OVERTURE, 1.

French pitch. An 18th-century *pitch standard about a tone below modern pitch.

French sixth chord. An *augmented 6th chord.

French time names. See GALIN–PARIS–CHEVÉ SYSTEM.

fresco (It.). 'Fresh'; *frescamente*, 'freshly'.

frettevole, frettoso, frettoloso (It.). 'Hurried'.

fricassée (Fr., 'jumble', 'medley'). A 16th-century name for a humorous *quodlibet, in which melodies from various sources, including chansons, folk tunes, urban popular songs, and street cries, are assembled for comic effect.

frisch (Ger.). 'Vigorous'.

fröhlich (Ger.). 'Joyful'.

frottola (It.). A form of secular song popular in Italy in the late 15th and early 16th centuries, the most important forerunner of the madrigal. It developed from the widespread practice of reciting poetry to an improvised musical accompaniment. Frottolas set verse, often light-hearted love poetry, in many different forms and rhyme schemes, some lighter, bawdy or sentimental, such as the frottola or barzelletta, *oda*, and *capitolo*, and some more serious, such as the sonnet, **strambotto*, and canzone. Frottolas are generally strophic and may include repeated lines of verse and their accompanying music within each strophe, often in the form of a refrain. Settings are for three or four voices, mainly syllabic and homophonic, with the melody in the top voice. Often the text is written out only in the top voice, which suggests that frottolas could be performed by one singer with the three lower parts taken by viols or by a single instrument such as a lute or keyboard.

Frühlingslied (Ger.). 'Spring song'.

fuga (Lat., It.). *'Fugue'.

fugato (It.). A passage in fugal style introduced into a non-fugal composition.

fughetta (It.). A short *fugue.

fuging tune [fuguing tune]. A style of singing metrical psalms and hymns used in English parish churches in the 18th and early 19th centuries and still found in parts of the USA. A typical fuging tune is constructed of alternating homophonic and contrapuntal musical phrases; in the latter, voices enter in imitation of each other in the manner of a fugue.

fugue (Lat., It.: *fuga*; Fr.: *fugue*; Ger.: *Fuge*). Literally, 'flight' or 'escape'. In music the word denotes a composition in which three or more voices (very rarely two) enter imitatively one after the other, each 'giving chase' to the preceding voice. Fugue is a style of composition rather than a fixed structure, but all fugues have features in common, and there is an accepted terminology to describe the roles of individual voices, the component parts of the fugue, and certain technical devices.

The first voice to enter carries the principal theme, known as the 'subject'. The second voice enters, transposing the subject to the dominant; this entry is called the 'answer'. The third voice enters with the original subject (in a different octave), and so on. This opening section is called the 'exposition'; it concludes when each voice has presented the subject or answer. It is usual to allocate the same version of the theme to alternate voices (in a typical four-voice fugue soprano and tenor have the subject, and alto and bass the answer, or vice versa), and to introduce the voices in an alternating sequence of subject and answer. Occasionally an exposition ends with an extra statement of the theme, known as a 'redundant entry'.

As the second voice enters (with the answer) the first voice provides a counterpoint against it; similarly the second voice provides a counterpoint to the third voice (subject), and so on. When this counterpoint is identical at each appearance in the exposition it is called a regular 'countersubject'; when either the subject (or answer) or the countersubject can serve as the bass line without grammatical error the counterpoint is said to be invertible. Additional counterpoint is called 'free', but such material may be restated in an identical form, as if it were a second countersubject. The exposition of a typical three-voice fugue could be represented as in Table 1. Sometimes a link is inserted between successive entries, most commonly the second (answer) and third (subject).

The answer may be 'real' or 'tonal'. A real answer is one that exactly transposes the subject to the dominant; a tonal answer modifies it in some way. The latter is most commonly used when a dominant note appears prominently at or near the beginning of the subject: this note is answered not with the home key's supertonic (an exact transposition) but with its tonic. In a C major fugue an initial G would become a C at the beginning of the answer, not a D. Similarly a leap from tonic to dominant (C–G) would be answered with a leap from dominant to tonic (G–C, not G–D). There are examples of tonal answers in the D♯ minor, F minor, and F♯ major fugues in book 1 of J. S. Bach's '48'. A tonal answer is also needed if the subject ends in the key of the dominant. A real answer would modulate to the supertonic key, far from the tonic in which the subject is about to return; an adjustment is made so that the answer ends in the tonic key. The E♭ major and G♯ minor fugues in book 1 of the '48' have modulating subjects.

After the exposition most fugues continue with an alternating sequence of episodes and middle entries—the latter in related keys—and conclude with a final entry in the tonic. (The first fugue of the '48' is exceptional in containing no episodes.) Episodes are generally based on the thematic material of the subject

TABLE 1

1st voice	subject	countersubject	free counterpoint
2nd voice		answer	countersubject
3rd voice			subject

or countersubject (or both), developing it in various ways and effecting a modulation for the next entry of the subject. Middle entries may incorporate counterpoints from the exposition or introduce new ones. Sometimes after the exposition the composer creates excitement by bringing the entries of the subject nearer to each other so that they overlap. This device is called 'stretto' (It., 'close' or 'compressed'); it is used with unusual frequency in the C major fugue of book 1 of the '48'. Other technical devices are *inversion, *diminution, *augmentation, and more rarely *retrograde.

Occasionally one or more countersubjects appear simultaneously with the subject at the beginning of the fugue. Such a fugue is often called a double (or triple, etc.) fugue; but this term is more properly applied to a fugue in which a second (third, etc.) independent subject appears in the course of the fugue and may subsequently be combined with the first subject. A short fugue is a *fughetta*.

Fugues are most common in Baroque music but also occur in Classical works. They were sometimes used by 19th-century composers in vocal music or operatic ensembles.

fuguing tune. *See* FUGING TUNE.

full anthem. An anthem written for full choir; *see* ANTHEM.

full close. *See* CADENCE.

full score. A *score in which each instrumental or vocal part is separately displayed.

Füllstimme (Ger.). **1.** A 'filling' part, without independent or functional significance, for example an extra orchestral part. **2.** The mixture stop of an organ.

functional analysis. A form of analysis, devised by Hans Keller (1919–85) for use in radio broadcasts, in which a musical structure was broken down into extracts (without verbal description) to demonstrate that the whole work proceeded from a cell-like basic idea.

functional harmony. A theory of tonal harmony, devised by Hugo Riemann (1849–1919), according to which each chordal identity within a tonality can be reduced to one of three harmonic functions—those of tonic, dominant, and subdominant. Thus, for example, a supertonic chord has the function of a subdominant.

fundamental bass (Fr.: *basse fondamentale*). An imaginary bass line, consisting not of the actual lowest notes of a series of chords but of the roots of those chords. The fundamental bass demonstrates that, even when inverted, a chord retains its harmonic nature and function.

funèbre (Fr.), **funebre** (It.). 'Funereal', 'gloomy'.

fuoco, con (It.). 'With fire', i.e. wild and fast.

furiant (Cz.). A quick, exhilarating Bohemian folk dance characterized by the alternation of 3/4 and 2/4 time. It was frequently used by 19th-century Czech composers.

furioso (It.), **furieux** (Fr.). 'Furious'; *furiosamente* (It.), *furieusement* (Fr.), 'furiously'.

furlano (It.). *See* FORLANA.

fusa (Lat.). An early note-value, from which the modern *quaver derives; *see* NOTATION.

Futurism (It.: *Futurismo*; Rus.: *Futurizm*). An artistic movement that saw the 20th century as a new age, a future it vigorously embraced. It was specially prominent in Italy and Russia, and was at its height in the second and third decades of the century. In Italy, Futurist artists were stimulated by the speed and energy of mechanized technology and of 20th-century city life. Among the Italian

Futurist composers was Luigi Russolo, who designed mechanical percussion instruments which he called *intonarumori* ('noise makers'). In Russia Futurists were initially concerned with spiritual regeneration, but after the Revolution they identified themselves with the country's technological and social change.

fz. Abbreviation for *forzando* or **sforzando.*

f

G. The fifth degree (dominant) of the scale of C major (*see* SCALE, 1).

gagliarda (It.). *See* GALLIARD.

gaillarde (Fr.). *See* GALLIARD.

galant (Fr.). A term used to describe the elegant style popular in the 18th century, not only in music but also in literature and the visual arts (as in Watteau's *Fêtes galantes*). The *style galant* (Ger.: *galanter Stil*) was typical of rococo rather than Baroque attitudes, and it served the Enlightenment ideals of clarity and naturalness. In music it resulted in an emphasis on melody with light accompaniment rather than on equal-voiced part-writing and fugal texture. In the 1770s the *galant* style was given a new lease of life in Germany in the sensitive, emotional *empfindsamer Stil* (*see* EMPFINDSAMKEIT).

Galanterien (Ger.; Fr.: *galanteries*). In the early 18th-century *suite, the *Galanterien* are extra movements not essential to the usual scheme of allemande, courante, sarabande, and gigue. They are generally taken from such dance forms as the minuet, gavotte, bourrée, or passepied and are mostly in a lighter vein than the larger-scale suite movements.

galanter Stil (Ger.). *See* GALANT.

Galin–Paris–Chevé system. A method of teaching sight-singing devised by Pierre Galin (1786–1821), Aimé Paris (1798–1866), and Émile Chevé (1804–64). They used a figure notation in which 1 represented the tonic, 5 the dominant, and so on, but in practice sang the sol-fa syllables (*do*, *ré*, *mi*, *fa*, *sol*, *la*, *si*). Their most important contribution was a series of note names for durations, pronounced rhythmically so as to represent the sound of the notes themselves. Commonly known as 'French time names' (Fr.: *langue des durées*), these were adopted by John Curwen in his sight-singing method (*see* TONIC SOL-FA).

gallarda (Sp.). A Spanish 16th- and 17th-century dance, often used as the basis for a set of variations.

galliard (Fr.: *gaillarde*; It.: *gagliarda*; Sp.: *gallarda*). A lively dance of Italian origin popular during the 16th and 17th centuries. It is a sectional dance similar to the *saltarello and **tordion*, with a five-step pattern, and is usually in moderate triple or compound duple time; bars in hemiola rhythm frequently occur, especially near cadence points. The galliard was normally paired with the *pavan (with the galliard placed second as the after-dance), and the two sometimes used the same melodic material. Examples occur in French ballets, English masques, and Italian *intermedi*. In England galliards flourished during the period 1590–1625, both for keyboard and for instrumental consort.

galop (Fr.). A fast and lively ballroom dance in 2/4 time which became popular in Paris and Vienna in the 1820s. It derived from an earlier German dance, the Hopser, and was popular in England in the mid-Victorian era, either as an individual dance or as a *quadrille movement.

gamme (Fr.; It.: *gamma*). *'Scale'; *see also* GAMUT, 3.

gamut. 1. The note G, at the pitch indicated by the bottom line of the bass staff. The word is a contraction of *gamma ut*, which might literally be translated as 'G-doh', the *solmization name for the lowest note recognized in the medieval *hexachord. **2.** By extension, the whole hexachordal system. The term was first used in this sense (in the form 'gamme') at the end of the 14th century. Although the hexachordal system was no longer in use at the end of the 17th century, hexachordal names for notes were common and the term 'gamut' (which seems to be peculiar to English) was still used to refer collectively to them. **3.** By further extension, range, compass (as in the modern French *gamme* and the Italian *gamma*). From an early association with the range of the *Guidonian hand, the term came to be used figuratively to refer to any extended range of musical sounds reckoned from the lowest to the highest. *See also* SOLMIZATION.

ganz (Ger.). 'Whole'; e.g. *ganzer Bogen*, 'whole bow', *gänzlich*, 'completely'; *ganze Note*, 'whole note', i.e. semibreve; *ganze Pause*, 'whole-note rest'.

gapped scale. A pentatonic scale; *see* SCALE.

garbo, con, garbato (It.). 'Graceful', 'elegant'.

gathering note. In hymn-singing, a note played by the organist before the first (or each) verse of a hymn to alert the congregation and establish the pitch. In the late 16th and the 17th centuries a gathering note often prefaced each line of the tune.

gavotte (Fr.; It.: *gavotta*). A French folk dance of Breton origin, absorbed into the repertory of court dances in the 16th century; in the Baroque era it also developed into an instrumental form. Baroque gavottes were in moderate duple metre and generally followed a simple binary structure with two repeated halves. They usually begin with an upbeat of two crotchets and the melodies move in stepwise quavers. Just as a minuet was generally followed by another minuet in contrasting style (*see* TRIO, 2), so the gavotte acquired a second gavotte, often in the style of a *musette. Before the mid-17th century a gavotte usually followed a series of *branles, a dance to which it was closely related. The gavotte was also adapted for inclusion in many dramatic works and ballets and was often associated with pastoral scenes. As an instrumental form, especially for keyboard, it appears as an optional movement in the 18th-century *suite, where it usually follows the sarabande, and as an independent piece. It was also often used as a movement in 18th-century solo and trio sonatas. In the 19th century, many lightweight drawing-room pieces were written in gavotte style.

G clef. *See* CLEF.

Gebrauchsmusik (Ger., 'music for use'). Music designed for children or amateurs and thus, by implication, simpler than that which the composer would write for concert performance (*Hausmusik*). The term arose in Germany during the 1920s, when *Hausmusik* gained political and social importance.

gebrochen (Ger,). 'Broken', i.e. arpeggiated.

gebunden (Ger.). 'Bound', 'tied', i.e. *legato*.

gedämpft (Ger.). 'Muted': an indication that an instrument should be muffled, damped, or deadened, by the appropriate means, i.e. muted (stringed and brass instruments), muffled (drums), or damped (keyboard instruments).

gedehnt (Ger.). 'Prolonged', 'sustained', i.e. slow.

gefällig (Ger.). 'Agreeable', 'pleasant'.

gefühlvoll (Ger.). 'With feeling'.

gehalten (Ger.). 'Sustained'.

gehaucht (Ger.). 'Whispered'.

geheimnisvoll (Ger.). 'Mysterious'.

gehend (Ger.). 'Going', i.e. at a moderate pace, **andante*.

Geisslerlieder (Ger.). *'Flagellant songs'.

geistlich (Ger.). 'Spiritual', 'sacred'; e.g. *geistliches Lied*, 'spiritual song'.

gekoppelt (Ger.). 'Coupled', as applied to organ stops.

gelassen (Ger.). 'Calm', 'quiet'.

Geläufigkeit (Ger.). 'Fluency', i.e. technical ability.

gemächlich (Ger.). 'Comfortable', i.e. unhurried; *gemächlicher*, 'at a more leisurely pace'.

gemässigt (Ger.). 'Moderate', i.e. at a moderate speed.

Gemeindelied (Ger.). *Chorale, congregational hymn.

g

gemendo (It.). 'Moaning', i.e. lamenting.

gemessen (Ger.). 'Measured', 'restrained', i.e. precise (in time-values), at a moderate speed, or in a restrained style.

genau (Ger.). 'Exact'.

Generalbass (Ger.). *See* CONTINUO.

Generalbasslied (Ger.). *'Continuo lied'.

Generalpause (Ger.) An indication in orchestral scores, often abbreviated G.P., that all the players are silent at that point. It commonly occurs after a climactic passage, and was one of the notable innovations of the 18th-century Mannheim school of orchestral playing.

German sixth chord. An *augmented 6th chord.

Ges (Ger.). The note G♭; *Geses*, the note G𝄫.

Gesamtausgabe (Ger.). A 'collected edition' of the complete works of a single composer.

Gesamtkunstwerk (Ger., 'total work of art'). A term formulated by Wagner, who believed that the 'three purely human arts' (music, poetry, and dance) should be united with 'the ancillary aids of drama' (architecture, sculpture, and painting), not merely in association but in a single expressive aim.

Gesang (Ger., 'song'). *See* LIED.

gesangvoll (Ger.). 'Songlike'.

geschwind (Ger.). 'Quick', 'agile'.

Gesellschaftslied (Ger., 'society song'). A song originating among the middle classes of Renaissance society, as opposed to *Hoflied* (a court or aristocratic song) or *Volkslied* (a folksong).

gesteigert (Ger.). 'Increased', i.e. *crescendo.*

gestopft (Ger.). 'Stopped': in horn playing, *stopped notes are produced when the bell of the instrument is more or less completely closed by the player's fist; the term is sometimes used interchangeably with **gedämpft*.

geteilt (Ger.). 'Divided': the same as **divisi*; it is sometimes abbreviated *get.*

getragen (Ger.). 'Solemn', 'slow'.

gewandt (Ger.). 'Agile'.

gewöhnlich (Ger.). 'Usual', 'normal': it is used to countermand a previous instruction that an instrument should be played in an unusual way, e.g. bowing on the fingerboard of a stringed instrument.

gezogen (Ger.). 'Drawn', i.e. sustained.

gezupft (Ger.). *Pizzicato.

gigue (Fr., 'jig'; It.: *giga*). A dance of British origin (*see* JIG), imported into France in the mid-17th century; as an instrumental form the French gigue was one of the four standard movements of the Baroque *suite. During the 17th century the French gigue and the Italian *giga* developed as two distinct styles. The former was typically in triple or compound duple metre, moderate to quick time, and with predominantly dotted rhythms—rather more elegant than its British forebear. The dance was popular with lutenists: later in the century it appeared in harpsichord suites and stage works. The Italian *giga* was nearly always in 12/8 time, much quicker and less contrapuntal than the French version. In Germany, the French version was commonly used as the last movement of keyboard suites. Bach and Handel used both the French and the Italian forms. The dance fell out of use in the Classical period.

gimel. *See* GYMEL.

giocoso (It.). 'Playful', 'humorous'.

gioioso (It.). 'Joyfully'.

Gis (Ger.). The note G♯; *Gisis*, the note G𝄪.

gitano, gitana (It., Sp.). 'Gypsy'; *alla gitana*, 'in Gypsy style'.

giù (It.). 'Down'; e.g. *arcata in giù*, 'down-bow'.

giustamente (It.). 'With exactitude', i.e. with unvarying speed and rhythm.

giustiniana (It.). A term derived from the name of the poet Leonardo Giustiniani. In the 15th century it was applied to songs setting texts by or ascribed to him, some of the earliest polyphonic examples being by Ciconia. In the 16th century the term was applied to a popular, comic type of *villanella or *canzone napolitana*.

giusto (It.). 'Just', 'exact'; *tempo giusto*, either the usual tempo for the type of music in question, or the return to a regular tempo after a passage of flexible tempo.

glänzend (Ger.). 'Brilliant'.

glee. A type of unaccompanied English *partsong composed in the 17th, 18th, and 19th centuries. The word derives from Old English *gliv* or *glēo*, meaning 'music'. The most characteristic period of the English glee was 1760–1830, when *c.*10,000 glees were composed. Like the *catch (the predominant English partsong form in the early 18th century), the glee was at first a male-voice genre; later, boys were paid to sing treble parts at meetings of glee clubs, and glees for SATB became more common. Glees are in certain respects similar to the earlier English madrigals. They were mainly written for from three to five voices, exceptionally for from six to eight; the lyrics were set one phrase at a time, with special attention to word-painting; and they contained a mixture of homophonic and contrapuntal writing. Between 1800 and 1820 composers experimented with 'virtuoso' glees for professional singers, and with glees accompanied by piano and harp. Descendants of the glee are the close-harmony folksong arrangement and the American *barber-shop quartet. Numerous glee clubs still survive in Britain and the USA.

glissade. *See* SLIDE, 1.

glissando (It.). A sliding movement from one note to another. The term is not an authentic Italian word but an Italianization of the French verb *glisser*, 'to slide'. On the piano the effect is achieved by drawing the thumb or the side of the index finger quickly up or down a series of adjacent notes (double glissandos, usually in octaves, and, very occasionally, triple ones also exist). The technique is also much used in harp music. With bowed instruments and voices, an infinite number of microtones are passed through in a glissando. The technique is also effective on the trombone. A glissando may be notated either by means of a written-out ascending or descending chromatic scale in the smallest note-values (in which case the composer generally intends each note to be heard), or by a diagonal straight or wavy line connecting the highest and lowest notes (in which case a *portamento is intended).

glissé (Fr.). 'Slid': in harp playing, a *glissando.

Gloria in excelsis Deo (Lat., 'Glory to God in the Highest'). The Great(er) Doxology, an ancient hymn of Christian praise beginning with the words of the angelic host to the shepherds (Luke 2: 14). Since the 8th century it has been a part of the Ordinary of the Roman *Mass, sung between the Kyrie and the collect except in Advent and Lent, when it is omitted. After the Reformation, vernacular versions were retained at the Eucharists of the Anglican and Lutheran Churches.

glosa (Sp., 'gloss'). **1.** A term used from the 16th century to the 18th for a kind of ornamentation in which a melody is broken up by fast figuration. **2.** A 16th-century term for the technique of writing variations, usually on a religious theme; such variations are generally simpler and less extensive than **diferencias*.

goat's trill (Fr.: *chevrotement*; Ger.: *Bockstriller*, *Geisstriller*). A badly performed vocal trill, reminiscent of the bleating of a goat.

g

gondola song (Ger.: *Gondellied*). *See* BARCAROLLE.

gopak. *See* HOPAK.

gorgheggio (It., from *gorgheggiare*, 'to trill'). A modern term applied to a long, rapid vocal passage in which one vowel takes many notes.

gorgia (It.). A term given to the art of improvised vocal ornamentation practised *c*.1600 in the performance of madrigals, motets, and other pieces.

G.P. Abbreviation for **Generalpause*.

grace notes. A term used for ornamental notes printed in small type and not included in the sum of notes in the bar. The simplest example is the *appoggiatura, especially in its short form (often called *acciaccatura). Some composers wrote long chains of grace notes, to be performed lightly and freely while maintaining a steady tempo overall.

gracieux (Fr.). 'Graceful'.

gracile (It.). 'Delicate'.

gradatamente (It.). 'Gradually'.

gradevole (It.). 'Pleasing', 'agreeable'.

gradito (It.). 'Pleasant'.

gradual (from medieval Lat. *graduale*). **1.** The liturgical book, used by the choir, containing the chants of the Mass. **2.** A responsorial chant, part of the Proper of the Mass, one of the chants between the readings; since the Second Vatican Council it is usually replaced by a longer text (a 'responsorial psalm'). It is sometimes also known as *responsorium graduale*, or simply *graduale*, perhaps because it was performed on the steps (Lat.: *gradus*) leading to the altar. Graduals are among the most elaborate of all chants and are performed by soloists and choir in alternation.

grail. English name for a gradual (*see* GRADUAL, 1).

grandezza, con (It.). 'With grandeur'.

grandioso (It.). 'Grandiose'.

grand opera. In common English usage, serious opera without spoken dialogue. In French, more precisely, *grand opéra* (as opposed to *opéra comique*) means a serious, epic work on a historical, mythic, or legendary subject, usually in five acts, which uses the chorus and includes a ballet, and frequently dramatizes the conflict between private emotion and public, religious, or political responsibility, with much emphasis on spectacle. It was the characteristic form of the Paris Opéra until the late 19th century.

graphic notation. A system developed in the 1950s by which visual shapes or patterns are used instead of, or together with, conventional musical notation.

grave (Fr.). **1.** 'Serious', 'solemn': a tempo indication which in the 17th century meant very slow but which by the 18th came to mean the same as *andante*. **2.** When applied to pitch, 'low'.

grazioso (It.). 'Graceful'; *graziosamente*, 'gracefully'.

great service. *See* SERVICE.

greghesca (It.). A light song of the mid-16th century, so called because the texts are in a 'language' derived from the dialect of the Veneto region and Greek.

Gregorian chant. *See* PLAINCHANT.

Gr. Fl. (Ger.). Abbreviation for *grosse Flöte* ('large flute'), the standard concert flute, as distinct from the piccolo (*kleine Flöte*, Kl. Fl.).

Griffbrett (Ger.). The 'fingerboard' of a stringed instrument.

groppo (It.). A cadential *trill.

gros, grosse (Fr.), **gross, grosse** (Ger.). 'Great', 'large'; when used of an organ stop it means 'of low pitch'; *grosse caisse*, *gros tambour*, 'bass drum'.

ground, ground bass. A short melody, usually in the bass, repeated continually with changing upper parts. The term 'ground' first appeared in England in the late 16th century and referred variously to the melody itself, the harmonic framework constructed round it, or the entire composition. It was the contrast between a fixed bass and freely moving upper parts that attracted 16th- and 17th-century composers to the ground, particularly in England, where elaborate extemporization in an upper part or parts above a ground bass were called 'divisions' and became a valued performing technique among viol players (*see* DIVISIONS, 2). A ground bass may vary in length from a few notes to a full-length, extended melody and its repetitions need not be rigidly fixed.

In Renaissance and Baroque dance music a ground bass was sometimes allied to a particular melody (e.g. in the **romanesca* and **folia*), and these paired tunes, often together with their implied harmonic scheme, formed the basis of a number of theme and variation sets which were occasionally described as grounds. The ground is in effect an element of *variation form. It can be regarded as an extension of *ostinato, and the *passacaglia and *chaconne can both be considered types of ground, even though their repeated motifs may be in parts other than the bass. It was as a variation technique that the ground persisted beyond the Baroque period, though often under the more specific title of chaconne or passacaglia.

Gr. Tr. (Ger.). Abbreviation for *grosse Trommel* ('large drum', i.e. bass drum).

gruppetto (It.). 'Small group'; in the 16th century, a *trill, but thereafter a *turn.

gruppo (It.). A cadential *trill.

gsp. Abbreviation for glockenspiel.

guida (It.). **1.** A fugue *subject. **2.** A *direct.

Guidonian hand. A visual teaching aid, showing the notes of the scale and their *solmization syllables at specific points on the human hand. It was named after the Italian theorist Guido of Arezzo (*b c.*991; *d* after 1033), who invented the musical staff.

gusto (It.). 'Taste', i.e. with appropriate speed, phrasing, etc.; *gustoso*, 'tastefully'; *con gusto*, 'with style', 'with zest'.

gymel [gimel] (from Lat. *gemellus*, 'twin'). A term used to describe a technique of late medieval and Renaissance polyphonic composition where one contrapuntal voice part temporarily divides to form two of equal range. The word 'semel', formerly thought to indicate a return to unison singing after a passage of gymel, is simply an alternative to that term.

H (Ger.). The note B (*H-dur*, 'B major'; *H-moll*, 'B minor'); B♭ is called B in German.

habanera (Sp.; Fr.: *havanaise*). A Cuban dance, possibly of African origin, that became popular in Spain. In slow 2/4 time, with the first quaver of the bar dotted, it was further developed in South American music as the quicker but similar *tango.

hairpins. A colloquial term for **crescendo* and **decrescendo* signs; *see* DYNAMIC MARKS, Table 1.

halb, Halbe (Ger.). 'Half'; e.g. *Halbe-Note*, 'half-note', i.e. minim; *Halbe Pause*, 'half-note rest'.

half-close. *See* CADENCE.

half-coloration. A term applied to a two-note *ligature in which only one of the notes is in *coloration. The 'uncolored' note has its normal length, the 'colored' note loses a third of its value.

half-diminished seventh chord. The diminished 7th is a full diminished chord, comprising three minor 3rds which together span a diminished 7th interval (e.g. D–F–A♭–C♭). A half-diminished chord spans a minor 7th, and is built from two minor 3rds and a major 3rd, as in D–F–A♭–C. The *'Tristan' chord is half-diminished, and may also be termed a 'secondary 7th', i.e. a 7th chord on a degree of the scale other than the dominant.

half-note (Amer.). *Minim.

half-trill. *See* TRILL.

hallelujah. *See* ALLELUIA.

halling. A lively Norwegian folk dance in duple or quadruple time, normally a solo dance for men.

hard hexachord. *See* HEXACHORD; SOLMIZATION.

hardi (Fr.). 'Rash', i.e. bold.

harmonic minor scale. *See* SCALE.

harmonic rhythm. The rhythm articulated by changes of harmony within a given phrase or structure. The term is often used for the rate of change of chords.

harmonics. *See* HARMONIC SERIES.

harmonic series. A series of frequencies that underlies music in many ways and features in the playing technique of stringed and wind instruments. The series 1, 1/2, 1/3, 1/4, etc. is musically represented in the divisions of the length of a string or, in wind instruments, of an air column. The corresponding frequency-values (and therefore the musical pitch) follow a reciprocal series 1, 2, 3, 4, etc., since twice the wavelength corresponds to half the frequency, and so on. To demonstrate the series musically, the note *C* (C below the bass staff) is conventionally taken as the root or fundamental. Ex. 1 illustrates the series up to the 24th harmonic, since this is found in some 18th-century music for brass instruments.

Except for certain stringed instruments, on which natural harmonics are produced by touching the string at particular points along its length, the standard scheme numbers the octave harmonic '2' (as in Ex. 1); this has the advantage of bringing the numbers in line with the interval ratios. For example, the Cs 1, 2, 4, 8, etc. are each an octave apart, i.e. in a ratio of 1:2. Every interval in the series is expressible as the ratio of the two notes involved: for example, the interval G–E (3:5) is the natural or 'just' major 6th, as is D–B (9:15 = 3:5).

The higher one goes through the series, the smaller the successive inter-

Harmonic series, Ex. 1

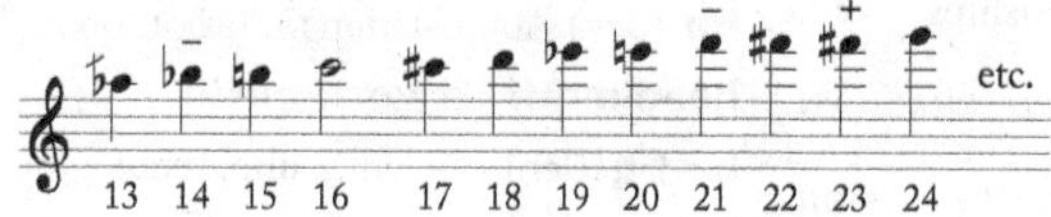

♭ = quarter-flat ‡ = quarter-sharp

vals become; thus, in Ex. 1, the intervals between harmonics decrease progressively from an octave (1:2) to about three-quarters of a semitone (23:24). The series therefore does not line up with a musical scale, in which the intervals are repeated in each octave. In practical music-making the differences are evened out by either *mean-tone or *equal-temperament tuning (*see also* TEMPERAMENT).

Harmonie (Fr., Ger.), **Harmoniemusik** (Ger.). A term used in France and Germany for a wind band, woodwind or mixed (as opposed to the French *fanfare*, a brass band). The wind section of an orchestra is sometimes referred to as the 'harmonie'. In France, *pièces d'harmonie* were generally collections of opera *airs* arranged for wind. The main tradition is however German and central European. In the late 18th century 'Harmonie' or 'Harmoniemusik' denoted a group of wind players or the music they played. Such bands were maintained by wealthy courts for performing serenades during dinner and on festive occasions, as a background to social activity.

harmony. The simultaneous sounding of notes, to produce chords and chord progressions; the 'vertical' element in music in several parts as opposed to the horizontal (*counterpoint). Since the time of the Ancient Greeks, writers on music have discussed the acoustical nature of harmony alongside its physical and emotional effects. Harmony texts share ideas and values which were closely bound up with the evolution of tonality and tonal composition between 1700 and 1900. The governing principle is that harmony embraces harmoniousness—that is, creates a pleasing effect—by observing certain compositionally established conventions, which derive from the perception that not all chords are the same and that combining different selections of notes of the scale creates different degrees of stability and instability, consonance and dissonance. However, in different eras there have been different notions as to what kinds of harmony are acceptable or desirable.

The shaping of musical forms and phrases in relation to the means of achieving convincing closure, or *cadence, was central to harmonic theory. The increasing 18th-century tendency to think of music as founded on a *fundamental bass of chordal roots, rather than on the *figured bass, contributed to the idea that rules of harmonic practice should be codified. Baroque, Classical, and Romantic harmonic practice kept to essentially vocal ideas about acceptable principles of motion, even in a bass line that was understood to need to move more by leap than by step. Dominant harmoniousness was reinforced by principles of rhythmic structuring and formal organization that emphasized regularity of phrase structuring as the norm and made clearly hierarchical distinctions between stronger, accented events within the prevailing metre and those weaker events which were inevitably perceived as moving between and therefore linking the strong ones in ways with which the hierarchies of tonal harmonic relationships could engage.

See also CADENCE; CHORD; CHROMATICISM; CLOSE HARMONY; CONSECUTIVE INTERVAL; CONSONANCE AND DISSONANCE; FALSE RELATION; INVERSION; PASSING NOTE; PREPARATION; RESOLUTION; SUSPENSION; TRIAD.

h

harmony of the spheres. *See* SPHERES, MUSIC OF THE.

hastig (Ger.). 'Hurried', 'impetuous'.

Haupt (Ger.). 'Head', 'principal'; e.g. *Hauptthema*, the 'principal theme' of a composition.

Hauptstimme (Ger.). 'Principal voice': the leading part, often the soprano. Schoenberg used the term to denote the principal part in a complex polyphonic texture (as opposed to the **Nebenstimme*, 'next voice'); it is often marked in the score by a bracket symbol formed from the letter H.

Hausmusik (Ger.). *See* GEBRAUCHSMUSIK.

haut, bas (Fr.). Terms used to describe early instruments and ensembles by their loudness, not their pitch. *Haut* ('loud') instruments such as shawms and slide trumpets played outdoor, festive music; *bas* ('soft') instruments—recorders, fiddles, lutes, and harps—played more intimately.

hautbois (Fr.). 'Oboe' or, before the mid-17th century, 'shawm'. The term was formerly used in English in the same two senses, frequently written 'hautboy' or 'hoboy'.

haute-contre (Fr.). A high tenor voice (or instrument of similar range), neither castrato nor falsetto, with a range of roughly *d–b′*. It was the leading male solo voice in French Baroque opera; by about 1820 it had been superseded by the normal tenor voice.

haute danse (Fr., 'elevated dance'). The opposite of *basse danse, i.e. a dance in which the feet were lifted off the ground as opposed to being kept close to it.

havanaise (Fr.). The *habanera.

Hb. (Ger.). Abbreviation for *Hoboe*, 'oboe'.

head-motif. *See* MOTTO THEME.

heftig (Ger.). 'Violent', 'impetuous'.

heighted neumes. Neumes placed in such a way as to give an idea of their relative pitch. *See* NOTATION.

heiter (Ger.). 'Cheerful', 'serene'.

Heldentenor (Ger., 'hero tenor'). A big-voiced tenor suitable for heavy operatic roles.

hemidemisemiquaver (𝅘𝅥𝅲). The note having 1/64 of the value of the semibreve, or whole note; hence the American usage '64th-note'.

hemiola [hemiolia] (from Gk. *hemiolios*, 'the whole and a half'). A term denoting the ratio 3:2. In modern notation, a hemiola occurs when two bars in triple metre (e.g. 3/2) are performed as if they were notated as three bars in duple metre (6/4), or vice versa. This rhythmic device is common in Baroque music, especially in the *courante. In early mensural music, the equivalent situation prevails when three imperfect notes are substituted for two perfect ones (*see* NOTATION). In the early theory of musical pitch, 'hemiola' was an interval of a 5th: the two lengths of vibrating string that produce this interval are in the ratio 3:2.

heptachord. A collection of seven pitches, especially the diatonic *scale.

heptatonic scale. A *scale of seven notes (e.g. the diatonic scale).

Herabstrich (Ger.). In string playing, 'down-bow'.

Heraufstrich (Ger.). In string playing, 'up-bow'.

Herbstlied (Ger.). 'Autumn song'.

Herstrich (Ger.). In cello and double-bass playing, 'down-bow'.

hervorgehoben (Ger.). 'Prominent', 'emphasized'.

hervortretend (Ger.). 'Brought out', 'prominent'.

herzlich (Ger.). 'Heartfelt', 'affectionate'.

Hes (Ger.). The note B♭. It is, however, more usually called B in German (*see also* H).

heterophony. A term coined by Plato, now used to describe the simultaneous sounding of a melody with an elaborated variant of it, and also the quasi-canonic presentation of the same or similar melodies in two or more vocal or instrumental lines. Such heterophony is a particular feature of 20th-century music influenced by Indonesian or other East Asian ensemble music, in which such textures are common.

hexachord (from Gk. *hex*, 'six', *chordē*, 'string'). A scale segment consisting of six adjacent notes. Although the term could denote such a series from any scale (just as 'tetrachord' means four adjacent notes from any scale), since the Middle Ages it has been most used to refer to six notes with the interval pattern tone-tone-semitone-tone-tone: the 'natural' hexachord (*hexachordum naturale*) C–D–E–F–G–A, the 'soft' hexachord (*hexachordum molle*) F–G–A–B♭–C–D, and the 'hard' hexachord (*hexachordum durum*) G–A–B–C–D–E. The notes of the hexachord were labelled *ut-re-mi-fa-sol-la*, a practice known as *solmization.

hinsterbend (Ger.). 'Dying away'.

Hinstrich (Ger.). In cello and double-bass playing, 'up-bow'.

His (Ger.). The note B; *Hisis*, the note B𝄪.

Hlzbl. (Ger.). Abbreviation for *Holzbläser* ('wood blowers', i.e. the woodwind section).

Hoboken. Abbreviation for the standard *thematic catalogue of the works of Joseph Haydn drawn up by Anthony van Hoboken (1887–1983). Haydn's works, especially those without distinguishing title or opus number, are often referred to by Hoboken number, as in the form 'Hob. XVII: 6'.

höchst (Ger.). 'Highest', 'in the highest degree'.

Hochzeitsmarsch (Ger.). 'Wedding march'; *Hochzeitszug*, a wedding procession.

hocket [hoquet]. A device of medieval polyphony whereby a melody is divided between two (or occasionally three) contrapuntal voice parts. One part rests while the other sounds, giving a fast alternation of single notes (or small groups of notes) and rests in each part and producing the effect of a vocal line 'jumping' from one voice to another (Ex. 1).

Hoflied (Ger.). A Renaissance song emanating from courtly or aristocratic circles, as opposed to *Gesellschaftslied*, a middle-class song, or *Volkslied*, a folksong.

Hoftanz (Ger.). A 16th-century German dance, counterpart of the French *basse danse.

Hocket, Ex. 1

hold. Another term for a fermata or *pause, mainly an American usage.

holograph. A manuscript wholly in the hand of its composer. *See also* AUTOGRAPH.

Holz (Ger., 'wood'). *Holzbläser*, 'woodwind players'; *Holzblasinstrumente*, 'woodwind instruments'; *Holzflöte*, 'wooden flute', an organ stop; *Holzharmonika*, 'xylophone'; *Holzschlägel*, 'wooden drumsticks'.

homophony. A term used to describe music in which one voice or part is clearly melodic, the others accompanimental and chiefly chordal. The converse is *polyphony, where the parts tend towards independence and equality. The term 'homophony' has also been used to describe part-writing where all the parts move in the same rhythm; a more precise term for this is *homorhythm. *See also* MONOPHONY.

homorhythm. A term used to describe music in which all the voices or parts move in the same rhythm (e.g. hymns, chorales, early organum).

hopak [gopak]. A Ukrainian folk dance, apparently deriving its name from the exclamation 'hop' uttered during performance. It is usually in a major key and fast duple metre. The solo dancing is improvised and acrobatic. There are examples in several 19th-century Russian operas.

Hopser. *See* GALOP.

hornpipe. A British dance similar to the jig, but usually in 3/2, 2/4, or 4/4 time, especially popular between the 16th and 19th centuries. It was usually performed by one person accompanied by bagpipes and fiddles. From the 16th century onwards, hornpipes appeared in dance suites and incidental music for the stage. The traditional association of the hornpipe with British seamen began in the late 18th century. (There is also a reed instrument called 'hornpipe'.)

Hr. (Ger.). Abbreviation for 'horns'.

Hrf. (Ger.). Abbreviation for *Harfe*, 'harp'.

humoresque (Fr.; Ger.: *Humoreske*). A name used as a title in the 19th century for a short, lively instrumental composition, often 'good-humoured' rather than 'humorous'.

hüpfend (Ger., 'hopping'). In string playing, with a springing bow (i.e. **spiccato*).

hurtig (Ger.). 'Quick', 'agile'.

hymn (from Gk. *humnos*; Lat.: *hymnus*). A term deriving from ancient Greek pagan religious song, later applied to (especially strophic and metrical) genres of Latin Christian song, and thence vernacular Christian song. 'Hymn' is now usually applied to Christian songs for worship, written in metrical verse in lines of regular length, whereas 'psalm' refers to the 'Psalms of David' in the Old Testament, whose poetry is neither metrical nor regular. In earliest Christian usage the terms were often interchangeable. Latin hymns are sung at the Divine Office, and are assigned to different liturgical occasions, according to time of day, season of the year, or Holy Day. From the 15th century, the melodies of Gregorian hymns often appeared in polyphonic arrangements, using the plainchant as a *cantus firmus.

The vernacular hymn, introduced with the Reformation, became fundamental to Lutheran congregational worship (*see* CHORALE). Calvinism, however, limited congregational singing to metrical versions of the psalms; this restriction operated in England and Scotland. In the 18th century, John and Charles Wesley represented a movement away from this practice towards a means of expressing the personal emotion of an evangelical congregation. By the 19th century the church was commissioning new hymns, culminating in *Hymns, Ancient & Modern* (1861). In Britain and America, different denominations developed their own hymnbooks in similar formats, notably *The English Hymnal* (1906).

idée fixe (Fr., 'fixed idea', 'obsession'). A term coined by Berlioz for a recurrent theme. Its use is related to *cyclic form, and is a forerunner of *leitmotif.

idyll. A literary description (in prose or verse) of happy rural life, applied by extension to a musical composition of a peaceful, pastoral character.

imitation. 1. The repetition—a process more technical than aesthetic—of a motif or idea in other voices: in fugal expositions, for example, the initial subject statement is answered and repeated as a way of reinforcing its importance to the contrapuntal structure. Imitation was instrinsic to certain medieval forms (e.g. the rota (*see* ROUND) and **caccia*) and pervaded Renaissance polyphony, especially the *motet. **2.** The representation in music of extra-musical sounds (e.g. birdsong, flowing water, a train, rumbling traffic).

immer (Ger.). 'Always', 'ever', 'still', e.g. *immer belebter*, 'ever more lively'; *immer schnell*, 'always quick'.

imperfect cadence. *See* CADENCE.

imperfect interval. An *interval of a 2nd, 3rd, 6th, or 7th.

impetuoso (It.). 'Impetuous'.

Impressionism. A term used for a style of late 19th-century French painting and extended to apply to music of a generation later. Monet's *Impression: Lever du soleil* ('Impression: Sunrise'), exhibited in 1874, led to the coinage of the term. The Impressionist school of painting was concerned with urban (often Parisian) and landscape subjects treated in a particular way: suffused and reflected light (the impression), sometimes hazy or smoky, is more important than outline or detail. The term was applied to early 20th-century French music that was similarly concerned with the representation of landscape or natural phenomena, particularly water and light imagery, through subtle textures suffused with instrumental colour. Debussy has traditionally been described as an 'Impressionist' (though he disapproved of the term).

impromptu. An instrumental (usually piano) composition, not necessarily (despite its name) of an improvisatory character; the title was common in the 19th century.

improvisation [extemporization]. A performance that is spontaneous, on inventive whim, rather than one given from a written or printed score or from memory. Improvisation, however, usually involves the imaginative reworking of a given theme or other musical material. It has been an important element in music since the Middle Ages (e.g. *discant, *faburden, *fauxbourdon). In the 17th and 18th centuries improvisation was required in the divisions of viol players (*see* DIVISION, 2). The Baroque and Classical concerto *cadenza gave the soloist an opportunity to display virtuoso technique in inventive use of material from the preceding part of the movement. Church organists are required to improvise for lengthy periods to fill in time during services and ceremonies. Certain pieces of unnotated *aleatory and *indeterminate music are effectively dependent on the performers' powers of improvisation.

in alt, in altissimo. *See* ALT, 1.

incalzando (It.) 'Pressing on', 'chasing', i.e. increasing the tempo.

incantation. In opera or oratorio, a scene in which spirits are conjured.

incidental music (Fr.: *musique de scène*; Ger.: *Bühnenmusik*; It.: *musica di scena*). Music played during a performance of a spoken drama. Incidental music is of secondary importance to the speech (though this does not necessarily mean it has no dramatic significance) and thus the term is not used with reference to such forms as the operetta, musical, *Singspiel*, or masque. It embraces not only the music 'outside' the drama, including the overture before the play and the *entr'actes, *interludes, or *act tunes between the acts, but also that performed as part of the action (fanfares, songs, dances, marches, and supernatural and mood music) whether on or off the stage. Such music was first used to accompany plays in ancient Greece.

incipit (Lat., 'begins'). **1.** The opening words or music of a work as presented in a catalogue or index. **2.** Occasionally, a synonym for intonation (*see* INTONATION, 1). **3.** The preliminary staff in modern editions of early music, giving the original clefs and time and key signatures, the opening note or notes in their original notation, and occasionally the range of the part.

indeterminate music. Music over which the composer has to some degree relinquished control, perhaps by leaving some aspects to chance (e.g. subject to the toss of a performer's coin) or to the performer's decision (e.g. using *graphic rather than conventional notation). Other possibilities include the use of texts to prompt a collective musical response or providing fixed material which may be played in sequences chosen by the performer. *See also* ALEATORY MUSIC.

inégales. *See* NOTES INÉGALES.

inequality. The convention, established during the Baroque period in France, whereby a sequence of notes written as equal in durational value was performed as alternately long and short. *See* NOTES INÉGALES.

inflection [inflexion]. A term referring to those parts of the melody that move away from the reciting tone in the simpler forms of *plainchant, recitation, or cantillation.

innig (Ger.). 'Heartfelt', 'sincere'.

In nomine (Lat.). An English form of instrumental *cantus-firmus composition that flourished during the 16th and 17th centuries. The cantus firmus is the Sarum antiphon *Gloria tibi Trinitas.* The title 'In nomine' is explained by the fact that the genre derives from John Taverner's cantus-firmus mass based on that antiphon: in the latter section of the Benedictus the words 'In nomine Domini' are set for four voices, with the cantus firmus in breves, and this passage gained separate currency in various arrangements. The two main *In nomine* traditions are for consort and for keyboard. After an early preference for four parts, five became the norm for the consort *In nomine*.

in relievo (It.). 'In relief', i.e. a direction to make a melody stand out.

insieme (It.). 'Together'.

instrumentation. *See* ORCHESTRATION.

intabulation (Ger.: *Intabulierung*; It.: *intavolatura*). An arrangement, usually for keyboard or plucked string instruments (e.g. lute), of an existing polyphonic vocal piece. Normally, all the voices of the original model were retained, though small omissions might occur, and the parts might be differently distributed for the convenience of a single player. Intabulations were the medieval and Renaissance equivalents of modern piano arrangements of orchestral scores, except that, in the earlier examples, the highest part was frequently embellished. The term 'intabulation' was also commonly applied to any piece written in a particular type of instrumental notation known as *tablature. The intabulated arrangements of early music provide valuable evidence for the addition of ornamentation in performance, and also (since the tablature notation tells the string player exactly where on the fret to put the fingers) for the use of accidentals in earlier times (*see* MUSICA FICTA).

intavolatura (It.). **1.** *'Intabulation'. When used to describe late 16th- and 17th-century Italian keyboard pieces, 'intavolatura' implies that the music was printed in 'keyboard score' format, i.e. with all parts compressed onto just two staves (*d'intavolatura*), rather than with each part allocated to a separate staff (*partitura*, 'score'). The term also indicates that such publications contain compositions originally written for voices but now arranged for instrumental performance. **2.** Any collection of solo instrumental music printed in *tablature.

interlude. Music, usually instrumental, played between the sections of a work. In church music, interludes are often short, improvisatory passages played on the organ between the verses of a hymn or psalm. In stage works, particularly operas, interludes are performed between scenes or acts and often serve to further the progress of the drama (*see also* ENTR'ACTE and ACT TUNE). The term is also used as a title of a musical work without the above connotations.

intermède. In the French theatre of the 16th and 17th centuries, music and dance performed between the acts of a play or opera—the French equivalent of the Italian **intermedio*. *Intermèdes* were spectacular presentations, often on mythological themes, in which, from the early 17th century, ballet was an important element. In the 18th century the term was also used to refer to a short one- or two-act comic opera in French.

intermedio (It.). A type of entertainment popular in the 16th and 17th centuries, particularly in Italy; it could involve music, drama, and dance and was performed between the acts of a play. The first known *intermedio* performances took place at the Ferrarese court in the late 15th century. They functioned as a means of distinguishing one act from the next and could consist simply of instrumental music performed by players who were not in view of the audience; *intermedi* were later added before and after the play. The more popular type of *intermedio*, however, involved singing, acting, and dancing and was usually based on a pastoral or mythological theme. *Intermedi* exerted considerable influence on the first operas, which themselves were developed in Florence and involved many of the same musicians and librettists. *Intermedi* continued to be performed even after opera was no longer a new genre. The French **intermède* tended to include more ballet than the Italian *intermedio*.

intermezzo (It., 'in the middle'). **1.** The 18th-century term for an **intermedio*. **2.** In the first half of the 18th century, a type of entr'acte performed between the acts of a spoken play or *opera seria*. The intermezzo was a development of the Italian 16th- and 17th-century **intermedio* but differed from its predecessor in having a single comic plot, usually presented in two parts, and the same cast of two or three characters. Although the first examples came from Venice, the genre was especially popular in Naples, where, in the 1720s, it acquired independence from the *opere serie* and spoken dramas to which it had formerly been attached. After *c.*1750 the intermezzo evolved further into *opera buffa*. **3.** In the 19th century, a term occasionally used as the title of a movement, usually of a light character, contained within a larger work. **4.** The term acquired a meaning similar to that of *interlude, and sometimes denoted a short orchestral piece inserted into an opera to indicate a lapse of time.

interpretation. The process by which a performer translates a work from notation into artistically valid sound. Because of the ambiguity inherent in musical notation, a performer must make important decisions about the meaning and realization of aspects of a work which the composer cannot clearly prescribe. These may include choices about dynamics, tempo, phrasing, and the like, or large-scale judgments concerning the articulation of formal divisions, pacing of musical climaxes, and so on.

interrupted cadence. *See* CADENCE.

interval. The distance in pitch between two notes. Precise measurement of intervals is expressible acoustically in terms of frequency ratios, but for ordinary purposes the diatonic scale is taken as a convenient yardstick. Table 1 shows examples of the most common intervals.

Each interval is named according to the number of notes of the scale it spans. Thus C–D (above) or C–B (below) is a 2nd (two notes), C–E (above) or C–A (below) is a 3rd (three notes), and so on. Intervals larger than an octave are compound intervals: thus C–D (in the next octave above) or C–B (in the next octave below) may be referred to either as a compound 2nd or, more usually, as a 9th, and so with compound 3rds (10ths), compound 4ths (11ths), and so on.

The intervals of a 4th, 5th, or octave are called perfect; they have a purity of tone and a bareness that makes them quite different from the others. The imperfect intervals—the 2nd, 3rd, 6th, and 7th—may be of two types, according to the number of semitones they span. Thus C–E and C–A, which both occur in the major scale on C, are a major 3rd (four semitones) and a major 6th (nine semitones) respectively, whereas C–E♭ and C–A♭, which both occur in the minor scale on C, are a minor 3rd (three semitones) and a minor 6th (eight semi-

TABLE 1

Intervals from middle C

	DIMINISHED	MINOR	MAJOR	PERFECT	AUGMENTED
UNISON					
2nd					
3rd					
4th					
5th					
6th					
7th					
OCTAVE					

tones) respectively. By extension, any major interval reduced chromatically by a semitone at either end becomes minor: thus C–D is a major 2nd, and C–D♭ and C♯–D are minor 2nds.

All intervals, perfect or imperfect, major or minor, may also be augmented or diminished. A major or perfect interval increased chromatically by a semitone at either end becomes augmented: thus C–G, a perfect 5th, becomes an augmented 5th in either of the forms C–G♯ or C♭–G, and C–A, a major 6th, becomes an augmented 6th in either of the forms C–A♯ or C♭–A. Similarly, any minor or perfect interval reduced chromatically by a semitone at either end becomes diminished: thus C–G, a perfect 5th, becomes a diminished 5th in either of the forms C–G♭ or C♯–G, and C–A♭, a minor 6th, becomes a diminished 6th in either of the forms C–A𝄫 or C♯–A♭. Very occasionally augmented or diminished intervals are increased or reduced by a further semitone, to become double augmented or double diminished.

While C–A♭ and C–G♯ are identical intervals on modern keyboard instruments, they none the less have different names: C–A♭ is a minor 6th (six note-names embraced) and C–G♯ an augmented 5th (five note-names). Although on the keyboard G♯ and A♭ are the same note, they are acoustically distinct; such intervals as that between G♯ and A♭ are called *enharmonic.

Intervals may be inverted by reversing the positions of the two notes relative to one another (i.e. if the upper note remains in position and the lower one steps over it to the pitch an octave above its previous position, or if the lower note remains in position and the upper one steps over it to the pitch an octave below its previous position). Inverted intervals, except for the unison and octave, change their quality and size on inversion: inverted major intervals become minor, minor become major, augmented become diminished, and diminished become augmented; and the size of an interval plus the size of its inversion always total nine, an inverted 4th becoming a 5th, a 6th becoming a 3rd, and so on.

In the context of modal or tonal composition, some intervals (3rds, 6ths, and all perfect intervals) are consonant, and others (2nds, 7ths, and all augmented or diminished intervals) are dissonant (*see* CONSONANCE AND DISSONANCE).

intonation. 1. The opening phrase of a plainchant melody, perhaps so called because it was sung by the priest or cantor alone, giving the pitch and, in the psalms, the 'tone' (*see* TONUS, 3) of what was to follow. **2.** The term used for identifying the state of a performer's tuning. It is thus possible to distinguish between 'good' and 'poor' intonation.

intonazione [intonatione] (It., 'intonation'). A short organ piece used as an introduction to a vocal item in a church service, designed to establish the pitch and mode of the following work.

intoning [monotoning]. Singing on one note, as practised by the clergy in parts of the Roman, Anglican, and other liturgies. *See also* INTONATION, 1.

Intrada (Ger., from Sp. *entrada*, 'entrance', 'beginning'). An instrumental piece played as a prelude to an occasion, the entrance of a character on stage, or to introduce choral items in the church service. In Spain the term was associated with the 'entries' of different polyphonic voices. In 17th-century Germany an *Intrada* was often included in the orchestral suite.

introduction (Ger.: *Einleitung*, *Eingang*; It.: *introduzione*). Any musical material that precedes the main structural substance of a composition. Introductions are usually slow and range from a single chord to a lengthy passage that develops its own theme. In sonata-form movements of the late 18th and early 19th centuries, introductions often precede the exposition. Composers have sometimes used the designation 'introduction' for a slow section of a work.

introit. 1. A chant accompanying the entrance of the clergy in Christian worship. The term most frequently refers to the initial chant of the Roman *Mass, normally consisting of an antiphon with one verse (usually of a psalm) and the *Gloria Patri* in the order: antiphon-verse-antiphon-*Gloria Patri*-antiphon. The introit is a part of the Proper of the Mass, and several Sundays are named after the first word of their introit. **2.** An organ piece replacing all or part of the sung introit of the Mass.

invariance. The property of remaining the same after some operation has been completed; the term is normally used in connection with atonal music. For instance, the set C-E-A♭ may be said to be invariant in content under transposition by a major 3rd, since such transposition results in the set E-G♯(A♭)-C.

invention (It.: *inventione*, *invenzione*). A name sometimes given to a short instrumental piece with no specified musical characteristics but which displays some kind of novelty; it occurs in many Italian works from the 17th and 18th centuries. Bach used it for sets of short two- and three-part imitative keyboard inventions, developing a brief melodic motif. In the 20th century the term was occasionally applied to works of a contrapuntal nature.

inversion. 1. Chords. According to theories of harmony that became prominent during the 18th and 19th centuries, chord construction was not simply a matter of particular intervals arranged in ascending order, but of particular intervals placed above a governing or *fundamental bass. The fundamental bass note, or *root, does not simply change when, for example, a *triad changes in vertical presentation from C-E-G to E-G-C. Rather, the functions of the notes in the chord that obtain when its fundamental bass note is the actual bass—the so-called *root-position chord (root, 3rd, 5th)—are retained even though the notes change position in the chord when read upwards. So, with E-G-C the bass (lowest) note remains the 3rd of the chord, and the position of the root is changed. Strictly speaking, this procedure is one of permutation in musical space, but in a simple sense, best experienced at the keyboard, shifting the root from bottom to top inverts the chord, turning it upside down. This, a first inversion (E-G-C), can in turn be inverted to give a second inversion (G-C-E). For chords with four different notes (e.g. secondary or dominant 7ths) a *third inversion is possible. **2.** Intervals. Inversion can be applied to intervals by reversing the positions of the two notes: the upper note remains and the lower note moves to the pitch an octave above its original position, or the lower note remains and the upper one moves to the pitch an octave below its original position. This is not literal inversion (see below, 4) but a complementation within the octave, and is the basis of *invertible counterpoint. *See also* INTERVAL. **3.** Melodies. An inverted melody follows the shape of the original in mirror image; where the original melody rises, the inversion descends, and vice versa. In tonal music the intervals between the successive pitches are not literally replicated (see below, 4) but become the equivalents within the diatonic scale. For example, the melody F-G-E-F would become F-E-G-F. Melodic inversion is a common feature of imitative forms, particularly fugue. **4.** 12-note rows. Inversion of a row or series of notes is fundamental to *twelve-note, or serial, music (*see* SERIALISM). Such inversions are literal: an ascending major 3rd becomes a descending major 3rd, a descending minor 2nd becomes an ascending minor 2nd, and so on. For example the inversion of F-G-E-F is F-E♭-G♭-F. In serial music any note in the series may occur at any octave register, so the inversion of a row may not necessarily be an inversion of its melodic contour.

inverted cadence. *See* CADENCE.

inverted interval. *See* INTERVAL.

inverted mordent. A *mordent that includes the upper rather than the lower auxiliary note.

invertible counterpoint. A technique of contrapuntal writing that allows the voices to change places (the higher becoming the lower, and vice versa) and still make musical sense.

invitatory (Lat.: *invitatorium*). In the Divine Office of the Roman and monastic rites, the opening chant of Matins, consisting of the psalm **Venite* and its corresponding antiphon.

Ionian mode. The authentic *mode on C; it has the same distribution of tones and semitones as the major scale.

irregular time signatures. Time signatures that do not indicate duple, triple, or quadruple time, the most common being quintuple (five beats in a bar, e.g. 5/4) and septuple (seven beats in a bar).

isomelic (from Gk. *isos*, 'equal', *melōidiā*, 'melody'). A term referring to repeated uses of the same pitch contour, though with variations in rhythm. The technique was much used by English and continental composers in the 15th century.

isometric (from Gk. *isos*, 'equal', *metron*, 'measure'). A term used to describe either works that have one rhythm simultaneously in all voices (i.e. homorhythm) or works that have the same time signature throughout.

isorhythm (from Gk. *isos*, 'equal', *rhythmos*, 'rhythm'). A modern term for the technique of using a repeated rhythmic and melodic pattern as a main structural component. In the 13th century the tenor part of a motet would frequently be organized according to a short repeated rhythmic pattern, derived from the *ordines* of the rhythmic modes (*see* NOTATION). These patterns increased in length as the century progressed. The melody in the tenor part was also often repeated, but not always to synchronize with the rhythmic repeat. The term *color* was used for the melodic pattern and *talea* for the rhythmic pattern. The two patterns were not necessarily the same length, however, so successive statements of the *talea* may occur with different pitches. Towards the end of the 14th century the use of isorhythm in all voices ('panisorhythm') was developed, especially by English composers.

istesso (It.). 'Same'; *l'istesso tempo*, 'the same tempo' as before. *See also* STESSO, STESSA.

Italian overture. *See* OVERTURE, 1.

Italian sixth chord. An *augmented 6th chord.

jácara [xácara] (Sp., Port.). An old Spanish ballad or dance tune. In the 17th century it was often used in the theatre, and it eventually developed into the **tonadilla*.

janissary music [Turkish music] (Fr.: *bande turque*; Ger.: *Janitscharenmusik*; It.: *banda turca*). Literally, a Turkish wind and percussion band of the Ottoman Empire. The term, however, has come to be used to describe supposedly Turkish elements in music of the Classical period. Janissary bands became known in Europe during the 17th century and janissary instruments were added to some Western military bands, in particular the bass drum. Composers used these to evoke a Turkish or a more generally exotic setting, or simply for military imagery.

jeté (Fr., 'thrown'). In string playing, a bowstroke (also known as *ricochet) in which the bow is dropped onto the string so as to bounce several times.

jeu-parti [partimen]. A type of troubadour or trouvère poetry cast in the form of a dialogue; as in the **tenso*, its most common topic is love. However, it is unlike the *tenso* in that the first speaker allows his opponent the choice of which of two positions he wishes to defend, then takes the opposite side.

jig. 1. A traditional dance of the British Isles, probably dating back to the 15th century. The word may be derived from the Old French verb *gigner* ('to leap', 'to gambol'). The best-known jig is the Irish, danced solo or by a couple to the accompaniment of the pipe and fiddle and usually in compound duple or triple time. *See also* GIGUE. **2.** From the 16th century to the 18th, the jig (or jigg) was also an often bawdy farce in rhyme, sung and danced to popular tunes, performed both in England and on the Continent.

jingle. A short and easily identifiable melody used to characterize a product or a broadcast programme.

Jodel (Ger.). *See* YODEL.

jongleur (Fr.). A medieval entertainer or *minstrel. The word derives from the Latin *jocus* ('jest') and has many variants within the Romance languages, not all of which imply musicianship.

jota (Sp.). A lively dance in triple time from northern Spain, accompanied by a guitar and castanets.

jouer (Fr.). 'To play'.

Jubilate (Lat., 'O be joyful'). The 100th Psalm (in the Hebrew and English numbering; 99 in the Greek Old Testament and the Vulgate). In the *Book of Common Prayer* it is provided as an alternative *canticle to the *Benedictus* at Morning Prayer; in the Roman Office since the Second Vatican Council and in the Anglican *Common Worship* it is an *invitatory alternative to the *Venite* and has been set by many composers.

jubilus. The name given in Latin antiquity to a joyful work sung without text. In modern scholarship it has been narrowly used for a long *melisma that concludes an alleluia.

just intonation. A system of tuning the scale to perfection, based on the ratios of the natural harmonics. Because there are two sizes of whole tone, the major tone 9:8 and the minor tone 10:9, keyboard instruments cannot change key and therefore require a tempered scale (*see* TEMPERAMENT). Other instruments and singers use just intonation whenever possible.

K. Abbreviation for *Köchel and *Kirkpatrick, used as a prefix to the numbers of Mozart's works and Domenico Scarlatti's keyboard sonatas respectively, as given in the standard *thematic catalogues of Ludwig Köchel and Ralph Kirkpatrick.

Kadenz (Ger.). **1.** *'Cadence'. **2.** *'Cadenza'.

Kammer (Ger.). 'Chamber', e.g. *Kammermusik*, 'Chamber music'; *Kammersymphonie*, 'Chamber symphony'; *Kammerton*, 'Chamber pitch' (*see* CAMMERTON; PITCH).

Kantor [Cantor] (Ger.). The director of music at a German Protestant church and usually also of any choir school or similar institution attached to such a church.

Kapelle (Ger.). 'Chapel'; *Hofkapelle*, 'court chapel'.

Kapellmeister (Ger., 'chapel master'). The director of music at a court or church.

Kassation (Ger.). *See* CASSATION.

Katzenmusik (Ger.). *See* CHARIVARI.

Kb. (Ger.). Abbreviation for *Kontrabass*, 'double bass'.

key. 1. The adherence in any passage to the elements of one of the major or minor *scales, or *tonalities. Compositions using the tonal system (and the individual movements of compositions) will normally have a principal key, understood as the one in which a movement begins and ends, and even those large areas of the music which deviate from the diatonic elements of the principal key may be regarded as ultimately dependent on it. **2.** A lever on an instrument which is depressed by finger or foot to produce a note, for example on a piano by finger, on an organ by foot, on woodwind by finger (the levers covering the airholes).

keyboard fingering. In the modern system of keyboard fingerings an octave is divided into one group of three notes and another of four, representing two distinct hand positions. The aim is to connect these as imperceptibly as possible by passing the thumb under the long fingers, or the fingers over the thumb. The system known as 'continental fingering', which numbers the thumb as 1 and the fingers 2 to 5, is now exclusively used. Methods of fingering have evolved since the 16th century. Modern principles were established in the early 19th century, particularly with the studies of Czerny. Fingering is a major element in articulation and phrasing and thus an important part of *performance practice.

key note. The principal (lowest) note of the scale out of which a passage is constructed; the *tonic. *See also* KEY.

key signature. A group of sharp or flat signs placed at the beginning of a composition (after the clef) or during a composition (normally after a double bar) to indicate the *key of the music that follows. By their positions on the staff the signs show which notes are to be consistently sharpened or flattened throughout, in all octaves, thus establishing the prevailing tonality of the music. Ex. 1 shows the 14 common key signatures, relating to all the diatonic major and minor keys. Each signature indicates one of two keys: the white note represents the major key, the black the minor key with the same signature (the 'relative' minor, its key note a minor 3rd below the major).

Key signature, Ex. 1

Key notes for the 'sharp' signatures rise a perfect 5th as each sharp is added, and the major key note is always a semitone above the last sharp; key notes for the 'flat' signatures fall a perfect 5th as each flat is added, and the major key note is always a perfect 4th below the last flat (i.e. the same pitch as the penultimate flat). The order of sharps in the signature is also by rising 5ths, the order of flats by falling 5ths and equivalent to the order of sharps reversed.

Keys with six sharps (F♯ major and D♯ minor) are the *enharmonic equivalents of keys with six flats (G♭ major and E♭ minor); keys with seven sharps (C♯ major and A♯ minor) are the enharmonic equivalents of keys with five flats (D♭ major and B♭ minor). Composers use either signature according to convenience and familiarity, but 'key colour' may also play a part in their choice: for example, sharp keys are thought to suggest bright colours, flat keys sober ones. In the late 19th and the 20th centuries, chromaticism and atonality contributed to the demise of the key signature's usefulness. At the same time, some composers experimented with 'hybrid' signatures, including both sharps and flats, to draw attention to special features of tonality in their music. *See also* ACCIDENTAL; CIRCLE OF FIFTHS; MUSICA FICTA; TONALITY.

Kinderstück (Ger.). 'Piece for children'.

Kirchencantate (Ger.). 'Church *cantata'.

Kirkpatrick. Abbreviation for the standard *thematic catalogue of the keyboard sonatas of Domenico Scarlatti drawn up by the American keyboard player and scholar Ralph Kirkpatrick (1911–84). The sonatas are often referred to by Kirkpatrick number, usually further abbreviated to K or Kk.

Kl. (Ger.). Abbreviation for *Klarinette*, 'clarinet'.

klagend, kläglich (Ger.). 'Lamenting', 'plaintive'; *Klaglied*, lament, elegy.

Klang (Ger.). **1.** 'Sound', 'sonority'; *klanglich*, sonorous. **2.** *'Chord'.

Klangfarbenmelodie (Ger., 'sound-colour melody'). A term introduced by Schoenberg for a 'melody' of timbre, in which the instrumentation of a piece is as important as the pitch and rhythm and has its own structural function.

klar (Ger.). 'Clear', 'distinct'.

klein (Ger.). 'Small'; when applied to intervals, 'minor'.

Kl. Fl. (Ger.). Abbreviation for *kleine Flöte*, 'piccolo'.

klingen (Ger.). 'To sound'; e.g. *klingen lassen*, 'allow to sound'; *klingend*, 'resonant'.

Köchel. Abbreviation for the standard *thematic catalogue of the works of Mozart drawn up by the Austrian music historian Ludwig Köchel (1800–77) and revised several times. A further revision, *Der neue Köchel* (NK), was begun in the closing years of the 20th century. Mozart's works, especially those without distinguishing title, are nearly always referred to by Köchel number, usually further abbreviated to K.

kolęda (Pol.; Rom.: *kolenda*). A Christmas song, the Polish counterpart of the carol, popular during the 17th and 18th centuries.

Kontretanz (Ger.). *See* COUNTRY DANCE.

Konzert (Ger.). **1.** *'Concert'. **2.** *'Concerto'.

Konzertmeister (Ger., 'concert master'). *See* LEADER.

Konzertstück (Ger.). *See* CONCERTINO, 2.

kräftig (Ger.). 'Strong', 'vigorous'.

krakowiak [krakoviak] (Fr.: *cracovienne*). A lively Polish dance, named after the Kraków region. It is in quick duple time with syncopated rhythms and has been described as a simple type of *polonaise. The *krakowiak* became popular in the early 19th century and featured in the works of Polish composers.

Krebsgang (Ger., 'crab motion'). *See* RETROGRADE.

Kreis (Ger.). 'Circle', 'cycle'; *Liederkreis*, *'song cycle'.

Kreuz (Ger., 'cross'). The sharp sign (*see* SHARP, 1).

Kuhreigen [Kuhreihen] (Ger.). *See* RANZ DES VACHES.

kurz (Ger.). 'Short'.

KV. Abbreviation for *Köchel-Verzeichnis, sometimes used as a prefix to the numbers of Mozart's works as given in the standard *thematic catalogue of Ludwig Köchel.

Kyrie eleison (Gk., 'Lord, have mercy'). An ancient acclamation adopted for use in Christian worship; it is part of the Ordinary of the Roman *Mass between the introit and the Gloria, where it was supplied with Latin verses (abolished after the Council of Trent) and sung in alternation with 'Christe eleison'. By the 10th century a ninefold pattern of performance ('Kyrie eleison' three times, 'Christe eleison' three times, 'Kyrie eleison' three times) had become customary for the Roman Kyrie.

la [lah]. The sixth degree of the scale in the *solmization system. In French and Italian usage it has become attached, on the fixed-*doh* principle, to the note A, in whichever scale it occurs. *See* TONIC SOL-FA.

lacrimoso, lagrimoso (It.). 'Lachrymose', 'tearful'.

Lage (Ger.). *'Position'. In string playing, the position: *erste Lage*, 'first position', *zweite Lage*, 'second position', etc. Of a chord, the spacing: *enge Lage*, 'close position', *weite Lage*, 'wide (open) position'. In reference to an instrument or voice, the register: *hohe Lage*, 'high', *tiefe Lage*, 'low'.

lah. *See* LA.

lai [lay] (Fr.; Ger.: *Leich*). A term that usually denotes an extended medieval song form featuring several stanzas ('strophes'), each using a different metrical form, rhyme scheme, and melody (the 'lyric *lai*'). However, *lai* might also be used merely as a synonym for 'song'; moreover, songs in similar form appear under different names, especially *descort*. The troubadour and trouvère 'lyric *lai*' repertory of the 12th and 13th centuries exhibits considerable variety in number and length of stanzas. In the 14th century the *lai*'s principal exponent was Machaut, who used a greater variety of tempos and introduced polyphony into what had been essentially a monophonic form. As well as the lyric *lai*, there existed the 'narrative *lai*', a different poetic and musical form.

laisser (Fr.). 'To allow', 'to leave'; *laisser vibrer*, 'allow to sound, do not damp'.

lament. 1. Specifically, music for bagpipes at Scottish clan funerals. **2.** Any piece of music expressing grief, usually at the loss of a friend or a famous person. *See also* APOTHÉOSE; DÉPLORATION; DIRGE; DUMP; ELEGY; EPICEDIUM; LAMENTO; PLAINTE; THRENODY; TOMBEAU.

Lamentations. The Lamentations of the prophet Jeremiah. Before the Second Vatican Council, readings from Jeremiah were sung at Matins during the week before Easter (known as 'Tenebrae'); they had their own plainchant melodies and were often set polyphonically. The Greek word *Threni* is sometimes used.

lamento (It.). A song of mourning. It was often an important item in 17th-century Italian opera, usually placed before the emotional climax of the plot, a vehicle for the composer's skills of expression and word-setting.

lancers. A simplified version of the *quadrille.

lancio, con (It.). 'With vigour'.

Landini cadence. *See* CADENCE.

ländler (Ger.). A rustic German and Austrian dance in slow *waltz tempo, which originated in the Landel district of Austria (now Upper Austria). It was a hearty country dance, with stamping and clapping; the dancers sometimes sang or yodelled, while the typical instrumental accompaniment consisted of violin and double bass. A more refined version became popular in Vienna and the dance soon began to resemble the waltz, which eventually superseded it. It was popular in the early 19th century and its rhythms and spirit were absorbed into several late 19th-century symphonies.

langsam (Ger.). 'Slow'; *langsamer*, 'slower'; *sehr langsam*, 'very slow'.

largamente (It.), **largement** (Fr.). 'Broadly', i.e. slow and dignified. *See also* LARGO.

largando. *See* ALLARGANDO.

larghetto (It.). 'Slow', but less so than **largo*.

largo (It.). 'Broad'. A tempo indication which, when it first appeared in the early 17th century, was regarded as the slowest. Purcell and his contemporaries considered it to be between *adagio* and *andante*. The term 'largo' is often also used as the title of a slow movement or piece.

lassú (Hung.). 'Slow'; *see* CSÁRDÁS; VERBUNKOS.

lauda spirituale (It., 'spiritual praise', pl. *laude spirituali*; the form *laude*, pl. *laudi*, is also found). A type of sacred song, usually with Italian words though sometimes partly or wholly in Latin, cultivated in Italy from the 13th century to the 16th. Like the Spanish **cantiga* and the English *carol, *laude* belong to the category of popular religious music sung by the laity, and never formed part of the formal worship of the church. Their performance was fostered by guild-like fraternities of singers (*laudesi*), which existed throughout Italy; *laude* were also popular within monastic communities, and were sometimes included in religious plays. Some of their characteristic features were taken over in the music of the *rappresentazione sacra* and the early *oratorio.

laudesi (It.). *See* LAUDA SPIRITUALE.

laut (Ger.). 'Loud'.

Laute (Ger.). 'Lute'.

lavolta. *See* VOLTA, 1.

lay. *See* LAI.

leader [concert master] (Fr.: *chef d'attaque*; Ger.: *Konzertmeister*). The principal first violinist in an orchestra, who plays the violin solos in orchestral works and is often a considerable virtuoso. He or she is responsible for phrasings and bowings in the string parts.

leading motif. *See* LEITMOTIF.

leading note. The seventh degree of the scale, a semitone below the tonic. It is so called because of its tendency to rise, or 'lead', to the tonic. In a minor key it is sometimes flattened in the descent, and is then called a 'flattened leading note'.

lebendig (Ger.). 'Lively'.

lebhaft (Ger.). 'Lively', **vivace*.

ledger lines [leger lines]. Short extra lines added below or above the staff to accommodate notes that are too low or too high to be placed on the staff itself.

legato (It.). 'Bound', i.e. played smoothly with no noticeable breaks between the notes. This may be indicated either by the use of a phrase mark over the passage in question or by placing the word *legato* at the beginning of it. The term does not imply an absence of articulation. The term *legatissimo*, 'extremely smoothly', is sometimes used. The opposite of *legato* is **staccato*.

legatura (It.). *'Ligature'.

legend (Fr.: *légende*; Ger.: *Legende*). A name given to a short composition of lyrical or epic character.

léger, légèrement (Fr.). 'Light', 'lightly'.

leger lines. *See* LEDGER LINES.

leggero, leggeramente (It.). 'Light', 'lightly', a direction that also implies a detached style of playing in quick passages.

leggiadro, leggiadretto (It.). 'Graceful'; *leggiadramente*, 'gracefully'.

leggio (It., from *leggere*, 'to read'). 'Music desk'.

legno (It.). 'Wood'; *col legno*, 'with the wood', a direction to string players to tap the strings with the wood of the bow instead of playing with the hair; *strumenti* [*stromenti*] *di legno*, 'woodwind instruments'.

Lehrstück (Ger., 'teaching piece'). A 20th-century musical work of a didactic, and often political, nature. The term first gained currency in the theatre, through the work of Bertolt Brecht, and acquired a musical dimension in his collaborations with Hindemith, Weill, and Eisler.

leicht (Ger.). 'Light', i.e. popular; 'easy'; *Leichtigkeit*, 'lightness', 'easiness'.

Leid (Ger.). 'Grief', 'pain'; *leidvoll, leidensvoll*, 'sorrowfully'.

leidenschaftlich (Ger.). 'Passionately'.

Leise (Ger.). A medieval German devotional song, perhaps owing its name to the frequent use made of the refrain 'Kyrie eleison', abbreviated to 'kirleis' or 'leis'.

leise (Ger.). 'Soft', 'gentle'; *leiser*, 'more softly'.

leitmotif (from Ger. *Leitmotiv*, 'leading motif'). A term coined in the mid-1860s to describe a musical motto or theme which recurs in a piece of music (usually an opera) to represent a character, object, emotion, or idea. It is particularly associated with the later operas of Wagner, though he did not use the term himself, preferring to call the themes *Hauptmotiv* ('principal motif'), *thematisches Motiv* ('thematic motif'), *Grundthema* ('basic theme'), and so on. The term should be distinguished from *'reminiscence motif', which had been a feature of opera at least as far back as the 18th century. Leitmotifs are used much more frequently, to the extent of becoming part of the basic thematic material of the work in question.

lent, lentement (Fr.). 'Slow', 'slowly'; *lenteur*, 'slowness'.

lento, lentamente (It.). 'Slow', 'slowly'; *lentando, lentato*, 'slowing', 'slowed' (the same as *rallentando*); *lentezza*, 'slowness'.

lesto (It.). 'Agile', 'quick'; *lestamente*, 'agilely', 'quickly'.

letzt (Ger.). 'Last'.

levalto. *See* VOLTA, 1.

levare (It.). 'To lift', 'to take off'; e.g. *si levano i sordini*, 'the mutes are taken off'; *levate*, 'take off'.

levet (? from It. *levata*, 'rising', 'getting up'). A trumpet call or musical strain to rouse soldiers and others in the morning.

L.H. Abbreviation for left hand, *linke Hand* (Ger.).

liberamente (It.). 'Freely', i.e. in a free rhythm or tempo.

libitum, ad (Lat., 'at pleasure'). An indication that a performer is at liberty, according to the context, to vary the tempo, or to improvise, embellish, or devise a cadenza; it was often used in the late 18th century to indicate that a part so marked could be omitted (the opposite of *obbligato).

libre, librement (Fr.). 'Free', 'freely'.

libretto (It., 'little book', dim. of *libro*, 'book'; Fr.: *livret*; Ger.: *Textbuch*). The name generally given to the book of the words of an opera, or other vocal dramatic work, and consequently to the text itself.

licenza (It.). **1.** 'Licence', 'freedom'; *con alcuna licenza*, 'with some licence', i.e. freedom with regard to tempo and rhythm. The term was used in the 17th and 18th centuries for a passage or cadenza improvised by the performer. **2.** An epilogue added to a stage work in honour of a patron's birthday or wedding or for some other festive occasion.

lié (Fr., 'bound'). Slurred or tied, i.e. **legato*.

lied (Ger.). The German word for 'song' that came into general acceptance in the 15th century. *Gesang*, also meaning 'song' (as in *Meistergesang*, the art of the *Meistersinger), became used less frequently. The greatest age of the lied was the 19th century, with Schubert, Schumann, Brahms, and Wolf being the supreme masters. *See also* CONTINUO LIED; SONG CYCLE; TENORLIED.

Liederbuch (Ger., 'songbook'). A word used for the songbooks of the German Middle Ages (most of which survive without music), for later poetry collections, whether printed or manuscript, for the German polyphonic songbooks of the 15th and 16th centuries, and for many later collections of songs with German text.

Liederzyklus (Ger.). *'Song cycle'.

Lied ohne Worte (Ger.). *'Song without words'.

lieto, lietamente (It.). 'Joyful'; *lietissimo*, 'most joyful'; *lieto fine*, 'happy ending' as of an opera.

lieve, lievemente (It.). 'Light', 'lightly'; 'easy', 'easily'.

ligature (from Lat. *ligare*, 'to bind'). A note form representing two or more notes. The use of ligatures was common in the medieval period, but the advent of music printing and other factors led to their demise *c.*1600. Ligatures originated in neumatic plainchant *notation, where a single ligature contained a group of notes sung to just one syllable of text. At the beginning of the 13th century, set ways of combining ligatures were established so as to indicate clearly the rhythmic patterns of the music. These set patterns were called 'rhythmic modes'; in the basic system, there were six. From the 14th century to the 16th, the rhythmic meaning of individual ligatures was fixed irrespective of their combination with other ligatures. In the 16th century it became common for several notes setting a single syllable to be written not as a ligature but as individual notes under a slur sign, as is done today. Modern editors of early music indicate groups of notes originally written as a single ligature by enclosing them under a square bracket.

light. An adjective applied loosely to music deemed of no great intellectual or emotional depth, intended for light entertainment, and usually for orchestra. There is a large repertory of British light music. Such music is often played by 'light orchestras'.

lining out. In metrical *psalmody, the practice in which a soloist sang each verse before its performance by the congregation.

liquescent neume. A form of neume associated with plainchant to indicate certain consonants and diphthongs. The singer produces a semi-vocalized sound when moving from one note to the next. *See* NOTATION.

liscio, liscia (It.). 'Smooth', 'even'.

l'istesso. *See* ISTESSO.

litany (Lat.: *litania, letania*, from Gk. *litaneia*, 'prayer'). A form of prayer consisting of a series of petitions to God, the Virgin Mary, or the saints, or the procession during which such supplications are made. One of the most popular was the *Litaniae lauretanae* ('Litany of Loreto') in honour of the Virgin Mary, which has attracted numerous polyphonic settings.

livret (Fr., 'little book'). *Libretto.

loco (It.). 'Place': an instruction to return to the normal register after a passage marked to be played in a different one, for example an octave higher or lower; it is also given in the form *al loco*, 'at the place'.

loin, lointain (Fr.). 'Distant'.

Lombardy style. *See* SCOTCH SNAP.

long. A note-value (¶) used in medieval and Renaissance music. *See* NOTATION.

lontano (It.). 'Distant'.

lourd, lourde (Fr.). 'Heavy'; *lourdement*, 'heavily'.

loure (Fr.). A dance popular in the late 17th and early 18th centuries. It resembles the *gigue, but is slower. It is characteristically in moderate triple time, with dotted and syncopated rhythms. (The term is also used for a bagpipe of 16th- and 17th-century Normandy.)

louré (Fr.). **1.** (It.: *portato*). In string playing, a type of bowing where several notes are taken in the same direction, but slightly detached from one another. **2.** *See* NOTES INÉGALES.

lower mordent. *See* MORDENT.

Luftpause (Ger., 'air break'). A pause for breath in wind playing or singing, often indicated by a V-shaped mark above the staff. *See also* ATEMPAUSE.

lullaby. *See* BERCEUSE.

lungo, lunga (It.). 'Long'; *lunga pausa*, 'long rest'.

lusingando (It.). 'Flattering', 'coaxing'.

lustig (Ger.). 'Merry', 'cheerful'; *Lustspiel*, 'comedy'.

lute-song. An accompanied song or ayre of the late 16th and early 17th centuries, peculiar to England; it is similar to the French **air de cour*. It is related to the native mid-16th-century partsong and near contemporary consort song and is generally strophic and musically concise.

Lydian mode. The *mode represented by the white notes of the piano beginning on F.

Lydian tetrachord. A *tetrachord spanning an augmented 4th, as in the first four notes of the Lydian *mode.

lyric. 1. Strictly speaking, vocal performance accompanied by the lyre, but in fact broadened in meaning to denote any kind of accompanied vocal music, e.g. **drame lyrique* (Fr., 'lyric drama', i.e. opera). **2.** A short poem, i.e. not epic or narrative. Composers adapted this meaning to music, e.g. Grieg in his *Lyrische Stücke* (Ger., 'Lyric Pieces'). **3.** A description of a voice-type, e.g. lyric tenor or lyric soprano, meaning somewhere between light and heavy in style. **4.** In the plural, the words of a song, especially used of popular present-day song and musical comedy.

lyrisches Stück (Ger., 'lyric piece'). *See* LYRIC, 2.

machicotage (Fr.). Extempore embellishment of sections of plainchant by a soloist, usually through the addition of passing notes. The practice was common in France and Italy in the Middle Ages.

mächtig (Ger.). 'Mighty', 'powerful'.

madrigal. A term with two distinct meanings: a poetic form and its musical setting as a secular song cultivated in Italy in the 14th century; a type of secular song that flourished in Italy in the 16th and early 17th centuries and spread to most other European countries, one of the most important genres of the late Renaissance. The madrigal did not adopt a more or less fixed form until the 1340s, some 20 years after its first appearance; it settled into a standard length of two or three stanzas, each of three lines and each set to the same music, the final stanza closing with a 'ritornello' of one or two lines, usually in a contrasting metre. The music is commonly in two, sometimes three, parts and is highly melismatic, particularly in the upper voice. The early madrigal is characteristically bright and attractive, apt for virtuoso singing and playing (the lower part, or parts, may have been performed by instruments). Towards the end of the 14th century the madrigal yielded in popularity to the **ballata*.

The 16th-century madrigal set a variety of verse types, usually a single verse without a refrain. These included the serious and lighter genres, such as sonnets, canzoni, and a poetic form known in the 16th century as 'madrigale', which consisted of one stanza of an unspecified number of lines of seven and 11 syllables in a free rhyme scheme. The madrigal was now essentially a serious form, setting verse of a high quality, much of it the courtly love poetry of Petrarch. Madrigals were composed by Italians, particularly those based in Rome and Florence, and were typically for between three and six voices, using both polyphonic, often imitative textures and chordal writing, and placing strong emphasis on tunefulness and on reflecting the mood and meaning of the text.

The range of note-values available increased with a new style of notation that involved the use of *note nere* ('black notes', i.e. crotchets and quavers) in addition to the existing 'white notes' (minims, semibreves, breves). This allowed composers greater flexibility in text-setting, making rapid declamatory patterns and quick imitative entries possible. The most renowned composer of the mid-century style was Cipriano de Rore, in whose highly developed *word-painting almost every significant word seems to suggest a corresponding image in sound. Minor intervals express sadder emotions, major ones joy; ascending notes symbolize such words as 'heaven', low registers 'earth'; dissonance and wide, jagged leaps express pain or struggle.

The genre developed in several different directions. One involved a rapprochement between the serious madrigal and such lighter forms as the *canzonetta, *villanella, and satirical **giustiniana*. Another, stimulated by the virtuoso court singers at Mantua and Ferrara, was the rich, ornamented, chromatic, and highly expressive style seen in the later madrigals of Marenzio, Gesualdo, and Monteverdi. While polyphonic madrigals continued to be written into the 17th century, the rise of the basso *continuo (or more accurately the *basso seguente*) and of *monody had important implications for the madrigal's development as a piece for one or two voices (sometimes more) with continuo. The presence of the continuo part (sometimes using strophic basses) and the reduced textures left the solo voice(s) free to explore much more virtuoso embellishment or dramatic representations of speech than was possible in the ensemble madrigal. By the mid-17th century the possibilities of madrigal writing had been more or less exhausted; composers of secular vocal music extended the techniques of ensemble writing in the *dialogue and the *cantata, and those of the solo madrigal in the solo cantata and the aria.

The lighter madrigal style that flourished in Italy in the 1580s enjoyed great popularity in England in the 1580s and 90s. Madrigals by English composers are typically lighthearted, setting pastoral and amorous English verse, and using a mixture of imitative and chordal writing. Thomas Morley was the master of this style. By the 1630s, however, the madrigal in England was being superseded by the native *lute-song and ayre.

m

madrigal comedy. A late 16th- and early 17th-century musical entertainment made up of a series of madrigals or lighter vocal forms that illustrate a story or a group of characters. Madrigal comedies are generally comic and were intended to be staged.

maestoso (It.). 'Majestic'; *maestevolmente, maestosamente*, 'majestically'.

maestro (It., 'master', 'teacher'). The *maestro di cappella* (Ger.: *Kapellmeister*) was the director of music at a court or church. Today 'maestro' is used as a mark of respect or when addressing or referring to an eminent conductor or soloist.

maggiore (It.). 'Major'.

maggot. In Old English, a fanciful idea. In the 16th and 17th centuries it was used as a title for a pleasant piece of music, such as a dance, with the name of a person attached, e.g. 'My Lady Winwood's Maggot'.

Magnificat. The *canticle of the Virgin Mary (Lat.: 'Magnificat anima mea', 'My soul magnifies the Lord'), Luke 1: 46–55. It became a fixed element of Vespers in the medieval Roman rite, and, following the Protestant Reformation, passed into the evening offices of the Anglican and Lutheran Churches. Between the 15th and 17th centuries, Western composers set the *Magnificat* to polyphony more frequently than any other liturgical text outside the Mass Ordinary. Anglican composers often set the *Magnificat* and **Nunc dimittis* together, either on their own or as part of a full service. During the Baroque and Classical periods the text was the subject of large-scale choral works.

main (Fr.). 'Hand'; *main droite*, 'right hand'; *main gauche*, 'left hand'; *à deux mains*, 'both hands'; *à quatre mains*, 'four hands', i.e. piano duet.

maîtrise (Fr.). 'Choir school', usually attached to a cathedral. The word can also apply, by extension, to the body of choristers in a church choir or to their choirmaster.

majeur (Fr.). 'Major'.

major interval. *See* INTERVAL.

major scale. *See* SCALE.

Mal (Ger.). 'Time'; *das erste Mal*, 'the first time'; *einmal*, 'once'; *zweimal*, 'twice', etc.

malagueña. An improvised Spanish song in free style and rhythm but based on a repetitive chordal accompaniment.

male alto. *See* ALTO VOICE.

malinconico (It.). 'Melancholy'; *malinconoso, malinconioso*, 'in melancholy fashion'.

man. Abbreviation for **mano*.

mancando (It.). 'Dying away'.

manica (It.). In string playing, a shift in position; *mezza manica*, 'half-shift'.

Manieren (Ger.). *'Grace notes'.

Männerchor (Ger.). 'Men's chorus'.

Mannerism. A term most often used with reference to the visual arts, to describe the extravagant subjects, contorted gestures, and virtuoso effects of certain 16th- and 17th-century painters, e.g. Giulio Romano and Caravaggio. It has also been applied to literature and, more recently, to music. It is apt when used to describe the works of late 16th-century 'avant-garde' madrigal composers such as Gesualdo, who in their attempts to depict words vividly used unusual harmonies and intervals, chromaticism, etc.

mano (It.). 'Hand'; *mano destra*, 'right hand'; *mano sinistra*, 'left hand'.

manualiter (Ger., from Lat. *manualis*). 'On the manuals'; in keyboard music, a direction to play with the hands only.

marcato (It.). 'Marked', 'stressed', i.e. emphasizing each note; it often indicates a melody that should be given prominence.

march (Fr.: *marche*; Ger.: *Marsch*; It.: *marcia*). A composition, commonly in duple time, with strong repetitive rhythms for accompanying military movements and processions. 17th- and 18th-century marches were generally ephemeral pieces, but the French Revolution and the Napoleonic Wars provided impetus. The great period of popular march composition came during the 19th century with the rise of specialist light-music composers, many of whom were military bandmasters as well as dance-band leaders. Their success culminated in the career of John Philip Sousa. Processional march music is a feature of operas and oratorios.

Märchen (Ger., 'tale'; pl. *Märchen*). A piece of music with some suggestion of traditional or legendary forms.

marcia (It.). *'March'; *alla marcia*, 'in the manner of a march'; *marcia funebre*, 'funeral march'.

Marian antiphon. One of the *antiphons of the Virgin Mary, customarily sung as a devotion at the conclusion of Compline.

markiert (Ger., 'marked'). **Marcato*.

markig (Ger.). 'Vigorous'.

marqué (Fr., 'marked'). **Marcato*.

Marsch (Ger.). *'March'.

martelé (Fr., 'hammered'). In string playing, a heavy, detached bowstroke on the string.

martellando, martellato (It., 'hammering', 'hammered'). Terms used most often (interchangeably with **martelé*) in string playing, but also applied to piano and vocal technique.

martellement (Fr., 'hammering'). A 17th-century term for a *mordent.

mascherata [mascarata, mascherada] (It.). 'Masquerade'. **1.** An entertainment, popular in Renaissance Florence, in which masked performers mimed to musical accompaniment from carnival floats. **2.** A kind of *villanella, also related to street performances in the Carnival season.

maske. An old spelling of *masque. When found as the title of an instrumental piece, it probably implied that the piece was suitable for use in a masque.

masque. A courtly entertainment celebrating special events (e.g. dynastic marriages, state visits) in England during the 16th and 17th centuries. It comprised dancing, speech, and song brought together in an allegorical 'device' in honour of the king or a prominent courtier. The masque differs from spoken drama or opera in that the action is carried forward by dance rather than by speech or song. The main characters ('masquers') were aristocratic amateurs who danced their roles, often led by a member of the royal family. During the reign of Charles I the masque increased in length, complexity, magnificence, and cost. After 1700 the term 'masque' was applied to short semi-operas.

Mass (Fr.: *messe*; Ger.: *Messe*; It.: *messa*; Lat.: *missa*). The eucharistic liturgy of the Roman Catholic Church. The various musical items belong either to the

Ordinary, whose sections make up the musical entity normally referred to as a mass and whose texts do not vary, or to the Proper, whose texts change according to the church calendar. Table 1 sets out the sequence of events at High Mass; capital letters indicate the sections of the Ordinary and lower-case those of the Proper, while the portions intoned by the clergy are in parentheses.

The earliest notated music for the Mass, both Ordinary and Proper, is plainchant. The solemnity of a mass during the Middle Ages could be heightened through the addition of a sequence or the improvisation of polyphony, a practice that continued in some locations into the Renaissance and beyond. The earliest notated polyphonic music for the Mass, such as the organa of Léonin and Pérotin, consists of settings of the Proper. In the 14th century this situation was reversed: most of the Mass music that survives consists of individual movements rather than complete settings of the Ordinary. The first extant complete setting by a single composer is Machaut's Notre Dame Mass from the later 14th century.

The 15th century saw an increasing tendency not only towards the composition of complete masses, but also towards giving these an overall unity, usually by the use in all the movements of some existing material, of various kinds: plainchant; secular melodies; invented themes drawn from the hexachord, or devised by applying *solmization syllables to the vowels in an appropriate phrase; *motto themes; complete pieces. The first four types are *cantus-firmus masses; the last became

TABLE 1

Mass of the Word

introit
KYRIE
GLORIA [except in Advent and Lent]
(collect)
(epistle [medieval usage]; Old Testament lesson [restored after Vatican II])
gradual
(epistle [after Vatican II only])
alleluia [or, in penitential seasons, tract]
sequence [if appointed]
(gospel)
CREDO

Mass of the Faithful

offertory
preface
SANCTUS/HOSANNA/BENEDICTUS/HOSANNA
(Pater noster)
AGNUS DEI
communion
(postcommunion)
ITE MISSA EST [or, in penitential seasons, BENEDICAMUS DOMINO; both are rarely set by composers]

known as a *'parody mass'. By the later 16th century this type was the most common.

The stylistic changes of the early Baroque era led to an increasing disparity between masses written entirely in the traditional polyphonic manner (*stile antico*), whose principal concession to modernity was the use of the basso continuo and the gradual adoption of a wider harmonic vocabulary, and those in modern style, with solo voices and instrumental obbligatos. A further disparity was that between the so-called *missa solemnis* (the term being used in this instance purely with reference to the degree of musical elaboration involved), on an extended scale, with the longer sections divided into several movements, and requiring a large number of performers, and the *missa brevis*, a more compact setting demanding less extravagant resources.

The so-called 'Neapolitan' or 'cantata' mass style, which owed much to contemporary opera, and in which the text was divided into many short sections set as self-contained solo arias and choruses in a variety of styles, had an important influence on 18th-century mass composition; in particular it established the tradition of ending the Gloria and Credo with an extended 'Amen' fugue. Bach's B minor Mass is the supreme example. Many of Mozart's masses are in the compact *missa brevis* form, as are some of Haydn's early ones. Beethoven's *Missa solemnis* is a successor to Haydn's late symphonic masses and, like them, was considered suitable for liturgical use on a festal occasion. The distinction between concert masses and those intended for liturgical use was to become more marked as the 19th century progressed. Renaissance polyphony continued to exercise a strong influence on 20th-century composers of masses.

mässig (Ger.). 'Moderate', 'moderately'; *mässiger*, 'more moderate'. It can also mean 'in the style of', e.g. *marschmässig*, 'in march style'.

Mastersingers. *See* MEISTERSINGER.

mattinata (It.). A morning song, similar to the French *aubade.

maxima (Lat.). 14th-century term for the *duplex long.

mazurka (from Pol. *mazur*). A traditional Polish folk dance, named after the Mazurs, who lived in the plains known as Mazovia around Warsaw. The name embraces several types of folk dance, including the *kujawiak* and the *oberek*; all are in triple metre, with dotted rhythms and a tendency to accentuate the weak beats. In the mid-18th century the mazurka spread to Germany, where it developed into a social couple dance for the ballroom. It became immensely popular throughout Europe during the 1830s and 40s. Chopin wrote over 50 mazurkas for the piano in a great variety of styles, often exhibiting a high degree of chromaticism.

The 'polka-mazurka', a combination of two dances, differs from the *polka in its triple rhythm and from the mazurka in having an accent on the third beat of each bar.

m.d. Abbreviation of *main droite* (Fr.), *mano destra* (It.), 'right hand'.

me. *See* MI.

meane [mean, mene]. In early English music, a term for the middle part of a three-part polyphonic work.

mean-tone temperament. A system of tuning keyboard instruments, used from *c.*1570 into the 19th century and revived in the 20th, in which each whole tone is half the size (the 'mean') of a pure 3rd. Most 3rds are pure, much better in tune than in *equal temperament, and the 5ths and 4ths are only slightly worse than in equal temperament. *See also* TEMPERAMENT.

measure. 1. In American usage, a term equivalent to the British 'bar' when used to refer to a metrical unit in notation; the American term for 'bar-line' is 'bar'. *See* BAR. **2.** In early English usage, a general term meaning 'dance'; more specifically, in 16th- and 17th-century England a moderately slow and stately dance in duple time.

medesimo (It.). 'Same', e.g. *medesimo movimento*, 'the same speed'.

medial cadence. *See* CADENCE.

mediant. The third degree of the major or minor scale, so called because it lies midway between the tonic and the dominant.

mediatio (Lat., 'mediation'). A subordinate cadence, occurring halfway through a verse in a psalm tone (*see* TONUS, 3).

medieval. A term borrowed from other branches of historical study which, when applied to music, denotes the period *c*.500–1430. The early boundary is hard to define as it predates musical *notation, but the period (and the concept of the Middle Ages) is taken to end with the rise of the Renaissance. *See also* ARS ANTIQUA; ARS NOVA; ARS SUBTILIOR.

m

medley (It.: *mescolanza*). **1.** A term first used by 16th-century composers, especially the Elizabethan virginal composers, for a piece that strings together several favourite tunes. *See also* POTPOURRI. **2.** In the second half of the 18th century the 'medley overture' combined well-known melodies from popular songs, dances, and folk music. Later, such an overture would usually contain tunes from the work it preceded. The term 'medley' today denotes a selection of pieces linked to form a single light-orchestral concert work. A medley differs from a *potpourri in that its components are more closely connected.

mehr (Ger.). 'More'; *mehrstimmig*, 'more (than one) voice', i.e. polyphonic; *Mehrstimmigkeit*, 'polyphony'; *mehrchörig*, 'polychoral'; *mehrsätzig*, 'multi-movement'.

Meistersinger (Ger., 'master singers'). German amateur poet-musicians from the burgher and artisan classes who, from the 14th century to the 17th, formed themselves into guilds for the practice of their musical skills. The most important was at Nuremberg. The leading figure among the 16th-century singer-poets was Hans Sachs (1494–1576), a Nuremberg shoemaker, whose extant works number over 6000; many of these are Meisterlieder, in which melismas (called *Blumen*) are used to decorate chosen words or syllables. The Meistersinger differed from their aristocratic predecessors, the *Minnesinger of the 12th–14th centuries, not only in their lower social status but also by their choice of sacred themes for their verse. However, various properties of the Minnelied—the **Bar* form, comprising two identical phrases (*Stollen*) and a contrasted final phrase (*Abgesang*), and the use of the ecclesiastical modes in the formation of melodies—featured consistently in songs from the earliest Meistersinger period. The Meistersinger guilds mounted public song contests.

melisma (Gk., 'song'). A group of notes sung to one syllable of text. It is used particularly to describe such passages in plainchant (*see*, e.g., CLAUSULA, 2), where the contrast between syllabic and melismatic passages is an important stylistic feature. However, it is also appropriate to later music.

melodic minor scale. *See* SCALE.

mélodie (Fr.). The 19th-century French term for 'art song', equivalent to the German *lied, as opposed to the lighter, less literary chanson. The *mélodie* developed in the early 19th century from such simpler forms as the *romance*, a strophic song with an undemanding tune, the *bergerette*, celebrating the activities of nymphs and shepherds, and the *scène*, imbued with melodramatic pathos. Practically every French composer from 1850 onwards wrote *mélodies*, but between 1870 and 1960 four composers made the most significant contributions to the genre: Fauré, Debussy, Duparc, and Poulenc.

melodrama. A composition or section of a composition, usually dramatic, in which one or more actors recite with musical commentary. If for one actor, the term 'monodrama' may be used; if two, 'duodrama'. The genre became popular in the second half of the 18th century. Melodrama was cultivated in the French *opéra comique* and the German *Singspiel*, and there are many 19th- and 20th-century examples.

melody. A succession of notes of varying pitch, with an organized and recognizable shape. Melody is 'horizontal' (i.e. the notes are heard consecutively) as opposed to 'vertical' (e.g. the notes of the *harmony, or chords, which are heard simultaneously). It is the result of the interaction of rhythm and pitch. The functions that define melody overlap with those used to define human speech, so that both may be regarded as fundamental capacities of the human species. Whereas speech is a form of communication, melody in all cultures has been used typically as a form of emotional expression. This use of melody may also be a capacity of other animals, since birds and dolphins, for example, produce organized sequences of varied pitch.

In the Western tradition, melody in the form of plainchant was the first aspect of music to be developed into an elaborate art form, before the last millennium of development of harmonic and rhythmic language. Since the first mature experiments in *polyphony (the combination of melodically differentiated voices) about a thousand years ago, monophony has played a relatively small part in our culture. In both sacred music and secular art music, medieval and Renaissance composers thought in terms of contrapuntal equality (*see* COUNTERPOINT). At the beginning of the 17th century in Italy, however, there was a change in attitude towards melody and its function; this arose from a desire to recapture, in secular music, a true marriage of word and melody. The resulting new art of *recitative, which spread rapidly, exploited a melodic style closer to the inflection and rhythm of speech, sustained by a melodically sparse bass which carried the harmonic structure. The principle of a two-part texture, melody against bass with 'inner' parts providing homophonic or imitative richness, was the prevalent style of the Baroque era and the fundamental nature of Classical and Romantic music.

Ex. 1

Ex. 2

The characteristics of melody in tonal music are the yardstick for discussion of melody in general. Ex. 1 illustrates this, showing that the second half of the clarinet melody which opens the third movement of Brahms's Symphony no. 1 repeats the first half upside down. It is an exact inversion, a procedure that became crucial in the melodic structure of 12-note music. Rhythmic articulation is another vital factor in the nature of melody. Melodic structure has to be described not only in terms of its overt linear properties, but also in terms of its harmonic implications. The English ballad *Greensleeves* (Ex. 2*a*) demonstrates how pure melody nevertheless unfolds a harmonic progression (Ex. 2*b*). In Classical music, the potential for harmonic and contrapuntal implication in melody becomes a sophisticated source of musical unity. Similarly, the form of a melody is inherently tied to other properties of musical structure. Melodic patterns like ABA and AAB are perceived as structural, even as textural, patterns.

Schoenberg paved the way for a new approach to melody, with *Sprechstimme*, midway between recitation and song, relying on pitch relationships to guide the declamation of the voice but specifically not 'singing' the notes, for which he devised special notation (*see* SPRECHGESANG, SPRECHSTIMME). Schoenberg and Webern also investigated the idea of **Klangfarbenmelodie* ('sound-colour melody'), in which variation of timbre is substituted for the variation of pitch which underlies the whole history of melody.

ménestrel (Fr., 'minstrel'). A French musical entertainer. *See* MINSTREL.

m

meno (It.). 'Less'; *meno mosso*, 'slower'.

mensural music, mensural notation. Terms meaning 'measured music' and 'measured notation'. They were used originally to distinguish polyphony and its notation from plainchant (which was sung in free rhythm). More technically, they apply to music in which each note-type has a clearly defined value. This system, established in the 13th century (*see* FRANCONIAN NOTATION), forms the basis of notational practices from that period to the present day. However, 'mensural music' is commonly applied in a more restricted sense to mean 15th- and 16th-century music. This music had no bar-lines, and the note shapes were written only in outline (like our modern minims and semibreves); thus it is referred to as 'white' mensural notation.

In mensural notation two relationships are carefully defined or 'measured'. First, the proportional relationship between a note and the next higher or lower in value. In modern notation this relationship is always duple (two crotchets in a minim, two minims in a semibreve, no matter what the time signature), though in earlier notations one or both of these relationships might be triple depending on the time signature. Second, the speed relationship between sections of music with different time signatures (*see* PROLATION; NOTATION).

Mensurstrich (Ger.). In editions of early music, the use of a line between the staves rather than through them, to divide the music into bars. The method is supposed to avoid the four-square, regular accentuation implied by the modern bar-line.

mente, alla. *See* ALLA MENTE.

menuet (Fr.; Ger.: *Menuett*). *'Minuet'.

mescolanza (It.). *'Medley'.

messa di voce (It., 'placing of the voice'; Fr.: *mise de voix*). A Baroque vocal technique, still used as a method of voice-training. It consists of a long-held note during which the tone swells to a climax, followed by a diminuendo to *pianissimo*.

Messa per i defunti (It.). 'Mass for the dead', i.e. *Requiem Mass.

Messe (Fr., Ger.). *'Mass'.

Messe des morts (Fr.). 'Mass for the dead', i.e. *Requiem Mass.

mesto (It.). 'Mournful', 'sad'.

mesure (Fr.). **1.** 'Measure', i.e. bar. **2.** Tempo, e.g. *à la mesure*, *en mesure*, 'in time' (*a *tempo*).

mesuré (Fr.). 'Measured'.

metamorphosis, thematic. *See* TRANSFORMATION, THEMATIC.

metre. The pattern of regular pulses (and the arrangement of their constituent parts) by which a piece of music is organized. One complete pattern is called a *bar. The prevailing metre is identified at the beginning of a piece (and during it whenever it changes) by a *time signature, which is usually in the form of a fraction; the denominator indicates the note-value of each beat and the numerator gives the number of beats in each bar. Thus 3/4 denotes three beats to a bar, each being a quarter-note (i.e. a crotchet). The sign **C** is the equivalent of 4/4 and ₵ of 2/2.

The perception of musical metre requires recognition of the first beat in the metrical pattern or bar. In a bar in 4/4 time, the first beat is the strongest (the downbeat), the third next strongest, with the weak beats being the second and fourth. In Western music metre is generally duple (in which the unit of pulse is in groups of two) or triple (in groups of three). 4/4, though it could be called quadruple metre, is considered a form of duple metre. If the units of pulse can be subvided into three, a piece is said to be in compound metre. A bar in 6/8 time and a bar in 3/4 may each contain six quavers; however, 6/8 is a compound duple metre because it consists of two groups of three quavers; 3/4 is a simple triple metre because it contains three groups of two.

Until the 20th century composers used simple and compound metres, occasionally writing in quintuple metre. During the last century composers experimented with metre, using odd numbers of beats in a bar, different metres simultaneously, or changing metres in quick succession. Some dispensed altogether with the regular organization of pulse. *See also* RHYTHM; TIME SIGNATURE.

metrical psalms. *See* HYMN; PSALMODY.

metric modulation. A technique by which changing time signatures effect a transition from one metre to another, just as a series of chords can effect a harmonic modulation from one key to another.

metronome (Fr.: *métronome*; Ger.: *Taktmesser, Zeitmesser*; It.: *metronomo*). A machine for establishing and regulating the speed of a performance; specifically, the clockwork-driven machine introduced by Johann Nepomuk Maelzel in 1815. Some composers indicate the intended speed of a piece by giving a metronome marking: MM, 'Metronome Maelzel' = beats per minute.

mettere (It.), **mettre** (Fr.). 'To put'; *mettete il sordino* (It.), *mettre la sourdine* (Fr.), 'put on the mute'. In organ playing *mettez* (Fr.) often means 'put (a stop) into action'.

mezza voce (It., 'half-voice'; Fr.: *demi-voix*). A direction to sing at half the vocal power.

mezzo, mezza (It.). 'Half', 'medium', 'middle'; *mezza voce*, 'half-voice', i.e. at half the vocal (or instrumental) power, restrained; *mezzoforte* (abbreviated *mf*), 'half loud', i.e. moderately loud; *mezzo-piano* (abbreviated *mp*), 'half soft', i.e. moderately soft.

mezzo-soprano (It., 'half-soprano'). A female voice (or artificial male voice) with a range midway between those of the contralto and the soprano, roughly *a*–*a''* (often *b''*). The distinction between a female soprano and a mezzo-soprano (colloquially 'mezzo') became pronounced only in the early 19th century, when the castrato voice (of approximately the same range as the female mezzo-soprano) rapidly became obsolete. A high mezzo-soprano is often similar to a dramatic or **spinto* soprano, and many roles can be sung by either. Occasionally a singer will describe herself as a mezzo-contralto, meaning a little lower in range than a mezzo-soprano.

mf. Abbreviation for *mezzoforte*; *see* MEZZO, MEZZA.

m.g. Abbreviation for *main gauche* (Fr.), 'left hand'.

mi [me]. The third degree of the scale in the *solmization system. In French and Italian it has become attached, on the fixed-*doh* principle, to the note E, in whichever scale it occurs. *See* TONIC SOL-FA.

mi contra fa (Lat.). Part of a short rhyme alerting singers to the awkward intervals, especially the tritone, that can occur when the two notes with the *solmization syllables *mi* and *fa* come together. The full rhyme is *mi contra fa / diabolus est in musica* ('*mi* against *fa* is the devil in music'). *See* MUSICA FICTA.

microtone. Any interval smaller than a semitone. Such intervals have long been used in Asian cultures, but their use in Western art music is a 20th-century phenomenon. Microtonal music can pose problems in performance, since it sometimes requires the construction of special instruments. In the electroacoustic field, however, there are no limitations: computer technology facilitates microtonal inflection.

middle C. The C nearest the middle of a piano or other musical keyboard. It is written on the first ledger line below any staff bearing the treble clef. Usually it is indicated by the letter *c*′, to distinguish it from the pitch C when it occurs in other octaves (*C*, *c*, *c*″, etc.). In the modern equal-temperament tuning system it has a frequency of 260 Hz.

military band and corps of drums. Wind and percussion ensembles, not necessarily belonging to the armed forces, though civilian ensembles usually prefer to be called *concert bands or wind orchestras. The instrumentation of the military band is similar to that of the symphony orchestra, minus the strings, but with the addition of cornets and saxophones, and a multiplicity of flutes and clarinets of various sizes.

minaccioso (It.). 'Menacing'; *minacciosamente*, 'menacingly'.

miniature score [pocket score]. A printed *score of pocket size for individual use or study. Such scores were marketed from the late 19th century onwards to meet the demand created by the rise in popularity of public concerts and, later, recordings.

minim (𝅗𝅥). The note having half the value of the semibreve, or whole note; hence the American usage 'half-note'.

minimalism. A term, borrowed from the visual art movement of the same name, applied to a style of composition that originated in the USA in the 1960s. It came about as a reaction to the prevailing modernist climate of the 1950s, with its dominant trends of indeterminacy and total serialism. The pioneers of the movement were La Monte Young and Terry Riley, quickly followed by Reich and Glass. Their aesthetic found expression in pared-down means of composition, with no sense of time-oriented direction. Stasis and repetition replaced the melodic line, tension and release, and climax of conventionally tonal music. Loops, *phasing, stasis, and tonality were all prominent features, used differently (though to similar effect) by each composer. In the 1990s a number of European composers exploited minimalism's qualities of timelessness to create what became dubbed 'spiritual minimalism'.

Minnesinger (Ger., pl. Minnesinger). German poet-musicians, often of aristocratic birth, of the 12th, 13th, and 14th centuries. Like the *trouvères of northern France, the Minnesinger modelled their culture on that of the *troubadours; their poetry reflects a social order of great refinement and education, dominated by a reverence for women and generally expressed in the language of courtly love. Although most of their verse was set to music, sung by the Minnesinger themselves and often accompanied by professional minstrels, few melodies have survived from the first two centuries of the movement's existence. *See also* MEISTERSINGER; MINSTREL.

minor interval. *See* INTERVAL.

minor scale. *See* SCALE.

minstrel. A professional secular musician or poet-musician, usually non-literate, either attached to a noble household or nomadic, who made music for financial reward and played or sang from memory. (The late medieval word *jongleur* has a similar meaning, but it can denote a professional entertainer of any sort—storyteller, juggler, buffoon, acrobat, instrumentalist.) The golden era of the minstrel is the later Middle Ages (roughly from the 12th century to the 15th). Some categories of minstrel continued to thrive after that time (e.g. the *waits) but the profession declined with the rise of performers who could read and play from music notation. Reciters of epic poetry in the bardic tradition can loosely be described as minstrels, as can the instrumentalists who worked alongside the *troubadours, *trouvères, and *Minnesinger.

minuet (Fr.: *menuet*; Ger.: *Menuett*; It.: *minuetto*). A stately dance in triple metre (usually 3/4) that flourished between the mid-16th century and the end of the 18th, and an instrumental form commonly used in such multi-movement works as the Baroque *suite and the Classical symphony, sonata, and string quartet. Typically in binary form, it is characterized by a regular phrase structure (usually of four bars), simple harmonies, and an uncomplicated melodic line.

The minuet first appeared at the French court in the 1660s. In the suite it was an optional movement and was, like the *bourrée and *gavotte, usually placed after the *sarabande. Many instrumental minuets are followed by a *double* (a varied repeat with ornaments); this led eventually to the traditional arrangement of minuet–second minuet in contrasting style (*trio)–first minuet repeated. In Italy a slightly faster version of the minuet, usually in 3/8 or 6/8 time, was preferred. This Italian style was also used in France. The minuet was quickly taken up in England, where it became especially popular as a ballroom dance and a regular component of the suite. Bach used both Italian and French types.

In the Classical period, the minuet was incorporated in the evolving forms of symphony, solo sonata, and string quartet. At first it acted as a finale, but eventually the standard tripartite minuet and trio was adopted as the third movement of the four-movement plan of symphonies and quartets, generally designed to provide light relief between the slow movement and the finale. From Beethoven onwards the traditional place of the minuet in symphonies and chamber music began to be taken over by the *scherzo, but it enjoyed a revival in the late 19th century, when French composers looked to the past for inspiration.

mirror canon. *See* CANON.

Missa (Lat.). 'Mass'. The *Missa solemnis* or 'solemn *Mass' is the most elaborate type, appropriate to high ceremonial occasions and most often set by composers. The *Missa cantata* ('sung Mass') is practically the same as the *Missa solemnis* in that it is 'sung' or chanted, but it is given with less ceremonial. The **missa brevis* is distinguished from these by its less imposing musical setting rather than by any liturgical difference.

missa brevis (Lat., 'short mass'). A short musical setting of the Ordinary of the Mass. This term applies variously to settings with textual omissions (e.g. Lutheran masses consisting only of the Kyrie and Gloria), of relatively brief duration, or both, as in 15th-century masses for the Ambrosian rite.

Missa pro defunctis (Lat.). 'Mass for the dead', i.e. *Requiem Mass.

mistero, misterio (It.). 'Mystery'; *misterioso*, 'mysteriously'; *misteriosamente*, 'in a mysterious manner'.

misura (It.). 'Measure', 'bar'; *alla misura*, 'in strict time'; *senza misura*, 'without strict time', i.e. in free tempo; *misurato*, 'measured', i.e. in strict time.

Mitte (Ger.). 'Middle'; *auf der Mitte des Bogens*, 'in the middle of the bow'.

mixed cadence. *See* CADENCE.

mixed media, multimedia. Terms invented in the 1960s to cover performances combining live music with other means of expression: recorded or electronic music, dance, speech, lighting, video or film display, etc.

mixed voices. A term used in choral music to denote a combination of male and female voices, such as the standard choral combination of sopranos, altos, tenors, and basses (SATB).

Mixolydian mode. The *mode represented by the white notes of the piano beginning on G.

MM. Abbreviation of *Metronome Maelzel.

mobile form. A form used in *aleatory music whereby the order of events is flexible. Players may be asked to choose the order on the spur of the moment, or be given instructions from which to create different permutations.

modality. *See* MODE.

m

mode. A term with two meanings in modern usage: that of the rhythmic modes, found in the theory of rhythm of medieval mensural music (*see* NOTATION); and that of 'scale' or 'melody type'. The latter covers a wide range of definition, from simple scales—arrangements of tones and semitones sometimes without any implication of a 'tonic' or main note—to a particular and typical melodic style or collection of motifs, perhaps with a definite 'tonic' and other notes in a hierarchy of importance.

In the late 8th and early 9th centuries musicians constructed a theoretical framework to accommodate the newly created repertory of Gregorian chant (*see* PLAINCHANT). A large part of the singers' duties consisted of the singing of psalm verses according to set formulas or 'tones' (*see* TONUS, 3). Each intonation was introduced and followed by an antiphon, and it was vital to use the tone that accorded best with the tonality of the antiphon. Thus there was effected a standardization of the chant repertory into eight modes, and correspondingly eight psalm tones. The psalm tones themselves do not all cadence on the finals of their corresponding modes. Because the psalm tones are always succeeded by a repeat of an antiphon, and a smooth transition must be made from the end of the psalm verse back to the beginning of the antiphon, each psalm tone is provided with several different cadences, or *differentiae*.

The first four modes ('authentic' modes: *protus*, *deuterus*, *tritus*, *tetrardus*) began on D, E, F, and G; they may be recreated by playing an octave scale on the white notes of the piano starting on these notes. The fifth note (the dominant) was used as a reciting tone in plainsong, and the first (the final) as a cadence note. To these four modes were added another four ('plagal' modes); they were new forms of the authentic modes, starting not on the final but on the dominant (i.e. A, B, C, and D). This was the foundation of the medieval and Renaissance modal system.

In the 11th century, the influence of Greek theory led to the naming of the modes as follows (with their ranges): Dorian, *c–e'*; Hypodorian, *a–b♭'*; Phrygian, *d–e'*; Hypophrygian, *c–c'*; Lydian, *f–f'*; Hypolydian, *c–d'*; Mixolydian, *f–g'*; Hypomixolydian, *c–e'*. Dissatisfaction with the inability of this eight-mode system to contain polyphonic procedures prompted the 16th-century theorist Heinrich Glarean to create a more comprehensive system with 12 modes. To the previous eight he added the Aeolian (*a–a'*) and the Hypoaeolian (*e–e'*), both with finals on *a*, and the Ionian (*c–c'*) and Hypoionian (*g–g'*), both with finals on *c*. *See also* SCALE.

mode of limited transposition. A term introduced by Messiaen to denote a mode that can be transposed only two or three times before it duplicates itself. The whole-tone scale can be transposed up one semitone to generate a different set of notes, but transposition at any other interval will duplicate the notes of one of these two versions of the scale. The mode of limited transposition that had the greatest compositional relevance during the 19th and 20th centuries is the *octatonic scale.

moderato (It.), **modéré** (Fr.). 'Moderate', i.e. at a moderate tempo; *moderatamente* (It.), *modérément* (Fr.), 'moderately'.

modernism. A current of compositional thought and practice characterized by innovation. Modernism was in evidence as an idea and as a term by the second decade of the 20th century, in association with the move towards atonality and the music of the Futurists. But although many modernist endeavours were born at the same time, there was no unanimity of motivation or outlook. *See also* FUTURISM.

modinha (Port.). A type of song, originating in Italian opera and other art-music traditions; it was sentimental and usually for solo voice and guitar. It became especially popular in Brazilian salons in the 18th century.

modo (It.). **1.** 'Manner'; *in modo di*, 'in the manner (style) of'. **2.** *'Mode'.

modulation. The contradiction of one key by the establishing of another. In the major-minor tonal system, a key may be either major or minor, with any of the 12 chromatic pitches as its tonic, so that 24 keys are available. A tonal piece of music begins and ends in one key, but during its course it may modulate to one other key or to several others. Modulation may be diatonic, where the notes of the first key are not contradicted and only the harmonic disposition of the music suggests a new key (Ex. 1*a*); chromatic, where 'foreign' notes are introduced and must be contradicted in turn when the music returns to the original key (Ex. 1*b*: B♮ to B♭ to B♮); or enharmonic, where the actual note names and notation are contradicted by the new intervals formed in the modulation (Ex. 1*c*: note the augmented 4th and the diminished 5th marked *). An important aspect of the harmonic theory that explains modulation is the 'pivot' chord (see, for example, the chord marked ** in Ex. 1*b*), which is common to both the old and the new key. More remote modulations reduce the possibility of pivot chords. As Ex. 1*d* illustrates, the keys

from and to which the progression in Ex. 1*c* modulates have no common triad: at opposite extremes of the *circle of 5ths, they are as remote from each other as is possible. Modulation plays an important part in a work's formal structure.

The term is also used in *electroacoustic music for processes of change, some by means of a ring modulator.

modus. *See* MODE.

modus lascivus (Lat., 'lascivious mode'). Medieval name for the Ionian *mode.

möglich (Ger.). 'Possible'; *so rasch wie möglich*, 'as quick as possible'.

moins (Fr.). 'Less'.

moll (Ger.). 'Minor', in the sense of key, e.g. *A-moll*, 'A minor', *moll Ton* (*Tonart*), 'minor key'. *See also* DURUM AND MOLLIS.

mollis. *See* DURUM AND MOLLIS.

molto (It.). 'Much', 'very'; *molto allegro*, 'very quickly'; *moltissimo*, 'extremely'.

moment form. An avant-garde form dating from the 1960s. Its first exponent was Stockhausen, who conceived each individually characterized passage in a work as a unit, or 'moment'. No moment has priority over another (even at the beginning or ending of a work), each is equally dispensable, and each is self-contained; they may be combined in a variety of ways often at the performers' discretion.

monocordo (It.). In string playing, the performance of a piece or passage on a single string, usually requiring upward shifts in position.

monodrama (It.). A *melodrama for one speaker only.

monody (from Gk. *monōidos*, 'singing alone'). **1.** The same as *monophony. **2.** More specifically, a modern term for the solo song with *continuo accompaniment that flourished in Italy in the first half of the 17th century. The members of the Florentine *Camerata had experimented with developing a new, direct style of singing in the late 16th century, aiming to recreate the power of Ancient Greek music which they felt had been lost in the elaborate music of their own time. Performances and arrangements of polyphonic music, such as madrigals, for solo voice and instrumental accompaniment were also popular. The prime exponent of the new monodic song was Giulio Caccini, whose madrigals and strophic arias for solo voice and continuo marked the beginning of monody's popularity and of a gradual decline in polyphonic song.

Freed by the presence of the continuo and the absence of other voices, the monodic vocal line could follow closely the meaning and rhythm of the text, being declamatory and often syllabic and recitative-like, and could be much more virtuoso and highly embellished than was possible in polyphonic song. Monody played an important role in the early operas of Caccini and Jacopo Peri. After *c*.1620 it spread from Florence to other regions of Italy. *See also* ARIA; MADRIGAL; OPERA; STILE RAPPRESENTATIVO.

monophony. A term used to denote music consisting of only one melodic line, with no accompaniment or other voice parts (e.g. plainchant, unaccompanied solo song), as opposed to *polyphony and *homophony (each having several parts).

monothematic. A term used to describe a composition or movement based on only one main theme. It is sometimes used in connection with movements in *sonata form, in which two themes, or subjects, are usually introduced in the exposition; some composers of the Classical period, however, would base the second subject on thematic material taken from the first.

monotoning. *See* INTONING.

monter (Fr.). 'To raise', e.g. the pitch of an instrument.

morbido (It.). 'Soft', 'gentle'; *morbidezza*, 'softness', 'gentleness'.

morceau (Fr.). 'Piece'; *morceau symphonique*, 'symphonic piece'.

mordent (from It. *mordente*, 'biting'; Fr.: *mordant*, *pincé*, *battement*, *martellement*, *tiret*; Ger.: *Mordent*, *Beisser*). An *ornament consisting in a rapid, often sharply rhythmic, alternation of main note, lower auxiliary note, and main note, indicated by the sign 𝆘; the inverted form uses the upper auxiliary note instead of the lower. Mordents with one or two repercussions (the latter termed 'double mordents') functioned primarily as rhythmic ornaments; those with multiple repercussions (sometimes indicated by an elongation of the sign: 𝆘𝆘) intensified and coloured the melodic note. Baroque composers often left the chromatic alteration of the auxiliary note to the discretion of the performer. Mordents, particularly short ones, gave brilliance to leaping and detached notes. Contrary to popular opinion, the inverted mordent (Ger.: *Schneller*) was not characteristic of the later Baroque period; the **Pralltriller*, or half-*trill, probably fulfilled this function. From the late 18th century onwards, however, the inverted mordent came into wide acceptance and was indicated by the sign formerly used for the trill; often it was intended to be performed before the beat.

The terminology concerning mordents is confusing: some modern writers have reversed the definitions of mordent and inverted mordent given above, while others refer instead to upper and lower mordents.

morendo (It.). 'Dying', 'fading away'.

moresca (It., Sp.), **moresque** (Fr.). A dance popular throughout Europe in the 15th and 16th centuries. Its performers wore Moorish costumes, had blackened faces, and wore bells on their legs; it frequently involved a mock sword fight between 'Christians' and 'Moors'. Also known as a *danse des bouffons*, it is probably related to the English morris dance and certainly to the *villanella.

Morgenlied (Ger.). 'Morning song'. *See* AUBADE.

mormorendo (It.). 'Murmuring', 'whispering'.

mosso (It.). 'Moved'; *più mosso*, 'more moved', i.e. quicker; *meno mosso*, 'less moved', i.e. slower.

motet. The most important form of polyphonic vocal music in the Middle Ages and Renaissance. Over its five centuries of existence there is no one definition that would apply throughout, but from the Renaissance onwards motets have normally had Latin sacred texts and have been designed to be sung during Catholic services.

The medieval motet evolved during the 13th century, when words (Fr.: *mots*) were added to the upper parts of *clausulae—hence the label 'motetus' for such an upper part, a term that came to be applied to the entire piece. Whereas the lower part of such a composition (a tenor cantus firmus) moved in slower notes and was derived from a plainchant with Latin text, the upper part or parts might carry unrelated Latin or even French secular texts, and such parts were being freely invented by *c.*1250. During the 14th century, the structural principle of *isorhythm was applied to the tenors of motets; up to the early 15th century, it was applied in some cases to all voices.

A freely composed type of motet, often in simple style and with a single text, came into being, and by the late 15th century the motet had become a choral setting of sacred works in four or more parts. Its choral texture was more unified, the individual voices moving at the same sort of pace. The practice of imitation, whereby each voice entered in turn with the same distinctive musical idea, became fundamental to the motet as to other types of polyphonic music; at the same time composers reflected a new humanist spirit in their choice of texts and attention to the way the words were enunciated in the music. The motet, unlike the mass, the psalm, the hymn, or the *Magnificat* setting, remained a form not strictly prescribed by the liturgy, but added (or substituted) at an appropriate place in the service on the appropriate day—in the same way as the English *anthem. The occasional 'ceremonial' type of motet survived.

The imitative motet style flowered with the generation after Josquin, and the device of 'pervading imitation', whereby successive phrases of the text are set to overlapping points of imitation, was refined by Palestrina and the other great late Renaissance polyphonists: Lassus, Byrd, and Victoria. Although the old style (**stile antico*) of Palestrina was still sometimes cultivated in motets written during the Baroque period (and even later), from 1600 onwards composers largely adopted the new styles for their motets, writing pieces for one or more voices with continuo and sometimes also including independent instrumental parts, usually for strings. This was especially so in Italy, where by 1700 the solo motet, a cantata-like piece for one voice and strings, often setting a picturesque non-liturgical text, had become the most common form of motet. In Louis XIV's France the *grand motet* for solo voices and chorus with instrumental accompaniment, produced for great occasions, was one of the chief forms of sacred music. Since the Baroque era motet composition has declined, though there are Classical and 19th- and 20th-century examples.

motetus (Lat.). **1.** *'Motet'. **2.** A term used from the 13th century to the 15th for the voice part immediately above the tenor in motets.

motif [motive]. A short melodic or rhythmic idea, the smallest part of a theme or phrase to have a specific identity. A motif is the main building-block for themes and melodic lines, and brings unity and comprehensibility to a work through its repetition and varied occurrence. *See also* LEITMOTIF.

m

motion. The linear pattern of a melody. Progression by step, ascending or descending, is described as 'conjunct' motion, by leap as 'disjunct' motion. In part-writing, simultaneous voice parts moving in the same direction are said to be in 'similar' motion; if, in addition, they move by the same intervals they are in 'parallel' motion. If they move in opposite directions the motion is described as 'contrary'. If one part is stationary (on the same pitch) while another moves away from it the motion is 'oblique'.

Motiv (Ger.). *'Motif'.

moto (It.). 'Motion'; *con moto*, 'with motion', e.g. *andante con moto*, faster than *andante*; *moto precedente*, 'preceding motion', i.e. at the same speed as before.

moto perpetuo (It.). *See* PERPETUUM MOBILE.

motor rhythm. Insistently regular rhythmic repetition. Motor rhythm has been a feature of many musical styles, from the Baroque toccata onwards. The metaphor of motoric, mechanistic reiteration is specifically a 20th-century one, and most appropriate when the music's subject matter is explicitly industrial.

motto theme. A recurring theme, similar to *leitmotif and **idée fixe*. The term is often used in connection with earlier music, however, for example with those 15th- and 16th-century masses that open each movement with an identical motif or motto (Ger.: *Hauptmotiv*, literally 'head-motif'). The 'motto arias' (Ger.: *Devisenarien*) of the 17th and 18th centuries worked on the same principle: a preliminary statement by the solo voice of the first motif of the melody would precede the instrumental introduction.

mouvement (Fr.). 'Movement', either in the sense of motion, or in the derived sense of a section of a composition. It is often abbreviated to *mouvt*. The term is sometimes used to imply a return to the original tempo after some deviation, such as a *rallentando*. *Mouvement perpétuel*, the same as **perpetuum mobile*.

mouvementé (Fr.). 'Animated'.

movable doh. *See* FIXED DOH.

movement (Fr.: *mouvement*; Ger.: *Satz*; It.: *movimento*, *tempo*). A term used in connection with musical forms (most commonly the sonata, symphony, concerto, string quartet, etc.) that consist of a number of substantial sections, each one being called a 'movement'. A movement is, in theory, self-contained and in most cases is separated from the other sections by a brief pause.

mp. Abbreviation for *mezzopiano*; *see* MEZZO, MEZZA.

M.S. Abbreviation for (1) *mano sinistra* (It.), 'left hand'; (2) manuscript (also MS or Ms.).

multimedia. *See* MIXED MEDIA.

multiphonics. Sounds in which more than one distinct pitch is discernible, but produced on instruments traditionally considered monophonic. Multiphonics usually occur when the single air column of an instrument is made to vibrate at several frequencies simultaneously. Alternatively, a performer may simultaneously play one note and sing another, particularly on the flute and on brass instruments; in many cases more than two notes can result.

multiple stopping. *See* STOPPING.

murky bass. An 18th-century name for bass accompaniments in *broken octaves.

muscadin. A dance occasionally encountered in English 16th- and 17th-century virginal music. It resembles the *allemande.

musette (Fr.). A dance of a pastoral character similar to the *gavotte. It was especially popular at the courts of Louis XIV and Louis XV. Its music is characterized by a bagpipe-like drone in the bass and conjunct motion in the upper parts. Musettes were also composed for keyboard. Several kinds of musical instrument are called 'musette'.

musica colorata. *See* MUSICA FIGURATA.

musica ficta (Lat., 'false music'). Before 1600 musical sources rarely indicated all the required accidentals, so it was necessary for performers to add them. Today, editors and performers of early music often insert what they consider to be the missing accidentals, and these are commonly called *musica ficta*. The term, however, properly refers to any accidentals (or chromatic alterations by the performer) that lie outside the standard system of notes used in the medieval and Renaissance periods. This system was based on three uniform interlocking scales, each of six notes, called *hexachords.

musica figurata (Lat., 'figured music'). **1.** Originally a term used to distinguish any type of polyphonic music from plainchant or other monophony. In the 15th and 16th centuries it was used to describe polyphony in which the voice parts are more florid and move more independently than in note-against-note counterpoint. **2.** In a more specialist sense, *musica figurata* denotes the decorated, florid style found in the polyphony of some early Flemish composers as distinct from the generally more sober **musica reservata* of Josquin and later composers. In this sense too the less common *musica colorata* is used, which may also suggest any sort of florid decoration (*see* COLORATURA). *See also* FIGURAL.

musical comedy, musical. A type of popular musical theatre. 'Musical comedy' was generally used in 19th-century America to describe loosely constructed musical shows. When the popularity of operetta and comic opera waned in the 1890s, the term was applied to a livelier type of show that featured fashionable modern dress and elements of burlesque and music hall as well as comic opera. British musical comedy flourished into the early 20th century. Its American counterpart developed along two lines: extended vaudeville sketches, and adaptations of European shows, containing light interpolated songs with vernacular American lyrics. The great period of the American musical was the 1940s and 50s.

musica mundana. *See* SPHERES, MUSIC OF THE.

musica reservata (Lat., 'reserved music'). A term used by music theorists between 1552 and 1625. It is never clearly defined in the original sources, and various interpretations of its meaning have been suggested. It appears to designate a particularly expressive style of composition, without unnecessary ornamentation, in which attention is paid to word-setting, often involving chromaticism, modulations, enharmonic shifts, and techniques associated with *Mannerism.

music drama. Wagner's term for his operas. *See also* GESAMTKUNSTWERK.

music hall. An entertainment made up of comic, vocal, acrobatic, and miscellaneous acts. The heyday of music hall lasted from the 1850s to World War I. The name was simply a description of the places where the entertainment was given in its formative days—in specially adapted or specially constructed halls added to public houses to provide entertainment while the customers ate and drank. Later it acquired its own theatres, players, and repertory, and the name 'variety' was frequently used, with 'vaudeville' becoming more common in the USA. The era of music hall ended when supplanted by new popular entertainments such as radio, gramophone, and cinema.

music of the spheres. *See* SPHERES, MUSIC OF THE.

musicology. Research in music. Musicology may cover a wide range of activities: acoustics, sociology, perception, ethnology, linguistics, logic, philosophy, and many other activities alongside the more traditional kinds of musicological study cultivated for much of the 20th century in English-speaking countries—primarily music history, source studies, criticism, and musical analysis.

music theatre. A term used since the 1960s to designate musical works (usually for restricted forces) which, though not staged in the conventional sense, incorporate such theatrical elements as costumes, gesture, and platform movement. Instrumentalists often occupy the same performance space as singers, becoming equal participants with them in the drama.

Musikwissenschaft (Ger.). *Musicology.

musique concrète (Fr.). A kind of *electroacoustic music which uses natural sounds, not electronically generated tones, as raw material. The recordings—of machinery, running water, musical instruments, etc.—are transformed by electronic means and joined to form a composition. Pierre Schaeffer coined the term in 1948 to describe his first electronic studies.

musique mesurée (Fr., 'measured music'). A French literary and musical experiment of the late 16th century. It began as an attempt to apply to contemporary French verse the principles of metrical accentuation found in classical poetry (*vers mesurés à l'antique*) with the aim of recreating the legendary powers and 'effects' of ancient music. *Musique mesurée* was devised by Jean-Antoine de Baïf and the group of poets known as the Pléiade, who enlisted the help of contemporary musicians to transfer these poetic principles to vocal music—*musique mesurée à l'antique*. Texts were set syllabically and homophonically so that the words were as clear as possible. The prime importance of *musique mesurée* lies in the transference of many of its characteristic features to the **air de cour*.

muta (It.). 'Change'. An instruction to change instrument, crook (in brass instruments), or tuning; *muta D in C* means 'change the tuning from D to C' on the timpani.

mutation. 1. In *solmization, a change from one *hexachord to another. **2.** The change in the male voice that takes place at puberty. **3.** In violin playing, a shift of position.

Muzak. A term for recorded background music played in public places and offices, to create a soothing atmosphere, to enhance workers' productivity, etc. Such music was first broadcast in 1922 by the American company Wired Music, later renamed Muzak; the term has also come to be applied pejoratively to any characterless recorded music.

nachdrücklich (Ger.). 'Energetic', 'emphatic'.

nachlassend (Ger.). 'Slackening', 'slowing'.

Nachschlag (Ger., 'afterstroke'). **1.** In modern German terminology, the final two notes of the turn that normally concludes a *trill. **2.** In 17th- and 18th-century music, the same as the English *springer.

Nachspiel (Ger.). *Postlude.

Nachtmusik (Ger., 'night music'). A term used in the late 18th century for a composition with the character of a *serenade. *See* NOTTURNO.

Nachtstück (Ger., 'night piece'). A term used in the 19th century for pieces in a style similar to that of a *nocturne. In the 20th century it was used to describe instrumental pieces that evoke the sounds and the atmosphere of night.

narrator (It.: *testo*). A character who tells the story in a dramatic work, in musical works usually to recitative. The custom is derived from early Greek tragedy. In Passion music the *Evangelist, traditionally sung by a tenor, is given the role of narrator.

national anthems. Hymns, marches, anthems, or fanfares used as patriotic symbols, like a national flag. They are played or sung at ceremonial and diplomatic occasions and at international sports events to salute winners.

nationalism. Patriotism, which may be expressed in music by composers or by those who control performance. It often involves the conscious use of elements that can be recognized as belonging to one's own nation (or would-be nation), with the object of arousing patriotic feelings. In Western art music, nationalism reached its height during the 19th century. It was given impetus by the political movements for independence (e.g. those of 1848) and as a reaction, particularly in eastern Europe, to German musical hegemony. In addition to using recognizably national genres (e.g. folksong, folk dance, folk rhythms), nationalist composers based their operas and symphonic poems on subjects that reflected national life or history. Nationalism flourished especially in Bohemia, Hungary, Poland, Russia, and Scandinavia.

natural (Fr.: *bécarre*; Ger.: *Auflösungszeichen, Quadrat*; It.: *bequadro*). **1.** A note which is neither raised (sharpened) nor lowered (flattened). **2.** The sign (♮) that, after a note has been raised by a sharp or double sharp or lowered by a flat or double flat, restores a note to its natural pitch. After a double sharp or double flat, the reversion to a single accidental is notated either by the use of the single sharp or flat alone, or occasionally by ♮♯ or ♮♭. For the origins of the natural sign and its early use, *see* NOTATION.

natural harmonics. *See* HARMONIC SERIES.

natural hexachord. *See* HEXACHORD; SOLMIZATION.

natural notes. The notes available on brass instruments without the use of valves.

Neapolitan sixth chord. Name given to one of the chromatic chords—the first inversion (i.e. the '6th' chord) of the triad built on the flattened supertonic. Ex. 1 shows an example in the key of C. It is often used to replace the subdominant chord in the cadential progression IV–V–I. Although it was already an established feature in music (not only Italian) of the second half of the 17th century, it appears to take its name from its use by composers of the 18th-century 'Neapolitan school', e.g. Alessandro Scarlatti and Pergolesi.

Ex. 1

Nebenstimme (Ger., 'next voice'). A term introduced by Schoenberg for the second part in a polyphonic texture, indicated in the score by the symbol N⌐. *See* HAUPTSTIMME.

neighbour note. *See* AUXILIARY NOTE.

nenia (It.). *'Dirge'.

neo-classicism. The conscious use of techniques, gestures, styles, forms, or media from an earlier period. In the history of art and literature, the term is most commonly used for the appeal to models from Ancient Greece and Rome made by painters and poets towards the close of the 18th century. In music history, however, that was the period not of neo-classicism but of the Classical style. Neo-classicism therefore has to be a return to that style (or others), and the term is particularly associated with the works Stravinsky wrote between the early 1920s and the early 1950s. These include dislocated arrangements of 18th-century Neapolitan music, concertos somewhat in the manner of Bach or of early Romantic music, and ballets suggestive of the French Baroque era. The influence of Stravinsky's neo-classical scores was felt by many composers who worked in or visited Paris between the wars. The leading neo-classicist of the Austro-German world was Hindemith.

neuma [pneuma] (Gk., 'gesture', 'breath'). A medieval term referring to a sign in plainchant notation (neume; *see* NOTATION) or to melismas appended to certain passages of plainchant: the concluding melismas of alleluias (*see* JUBILUS), graduals, and responsories; the textless repetition of verses within a sequence; and the florid endings given to intonation formulas and model antiphons in some tonaries. The word is sometimes used more generally for melody (irrespective of words) as notated.

neume (from Gk. *pneuma*, 'breath'). An early note form; *see* NEUMA; NOTATION.

night music. *See* NACHTMUSIK.

ninth chord. A triad with a 7th and 9th added. *See* DIMINISHED SEVENTH CHORD; DOMINANT SEVENTH CHORD.

nobilmente (It.). 'Nobly'.

nocturne (Fr., 'of the night'; Ger.: *Nachtstück*). A 19th-century, Romantic piano piece of a slow and dreamy nature in which a graceful, highly embellished melody in the right hand is accompanied by a broken-chord pattern in the left. The title was first used by John Field, and was taken up by Chopin. In the 20th century the term was also applied to pieces that depicted musically the sounds of night.

noël (Fr.; Burgundian: *noé*) [nowell] (from Lat. *natalis*, 'of birth'). 'Christmas'. The word was used as an expression of joy and often appears in the texts of French *noëls* and English *carols. In France since the 15th century the term has referred to strophic, popular Christmas songs, whose music might be taken from liturgical chant, or well-known songs or dance tunes. From the 16th century to the 18th, however, a large number of vernacular French texts were printed, with suggestions as to appropriate melodies. From the 17th century, organists played instrumental variations on *noël* melodies; many surviving keyboard transcriptions of these survive. New organ *noëls* were composed in France in the 19th and 20th centuries.

nomine, In. *See* IN NOMINE.

nonet (Fr.: *nonette*; Ger.: *Nonett*; It.: *nonetto*). An ensemble of nine instruments or voices, or music written for it. Frequently encountered is the combination of two standard ensembles: a string quartet (two violins, viola, and cello) and a wind quintet (flute, oboe, clarinet, horn, bassoon), or the same but with a double bass replacing the second violin.

non-harmonic note. A note that is not part of the chord with which it sounds, e.g. a *passing note or an *appoggiatura.

nota cambiata (It.). 'Changing note' (literally 'changed note'); an idiomatic melodic formula whose salient feature is the leap of a 3rd away from an unessential note. The *nota cambiata* should not be confused with the *cambiata* (*see* ÉCHAPPÉE).

notation. The methods of writing down music to indicate how sounds and silences intended as music should be reproduced in performance. The origins of the present-day notational system lie in the various plainchant sources and theoretical treatises of the 9th and 10th centuries. Plainchant was first notated with 'neumes': small dots and squiggles probably derived in part from the accentual signs once used in the Latin language. Their various shapes represent either single notes or groups of notes. Those that represent groups of notes strung together are called *'ligatures' (from Lat. *ligare*, 'to bind'), and this term continues to be used for all compound note forms found in various notations up to the 17th century. The basic plainchant neumes acted as a memory aid, suggesting (but not precisely indicating) changes of pitch within the melody. There were also *'liquescent' neumes—ornamental neumes that required special types of vocal delivery.

By the end of the 10th century, some sources were arranging the neumes vertically on the page to show their relative pitch (*see* DIASTEMATIC NEUMES). Shortly after, Guido of Arezzo (*c*.991–after 1033) recommended that a staff should be used with spaces as well as lines indicating pitches, and that at least one of the lines should be identified by a pitch letter (i.e. *clef). Guido also suggested that two different forms of the letter b be used to describe the pitches B♭ and B♮. These letter signs are the earliest known accidentals in Western music (*see* DURUM AND MOLLIS). This attention to precise pitch notation and chromatic inflection coincided with the first written polyphonic music and its inevitable concern with vertical (harmonic) relationships.

An important development *c*.1200 was the codification of set ways of combining ligatures so as to indicate clearly rhythmic patterns. These set patterns were called 'rhythmic modes' and in the basic system there were six. Thus, if a composer wished to write the ♩♪♩♪ rhythm (first mode) he would use a three-note ligature followed by a two-note group, e.g. . The smallest unit in each modal pattern was called an *ordo*, and the ligature pattern that signalled the mode was sufficient for at least two *ordines*. The meaning of any particular note or rest still depended on its context, and not until *c*.1260 was there an attempt to stabilize the relationship between the shape of a note and its value (*see* FRANCONIAN NOTATION; MENSURAL MUSIC, MENSURAL NOTATION). This was the beginning of modern notation. Unlike modern notation, however, which is based on duple relationships (two crotchets in a minim, two minims in a semibreve, etc.), this music also had triple relationships (three minims in a semibreve, and so on; *see* PROLATION). In such triple-time music, notes could be made duple only by being 'imperfected' in some way, for example by writing the note in red (*see* COLORATION).

The 14th-century French notational system is described in a collection of writings based on the theories of Philippe de Vitry. For the first time the minim is now fully accepted as a note-value in its own right rather than as a special (i.e. 'minimum') kind of semibreve. Moreover, the relationship between the semibreve and the minim is given exactly the same status as that previously accorded to both the long and breve, and the breve and semibreve. A series of 'time signatures' (mensuration signs) eventually came into being which defined precisely the relationships between the various note-values. If there were three semibreves in the breve (i.e. perfect *tempus*) this was shown by a perfect circle, O; imperfect *tempus* (two semibreves in the breve) was shown by the half-circle C. Furthermore, a perfect or imperfect relationship between the semibreve and minim (prolation) was indicated by the presence or absence of a dot respectively. Thus, when both the *tempus* and prolation were imperfect, for example, the appropriate symbol was the half-circle on its own. (This is the origin of the time signature **C** for 2/4 and 4/4 time—it does not come from the initial letter of 'common time'.)

Around 1450 the solid black notes of earlier periods were replaced by void notes. This was because paper had replaced parchment as a writing surface, and the concentration of ink needed for black notation tended to eat through the paper rather quickly; the solution was simply to put the notation in outline. Also there was a decline in the use of *ligatures due partly to the establishment of music printing (1501), which could not cope well with them, but also to the new tendency to print music in score format which required notes to be synchronized vertically—almost impossible with ligatures.

Many details of modern notational usage (ties, slurs, ledger lines) were established in 16th-century instrumental music. Bar-lines, somewhat inconsistently used, occur as early as the 14th century, but not until the mid-17th century are they arranged to coincide with regularly recurring accents in the music. By the 15th century the natural sign ♮ is used almost as frequently as the sharp ♯ and flat ♭ signs, and composers are also beginning to use sharp 'key signatures' as well as the flat ones common in the medieval period.

The consistent use of tempo markings began in the 16th century. In the Baroque period such archaic devices as coloration, proportions, and ligatures are still found, particularly in works by 'learned' composers writing in the **stile antico*. But it was in instrumental music and secular vocal music that far-reaching notational experiments took place. The G clef gained wide acceptance in French and English harpsichord music, but it was not until the end of the 18th century that there was a real attempt to make G and F clefs standard for all music. Tempo was usually indicated by descriptive words in Italian.

The preoccupation with expression and articulation led not only to more dramatic styles of music and performance—*empfindsamer Stil* (*see* EMPFINDSAMKEIT), **Sturm und Drang*, and so on—but also to a host of ancillary symbols and instructions within the notation. We find bowing marks, fingering indications, and, in the late 18th century, pedalling signs for the pianoforte. No aspect of Baroque notation is more contentious than the interpretation of dotted rhythms. A *dot after a note ordinarily meant that it was half as long again as its normal value, but otherwise it simply signified that the notes on either side were irregular in some way.

Over the last 200 years the gradual separation of the role of composer and performer has contrived to increase the level of explicit instruction in music, and the printed score has become the paramount intermediary between composer and public. Moreover, the layout of scores became more standard. The treatment of tempo and pulse gradually grew more erratic and extreme. The 19th-century concern for virtuosity and expressiveness naturally resulted in increased attention to the notation of articulation, phrasing, and expressive nuance. Dynamic levels too have become more extreme, and experiments have been made to indicate dynamics not by traditional methods (*ff*, *pp*, etc.) but by the size of note-head, numerical scales, and other devices. In the 19th century, ornamentation was gradually absorbed into the style so that in Chopin's music, for example, the main melody is picked out in larger notes with the ornamental decoration fully written out in smaller ones. Electronic scores are often, in part, instruction manuals showing precisely how sounds are to be reproduced. The notation still bears some resemblance to conventional scores, but some more recent computer notations are highly sophisticated 'machine languages' for controlling and manipulating acoustical equipment; their visual appearance is no longer obviously analogous to the gestures in the resultant music. Some types of *aleatory music allow random events outside the control of the performer to become part of the music, while others attempt to provoke the musician into a subjective response, using *graphic notation.

The 20th century spawned a number of didactic and academic notations. For example, the disciplines of *ethnomusicology and music *analysis have developed their own notations, the former for recording non-Western musics, the latter for distinguishing between foreground and background materials and more or less significant harmonic events.

note. A written sign representing the pitch or duration, or both, of a musical sound. In English terminology the word has two further meanings: (1) the key of a keyboard instrument; and (2) the actual sound produced.

note-against-note. *See* HOMORHYTHM. ('Homophony' is sometimes used incorrectly to describe note-against-note writing.)

note-head. In notation, the part of a note that, through its position on the staff, indicates pitch.

note nere (It., 'black notes'). A style of notation, common in mid-16th-century madrigal collections, in which short note-values (semiminims and *fusae*, equivalent to crotchets and quavers) were used with the mensuration sign C, instead of the more usual long values with ¢. This made the page seem rather 'blackened'; an alternative name for this notation was 'cromatico' ('coloured').

note row. Synonym of *series.

notes inégales (Fr., 'unequal notes'). In performance, the rhythmic alteration of groups of notes that are written evenly, generally involving the lengthening of the first of a consecutive pair of notes and the corresponding shortening of the second; rarely the reverse happens, giving a rhythm like the *Scotch snap. Such a convention was prevalent in French music from the mid-16th century to the late 18th and was regarded as an important means of increasing the beauty of a vocal or instrumental work. It is also a common feature of jazz. Inequality was rarely notated in French music, but was sometimes indicated by the written word *pointé* and cancelled by *égales*. Disjunct notes were rarely played as *inégales*, and, when they were intended to be, were usually written out. *See also* DOT, 3.

notturnino (It., dim. of *notturno*). A miniature **notturno*.

notturno (It., 'of the night'; Ger.: *Nachtmusik*). An 18th-century composition, usually instrumental, written for performance at night. Such pieces generally consisted of between two and six movements of a light character. The German equivalent *Nachtmusik* was applied to music that was similar but played by a smaller ensemble. *See also* SERENADE; DIVERTIMENTO.

nourri, bien (Fr.). *See* BIEN NOURRI.

novelette (Fr.; Ger.: *Novellette*). A term first used by Schumann as the title of his op. 21 for piano. Several other composers subsequently adopted the term, which carries no particular connotation of form.

nowell. *See* NOËL.

number opera. Opera in which there is a clear distinction between self-contained 'numbers' (arias, ensembles, or choruses) and recitative or spoken dialogue. The term is applied to 18th-century operas, especially **opera seria*.

Nunc dimittis (Lat., 'Now let [thy servant] depart'). The *canticle of Simeon

(Luke 2: 29–32). It is sung at the Roman Catholic service of Compline, and was taken over from that Office to be sung at Evensong in the Anglican Church, where composers frequently coupled it with the *Magnificat, either as a self-contained work or as part of a full service.

n

obbligato (It., 'necessary'; Fr.: *obligé*; Ger.: *obligat*). An accompanying part that cannot be omitted. In the 17th and 18th centuries the term often referred to a keyboard part that was fully written out rather than notated as a figured bass. In a keyboard piece with 'violino obbligato' the violin part is essential to the structure; an optional violin part would be marked *ad *libitum*. The term has subsequently come to refer to prominent instrumental countermelodies, a common feature of 19th-century opera arias, where an orchestral instrument has a semi-solo role accompanying the voice.

obligat (Ger.). *See* OBBLIGATO.

obligato. An incorrect spelling of *obbligato.

obligé (Fr.). *See* OBBLIGATO.

oblique motion. *See* MOTION.

obra (Sp.). **1.** A general term for a musical work. **2.** In the early 18th century *obra* was sometimes used more specifically to refer to a *tiento.

octatonic scale. A succession of eight notes within the octave in which tones and semitones, or semitones and tones, alternate. The scale came into regular use during the 19th century, especially as a means of establishing an exotic atmosphere in Russian Romantic music, and retained a strong influence during the 20th century, notably in the music of Stravinsky and Messiaen (his second *mode of limited transposition).

octave (from Lat. *octavus*, 'eighth'; Fr.: *octave*; Ger.: *Oktave*; It.: *ottava*). **1.** The eighth note of the diatonic scale. **2.** The *interval of an octave is the most consonant interval of all, and one that gives the impression of duplicating the original note at a higher or lower pitch. Acoustically, the octave above a note is one with twice the frequency of the original (e.g. $a = 220$, $a' = 440$, $a'' = 880$). *See* HARMONIC SERIES.

octet. An ensemble of eight instruments or voices, or music written for it. The string octet is usually a double *quartet, sometimes with a double bass replacing one of the cellos. The classical wind octet was known in the 18th century as the *Harmonie or Harmoniemusik and consisted of pairs of oboes, clarinets, horns, and bassoons. Schubert's famous Octet is scored for clarinet, horn, bassoon, string quartet, and double bass.

ode (from Gk. *oidē*, 'song'; Lat.: *oda*). **1.** In Ancient Greece, a lyric poem accompanied by music. In Greek drama and in the works of Pindar, odes were sung by a chorus and performed with dance. Several of the Latin *Odes* and *Epodes* by Horace were set to music during the Renaissance. **2.** In England, from the Restoration to the early 19th century, a ceremonial *cantata composed for the monarch in celebration of a particular occasion. Such works include odes for royal birthdays, coronations, funerals, banquets, the return of the monarch from a journey, and pieces for New Year and St Cecilia's Day.

oeuvre (Fr.). 'Work', 'composition'. *See* OPUS.

offertory (from Lat. *offertorium*). The offering of bread and wine on the altar at a Christian Eucharist and, in the Roman rite, the chant sung to accompany this action. Gregorian and Old Roman offertories are melismatic responsorial chants, the majority taken from the psalms. Their music originally consisted of a refrain, the latter half of which (the *repetendum*) would be repeated after each of a series of solo verses (later suppressed). Renaissance musicians set offertories to freely composed polyphony; later generations often ignored the canonical texts or replaced them with instrumental works.

Oktave (Ger.). 'Octave'; *Oktavflöte*, 'octave (above) flute', i.e. piccolo; *Oktavfagott*, 'octave (below) bassoon', i.e. contrabassoon; *Oktavkoppel*, 'octave coupler'.

ondeggiando (It.), **ondeggiante, ondeggiamento.** 'Undulating', i.e. tremolo or vibrato.

ongarese, all'. *See* ALL'ONGARESE.

op. Abbreviation for *opus.

open form. A structural procedure whereby the sequence or construction, or both, of parts of a notated work are variable. It was first used by American composers in the early 20th century and was developed as indeterminacy (*see* INDETERMINATE MUSIC).

open harmony. The converse of *close harmony.

O

open notes. 1. Notes on the unstopped (or 'open') string of any bowed or plucked instrument. **2.** On valved brass instruments, the notes of the *harmonic series, which are produced without lowering (or closing) any valve. **3.** In brass parts generally, the direction 'open', or 'ouvert', countermands 'muted' or 'stopped'.

open score. A *score, normally comprising more than two staves, that shows each voice of a polyphonic composition on a separate staff. Open scores of four staves were used for some Renaissance and Baroque keyboard pieces.

open string. A string of a bowed or plucked instrument not 'stopped' by the fingers.

opera. A staged drama in which accompanied singing has an essential function. Liturgical music drama and mystery plays contain the seeds from which opera grew, and another antecedent was the **intermedio*. However, the form in which opera first appeared was a Renaissance phenomenon, the product of speculation by intellectuals, living mainly in Florence, who wanted to revive the glories of the art of Ancient Greece (*see* CAMERATA). They aimed to emulate Greek drama, which was sung, or said, in such a way that the words were emotionally heightened but always clearly audible. They experimented with this principle in vocal chamber music (*see* MONODY).

The new **stile rappresentativo*, as it was called, spread to other Italian courts, notably Mantua, where Monteverdi worked. In 1637 the first public opera house opened in Venice. The genre changed to meet the demands of new audiences, embracing virtuoso singing and spectacle; the unity and simplicity of Florentine opera gave way to diversity and discontinuity, with songs, duets, and instrumental pieces dispersed among the *recitatives. By the end of the 17th century opera was popular throughout Italy. To satisfy public taste, the *aria now became lengthier, with a reprise of the **da capo* giving the 'star' singers an opportunity to provide virtuoso embellishments. Plots and action became more varied and spectacular stage effects were featured.

Thereafter different operatic genres, serious and comic, some with spoken dialogue, some featuring dance, grew up in different countries, notably *ballad opera, **comédie-ballet*, *grand opera, **opéra-ballet*, **opera buffa*, **opéra comique*, **opera seria*, **opera semiseria*, *operetta, *pasticcio, **Singspiel*, **tragédie lyrique*, and *zarzuela.

See also AZIONE TEATRALE; FARSA; FESTA TEATRALE; GESAMTKUNSTWERK; INTERMEDIO; INTERMEZZO; MASQUE; MELODRAMA; NUMBER OPERA; RESCUE OPERA; VERISMO.

opéra-ballet (Fr.). A form of entertainment combining music, drama, and dance that was popular at the French court from the end of the 17th century to the late 18th. It usually consisted of a prologue and three or four acts (*entrées*), each of which had a separate plot (though often on a common theme). *Opéras-ballets* were generally light-hearted, treating mythological or pastoral subjects rather than tragedy, and included instrumental pieces, dances, solo and choral song, and recitatives.

opera buffa (It.; Fr.: *opéra bouffe*). 'Comic opera', the opposite of **opera seria*. It began in early 18th-century Naples as an entertainment involving characters drawn from low life. The purely comic but all-sung *intermezzo was often played between the acts of an *opera seria*. The dramatist Carlo Goldoni added 'high' characters, especially a high-minded heroine, and more serious or sentimental episodes in the mid-18th-century *dramma giocoso*. Characteristic features of the genre are the rapid-firing *secco* *recitative accompanying vigorous stage business, and the multi-sectional concerted finale with dramatic surprises. With the demise of *secco* recitative after the mid-19th century, *opera buffa* ceased to be a separate genre.

opéra comique (Fr., 'comic opera'). The word 'comique' is not identical in meaning with the English 'comic', or with the Italian 'buffa', having more to do with the Ancient Greeks' dramatic category of 'komoidia' (comedy). The French understood different things by it according to the date of its use. Beginning in the early 18th century with farces and satires using spoken dialogue with well-known *airs* (vaudevilles), the genre developed into the sentimental *comédie mêlée d'ariettes*. Thence, in the 19th century, it drew closer to serious opera, handling serious or Romantic themes, but still did not conform to the traditional requirements of French opera proper (five acts, all-sung). The use of spoken dialogue remained a distinctive characteristic.

opera semiseria (It., 'half-serious opera'). A sub-genre of Italian opera in the early 19th century. The term was first used for *rescue operas but the more lasting meaning was an *opera buffa* with an unusually serious plot. In particular, the principal bass became a genuine villain rather than merely a comic figure.

opera seria (It.). 'Serious opera'. The grandest form of Italian opera from the late 17th century to the early 19th. At the time it was generally termed *dramma per musica* ('drama in music'). Its audience tended to be royal or aristocratic. The subjects were drawn from mythology or Greek or Roman history, turned into elegant verse and organized in three acts. The music was largely a series of formal *arias separated by *secco* *recitatives. The prima donna (heroine) and primo uomo (the hero, generally a *castrato) each had at least one large-scale display aria in every act, followed by an exit. Tenor and bass soloists, if present, were generally gods, father figures, or villains. There were very few ensembles, and choruses began to play a major part only in the later stages. A sub-genre was the **festa teatrale* ('theatrical celebration'), often written for a royal occasion; unlike the *dramma per musica* it included much dancing and choral singing.

operetta (It., dim. of *opera*; Fr.: *opérette*; Ger.: *Operette*). Literally meaning 'little opera', the term came during the 19th century to describe a form of light opera in which spoken dialogue replaced recitative and the musical numbers were memorably tuneful. Operetta led in turn to *musical comedy and the modern musical. The first developments of the genre took place in France. The chief propagator of the classical operetta was Jacques Offenbach, who began with one-act works before expanding into evening-long scores. Offenbach was also a source of inspiration to Franz von Suppé and Johann Strauss in Vienna. The latter wrote one of the supreme operettas in *Die Fledermaus* (1874), and his background in the dance hall led to the waltz becoming the centrepiece of the romantically inclined Viennese operetta. The influence of Offenbach was also felt in Spain, which enjoyed a simultaneous boom in popularity of the *zarzuela; in London his works inspired those of Gilbert and Sullivan.

As operetta began to place increasing emphasis on contemporary plots and catchy musical numbers, musical comedy came to the fore. Through various influences 'operetta' came to imply not only a more operatic 19th-century musical style but also Ruritanian settings and aristocratic characters.

opp. The abbreviated plural of *opus.

op. posth. A designation used instead of an *opus number to show that a work was published after the death of its composer.

opus (Lat., usually abbreviated op., pl. *opera*, usually abbreviated opp.; Fr.: *oeuvre*; Ger.: *Opus*; It.: *opera*). 'Work'. The custom of numbering a composer's works as they appear 'opus 1' and so on is useful both as a means of identification and to show the place a particular work occupies in that composer's career, but the unsystematic application of the numbering has made it less helpful in practice than it is in theory. Some composers' works have been catalogued by different systems of numbering (*see*, e.g., BWV; DEUTSCH; HOBOKEN; KIRKPATRICK; KÖCHEL; RYOM).

oratorio. A sacred work for soloists, chorus, and orchestra on a large scale, neither liturgical nor theatrical, but intended for concert performance. S. Filippo Neri, who founded one of several religious orders which came into being in the 16th century believed that the spiritual health of the laity would be helped if the Latin liturgy were supplemented with meetings at which religious matters would be expounded in the vernacular and in which the congregation would take part. He therefore established an 'oratory' (*oratorio*, from Lat. *oratio*, 'prayer') in which it became the custom to hold an *oratorio vespertino* after Vespers; a sermon was given and motets and hymns sung. These hymns or **laude* sometimes told a story or had a framework of dialogue. At about the same time, the Society of Jesus, in charge of the Collegio Germanico in Rome, gave plays in the vernacular on religious themes, with music.

From these two roots sprang the first musical oratorios. The most remarkable was the *Rappresentatione di Anima, et di Corpo* (performed 1600), a lavish, fully staged entertainment with dancing; its allegorical story was in the tradition of medieval mystery plays and its spectacular elements were after the manner of the **intermedio*. The word 'oratorio' was used of the building, rather than the composition designed for it, until as late as 1640.

By the late 1640s oratorios were attracting crowds in Rome, and oratories were soon set up in many cities in Roman Catholic countries. Performances began to take place elsewhere than in the oratory churches, sometimes in the cardinals' palaces, especially during Lent or when for some reason the theatres were closed. In these circumstances scenery was possible (though usually restricted to a backcloth and drapes) but there was no acting. Since this was the period of the growth of opera companies it was natural for composers to write both operas and oratorios, with the result that the two genres became closer in style. The role of narrator, common around 1660, had disappeared by the end of the century, and the popular subjects became hagiographical: the similarity of the lives of saints to those of operatic heroes and heroines provided an opportunity for love scenes in a genre nicknamed the *oratorio erotico*.

The history of oratorio music at this time runs parallel to that of opera. In the period 1660–80 there was still a flexible alternation of recitative (not the perfunctory *secco* recitative of the later 18th century, but measured and expressive), arioso, and arias (most of them still rather short). By 1700 a more regular alternation of recitative and *aria was usual, the arias being more extended and in *da capo* form. The chorus was virtually abolished, though all the characters often joined in a finale or *arietta allegra*. The role of the orchestra—sometimes a large band of 30 or 40 players—increased, with grand overtures and full accompaniment in arias. It was in this form, of which Alessandro Scarlatti was the master, that Handel found the oratorio on his Roman visit.

Outside Italy, oratorios were performed in Roman Catholic courts, notably Vienna, as a substitute for opera during Lent. A related genre was the *sepolcro*, a dramatic enactment of the Passion story with scenery and costumes. Oratorio reached Protestant countries much later. In Germany, the *Passion and *historia* (a musical setting of a biblical story) prevailed, along with the **actus musicus*.

The English oratorio was essentially created by Handel, who combined the Italian operatic style (with its arias and recitatives), the German Passion, with its chorus as character, and the English *anthem and ceremonial *ode. It was in three acts, and offered a highly dramatic treatment of a biblical subject. The oratorio changed little in the 18th century. During the 19th it declined, but the genre remained popular in Germany and England, particularly for massive forces for performance at festivals.

orchestra (Fr.: *orchestre*; Ger.: *Orchester*). An ensemble of woodwind, brass, string, and percussion instruments in fairly standard proportions, used for accompanying opera and playing the Western concert repertory. The term is also used of other large ensembles including dance orchestras, jazz orchestras, and wind orchestras. In classical Greece the *orchēstra* ('dancing-place') was the area in front of the stage where the chorus danced and sang during theatrical performances. Because the first operas, dating from the beginning of the 17th century, were based on classical drama, it seemed logical to retain the term, which came to be used for the ensemble that played there.

Although composers may vary the number and kind of instruments used in an orchestral piece, the standard forces required by late 19th- and early 20th-century orchestral music are as follows. Woodwind: 3 flutes, 1 doubling piccolo; 3 oboes, 1 doubling cor anglais; 3 clarinets, 1 doubling bass clarinet; 3 bassoons, 1 doubling contrabassoon. Brass: 4 (or 6) horns; 3 trumpets; 3 trombones (2 tenor, 1 bass); 1 tuba. Percussion: 3 timpani (1 player); snare drum, bass drum, cymbals, gong, triangle, xylophone, vibraphone, etc. (2 or more players). Other: 2 harps; 1 piano. Strings: 1st violins (*c*.14); 2nd violins (*c*.14); violas (*c*.12); cellos (*c*.10); double basses (*c*.8).

orchestral score. A *score in which each instrumental or vocal part is separately displayed.

orchestration. The art of combining instruments and their sounds in composing for the orchestra, or, more simply and practically, the act of scoring a sketch or an existing work for orchestral forces. By extension, the term may also be used in the context of music for chamber forces or even for chorus or solo piano, since the basic concerns of orchestration—with balance, colour, and texture—are common to music of all kinds.

ordinaire (Fr.), **ordinario** (It.). 'Ordinary', 'normal'. An instruction to return to playing in the normal way after a passage in which an unusual playing technique has been required, e.g. bowing *col legno*. *See also* TEMPO ORDINARIO.

Ordinary of the Mass. The sections of the Mass whose texts do not vary; *see* MASS; PLAINCHANT.

ordo (Lat., pl. *ordines*). The smallest unit forming part of one of the rhythmic modes. *See* NOTATION.

ordre (Fr.). *'Suite'.

organ chorale (Ger.: *Orgelchoral*). A term that encompasses a network of related genres, all of which treat sacred melodies at the organ using predominantly contrapuntal textures. They often either served as an introduction to congregational singing of the chorale ('chorale prelude', 'organ prelude') or were heard in alternation with the singing of individual chorale verses. The organ chorale flourished in Germany in the 16th, 17th, and 18th centuries.

Types of approach to the organ chorale included: setting individual lines of the melody imitatively; presenting the chorale melody in long notes as a cantus firmus, with the accompanying voices engaging in contrapuntal and figurative elaboration which was often thematically related to the chorale itself; free chorale fantasias, often combining these two methods and frequently also including more improvisatory tendencies; and sets of variations (often called partitas, a term with a number of meanings; *see* CHORALE VARIATIONS).

organ mass. *See* VERSET.

organology. The study of musical instruments. Important aspects of organology include the analytical classification of instruments, the science of instruments, their historical development, and their musical and cultural uses.

O

organ prelude (Ger.: *Orgelvorspiel*). Alternative term for *chorale prelude. *See also* ORGAN CHORALE.

organ score. A reduction of a full *score of any ensemble composition to form an arrangement for organ. The term has also been used in the past to denote an *open score (often of four staves) of a piece of organ music.

organ tablature. *See* TABLATURE.

organum (Lat., from Gk. *organon*, 'tool', 'instrument', also 'system of logic'). Early polyphonic vocal music. The term was originally connected with the organ and later with 'consonant music'. The earliest surviving source calls polyphony 'organum', and this terminology was to be standard up to the 13th century; hence the term *vox organalis*, meaning the part added to a previous one (or *vox principalis*) to create polyphony.

Four types of organum are known from between the 9th and 13th centuries; all involve adding a part to a line of plainchant. **1.** In parallel organum the added voice or voices begin, move, and end at the constant interval of a 4th, 5th, or octave (or a combination of these) from the main voice. **2.** The added voice begins in unison with the main voice. It repeats its opening note until the main voice has moved up and away to the distance of a 4th above it. It then moves in parallel 4ths with the main voice. At cadences it repeats the sub-final while the main voice nears the final, then both voices merge in the final unison. **3.** The added voice complements the given voice by contrary motion, one part ascending while the other descends, one moving in the top part of the available range, the other in the lower part. The term *'discantus' came to be preferred to designate this style. **4.** The chant is drawn out into long held notes, while the added voice floats in faster motion above and around it. The chant is usually split into two- or three-note segments, the two voices starting together and ending with a simultaneous movement onto their respective final notes (usually a unison).

organ verset. *See* VERSET.

Orgel (Ger.). 'Organ'; *Orgeltabulatur*, 'organ tablature'.

orgue (Fr.). 'Organ'.

ornaments and ornamentation. The decoration of a melodic or, less commonly, harmonic line. The art of ornamentation was at its zenith between the 16th and 19th centuries, when it was regarded as essential to virtuoso technique. Ornamentation was characteristically used to vary repeated material, whether whole sections or shorter passages. Two broad categories are distinguished: small-scale ('simple') ornaments or 'graces' added to single notes; and more extensive ('compound') or florid decorations applied to entire passages, in which the original melody might be almost entirely disguised. The latter was largely the preserve of the virtuoso. Cadences in particular invited elaboration, from which the solo *cadenza evolved. During the 16th century, ornamentation was left mainly to the improvisational skill of the performer, but in the 17th and 18th centuries this freedom was tempered to varying degrees by more precise indications in the notation. In France these were known as *agréments*. 19th-century composers made their intentions clearer still. Later developments included the adoption of standard signs for such frequently used ornaments as appoggiaturas, mordents, slides, trills, or turns. No single interpretation of ornament signs has been followed throughout the centuries, or in any one country. The performance context (both date and place) of any given ornament must therefore be taken into account. *See also* ACCIACCATURA; APPOGGIATURA; MORDENT; RELISH; TRILL; TURN.

ossia (It., 'or'). A term used to designate passages added as alternatives to the original (and usually easier).

ostinato (It., 'persistent'). A fairly short melodic, rhythmic, or chordal phrase repeated continuously throughout a piece or section. Although it is one of the most common and effective continuity devices in music, ostinato is not merely repetitive: it also has a structural or thematic function, or both. It is present from medieval times to the present day, and is often a characteristic of a more specific compositional procedure, as in the *chaconne, *passacaglia, and *ground, and in *isorhythm and *minimalism. Where it is applied to a set bass pattern it is known as *basso ostinato*.

ôtez (Fr.). 'Take off', e.g. *ôtez les sourdines*, 'take off the mutes'.

ottava (It.). 'Octave'; *all'ottava*, 'at the octave', an indication to play an octave above (*all'ottava alta*) or below (*all'ottava bassa*) the written pitch; *coll'ottava*, 'with the octave', found in orchestral scores to show that one instrument should play in octaves with another (*ottava alta*, *ottava sopra*, 'octave above'; *ottava bassa*, *ottava sotto*, 'octave below').

ottone (It.). 'Brass'; *stromenti d'ottone*, 'brass instruments'.

ouvert and clos (Fr., 'open' and 'closed'; It.: *aperto*, *chiuso*). In some 14th- and 15th-century vocal forms, such as the *ballade* and the *virelai*, repeated sections are given alternative endings; these are labelled *ouvert* and *clos*, or *aperto* and *chiuso*, and correspond to the present-day use of *prima volta* and *seconda volta*, or 'first-time bar' and 'second-time bar'.

ouverture (Fr.). *'Overture'.

overblowing. The technique whereby woodwind players reach the upper registers of their instruments, made possible by a tube's ability to sound certain intervals above its fundamental vibrating frequency through increased air pressure.

overdotting. The exaggeration in performance of dotted rhythms, a practice adopted for much Baroque music (*see* DOT, 3).

overture. A piece of instrumental music composed as an introduction to an opera, oratorio, ballet, or other dramatic work, or intended for independent concert performance. In the Baroque period the title 'Ouvertüre' was sometimes applied to a keyboard or orchestral suite (Bach), or to its opening movement; and in 18th-century England 'Overture' could serve as an alternative title for a symphony. **1.** As opera and oratorio developed and became more organized, so did the introduction. Mid-17th-century operas often began with a slow, duple-metre one; this was to form the basis of a standard overture-type which, through its later association with French opera, came to be known as the French overture. It is characterized by a grave, sometimes pompous opening, with plentiful dotted rhythms and suspensions, leading straight into a fast, lively section in imitative, even fugal style, which often closes by echoing the mood of the first section. This pair of movements was sometimes followed by a moderately slow dance movement, or the entire first section might be repeated.

Late in the 17th century a tripartite overture appeared in Naples, cast in short fast–slow–fast sections, which came to be known as the Italian overture, though it was almost invariably entitled 'Sinfonia'. It was the ancestor of both the Classical symphony, in which all three sections became fully developed movements and were often supplemented by a slow introduction and a minuet and trio, and of the Classical opera overture, in which the second and third movements were reduced and then discarded.

Until the mid-18th century there was little connection, beyond a general spiritual conformity, between an overture and what followed. Gluck sought a more intimate correspondence between the two. The typical Classical opera overture consisted of a brief slow introduction followed by a fast movement closely related to *sonata form, but without a repeated exposition and generally with an abbreviated development section.

The form continued to evolve in Italian operas of the early 19th century. Wagner's early opera overtures still conformed to the Classical pattern, but later he preferred a short, independent prelude ('Vorspiel'). An effective type of overture that served well for 19th-century comic or light opera and operetta was one put together from a *medley or *potpourri of tunes taken from the opera, with little or no linking material. **2.** The concert overture had its precursors in the performance, as separate concert pieces, of Mozart's later opera overtures and of those that Beethoven wrote for stage plays. Other early 19th-century concert overtures were 'occasional' or abstract, but it is the descriptive, poetic pieces that typify the Romantic concert overture. Some were written to commemorate events, others were inspired by literature or art; still others have no known extra-musical connections. In the 19th century the concert overture gave way to the freer, more flexible *symphonic poem, or tone-poem.

P, p. 1. Abbreviation for *piano*. **2.** Abbreviation for 'pedal' in piano music. **3.** Abbreviation for *pédalier* (Fr.), the pedalboard of an organ, or for *Positiv* (Ger.), 'choir organ'.

pacato (It.). 'Calm'.

padovana (It.). *'Pavan'.

paduana (It.). *'Pavan'.

Palestrina, alla. *See* ALLA PALESTRINA.

palm court music. A term adopted to identify a style of *light-music repertory and performance that developed in Victorian times in resorts and spas, on piers and in floral halls, and in bandstands. It is particularly associated with groups that played in grand hotels for diners in rooms furnished with potted palms.

pandiatonicism [pandiatonism]. A term coined by Nicolas Slonimsky to describe the free use of all seven degrees of the diatonic scale, melodically, harmonically, or contrapuntally. The *added 6th chord is a pandiatonic device.

panisorhythm. *See* ISORHYTHM.

pantonality. Synonym for *atonality. Schoenberg preferred this term as indicating the combination of all keys rather than the absence of any, but it is rarely used.

paradiddle. A rudimentary side-drum technique involving the alternation of the leading hand, as follows: LRLL RLRR. It creates a semblance of *legato* or smooth transition between two drums (often timpani).

parallel [consecutive] **fifths.** The stepwise movement of two parts a perfect 5th apart to an adjacent position also a perfect 5th apart. Such motion is 'prohibited' in tonal harmony and *counterpoint.

parallel interval. *See* CONSECUTIVE INTERVAL.

parallel motion. *See* MOTION.

paraphrase. 1. In the 15th and 16th centuries, a contrapuntal technique involving the quotation in one or more voices of a plainchant melody. *See* CANTUS FIRMUS. **2.** In the 19th century the term was applied to works based on existing melodies or pieces, often used as virtuoso showpieces. The supreme master of this type of recomposition was Liszt, who wrote numerous piano paraphrases of Italian operas and even of Wagner's operas.

parlando, parlante (It.). 'Speaking'. In singing, a speech-like style, with one syllable for each note, often used in dialogues in certain kinds of comic opera. In instrumental music, an instruction for expressive, 'eloquent' playing.

parody mass. A 16th-century polyphonic cyclic setting of the Ordinary of the Roman *Mass based on the imitative texture of a pre-existing polyphonic composition.

part (Fr.: *partie*, *voix*; Ger.: *Part*, *Stimme*; It.: *parte*, *voce*). **1** [voice part, voice]. In polyphonic vocal music, the designation for each individual line. In early polyphony the names for the voice parts did not imply a precise range in the way that they do today: they were named according to their function and their place in the compositional scheme. In present-day choral music the standard formation (from the highest voice downwards, as is customary) is: soprano, alto, tenor, bass (usually abbreviated to SATB). **2.** The music for one particular instrument (e.g. first violin, flute) or voice, as opposed to a score, which contains all the parts involved in a work. **3.** A section of a composition; binary form, for example, can be said to be in two parts, ternary form in three (a better word is 'section'). In certain large-scale genres, e.g. oratorios, 'Part' is used to designate the main division of the work.

partbooks (Fr.: *parties séparées*; Ger.: *Stimmbücher*). Manuscript or printed books containing the music for an individual part of a work, whether vocal or instrumental (*see* PART, 1 and 2). *See also* CHOIRBOOK.

parte, parti (It.). *'Part', 'parts'; *colla parte*, 'with the part', i.e. an indication that an accompaniment should follow a solo line closely with regard to flexible rhythm, tempo, etc.; *a tre parti*, 'in three parts', i.e. three vocal or instrumental lines.

partials. Constituents of the notes of the *harmonic series, the main (fundamental) note being the first partial and the others the upper partials.

partial signature. *See* KEY SIGNATURE; MUSICA FICTA.

partimen. *See* JEU-PARTI.

P

partimento (It.). 17th- and 18th-century term for improvising melodies over a written bass.

partita [parte] (It.). **1.** In the late 16th and the 17th centuries, one of a set of *variations, as in the titles of a number of volumes of instrumental (especially keyboard) music. Italian and, later, other composers customarily based sets of variations ('parti' or 'partite') on the bass lines of such well-known tunes as the *folia* or *romanesca*. It may have been from this usage that 'partita' came occasionally to be used to describe any sort of piece that was part of a larger collection. **2.** In late 17th-century Germany, an alternative title for a *suite, usually occurring in the form 'Partia' or 'Parthia'. In the 18th century it could be applied loosely to any sort of multi-movement instrumental piece of the suite or sonata type, which might include movements headed 'Largo' or 'Allegro', for example, as well as the dance movements (allemande, courante, etc.) that traditionally make up the suite.

partition (Fr.; Ger.: *Partitur*; It.: *partitura, partizione*). *'Score'.

partsong. In its broadest sense, any composition for two or more voices; more commonly, a vocal composition intended for choral rather than solo performance, tending more to homorhythm than polyphony, and usually without accompaniment. Although the term has been used in connection with 16th-century secular music for solo voices (e.g. the *madrigal), and with the 18th-century *glee for men's choir, it is more usually and correctly applied to 19th-century unaccompanied works for male, female, or mixed choruses, principally songs composed as a response to the growing interest in amateur choral singing in Britain, Germany, and the USA.

part-writing (Amer.: voice-leading). The art of composing contrapuntal music (*see* COUNTERPOINT).

pas (Fr.). **1.** 'Not', 'not any'. **2.** In dance or ballet, a 'step'; the term is also used to denote a certain form or movement, e.g. *pas d'action*, a dramatic scene; *pas seul*, *pas de deux* (*trois*, etc.), a dance for the number specified.

passacaglia (It., from Sp. *pasar*, 'to walk', *calle*, 'street'; Fr.: *passacaille*, *passecaille*; Sp.: *pasacalle*, *passacalle*). A through-composed variation form constructed over formal harmonic progressions, normally I–IV–V(–I), used widely in the Baroque era but with origins in the Spanish street dance, the *pasacalle*. Like the *chaconne, which also used specific *basso ostinato* formulas, the passacaglia became a separately identifiable extended late Baroque instrumental form. It was favoured by Italian and French composers, whence it spread to Germany.

passage-work. A 'passage' in a musical composition is simply a section. The term 'passage-work' is more specifically applied to transitional sections (especially in keyboard music) that have no intrinsic musical value and little, if any, thematic substance, but rather serve as 'padding', often consisting of brilliant figuration and thereby offering an opportunity for virtuoso display by the performer.

passaggio (It., 'passage'). **1.** Used in the plural (*passaggi*), a kind of ornamentation. **2.** Transition or modulation. **3.** A passage of music intended to display the performer's virtuosity.

passamezzo [passemezzo, pass'e mezzo, etc.] (It.). An Italian dance of the 16th and 17th centuries, similar to, but quicker than, the *pavan and, like that dance, in duple metre. Its name is possibly derived from *passo e mezzo*, meaning 'a step and a half'. Most passamezzos were composed on one of two standard chordal basses: the *passamezzo antico* was based on the progression i–VII–i–V–III–VII–i–(V–)I; the *passamezzo moderno* (known in England as the 'quadran pavan') had the chordal framework I–IV–I–V–I–IV–I–(V–)I.

passecaille (Fr.), **pasacalle** (Sp.). *Passacaglia.

passepied (Fr.). A French 17th- and 18th-century dance resembling a fast *minuet. It was usually in binary form, in 3/8 or 6/8 time, and with continuous running movement in small note-values. It became one of the optional dances in the 18th-century *suite.

passing note. In part-writing, a note moving stepwise between two chords but belonging to neither of them.

Passion music. Settings to music of the account of Christ's Passion, as recorded in the four gospels. The earliest were composed in the 16th century. Over time the genre evolved and expanded, reaching a culmination in the Passions of J. S. Bach.

pasticcio (It., 'pie', 'pastry', 'mess'). A piece assembled from several pre-existing sources; the term is applied particularly to Italian opera from the late 17th century to the end of the 18th, when it was common practice to recombine favourite airs from earlier operas into a new scheme. *Ballad opera is sometimes considered a variety of this type of pasticcio. The term is occasionally also applied (inaccurately) to new works on which several composers have collaborated.

pastiche (Fr.). 'Imitation', 'parody'; not the same as *pasticcio. A work written partly in the style of another period.

pastoral (Fr.: *pastourelle*; It.: *pastorale*). **1.** In the 15th–18th centuries, a type of stage work dealing with rural themes. **2.** A type of instrumental or vocal work resembling the *siciliana, generally in 6/8 or 12/8 time and often suggesting a rustic or bucolic subject by the imitation of the drone of a shepherd's bagpipe or musette. In many countries pastoral music is associated with the Christmas season. *See also* PASTORELLA.

pastorella [pastorela, pastoritia] (It. or Lat., dim. of *pastorale*). A Christmas composition for performance in church between Christmas Eve and the Purification, which originated in the second half of the 17th century. In one or more movements, it is usually for singers and small orchestra and tells the story of the shepherds. As well as such characteristic features of the Baroque *pastoral as drone basses and melodies harmonized in 3rds and 6ths, pastorellas include rhythmic and melodic elements probably deriving from folk music.

patter song. A type of comic song, usually found in opera, which depends for its effect on the speed of the singer's delivery. Most patter songs are in Italian or English, and they became common from the second half of the 18th century.

pausa (It.). 'Rest' (not *pause).

pause. 1. (Fr.: *point d'orgue*; Ger.: *Fermate*; It.: *fermata*). A sign (𝄐) indicating that the note, chord, or rest over which it appears is to be prolonged at the performer's discretion. It is sometimes placed over a barline to indicate a short silence. It may also be used to indicate the end of a phrase, section, or composition. *See also* GENERALPAUSE. **2.** (Fr.; Ger.: *Pause*; It.: *pausa*). 'Rest', especially a semibreve rest; a *demipause* is a minim (half-note) rest.

pavan [pavane, pavin] (Fr.: *pavane*; Ger.: *Paduana*; It.: *pavana*, *padovana*). A 16th- and 17th-century processional dance in duple time, probably originating in Italy and named after the town of Padua. It was generally coupled with another, quicker dance, which was usually in triple time and sometimes had thematic links with the pavan; in Italy the accompanying dance was a *saltarello, in France and England a *galliard. The pavan reached the height of perfection in the hands of the English virginal composers. In the late 16th century it was superseded by the *passamezzo.

pedaliter (Ger., from Lat. *pedalis*). 'On the pedals'; in keyboard music, a direction to play with both hands and feet.

pedal note. A term (derived from the deep notes of the pedal rank of the organ) used for the lowest note that can be produced on a brass instrument for any given slide position or valve setting, usually the fundamental of the *harmonic series for that setting of the instrument.

pedal point (Fr.: *point d'orgue*). The device of holding on a bass note (usually the tonic or dominant) through a passage including some chords of which it does not form a part. An inverted pedal follows the same principle, but the long held note is placed in the treble. If two different notes are held together (usually tonic and dominant) the term 'double pedal' is used.

peine, à (Fr.). 'Scarcely'; *à peine entendu*, 'barely audible'.

pentachord. A five-note section of the diatonic scale, e.g. from C to G.

pentatonic scale. A scale of five notes. *See* SCALE, 4.

perdendosi (It.). 'Losing itself', i.e. gradually dying away.

perfect cadence. *See* CADENCE.

perfect interval. An *interval of a 4th, 5th, or octave.

perfect pitch. *See* ABSOLUTE PITCH.

performance practice. A term borrowed from the German 19th-century *Aufführungspraxis* to describe the way music is and has been performed. Its study covers notation (and its interpretation), ornamentation, improvisation, the structure and playing techniques of instruments, instrumentation and scoring, voice production, tuning and temperament, and the size and disposition of performing forces. It is important for those interested in past, 'authentic' performing styles.

period. A section of a composition that achieves a significant degree of harmonic closure. The term has been used in various ways by theorists. Unlike a sentence, which contains an element of small-scale variation or development, a period consists of two *phrases, *antecedent and consequent, each of which begins with the same basic motif, but which need not, as a whole, cadence in the tonic.

period performance. The application of historical *performance practice, not only in music but also in theatre and dance.

perpetual canon. *See* CANON.

perpetuum mobile (Lat., 'perpetually in motion'; It.: *moto perpetuo*). A title sometimes attached to a rapid instrumental composition that proceeds throughout in notes of equal value.

pes (Lat., 'foot'). A term used in some English 13th-century manuscripts to describe the tenor part; in most cases the *pes* carries a melodic ostinato figure. The two lowest voices of the rota *Sumer is icumen in* are called *pes* in the original manuscript.

pesant (Fr.), **pesante** (It.). 'Heavy', i.e. with emphasis; *pesamment* (Fr.), *pesantemente* (It.), 'heavily'.

petto (It.). 'Chest'; *voce di petto*, *'chest voice'.

peu (Fr.). 'A little', 'rather'; *un peu*, 'a little'; *peu à peu*, 'little by little'; *un peu plus lent*, 'a little slower'.

pezzo, pezzi (It.). 'Piece', 'pieces', in the sense of 'composition'.

pf., pfte. Abbreviations for 'pianoforte'.

phantasie, phantasy. *See* FANTASIA.

phasing. A term denoting the effect achieved when two instrumentalists or singers perform the same musical pattern at different (slightly increasing or decreasing) intervals of time, moving in or out of phase. The technique is used in so-called minimalist compositions. Phasing can also be achieved electronically.

phrase. A musical unit, defined by the interrelation of melody, rhythm, and harmony, that ends with a *cadence of some kind. Musical phrases combine to form larger, more complete units known as periods, and may themselves be subdivided. The length of a phrase varies, but is most frequently of four bars, often followed by an 'answering' phrase of the same length. In notation, phrasemarks are the slurs placed over or under the notes as a hint of their proper punctuation in performance.

The term 'phrasing' refers to the way in which a performer interprets both individual phrases and their combination in the piece as a whole.

Phrygian cadence. *See* CADENCE.

Phrygian mode. The *mode represented by the white notes of the piano beginning on E.

Phrygian tetrachord. A *tetrachord made up of the first four notes of the Phrygian mode. The intervals of the Phrygian tetrachord are semitone-tone-tone (e.g. E-F-G-A), as opposed to the tone-tone-semitone of the diatonic major scale.

piacere, a (It.). 'At pleasure', i.e. *ad *libitum*.

piacevole (It.). 'Pleasing', 'agreeable'.

piangendo, piangente (It.). 'Weeping', 'plaintive'; *piangevole*, *piangevolmente*, 'plaintively'.

pianissimo (It.). 'Very quiet'; it is abbreviated *pp*.

piano (It.). 'Soft'; it is abbreviated *p*.

piano duet. A work for two pianists at the same piano, or, more rarely, two pianists playing two pianos. The genre became particularly popular from the second half of the 18th century. Piano-duet reductions of operas and opera highlights, as well as symphonies and other orchestral works, were made in large number in the 19th century.

piano quartet. An ensemble consisting of a pianist and three stringed instruments (typically violin, viola, and cello), or music written for it.

piano quintet. An ensemble consisting of a pianist and four other instruments (often a string *quartet), or music written for it.

piano reduction [piano score]. A reduction of a full *score of any ensemble composition to form an arrangement for piano. Piano reductions, particularly of opera scores, were popular from the late 18th century and throughout the 19th, before the advent of sound recording.

piano trio. An ensemble consisting of a piano and two other instruments (often violin and cello), or music written for it. *See* TRIO, 1.

piano-vocal score. Another name for a *vocal score.

pianto (It.). 'Lament', 'plaint'.

piatti (It). 'Cymbals'.

Picardy third. *See* TIERCE DE PICARDIE.

picchettato (It., 'knocked'). In playing stringed instruments, **spiccato*.

pied (Fr.). 'Foot', as in organ stops, etc.

pieno, piena (It.). 'Full'; *organo pieno*, 'full organ'; *coro pieno*, 'full choir' (as opposed to passages for soloists); *a voce piena*, 'with full voice'. *See also* RIPIENO.

pietoso (It.). 'Pitifully', i.e. tenderly.

pincé (Fr., 'pinched'). **1.** An occasional term for *pizzicato. **2.** An old term for the *mordent; *pincé renversé*, a *trill; *pincé étouffé*, an *acciaccatura. **3.** *Vibrato.

piqué (Fr., 'pricked'). In playing stringed instruments, **spiccato*; an indication in French Baroque music that a passage of even notes should be played in dotted rhythm.

pitch. A basic dimension of musical sounds, in which they are heard to be high or low. The subjective sense of pitch is closely correlated with frequency. The measurement of frequency is in cycles per second, or Hertz (Hz). Frequency is a 'ratio' scale of measurement: each time the pitch goes up by an octave, the frequency is doubled. Thus if c' is 256 Hz, c'' is 512 Hz. Another means of measuring pitch is 'arithmetical', and simply divides the octave into 1200 equal parts called 'cents' (100 per equal-tempered semitone).

The present International Standard Pitch, a' = 440 Hz, was agreed in 1939 and renewed and extended in 1960. Before that the general standard (*diapason normal*), was 435, a fifth of a semitone lower, except in Britain where it was 439, virtually the same as the modern. There is a tendency for pitch to rise very gradually with the passage of time. From *c.*1740 to 1820 concert pitches lay within the region of a' = 420–8 (i.e. about a quarter-tone below the present 440). This was the German *Cammerton* ('concert pitch').

pitch aggregate. A collection of pitches, whether or not they are sounded simultaneously.

pitch class. The property held in common by all pitches with the same name; thus middle C and every other C can be said to be a member of the pitch class C.

più (It.). 'More'; *più forte*, 'louder'; *più allegro*, 'faster', etc.

piuttosto (It.). 'Rather'; *piuttosto allegro*, 'rather fast'.

piva (It.). A 15th-century Italian couple dance, with improvisation by the male partner; it could be part of a **ballo*. The *piva* was also a basic step in Renaissance dance and the fastest of the four *misure* (metres with characteristic tempos and movement), the others being the saltarello, quadernaria, and bassadanza. (A *piva* is also an Italian bagpipe.)

pivot chord. In the process of *modulation, a chord that has a particular harmonic function in the initial key but a different function in the second key; the harmony following the pivot chord is in the new key.

pizzicato (It.). 'Plucked'; usually abbreviated in printed music to 'pizz.'. A technique, used most often on stringed instruments (usually of the violin family), in which the strings are made to vibrate by being grasped by the fingers of the right hand rather than bowed. The action usually takes place towards the end of the fingerboard, or just beyond it. The effect is possible with single notes, or with a number in quick succession, as a variant of *double stopping or multiple *stopping. Many other varieties of pizzicato are found, such as left-hand pizzicato; the 'snap' pizzicato (where the string is pulled upwards and allowed to snap against the fingerboard) indicated by the sign ⌽; and the pizzicato slide, in which the left hand slides up or down the string after the string has been plucked, producing a range of notes which sound as the string continues to vibrate.

Pk (Ger.). **1.** Abbreviation for *Pauken*, 'timpani'. **2.** In organ music, the abbreviation for *Pedalkoppel*.

placido (It.). 'Placid', 'tranquil'.

placito (It.). 'Judgment'; *a bene placito*, 'at one's own judgment', i.e. *ad *libitum*.

plagal cadence. *See* CADENCE.

plainchant [plainsong]. The monophonic and, according to ancient tradition, unaccompanied music of Eastern and Western Christian liturgy. In its final form it was called Gregorian chant. The term derives from *cantus planus*, in contrast to *cantus figuratus* ('florid chant', in which a counterpoint is added to the original melody) or *cantus mensuratus* ('measured chant', i.e. with a regular rhythm). The plainchant repertory is by far the earliest and largest to have been codified from oral traditions. Each melody consists of a single unaccompanied vocal line, notated on a four-line staff using neumatic *notation. The rhythm is free, following the prose of the psalm, prayer, etc. being chanted. Psalms chanted by a large community use simple melodic formulas, while those sung by soloists or trained choirs are more ornate. In antiphonal psalmody, as distinct from *responsorial psalmody, the text is chanted by alternating groups with one or more refrains (*antiphona*) after each verse. *See also* SEQUENCE, 2; TROPE.

plainchant mass. Either a mass in plainchant or a polyphonic mass composition in which each movement is based on the corresponding item of the plainchant. The term is sometimes broadened to include a mass using any item of plainchant as a cantus firmus.

plainsong. *See* PLAINCHANT.

plainte (Fr., 'complaint'). A mournful piece lamenting a death or some other unhappy occurrence. The term was used in the 17th and 18th centuries for some keyboard works.

plaisanterie (Fr.). A light movement—not a dance—in an 18th-century suite.

planctus (Lat., 'lament', 'plaint'; Provençal: *planh*). A medieval lament form (widespread from about the 9th to the 15th centuries), with either a Latin or a vernacular text.

planh (Provençal, 'lament'). *See* PLANCTUS.

plaqué (Fr.). 'Laid down': an instruction that the notes of a chord should be played simultaneously rather than as an *arpeggio.

plenary mass. An 'entire' mass composition, i.e. one comprising both the Ordinary and the Proper of the Mass. Such a work is rarely composed (except in the case of the *Requiem), for reasons of economy, since the Proper varies for particular festivals and occasions whereas the Ordinary remains the same.

plica (Lat., 'fold'). A term used in the medieval period for a *liquescent neume.

plötzlich (Ger.). 'Suddenly'.

plus (Fr.). 'More'.

pneuma. *See* NEUMA.

pocket score. *See* MINIATURE SCORE.

poco (It.). 'A little', 'rather'; *un poco*, 'a little'; *poco a poco*, 'little by little'; *poco lento*, 'rather slow'; *fra poco*, 'shortly'; *pochetto*, *pochettino*, 'very little'; *pochissimo*, 'the least possible'.

poem. A designation given to an orchestral piece, usually in one movement, with a strong programmatic element. The term was particularly common during the latter half of the 19th century and the early 20th, appearing most frequently in the descriptions *symphonic poem and tone-poem.

poème symphonique (Fr.; It.: *poema sinfonica*). *'Symphonic poem'.

poi (It.). 'Then'; e.g. *poi la coda*, 'then (play) the coda'.

point. **1.** A 'point of imitation' is a melodic motif taken as a subject for imitation. **2.** *See* DOT, 2. **3.** On a stringed instrument, the opposite end to the heel of the bow.

point d'orgue (Fr.). **1.** The *pause sign. **2.** A harmonic pedal; *see* PEDAL POINT. **3.** A cadenza in a concerto, probably so called because cadenzas were generally indicated by pause signs.

pointé (Fr.). 'Pointed', 'detached', i.e. not **legato*.

pointe d'archet, à la (Fr.). In string playing, an instruction to play 'at the point of the bow'.

pointillism. A compositional technique, named after Georges Seurat's method of painting with tiny dots of colour, in which each note has a distinct quality of timbre, loudness, etc. Sometimes pointillism is a by-product of advanced *serial procedures.

pointing. In *Anglican chant, the marking of texts with signs to show changes of melodic direction.

polacca (It.). *See* POLONAISE.

polka. A ballroom dance that became especially popular during the 19th century. Originally a peasant round dance from Bohemia, it was adopted in Prague in the late 1830s and soon spread throughout Europe. It was a lively couple dance in 2/4 time, generally in ternary form with regular phrases, and was characterized by short rapid steps for the first beat and a half of the bar, followed by a pause or hop. In Vienna during the 1850s several distinct types came into being, including the *schnell-Polka*, a particularly fast and lively variety similar to the galop; the *polka française*, a slower and more graceful version; and the polka-mazurka, in 3/4 time. All the leading dance composers of the mid-19th century wrote polkas, especially the Strauss family and Adolphe Jullien.

polonaise (Fr., 'Polish'; Ger.: *Polonäise*; It.: *polacca*). A Polish dance in triple time and of moderate speed. It originated in courtly 16th-century ceremonies. It is characterized by triple time, phrases starting on the first beat of the bar, the repetition of short, rhythmic motifs, and a cadence on the third beat of the bar. There are many 18th-century examples but the genre was most popular in the 19th century, when it became a virtuoso concert piece for piano. The composer most associated with it is Chopin. The polonaise was included in several dance scenes in opera.

polychoral. A term applied to music composed for two or more choirs, usually positioned to emphasize an element of contrast or *antiphony.

polychord. A chord made up of two or more simpler chords, e.g. triads.

polymetre. The simultaneous use of two or more metres; occasionally the term is used for the successive use of different metres in one or more parts. It is a characteristic feature of some 14th-century music, but then died out. Polymetre became prevalent in much music of the 20th and 21st centuries.

polyphony (from Gk. *polyphonia*, 'of many sounds'; Ger.: *Mehrstimmigkeit, Vielstimmigkeit*). Musical texture in two or more (though usually at least three) relatively independent parts. The term is generally applied to vocal music, but its usages are many and varied in the history of Western art and folk music and in ethnomusicology. Polyphony, in the sense of vocal music in more than one part, as opposed to *monophony, developed between the 10th and 13th centuries. The earliest manifestation was *organum. In the 14th century there was a rapid development of this rudimentary polyphony, as the independence of the parts grew; the three or four parts would often sing different texts together, in both Latin and the vernacular. A particular meaning of the term 'polyphony' is reserved for 16th-century sacred music, the 'golden age' of polyphony, epitomized in the music of Palestrina.

polyrhythm. Simultaneous use of different rhythms in separate parts of the musical texture. It is a characteristic feature of some 14th-century music, and also of some 20th-century pieces.

polytextuality. Simultaneous use of different texts in the various parts of a vocal composition. It was particularly common in the early *motet.

polytonality. Simultaneous use of two or more keys. If two keys are superposed the technique is known as *bitonality; more complex combinations are rare.

portamento (It., 'carriage'). **1.** The process of gliding from one note to another through all intermediate pitches. Its use is widespread in string, vocal, and trombone technique. As an expressive device by which instrumentalists might emulate the inflections of the voice it was used extensively in the 19th and early 20th centuries, particularly by violinists. **2.** A synonym for *appoggiatura.

portato (It.). 'Carried'; a kind of bowstroke between *legato* and *staccato*.

port de voix (Fr., 'carriage of the voice'). *See* PORTAMENTO, 1.

Pos. (Ger.). Abbreviation for *Posaune*, 'trombone'.

position (Eng., Fr.; It.: *posizione*). **1.** In the playing of stringed instruments the left hand is moved continually so that the fingers may fall onto a different set of points on the fingerboard, thus producing a different set of notes. Each of these locations is called a 'position' ('first position', 'second position', etc.). The movement of the left hand is termed 'shift' (It.: *manica*). **2.** Chords may be described as being in 'close' or 'open' position, depending on their layout. A chord of C major written as in Ex. 1*a* would be described as being in 'close' position, while one notated as in Ex. 1*b* would be in 'open' position.

Ex. 1

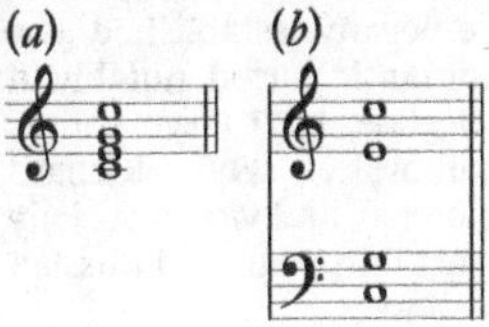

(*a*) (*b*)

postlude (Lat.: *postludium*; Ger.: *Nachspiel*). The converse of a *prelude, i.e. a composition played as an afterpiece. Many lieder end with an extended section for piano alone, referred to as a postlude, 'commenting' on the emotions expressed in the song's text. In organ music, the postlude is the voluntary concluding a church service. *See also* CODA.

postmodernism. A response or antidote to *modernism, whose commitment to the new is replaced by a concern with the old. Postmodernism originated as a term in the 1980s, when many younger composers were contradicting their revolutionary elders by turning to the past for styles, quotations, and other points of departure.

potpourri (Fr., 'rotten pot', 'stew'). A composition that consists of a string of pre-existing tunes. In the early 18th century the term was applied to collections of songs assembled for performance on stage. Later that century it denoted an instrumental arrangement of opera tunes. *See also* MEDLEY; QUODLIBET.

poussé (Fr.). 'Pushed': in string playing, the up-bow.

pp, ppp. Abbreviations for **pianissimo*.

praeambulum (Lat.). *'Prelude'.

praeludium (Lat.). *'Prelude'.

Pralltriller (Ger., 'tight (or compact) trill'). **1.** In modern German terminology, the inverted *mordent. **2.** Until *c*.1800, a rapid *trill of four notes, beginning on the upper note of a descending 2nd. It was usually indicated with the sign now used for the inverted mordent. In extremely quick passages the two ornaments sound almost identical, since there is not time to sound the first note of the *Pralltriller*, and it must be omitted, or tied to the preceding main note.

precentor. A term (dating back at least as far as the 4th century) meaning 'first singer'; it is attached to the official in charge of the singing in a cathedral or monastic establishment or a church (the equivalent of the cantor in a synagogue).

precipitato (It.). 'Hurried'.

preghiera (It., 'prayer'; Fr.: *prière*; Ger.: *Gebet*). A solo aria or chorus in which the singer or singers pray to God or supernatural powers for salvation from impending danger. The 'preghiera' scene became a feature of 19th-century Italian opera.

prelude (from Lat. *praeludium*, 'something played before'; Fr.: *prélude*; Ger.: *Vorspiel*; It.: *preludio*). A comparatively brief instrumental composition intended as an introduction to something further, e.g. a fugue. The term is often used for the overture or introductory scene of an opera. It also refers to a genre of music for soloistic instruments, especially the keyboard. An improvisatory style is central to the prelude throughout its history. In the 16th century works called 'prelude' or 'ricercar' became separated from their introductory function, and to a large extent became difficult to distinguish from other genres such as the *fantasia and the *toccata. The *prélude non mesuré*, in which pitch was fully specified but rhythm and metre were only minimally notated, was cultivated in 17th-century France. In the hands of Chopin and his followers the prelude was developed as an independent character piece for piano, exploring a particular expressive mood or technical device. *See also* CHORALE PRELUDE.

prélude non mesuré. *See* PRELUDE.

prendere (It.), **prendre** (Fr.). 'Take up', i.e. prepare to play; *prendere il flauto*, take up the flute (after a passage for piccolo).

preparation. The introduction of a pitch as a consonance immediately preceding its statement as a dissonance, especially as part of a *suspension.

près (Fr.). 'Near'; e.g. *près de la touche*, 'near the fingerboard' of a stringed instrument.

pressante (It.), **en pressant** (Fr.). 'Hurrying'.

presto (It.). 'Quick', i.e. faster than **allegro*; *prestissimo*, 'very quick'.

prick-song. 'To prick' is an obsolete English verb meaning 'to mark', and thus 'prick-song' came in the 15th and 16th centuries to be applied to music that was written down, or notated, as opposed to extemporized.

prima pratica, seconda pratica (It.). Terms used in the early 17th century to describe two different 'practices' in music. In the *prima pratica* as exemplified in the works of such composers as Josquin, the perfection of the part-writing was more important than the expression of the words; in the *seconda pratica*, in works by Gesualdo, Marenzio, etc., irregular harmonies, intervals, and melodic progressions were used to convey the meaning of the text.

prima volta (It.). 'First-time (bar)'; *see* DOUBLE BAR.

prime. A term with several applications: (*a*) the lower of two notes forming an interval; (*b*) the generator of a series of harmonics; (*c*) the root of a chord; (*d*) a unison; (*e*) the first note of a scale; and (*f*) the interval formed by two notes written on the same line or space, e.g. F and F♯.

Primgeiger (Ger.). The *leader of an orchestra or its principal first violin.

profondo (It., 'low', 'deep'). *See* BASSO PROFONDO.

programme music. Music which expresses an extra-musical idea, whether of mood, narrative, literary, or pictorial image, as opposed to *'absolute music'. The term originated with Liszt, but there are examples of such illustrative music from earlier periods. Programme music became established as a genre in the Romantic period, notably in the music of Berlioz, Liszt (*symphonic poems), Tchaikovsky, and Richard Strauss (tone-poems), and was especially popular with east European and Russian nationalist composers.

programme symphony. A work that matches a narrative or descriptive programme to symphonic form. *See* PROGRAMME MUSIC.

progression. In harmonic theory, the movement of one note to another or of one chord to another. The term is frequently encountered as 'cadential progression', describing typical ways of leading up to a *cadence.

prolation (from medieval Lat. *prolatio*, 'bearing', 'manner'). In early musical notation the term usually referred to the relationship between the minim and the semibreve. If prolation was 'major' there would be three minims in the semibreve, if 'minor', two.

pronto (It.). 'Quick'; *prontamente*, 'quickly'.

Proper of the Mass. The sections of the Mass whose texts change according to the church calendar; *see* MASS.

proportion. In mensural notation (*see* MENSURAL MUSIC, MENSURAL NOTATION), a ratio expressing the relationship between the note-values following that ratio and those preceding it, or between the note-values of a passage or work and an assumed normal relationship of note-values to the metrical pulse (*tactus*).

prosa (Lat.), **prose** (Fr.). The medieval name for the text of a *sequence, applied also to the sequence with its melody or, occasionally, to *prosulas.

prosula (Lat.). Diminutive of **prosa*, referring to the addition in medieval manuscripts of new words to the *melismas of offertories, alleluias, and other pre-existing chants of the Roman rite. *See* TROPE.

protus. *See* MODE.

Ps. 1. (Ger.). Abbreviation for *Posaunen*, 'trombones'. **2.** Abbreviation for 'Psalm'.

psalm (from Gk. *psalmos*). A sacred song, specifically one found in the Old Testament book of Psalms. They have been sung in various ways in the Jewish and Christian traditions. *See* ANGLICAN CHANT; FALSOBORDONE; PLAINCHANT.

psalmody. The practice of singing psalms and other forms of chant in the Jewish and Christian liturgical traditions, according to the metrical *psalter. By extension, the performance of any concerted sacred vocal music, whether for worship or recreation.

psalm tones. Plainchant recitation formulas for the psalms; *see* TONUS, 3.

psalter. A translation of the 150 Hebrew biblical psalms arranged for Christian liturgical or devotional use.

psaume (Fr.). *'Psalm'.

pulse. A term sometimes used as a synonym for 'beat', but a distinction is occasionally made: for example, 6/8 time may be said to have six 'pulses' but only two 'beats'.

punta, punto (It.). 'Point'; *a punta d'arco*, 'with the tip (point) of the bow'.

punteado (Sp.; Fr.: *pincé*; It.: *pizzicato*). A term used mainly with reference to Baroque guitar technique, denoting the 'plucking' of individual strings with the fingertips, as distinct from **rasgueado*, or strumming.

puy (Fr.). A name given to medieval French musical or literary societies, or guilds, that flourished in northern France up to the early 17th century. Their roots sprang from the *troubadour tradition, and they held annual song or poetry competitions (also known as *puys*) originally dedicated to the Virgin Mary.

Pythagorean intonation. A system of tuning in which the 4ths and 5ths are untempered. It is named after the Ancient Greek philosopher Pythagoras, whose calculations of intervals in terms of string-length ratios (octave = 2:1, 5th = 3:2, etc.) formed the basis of much medieval and Renaissance theory. A distinguishing feature of Pythagorean intonation is that the major 2nds and 3rds are larger, and the minor 2nds and 3rds smaller, than those of other tuning systems.

Quadrat (Ger.). The natural sign (*see* NATURAL, 2).

quadrille. A square dance that became popular in France during the reign of Napoleon I and arrived in England *c.*1815. It consists of a group of five dances, each of 32 bars, of different rhythms and tempos, originally using folk tunes but later using arrangements of popular songs and operatic arias.

quadruple concerto. A concerto for four solo instruments and orchestra or other instrumental ensemble.

quadruplet. A term for four notes that are to be performed in the time of three; they are indicated by the figure '4' placed above or below the four notes (*see* Ex. 1).

Ex. 1

4

quadruple time. *See* TIME SIGNATURE.

quartal harmony. Harmony based on chords built up from 4ths. Such chords are more dissonant than those built from 3rds and are more difficult to classify in relation to particular harmonic functions. They are found mostly in early 20th-century works and in post-tonal music.

quarter-note (Amer.). *Crotchet.

quarter-tone. Interval of a quarter of a tone, i.e. half a semitone. *See also* MICROTONE.

quartet (Fr.: *quatuor*; Ger.: *Quartett*; It.: *quartetto*). An ensemble of four singers or instrumentalists, or music written for it. The quartet normally consists either of voices or of families of like instruments (e.g. recorders, woodwinds, or the string quartet of two violins, viola, and cello) in graduated sizes covering the soprano, alto, tenor, and bass (SATB) ranges. In other groups (piano quartet, flute quartet, oboe quartet, etc.) one of the violins of the string quartet is replaced by the named instrument.

quasi (It.). 'As if', 'almost'.

quatreble. In medieval vocal music, a voice part pitched at a fixed interval above the treble. The name derives from a conflation of 'quadruple' and 'treble', denoting a fourth voice part added above the triplum, or treble.

quaver (♪). The note having an eighth of the value of the semibreve or whole note; hence the American usage 'eighth-note'.

quilt canzona. A rare type of *canzona in which short, sharply contrasting sections follow each other in quick succession, as in a patched piece of fabric.

quinte (Fr., 'fifth'). A term used for the fifth part of a string ensemble in 17th-century France. By extension, the instrument playing that part—usually the first viola—also became known as the *quinte*.

quintet. An ensemble of five singers or instrumentalists, or music written for it. Vocal quintets usually consist of soprano, alto, tenor, and bass (SATB) with either a second soprano or a second tenor. String quintets usually consist of a string *quartet with a second viola. A piano (or clarinet, etc.) quintet is usually a string quartet supplemented by the named instrument. The wind quintet consists of flute, oboe, clarinet, horn, and bassoon.

quintuplet. A term for five notes that are to be performed in the time of four or of three; they are indicated by the figure

Quintuplet, Ex. 1

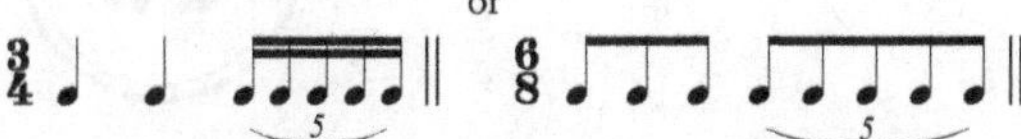

'5' placed above or below the five notes (see Ex. 1).

quintuple time. *See* TIME SIGNATURE.

quire. An obsolete spelling of 'choir'.

quodlibet (Lat., 'what you will'). A piece of music in which well-known tunes or texts (or both) are quoted, either simultaneously or in succession, generally for humorous effect.

rabbia, con (It.). 'With rage', i.e. furiously.

raddolcendo (It.). 'Becoming softer, sweeter'.

raddoppiare (It.). 'To double'; *raddoppiato*, 'doubled', *raddoppiamento*, 'doubling'.

radical cadence. *See* CADENCE.

raffrenando (It.). 'Slowing down'.

ralentir (Fr.). 'To slow down'.

rallentando (It.). 'Becoming slower'; it is often abbreviated *rall.*

ranz des vaches (Fr.; Ger.: *Kuhreigen*, *Kuhreihen*). A Swiss mountain melody sung or played on the alphorn by herdsmen to call their cows in. Every district has its own version, the most celebrated being that of the district of Gruyère. The *ranz des vaches* has been introduced into various orchestral works and operas.

rapsodia (It.), **rapsodie** (Fr.). 'Rhapsody'.

rasch (Ger.). 'Quick'; *rascher*, 'quicker'; *sehr rasch*, 'very quick'.

r

rasgueado (Sp.; Fr.: *batterie*; It.: *battute*). A term used mainly with reference to Baroque guitar technique, denoting the 'strumming' of several strings, either upwards with the fingertips or downwards with the back of the fingernails, as distinct from **punteado*, or plucking.

rastrology. The study of the use of the rastrum (Lat., 'rake'), a pen with several nibs designed to rule staves for music manuscripts. Evidence from rastrology can be used to determine the origins of a manuscript.

ratamacue. A rudimentary side-drum technique consisting of a pair of short strokes and a triplet preceding the main note, played LLRLRL or RRLRLR.

rattenendo, rattenuto (It.). 'Holding back', 'held back'.

ravvivando (It.). 'Quickening'.

ray. *See* RE.

re [ray]. The second degree of the scale in the *solmization system. In French (*ré*) and Italian usage it has become attached, on the fixed-*doh* principle, to the note D, in whichever scale it occurs. *See* TONIC SOL-FA.

real answer. *See* FUGUE.

realize. To improvise or compose an accompaniment over a bass line, with or without the aid of *figured-bass notation. For several centuries until the early 19th it was the task of players of keyboard, plucked, bowed bass, and sometimes even treble instruments to realize accompaniments in different styles according to context. These might include arpeggiated and non-arpeggiated chords of varying texture and rhythms, as well as melodic and ornamental figurations supplementing the upper parts.

A 'realization' is also a version by a modern scholar or composer of an older work in which the original skeletal indications are filled out to provide a fully notated and harmonized score for performance.

real sequence. *See* SEQUENCE, 1.

recapitulation. In *sonata form, the final section of the movement, in which the thematic material of the exposition is restated in such as way as to end in the tonic.

recit. Abbreviation for *recitative.

recital. A concert given by one performer or a small group. The term first gained currency in the mid-19th century. It was initially reserved for a solo performance (or accompanied solo), but it can now refer to various sorts of chamber or song programme, public or private. *See also* CONCERT.

recitative (from It. *recitativo*). A form of speech-like solo singing, free in rhythm and lacking in structured melodies. It was invented in Italy shortly before 1600 as a way for music to be more subservient to the text; basso *continuo, or *figured bass, was the means by which the accompaniment could follow a singer's spontaneous expression in the absence of a strict beat. In early 17th-century opera, recitative was the principal mode of expression and was often freely mixed with short passages of *arioso. Towards 1700, with the development of *opera seria*, it became more standardized, with predictable melodic patterns and set cadences. The more important dialogues and soliloquies were often accompanied by the orchestra: this was called *recitativo stromentato* (It., 'orchestrated recitative', also called *recitativo accompagnato*, 'accompanied recitative'), in contrast to *recitativo secco* ('plain recitative'), the more usual type with continuo accompaniment only. Now clearly separated from the more static and melodious *aria, recitative in *opera seria* lasted until the mid-19th century, and was imitated in the serious opera of other languages. In *opera buffa* it became a rapid-fire, light dialogue which was primarily a vehicle for the complex stage business. Recitative was also a feature of oratorios, cantatas, Passion settings, and anthems, and was sometimes imitated in instrumental music. It died out in the 19th century.

reciting tone. In plainchant, a melodic formula of varying complexity (though usually rather simple) used for the recitation by verse of psalms, canticles, lessons, and other liturgical texts.

recueilli (Fr.). 'Meditative', 'contemplative'.

redoute (Fr.). *See* RIDOTTO, 2.

reduction. *Arrangement. The term is most commonly used of a piano arrangement (for rehearsal purposes) of the accompaniment to a work for one or more soloists, or chorus, with orchestra or other instrumental ensemble.

reel. An ancient Scottish dance, in 2/2, 2/4, or 6/8 time divided into clear eight-bar sections.

refrain. A term originating in poetry, where it describes a recurrent phrase in the text, which can be applied to music in various ways: in song it can refer to a section of recurrent text, usually with the same music; in instrumental music it refers to recurrent sections of a piece. The repertory with which it is most commonly associated is that of 12th- to 14th-century French song, where refrains may be found in courtly *romances*, dance-songs (*caroles*), and plays; they are also found incorporated into polyphonic motets. The *rondeau*, *virelai*, and *ballade* have refrains as part of the poetic structure of their texts; these are distinct, though related. Some other forms give their refrains specific names; the refrain of a medieval carol, for instance, is known as a 'burden'. In modern times, a refrain is often synonymous with 'chorus', because it is usually sung by a group as opposed to a soloist.

registration. In keyboard playing, the selection of manuals or stops to enhance tone-colour, timbre, and volume.

Reigen (Ger., 'dance'). A term found in such titles as *Gnomenreigen* and in *Kuhreigen* (*see* RANZ DES VACHES).

Reigenlied (Ger.). A medieval round-dance song, characterized by triple metre, repeated notes, and phrase repetition, celebrating the vitality of springtime.

réjouissance (Fr.). 'Rejoicing', 'celebration'. Bach, Handel, and others used it as the title of a lively movement.

related keys. In harmonic theory, keys seen in terms of their 'relationship' to the tonic. For example, in C major the closest related keys are the dominant major (G), the mediant minor (E), the subdominant major (F), the supertonic minor (D), and the relative minor (A). The first four of these keys have a difference in key signature from C major of only one sharp or flat and the last has the same key signature as C major. *See also* CIRCLE OF FIFTHS; MODULATION.

relative major, relative minor. *See* KEY SIGNATURE.

relish. English name for an ornament used in instrumental music of the 17th and early 18th centuries. A single relish (usually indicated thus: .˙.) was simply a short *trill with a turn, but a double relish was more complex, consisting usually of a trill on each of two successive notes, closing with a turn and an appoggiatura; it was indicated by a cluster of dots (e.g. :˙:), or by two such clusters separated by two diagonal strokes (⑊).

remettre (Fr.). 'To put back': an instruction in French organ music to take off a stop.

reminiscence motif (Ger.: *Reminiszenzmotiv*, *Erinnerungsmotiv*). In opera, a theme or other musical idea which returns in an unaltered state to identify a character or signify a character's recollection of the past; it is a precursor of the *leitmotif.

Renaissance. A term applied to the period from *c.*1430 to the end of the 16th century, an era of 'rebirth' during which artists, writers, and musicians were adopting a new set of aesthetic and philosophical ideas derived from the ancient, classical world. This movement coincided with the beginnings of humanism. The relationship between words and music was central to Renaissance composers: textual intelligibility and vivid imagery (*word-painting) were paramount. The *chanson, *madrigal, *mass, and *motet epitomized the era, in which smooth, homogeneous, imitative polyphony was predominant. It was at this time that opera developed, out of the activities of the Florentine Camerata, and that the invention of printing allowed music to be published and thus disseminated more widely. The Renaissance was succeeded by the *Baroque era. *See also* PRIMA PRATICA, SECONDA PRATICA.

renforcer (Fr.). 'To reinforce', i.e. make louder.

repeat. The sign (:‖) that appears at the end of a piece or section of music to indicate a return to the opening. If there is a reversed sign (‖:) at the beginning of a section of music, the repeat sign at the end indicates a return to that sign only, not to the beginning of the piece. *See also* DA CAPO.

répétiteur (Fr.; It.: *repetitore*; Ger.: *Repetitor*). One who coaches the singers or instrumentalists, or both, in an opera house.

répétition (Fr.). 'Rehearsal'.

repiano. A corruption of *ripieno.

replica (It.). *'Repeat', 'repetition'; *senza replica*, without repeat, e.g. when a minuet or similar piece is played **da capo*.

reprise (Fr.). 'Repeat'. A return to a first section of music after an intervening and contrasting section; the repeat can be exact or varied. In 17th- and 18th-century French harpsichord music, 'reprise' indicates the point to which the performer should return (e.g. at the beginning of the second section in binary form movements and at the head of the refrain in a *rondeau*).

Requiem Mass (Fr.: *Messe des morts*; Ger.: *Totenmesse*; It.: *Messa per i defunti*; Lat.: *Missa pro defunctis*). The votive Mass for the dead of the Roman rite, the Tridentine version of which begins with the introit 'Requiem aeternam dona eis Domine' ('Give them eternal rest, O Lord'). Its format is basically identical with that of the normal Latin *Mass, but with the more joyful parts omitted (e.g. the alleluia, which is replaced by a tract, and the Credo) and the long 13th-century sequence *Dies irae* ('Day of wrath', suppressed after the Second Vatican Council) interpolated. Certain small changes occur in the text of some sections—for example, in the Agnus Dei the words 'Dona eis requiem' ('Give them rest') replace 'Miserere nobis' ('Have mercy upon us'). Liturgically the Requiem Mass has its place at funerals and memorial services and on All Souls' Day (2 November).

There are many musical settings, the earliest complete ones dating from the 15th century. Renaissance settings stylistically resemble those of the normal Mass, but favour the conservative compositional devices of cantus firmus and plainchant paraphrase over *parody. Numerous requiems were composed in the 17th and 18th centuries. Mozart's unfinished setting (1791) is the first large-scale one, with orchestra, intended for non-liturgical use. Of the 19th-century requiems, two stand out for their highly dramatic, quasi-operatic treatment: Berlioz's (*Grande Messe des morts*, 1837) and Verdi's (1874). Fauré's setting has gained a similar niche in the concert repertory, as has Britten's *War Requiem* (with settings of poems by Wilfred Owen interpolated in the text; 1961). Schütz's *Musikalische Exequien* (1636) and Brahms's *A German Requiem* (1865–8) are large-scale Protestant memorial works.

rescue opera. An opera in which an essential part of the plot turns on the rescue of the hero or heroine from prison or some other threatening situation. Beethoven's *Fidelio* (1805) is the best-known example. Most are from the second half of the 18th century, particularly during the period of the French Revolution.

resolution. The process by which dissonant elements in intervals move to consonant ones, ensuring closure. In counterpoint a resolution converts a dissonant configuration (e.g. a *suspension) into a consonance. *See* CADENCE.

resoluto, risoluto (It.). 'Resolute'.

respond (Lat.: *responsa*). **1.** An alternative name for *responsory or *response. **2.** More specifically, the section sung by the choir or congregation in responsorial chant (*see* RESPONSORY). The responds, alternating with the verse or verses, are usually marked R or ℟.

response. In Christian worship, the reply of the congregation or choir to a versicle (a short sentence said or sung by the priest). In Elizabethan times English composers made choral settings of the responses.

responsorial psalmody. The ancient practice of performing a psalm text with a congregational or choral refrain after each verse.

responsory (from Lat. *responsorium*). A type of Western liturgical chant, consisting in the responsories of the Roman Office of alternating respond and verse, especially the great responsories (Lat.: *responsoria prolixa*) of Matins and the lesser responsories (Lat.: *responsoria brevia*) of the daytime Hours. The term is sometimes used broadly to encompass other responsorial chants, including those of the Roman Mass. Polyphonic settings of the responsories maintained the principle of alternation. Many continental settings are through-composed in ABCB form. By the 16th century, texts were often set as elaborate motets. Responsories continued to be composed into the 18th century.

rest. In musical notation, a sign indicating a momentary absence of sound. Every standard note-value has a corresponding rest which, like the note itself, may be lengthened in value by the addition of a *dot or dots. Ex. 1 shows the common forms of rest. A whole bar's silence in any time signature is traditionally indicated by a semibreve rest (Ex. 1*b*). In individual instrumental parts two bars' rest may occasionally be indicated by a breve rest with a figure '2' above it (Ex. 2*a*), but more extensive periods of silence are normally represented by a horizontal line with a figure above it showing the number of bars' rest (Ex. 2*b*). *See also* GENERALPAUSE; PAUSE, 2; TACET.

r

Rest, Ex. 1

Ex. 2

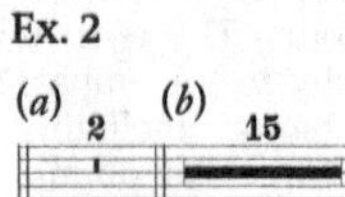

restringendo (It.). 'Becoming faster'.

retardando (It.). *See* RITARDANDO.

retardation. A *suspension resolved by rising a degree rather than falling.

retenant, retenu (Fr.). 'Holding back', 'held back', i.e. slowing down, but immediately, like **ritenuto*, rather than gradually like **rallentando*.

retirada (It.). In 17th-century ballets and suites, a closing movement.

retrograde [cancrizans (Lat., 'crab-like'), *Krebsgang* (Ger., 'crab motion')]. The backward-read version of a melody or, in serial music, of a series (i.e. the form obtained by reading the original from right to left; *see* SERIALISM). As serial music allows any note in the series to be placed at any octave level, the retrograde form of a serial melody need not give rise to a reversal of melodic contour.

retrograde canon. *See* CANON.

retrograde inversion. A version of a melody or series that is both inverted and reversed (*see* INVERSION, 3; RETROGRADE).

réunis (Fr.). **1.** 'United', 'reunited', e.g. in string playing to countermand *divisés*, 'divided'. **2.** In organ music, 'coupled'. **3.** In 18th-century French music, the term *les goûts réunis* ('reunion of tastes') was used to describe an ideal kind of music towards which composers should strive—the union of the best elements of French and Italian music, as opposed to the specifically French style adopted by the followers of Lully.

reveille (from Fr. *réveil*, 'awakening'). The military signal (pronounced 'revelly' or 'revally' by the British) that begins the day in the army.

revue. A theatrical entertainment consisting of songs and sketches, usually of a satirical nature: a variety show with an intellectual flavour. A revue is usually a miscellany by many hands. It was of French origin and became popular *c.*1840. A similar entertainment flourished in England a few years later. Modern revue has followed two courses: the 'intimate' revue (as above), with a small cast and nearly always satirical content; and the lavish spectacular, glorifying song and dance and visual effects.

rf, rfz. Abbreviations for **rinforzando*.

R.H. Abbreviation for right hand, *rechte Hand* (Ger.).

rhapsody (from Gk. *rhapsodia*; Fr.: *rapsodie, rhapsodie*; Ger.: *Rhapsodie*; It.: *rapsodia*). An instrumental piece in one movement, often based on popular, national, or folk melodies. The term (which in Ancient Greece denoted the recitation of epic poetry, especially that of Homer) was first used by Tomášek, as a title for a set of six piano pieces (*c.*1803). Rhapsodies may be passionate, nostalgic, or improvisatory. 19th-century interest in Hungarian and Gypsy violin playing led to the composition of pieces in that style, for example by Liszt.

rhetoric. Originally a term referring to the skills associated with public oratory, 'rhetoric' has come to mean the art of verbal discourse. There are obvious parallels between persuasive oratory and eloquent musical performance. Towards the end of the 15th century, new vernacular translations of classical texts on rhetoric had a profound effect on musicians. During the Baroque era rhetoric pervaded musical thought and practice: the ultimate goal of Baroque music was to move the listener to an idealized emotional state, and all elements of music were deployed in the service of affections (*see* AFFECTIONS, DOCTRINE OF).

rhythm. The perceptible organization of musical events in time, however flexible in metre and tempo, irregular in accent, or free in durational values. With melody and harmony, rhythm is one of the basic elements of music. It is an important element in melody, it influences harmonic progression, and it affects texture, timbre, and ornamentation. Many of the most common rhythmic patterns have been influenced by dance patterns. Rhythm is a compound of interdependent elements: a *metre, indicated by the time signature, which remains unchanged throughout, and which carries with it the implication that the strongest accents will normally fall on the first beat of the bar; a *pulse, or tempo, which also remains basically constant, and which relates to the time signature—it may be indicated by a metronome mark, a form of words, or by both; the durations used for the various musical events (minims, semiquavers, etc.), which combine to produce a rhythmic 'profile'; and the phrases that result from the arrangement of musical material in groups of beats and bars—bars tending, as here, to be grouped in multiples of two and four. These features of regularity and equality will naturally be modified at times by the use of syncopation, cross-accents, or those 'irrational' durational values which temporarily override the units indicated in the time signature, as well as by modifications of tempo—rubato, *accelerando*, or *ritardando*. But such deviations make their effect precisely because the music has its basis in equality and regularity. Most Western music up to the 20th century has a regular pulse, exceptions being plainchant and recitative.

rhythmic modes. In the 13th century, a set of six short rhythmic patterns defined by music theorists and associated particularly with the music of the Notre Dame school. In each mode, long and short values are arranged in a distinctive order similar to those of the poetic feet. *See* NOTATION.

ricercar (from It. *ricercare*, 'to seek'; Fr.: *recherché*; Ger.: *Ricercar*; Sp.: *recercada*). A type of instrumental piece common during the 16th and 17th centuries. The earliest were improvisatory in style, often for solo instruments such as the bass viol or lute. They consisted of highly embellished, unaccompanied melody, often containing many scalar passages, and were not very different from the early 16th-century *prelude. They usually lack a distinct shape and are seemingly designed as an exercise for the fingers (*see also* TIENTO; TOCCATA). The composers of these pieces were usually themselves virtuoso players or teachers, and they include the first writers of treatises on individual instruments.

Another type, which flourished late in the 16th century, was the duo, written for the instruction of beginners in part-music. The instruments are rarely specified, but the frequent use of themes based on easily remembered *solmization syllables suggests that they were exercises in sight-reading, perhaps for singers as well as instrumentalists. The best-known and most durable kind of ricercar was the instrumental equivalent of the vocal *motet. The earliest, dating from the mid-16th century, are conceived in the same tradition as polyphonic church music, with flowing melodic lines organized by imitative points. At first they were written mainly in four parts. The vogue for this kind of ricercar was at its height in the latter part of the 16th century, and by 1600 the genre was overtaken in popularity by the more tuneful *canzona. From about 1610, motet-like instrumental pieces are more often called 'sonata' and the term 'ricercar' tends to be associated with works that display some form of contrapuntal learnedness. In this sense, the word persisted until the end of the Baroque period.

ricochet (Fr., 'rebound'). A type of bowing applied to instruments of the violin family. The upper half of the bow is 'thrown' onto the string from a distance, causing it to bounce several times, resulting in a series of rapid staccato notes. The effect is a staple of 19th-century virtuoso technique. *See also* VOLANTE, 2.

ridotto (It.). **1.** 'Reduced', 'arranged'. **2.** A form of musical entertainment (Fr.: *redoute*) that was popular in the 18th century. It consisted of a selection of songs, followed by a ball in which the audience joined the performers.

riduzione (It.). *'Reduction', *'arrangement'.

rigaudon (Fr.). A 17th- and 18th-century dance in duple time, resembling the *bourrée. Like other French dances of folk origin (e.g. the *gavotte) it became more elegant when it was taken up in courtly circles, though it retained its liveliness. It was adopted into French stage works, especially *opéras-ballets*, and also became popular in Germany and England (where a variant in 6/8 came into being). In the mid-18th century it appeared as an optional dance in the *suite.

rigoroso (It.). 'Rigorous', i.e. in strict time.

rilasciando, rilasciante (It.). 'Releasing', i.e. getting gradually slower, the equivalent of **rallentando*.

rim shot. A side-drum technique involving the simultaneous striking of drumhead and rim to produce a gunshot-like sound.

rinforzando, rinforzato (It.). 'Reinforcing', 'reinforced': a stress or accent applied to individual notes or chords, similar to **sforzando*; it is sometimes abbreviated *rf* or *rfz*.

ripetizione (It.). 'Repetition', 'rehearsal'.

ripieno (It., 'filled'). A term used in Baroque music to denote the tutti (or concerto grosso), as opposed to the solo (or concertino) group in an orchestra. In vocal music, the concertino string group generally accompanied the arias, with the ripieno joining in for choruses. *Senza ripieno*, all players except those at the leading desks should be silent; *ripienista*, an orchestral player who is not a leader or a soloist. Various corruptions of the term have arisen, such as *ripiano* or *repiano* in brass or military band music, to denote players not at the leading desk. It is also the name of an organ stop.

riposato (It.). 'With repose'.

riprendere (It.). 'To resume', i.e. go back to the normal tempo.

ripresa (It.). *Reprise.

risoluto (It.). 'Resolute', 'energetic'.

rispetto (It.). A type of Italian poetry, also known as **strambotto*, with eight 11-syllable lines to the stanza, set by *frottola and madrigal composers.

risposta (It.). 'Answer' in *fugues.

rit. Abbreviation for **ritardando*.

ritardando, ritardato, ritenendo, ritenente (It.). 'Holding back', 'held back', i.e. becoming gradually slower, the same as **rallentando*; it is sometimes abbreviated *rit*.

ritenuto (It.). 'Held back', 'slower', i.e. slowing down, but immediately, rather than gradually like **rallentando*.

ritmo (It.). 'Rhythm'; *ritmico*, 'rhythmic'.

ritornello (It., dim. of *ritorno*, 'return'; Fr.: *ritournelle*; Ger.: *Ritornell*) [ritornel]. **1.** In the 14th-century **caccia* and *madrigal the ritornello was the concluding couplet of a poem; it was usually treated in musical settings as a separate section, often with a change of metre. It was not a refrain. **2.** In 17th-century operas and cantatas, the term came to be applied to the short instrumental conclusion added to an aria or other type of song. Sometimes the ritornello also occurred at the beginning. Apart from sinfonias, these ritornellos were the only instrumental portions of early operas. **3.** 'Ritornello form' is a term used to describe the first and often the last movements of the Baroque concerto, especially the concerto grosso. Such movements were characterized by the alternation and contrast between solo and tutti sections, the tuttis being based always on the same material. Thus these sections were equivalent to ritornellos.

ritournelle (Fr.). **1.** A 17th-century dance in quick triple time, found in the ballets of Lully. **2.** *See* RITORNELLO.

riverso, al (It.). 'Turned back', 'reversed'. The term is used both for inversion and for retrograde motion.

rococo (from Fr. *rocaille*, 'rockwork', and possibly *coquille*, 'shellwork'). A term used to describe a late 17th- and early 18th-century French style of decorative art and architecture characterized by delicacy, elegance, and wit, in contrast to the more severe lines of the *Baroque era. By analogy it has been loosely applied to the lighter, often small-scale French music of the period, notably the works of François Couperin. The style was widely imitated, particularly in southern Germany and Austria.

romance (Fr., Sp.; Ger.: *Romanze*; It.: *romanza*). **1.** In Spain, a form of long epic ballad dating back to at least the 14th century, when *romances* on legendary or historical subjects were sung for the entertainment of aristocratic patrons, usually by solo professional musicians. They were mostly for three or four voices but there are examples for solo voice with vihuela accompaniment. In the 17th century the genre became virtually synonymous with the *villancico, and in the 18th it expanded into a miniature cantata. Thereafter it survived in folk music. **2.** In France, the word acquired a musical connotation in the 18th century. It was an unpretentious strophic verse: a short, often tragic, love poem, the melody simple and unaffected, with unobtrusive instrumental support. Used extensively in France in the late 18th and early 19th centuries, especially in *opéra comique*, it had ousted the **air* before yielding in turn to the **mélodie*, which, however, bore a somewhat different meaning. The chief exponents of the French *romance* were lesser composers. The term became common as a title of 19th-century German songs. The typical *romance* of the salon or drawing-room, however, made little demand on the performers.

romance sans paroles. (Fr., 'song without words'.) A *character piece for piano, musically akin to the *nocturne.

romanesca (It.). A type of *ground bass, using a specific bass pattern and its associated harmony. Supposedly of Roman origin, it was especially popular from the mid-16th century to the mid-17th, and is found in both instrumental and vocal music.

Romanticism. In its original meaning, the word 'Romantic' derived from 'Romance', the ancient language of France, and hence the term applied to the poems or tales, characterized by imaginative adventurousness, that were typical of its literature. It was not until the 19th century that the word was needed to describe a new spirit which embraced the arts, philosophy, politics, and even the sciences. The age of Romanticism is now generally thought of as extending from the closing years of the 18th century to the early years of the 20th.

Romanticism emphasized the apparent domination of emotion over form and order: value was set on novelty and sensation, on technical innovation and experiment, and on the cross-fertilization of ideas from different disciplines. In music, Romantic ideas led to the cultivation of the *symphonic poem, the expressive miniature (e.g. the *nocturne) and the art song (e.g. the *lied); to works expressing national identity or exotic topics; and to large-scale opera, often featuring the supernatural, the fates of oppressed groups, or personal and political freedom (e.g. *rescue opera). It also saw the rise of the virtuoso performer.

romanza (It.; Ger.: *Romanze*). *See* ROMANCE.

ronde (Fr., 'round'). **1.** *Semibreve. **2.** *See* ROUND.

rondeau (Fr.). One of the three standard poetic forms used for 14th- and 15th-century chansons (*see also* BALLADE; VIRELAI). Unlike the other two, its structure was already established in the 13th century. The *rondeau* is a single-stanza poem of four couplets. The first, the refrain, is repeated at the end; the first line of the refrain is always used as the second line of the second couplet. The musical setting of a *rondeau* is divided into two sections (a and b), each of which carries one of the refrain lines. The remaining lines of text are allocated to the two musical sections according to their rhyme, and this yields the characteristic form of the *rondeau* in performance: ABaAabAB (capital letters indicate the position of the refrain). The refrain attained particular importance, as examples were quoted in their entirety in other works, as refrains, as motet tenors, or in more complex forms of quotation.

rondellus. A compositional technique making use of imitation and *voice exchange; also a complete work written using this technique. Most common in the 13th century and confined almost exclusively to Britain, it involved the composition of a simple melody that is consonant when combined with itself in imitation. The technique is found most frequently in three-part textures, in which either two upper voices are combined with a repeating phrase in the lower voice (known as a *pes*) or three voices stand alone. The best-known (but a rather uncharacteristic) example of *rondellus* technique is the rota *Sumer is icumen in*, in which a texture of many voices can be created from a long melody and a short *pes*.

rondo form. A fundamental form in music, in which a repeated section alternates with at least two different episodes. At its simplest it can be represented as ABACA. It is found in many cultures and periods, for example in the medieval carol, where the *burden represents the A section. The term 'rondo' (Fr.: *rondeau*) was first used in conjunction with this form in late Baroque suite movements, and then in Classical instrumental works, where it became typical for the last movement of a multi-movement work. Self-contained rondos were also published, and the form was sometimes used in songs, dances, and opera movements.

In the Classical rondo, the A section, or 'rondo theme' (which may be preceded by an introduction), always recurs in the tonic key, whereas the episodes modulate to related keys and may include new themes in those keys. In the more popular type of work, such as the *divertimento, and in many dances and marches, each section of the rondo is of strict duration, usually a multiple of eight bars, and is repeated; sections may be arranged in small *binary units. In more sophisticated movements, the sections, especially the episodes, are of unpredictable length, and may include *development and other sonata-like processes. Movements often end with a *coda. *See also* SONATA RONDO FORM.

root, root position. The root of a chord is the note from which it takes its name. Thus the C major chord has C as its root, even though the chord may be in first or second *inversion, with E or G respectively as its lowest note. If a chord is in root position, the lowest note is also the root. *See also* FUNDAMENTAL BASS.

rosalia. A type of sequence; *see* SEQUENCE, 1.

rota (Lat.). *See* ROUND.

roulade (Fr.). A vocal *melisma. It originally referred to a specific ornament of quick passing notes connecting two melodic notes.

round (Fr.: *ronde*; Lat.: *rota*). A short, circular *canon at the unison or octave, normally for three or more unaccompanied voices. In its simplest form, the round consists of a brief melody divided into sections of equal length that serve as the points of entry for each voice. As each singer reaches the end of the melody he or she begins again, so that the round is self-perpetuating and can be repeated as many times as desired. *Three Blind Mice*, which dates from the 16th century, is a well-known example. The *catch, a form of round based on word-play, was especially popular in Restoration England. (The term is also used for a traditional circle dance.)

roundelay (Fr.: *rondelay*). A 14th-century ballad, so called because of the constant recurrence of the first verse.

round O. A 17th- and 18th-century anglicization of the French word *rondeau* (*see* RONDO FORM).

rovescio, al (It.). 'In reverse'. The term can mean either *retrograde motion or *inversion.

row. Synonym of *series.

rubato (It., 'robbed'; *tempo rubato*, 'robbed time'). The practice in performance of disregarding strict time, 'robbing' some note-values for expressive effect and creating an atmosphere of spontaneity. Rubato is generally achieved in one of two ways: the pulse remains constant but expressive nuances are created by making small changes to the rhythmic values of individual notes; changes in tempo are made to all parts simultaneously, the performer applying **accelerando* and **ritardando* at his or her own discretion.

ruff. One of the ornamental rudiments of side-drum playing, consisting of a rapid triplet of strokes before the main one.

Ruggiero (It.). A characteristic harmonic bass line popular in Italy in the late 16th and the 17th centuries, chiefly as the basis of sets of instrumental variations. It may have served originally as a harmonic pattern over which a singer could improvise a melody: this connection supports the theory that the name derives from the first word of a stanza of Ariosto's epic poem *Orlando furioso*, 'Ruggier, qual sempre fui'. The *Ruggiero* eventually became standardized as a type of *ground bass for songs and dances.

ruhig (Ger.). 'Peaceful'.

RV. Abbreviation for *Ryom-Verzeichnis, used as a prefix to the numbers of Vivaldi's works as given in the standard *thematic catalogue of Peter Ryom.

Ryom. Abbreviation for the standard *thematic catalogue of the works of Vivaldi drawn up by the Danish scholar Peter Ryom (*b* 1937). Vivaldi's works are commonly referred to by Ryom number (often further abbreviated to RV, standing for Ryom-Verzeichnis).

S. **1.** Abbreviation for *segno* (*see* AL SEGNO; DAL SEGNO), **subito*, or **sinistra*. **2.** Abbreviation for *soprano or *superius. **3.** Abbreviation for Schmieder; *see* BWV.

saccadé (Fr.). 'Jerked', i.e. sharply accented, particularly a bowstroke.

sacra rappresentazione (It., 'sacred performance'). In 15th- and 16th-century Italy, a religious drama performed with music. The genre was a forerunner of opera and the oratorio.

sainete (Sp.). A type of late 18th-century Spanish comic opera in one act. It is the Spanish equivalent of *opera buffa* but has at times approximated more closely to farce.

Saite (Ger.). 'String'.

salmo (It., Sp.). *'Psalm'.

salon music. Music composed for performance in a domestic context rather than a concert hall, church, or theatre. It embraces most solo and chamber music, but usually denotes undemanding compositions (particularly those of the 19th and 20th centuries) of a lightweight character.

saltando, saltato (It.). 'Leaping', 'leapt': term used in the bowing of stringed instruments to mean **sautillé*.

saltarello (modern It.: *salterello*). A lively dance of Spanish and Italian provenance, characterized by triple metre and jumping movements. In the 16th century it frequently occurred as the 'afterdance' (Ger.: *Nachtanz*) to a *pavan or *passamezzo, the music often being indistinguishable from that of a *galliard.

sampling. The analysis of sounds by digital synthesizers. Sampling techniques have been widely used in the production of individual voices for commercial synthesizers: instead of generating sounds artificially from first principles, short extracts from acoustic instruments or other suitable sources are digitized, edited, and stored in a memory bank, ready for resynthesis.

Sanctus (Lat., 'Holy'). An ancient hymn sung throughout the undivided Church, East and West. It is part of the Ordinary of the Roman *Mass, sung during the Eucharistic prayer. In plainchant settings the Sanctus and Benedictus form a continuous whole, but in polyphonic settings and more recent compositions the Benedictus is usually a separate 'movement'.

sanft, sanftmütig (Ger.). 'Soft', 'gentle'; 'softly', 'gently'.

sanglot (Fr., 'sob'). 18th-century name for a descending *appoggiatura, usually sung to plaintive words.

sarabande (Fr., Ger.; It.: *sarabanda*; Sp.: *zarabanda*) [saraband]. A dance popular from the late 16th century to the 18th; as an instrumental form, it was one of the principal movements of the Baroque *suite, in which it usually followed the courante. Like the *chaconne it originated in Latin America and appeared in Spain during the 16th century. During this period it was a fast, lively dance alternating between 3/4 and 6/8 metre. In the early 17th century it was introduced to Italy, from where the first notated examples survive as tablatures for the Spanish guitar. It soon spread to France, where it appeared in the *ballet de cour* and other theatrical entertainments, as well as in the ballroom, where the much slower and more stately version evolved; this was in triple time with emphasis on the second beat, which was often dotted. This form of sarabande was also popular among German composers. In England, both types were known.

SATB. Abbreviation for sopranos, altos, tenors, and basses, the most common combination of voices in a choir or chorus.

Satz (Ger.). A term most commonly used to denote 'movement', for example of a sonata or symphony. It can also mean 'theme' or 'subject'; *Hauptsatz* (literally 'head-theme') is the main theme or first subject, *Seitensatz* or *Nebensatz* the second subject. *Satz* can also mean phrase or period, or structure, style, or texture; *freier Satz*, 'free style'. A *Schlusssatz* is a finale or a coda.

sautillé (Fr.; Ger.: *Springbogen*; It.: *saltando, saltato*). A short bowstroke played with the middle of the bow so that it bounces slightly. It is generated by a separate wrist movement for each note—unlike the *jeté* or *ricochet strokes, in which the bow, once set in motion, bounces naturally.

scala enigmatica (It., 'enigmatic scale'). A *scale invented by Verdi, consisting of the notes C–D♭–E–F♯–G♯–A♯–B–C.

scale (Fr.: *gamme*; Ger.: *Tonleiter*; It.: *gamma, scala*). A sequence of notes, ascending or descending stepwise. It defines a *mode or tonality, on the fundamental note of which it begins and ends. In addition to their role in composition, scales are played as an exercise to improve performing technique and musical understanding. There are numerous scales in different musical cultures, but the following are the principal ones used in Western art music. **1.** The diatonic scale is a set of seven pitch intervals of unequal size, adding up to an octave, that can be repeated indefinitely in other octaves. One form of the diatonic scale is represented by the white notes of the piano keyboard, conventionally beginning and ending on a C: in this form, the seven intervals are of two sizes, the whole tone (or whole step) and the semitone (or half-step), as in Ex. 1*a*. The semitones, slurred in the example, are exactly half the size of a whole tone; this precise relationship, called equal *temperament, is comparatively recent in origin. The diatonic scale on the white notes can be transposed to other pitches, using black notes as well, provided that the pattern of tones and semitones is unchanged.

A *mode is a subset of a scale (in this case the diatonic scale) that treats a particular pitch, and its octave transpositions, as the final or 'tonic'. Two modes, the Ionian (with its final on C) and the Aeolian (on A), have survived as the modern major and (natural) minor scales respectively (Ex. 1). However, the natural minor scale seen in Ex. 1*b* and transposed to two other pitch levels in Ex. 2 has not been much used in music of the last 300 years. The sixth and seventh degrees of the minor scale are unstable and result in two forms, neither of them diatonic: the harmonic minor, with the characteristic interval of an augmented 2nd (marked with a square bracket in Ex. 3*a*); and the melodic minor, in ascending form with sharpened sixth and seventh degrees avoiding the augmented 2nd and 'leading' to the tonic (Ex. 3*b*), and in

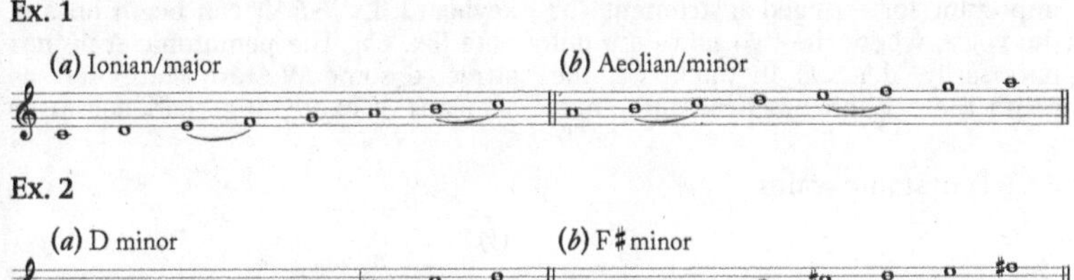

Ex. 3

Ex. 4

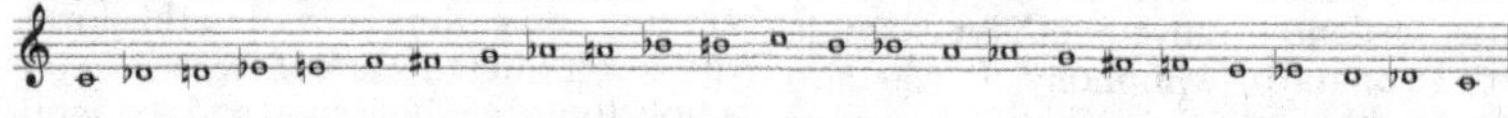

Ex. 5 Whole-tone scale

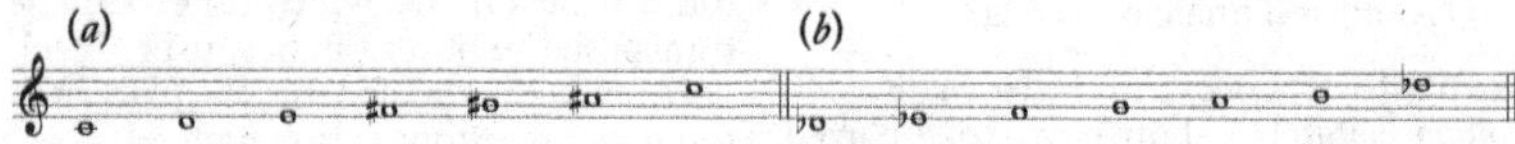

descending form equivalent to the natural minor. All three forms have in common the flattened third scale degree, producing a characteristic minor 3rd with the keynote. **2.** The chromatic scale consists of all 12 notes in an octave on the piano keyboard. Like the diatonic scale, it may begin on any degree. Ex. 4 shows an octave of the chromatic scale beginning on C, notated in sharps ascending and flats descending. The chromatic scale evolved with the rise of tonality. Melodically speaking, it is a diatonic scale with added 'chromatic' notes which are properly extraneous to the key but serve to 'colour' it. Harmonically, the added notes are needed to provide a major or minor *triad for each note of the diatonic scale.

There are many ways of notating the chromatic scale; in tonal music, the choice of G♯ or A♭ (for example) may be important for stringed instruments or the voice, where the two notes are not necessarily identical in pitch. On the piano there is no practical difference. **3.** The whole-tone scale divides the octave into six equal steps, each a whole tone apart. In equal temperament, it exists in only two forms (Ex. 5). Its lack of semitones (particularly leading note to tonic) and of perfect 5ths, both basic materials of tonal music, gives it an impression of tonal vagueness, which made it particularly attractive to Impressionists and other 20th-century composers seeking to avoid tonal centres and functional harmony. **4.** The pentatonic divides the octave into five steps, and exists in several forms. They are sometimes misleadingly termed 'gapped' scales, by comparison with seven-note diatonic scales (which however are themselves 'gapped' in terms of microtonal scales: see below, 5). The most familiar form is the tonal pentatonic, the order of its intervals corresponding (by coincidence) to that of the black notes of the piano keyboard (Ex. 6*a*). It can begin on any note (Ex. 6*b*). The pentatonic scale has attracted some Western composers as a means of expressing *nationalism or

Ex. 6 Pentatonic scales

creating special effects. **5.** Invented scales have been formed by combining elements of pre-existing ones. Microtonal scales, in which the octave is divided into intervals of less than a semitone, have long been used in Eastern cultures and they have been adopted by a number of Western composers (*see* MICROTONE). *See also* OCTATONIC SCALE.

scemando (It.). 'Dying away', i.e. becoming quieter, the same as **diminuendo*.

scena (It.). In opera, an extended episode consisting of a loosely constructed sequence of related sections (e.g. introduction, recitative, arioso, one or more arias), often for a solo singer and principally dramatic in intent. In the 18th and 19th centuries the title was given to specially composed dramatic episodes intended for concert performance by a solo singer, in the style of a cantata. These were normally settings either of an extract from an opera libretto or of some other dramatic text.

scène (Fr.). A vocal form, precursor of the **mélodie*.

schalkhaft (Ger.). 'Roguish'.

Schall (Ger.). 'Sound'.

scharf (Ger.). 'Sharply'; e.g. *scharf betont*, 'sharply accented'.

Schenkerian analysis. A system of musical *analysis, devised by Heinrich Schenker (1868–1935), which divides a composition into structural layers: background, middleground, and foreground.

scherzando, scherzante, scherzevole, scherzevolmente (It.). 'Jokingly', 'playfully'.

scherzetto [scherzino] (It.). A short *scherzo.

scherzo (It., 'joke', 'game'). A quick, light movement or piece, often in triple time. Like the *minuet, which it replaced in the late 18th century as the traditional third movement of such large-scale forms as the symphony and string quartet, it is generally in ternary form, with a contrasting middle section, or trio (*see* TRIO, 2). The term was first applied, in the 17th century, to vocal music. From the later Baroque period, it was used mainly for instrumental music. In the 19th century, the term was used as a title for short instrumental pieces, particularly for the piano.

scherzoso, scherzosamente (It.). 'Playful', 'playfully'.

schietto, schiettamente (It.). 'Open', 'sincere'; 'openly', 'sincerely'.

Schlag (Ger.). **1.** 'Stroke', 'blow'. **2.** 'Beat' (in the sense of 'three beats to the bar', etc.); *see* BEAT, 1.

schleppen (Ger.). 'To drag'; *nicht schleppend*, 'do not drag'.

Schlummerlied (Ger., 'slumber song'). A lullaby or *berceuse.

Schluss (Ger.). **1.** 'End', 'conclusion'; *Schlusssatz*, 'last movement', 'coda'; *Schlusszeichen*, the signal to end a piece, i.e. a double bar. **2.** *'Cadence'.

Schlüssel (Ger.). *'Clef'.

schmachtend (Ger.). 'Languishing'.

schmeichelnd (Ger.). 'Coaxing', 'flattering'.

schmerzlich (Ger.). 'Painful', 'sorrowful'.

schmetternd (Ger.). 'Blaring', especially in horn playing.

Schmieder. Abbreviation (sometimes further shortened to s) for Schmieder-Verzeichnis, used as a prefix to the numbers of J. S. Bach's works in the standard *thematic catalogue of Wolfgang Schmieder; *BWV is now more widely used.

schnell, schneller (Ger.). 'Quick', 'quicker'.

Schneller (Ger.). The inverted *mordent.

schola cantorum (Lat., 'school of singers'). A medieval Roman choir that provided the music for papal ceremonies and services.

Schottische (Ger., 'Scottish'). A round dance similar to, but slower than, the *polka. It is sometimes coupled with the *écossaise, but, despite the similarity of name, the only resemblance is that both are in duple time. The *Schottische* was called the 'German polka' when it first appeared in England in the mid-19th century.

Schrammel. A style of Viennese popular music; it owes its name to the violinist brothers Johann (1850–93) and Joseph Schrammel (1852–95), who formed a quartet with a clarinettist (later a piano accordionist) and a guitarist.

schrittmässig, schrittweise (Ger.). 'Stepwise', i.e. at a walking pace (the equivalent of **andante*).

Schusterfleck (Ger., 'cobbler's patch'). A derogatory name for a sequential passage (*see* SEQUENCE, 1) in which each repetition is one scale degree higher than the last.

schwach, schwächer (Ger.). 'Weak', i.e. soft, 'weaker'.

schweigen (Ger.). 'To be silent'; *schweigt* means the same as **tacet*; *Schweigezeichen*, a rest.

schwer (Ger.) 'Heavy', 'ponderous', 'difficult'; *schwermütig*, *schwermutsvoll*, 'heavy-hearted'.

schwindend (Ger.). 'Dying away', i.e. becoming quieter, the same as **diminuendo*.

S

schwungvoll (Ger.). 'Vigorous', 'energetic'.

sciolto, scioltamente (It.). 'Free', 'unconstrained', 'loosely'.

scordatura (It., 'mistuning'; Fr.: *discordé*, *discordable*, *discordant*; Ger.: *Umstimmung*, *Verstimmung*). A tuning in which one or more of the strings is at a different pitch from the normal. It was first used in the 16th century. Its purpose is to make passages easier to play by bringing notes, especially double-stopped chords, more easily under the hand. It can brighten the tone by allowing strings to resonate sympathetically with each other. Scordatura is sometimes used to extend the range downwards, for example tuning the lowest (C) string of a viola or cello to B or B♭, or the double bass E string to C.

score (Fr.: *partition*; Ger.: *Partitur*; It.: *partitura*). A printed or manuscript copy of a piece of music which shows the parts for all the performers arranged on separate staves. A 'full' score has each instrumental or vocal part separately displayed, with full performance details (though two parts for instruments of the same kind may be written on a single staff); this is the type normally used by a conductor. An alternative term is 'orchestral' score.

A 'vocal' or 'piano-vocal' score shows all the vocal parts (usually of an opera or a choral work) on separate staves, with the orchestral parts reduced to a keyboard arrangement. A 'piano' score is a full score reduced to form an arrangement for piano. A 'short' or 'condensed' score is a reduction of a full score to a smaller number of staves (related parts, for example woodwind, may be combined on one staff) but not necessarily arranged for piano. A *'miniature' score is a printed score of pocket size, in which, conventionally, any voice or instrument that rests for an entire system (see below) is omitted from that system. A 'study' score may be either a miniature score or a full score of reduced dimensions.

The act of 'scoring' is deciding on and writing down the instrumentation of a work that is already conceived for another medium (e.g. for the piano) or assembling in score form the individual instrumental or vocal parts of a work. A set of all the necessary staves printed on a page is called a system; each system is linked at the right- and left-hand ends by a continuous bar-line. Each individual staff has its own bar-lines, but these may extend through the staves of related instruments. There may be more than one system on a page, in which case they are separated at the left-hand side by a pair of strokes in bold type.

The modern vertical arrangement of instrumental parts in a full score of a work for standard orchestra, from top to bottom, is: woodwind (piccolo, flutes, oboes, clarinets, bassoons); brass (horns, trumpets, trombones, tuba); percussion (timpani, side drum, bass drum, triangle, etc.); strings (first violins, second violins, violas, cellos, double basses). A cor anglais part is normally placed below the oboes, bass clarinet below clarinets, and double bassoon below bassoon. A harp or celesta part is placed between the percussion and string sections, and any solo part in a concerto immediately above the first violins. Voice parts, if any, are placed above the string section, with soloists above the chorus, which is arranged in descending order of voices. *See also* NOTATION.

scorrendo, scorrevole (It.). 'Flowing'; a *glissando.

Scotch snap [Scotch catch]. A rhythmic feature in which a dotted note is preceded, rather than followed, by a note of shorter value, e.g.: ♪♩. as opposed to ♩.♪. It is a characteristic feature of the Scottish strathspey. It appears in late 16th-century French songs as a feature of **musique mesurée*, and in the performance of 17th-century **notes inégales*. In 17th-century Italian music it was known as the *stile lombardo* (Lombardy style).

scucito (It.). 'Detached', i.e. not *legato*.

sdrucciolando (It.). 'Sliding'; in harp playing, a *glissando.

sea shanty. *See* SHANTY.

sec, sèche (Fr.). 'Dry': a term used by French composers to indicate that a note or chord should be struck and then quickly released.

secco (It.). 'Dry', i.e. **staccato*. *See also* RECITATIVE.

seconda pratica. *See* PRIMA PRATICA, SECONDA PRATICA.

secondary dominant chord. A *dominant of a scale degree other than the tonic. In C major, for example, in which the dominant is G, the introduction of an F♯ into the chord on the supertonic (D) gives that chord the function of a secondary (or applied) dominant without creating a modulation.

secondary seventh chord. A *seventh chord on a degree of the scale other than the dominant.

seconda volta (It.). 'Second-time (bar)'; *see* DOUBLE BAR.

second inversion [6-4 chord]. A term describing the vertical presentation of a chord when the 5th rather than the root is the lowest note, the other notes being a 4th and a 6th above it (hence 6-4). *See also* INVERSION, 1.

second subject. The first or principal theme of the second group of a *sonata-form movement.

second-time bar. *See* DOUBLE BAR.

Seele (Ger.). 'Soul', i.e. feeling; *seelenvoll*, 'soulful'. (*Seele* has also been used to mean the soundpost of a bowed string instrument, fancifully considered the instrument's 'soul'.)

segno (It.). 'Sign'. *See* AL SEGNO; DAL SEGNO.

segue (It.). 'Follows': an instruction to play the following section or movement without a break; *segue la coda*, 'the coda follows'; *seguente*, *seguendo*, 'following'. The term may also be an indication to 'follow the same way', i.e. continue with a pattern that is at first written out in full but then abbreviated.

seguidilla (Sp.). A Castilian folk dance in quick triple time. It alternates *coplas* (verses sung by the dancers) with passages played on guitar and castanets, and is still performed in Andalusia.

Sehnsucht (Ger.). 'Longing'; *sehnsüchtig*, *sehnsuchtsvoll*, 'longingly'.

Seite (Ger.). 'Side', e.g. a page of a book or one skin of a drum; *Seitenthema*, 'second theme', e.g. in a sonata-form movement.

semel. *See* GYMEL.

semibreve (𝅝). The note having half the value of the breve and double the value of the minim; in American terminology it is known as 'whole note'.

semidemisemiquaver. *See* HEMIDEMISEMIQUAVER.

semifusa (Lat.). An early note-value, from which the modern *semiquaver derives.

semiminima (Lat.). An early note-value, from which the modern *crotchet derives.

semi-opera. A type of late 17th- and early 18th-century English drama in which the principal characters, usually played by actors, spoke, but the minor characters (often trained singers) used song and dance. The development of the semi-opera was influenced by the French *comédies-ballets* and *tragédies lyriques* as well as the earlier English *masque, but the genre declined with the growing popularity of Italian opera in England from the beginning of the 18th century.

semiquaver (𝅘𝅥𝅯). The note having 1/16 of the value of the semibreve, or whole note; hence the American usage '16th-note'.

semitone. The smallest interval in common use in Western music, covering half a tone.

S

semplice, semplicemente (It.). 'Simple', 'simply'.

sempre (It.). 'Always'; e.g. *sempre legato*, the whole passage or movement should be played smoothly.

sennet. A stage direction in Elizabethan plays indicating a type of fanfare, played by cornetts or trumpets, before actors entered or left the stage. *See also* TUCKET.

sensibile (It.), **sensible** (Fr.). *Leading note.

sentito (It.). 'Felt', 'with expression'.

senza (It.). 'Without', e.g. *senza sordini*, 'without mutes' (in string playing), or 'without dampers' (in piano playing); *senza tempo*, *senza misura*, 'without strict tempo'.

séparé (Fr.). 'Separated'; in French organ music, uncoupled.

septet. An ensemble of seven instrumentalists or, more rarely, singers, or music written for it.

septuplet [septimole, septolet]. A term for seven notes that are to be performed in the time of four or of six; they are indicated by the figure '7' placed above or below the seven notes (see Ex. 1).

Ex. 1

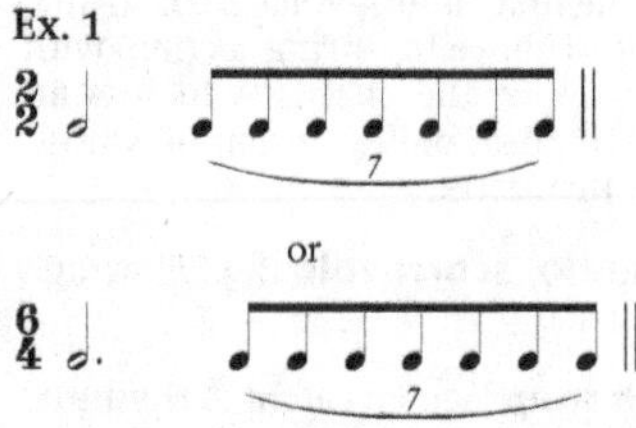

sequence. 1. The more or less exact repetition of a melody at another level, higher or lower. If the repetition is only in the melody, with changed harmony, it is called a melodic sequence, and if the repetition is followed also in the harmony, a harmonic sequence. If the repetition is made without leaving the original key, which necessarily means that some of the intervals become larger or smaller by a semitone, it is called a tonal sequence. If, in order to preserve the exact intervals, the key is changed, the name given is 'real sequence' (*see* FUGUE for a corresponding use of 'tonal' and 'real'). Sequences that are real in some repetitions and tonal in others (in some instances to avoid carrying the modulation too far) are called mixed sequences. A sequence that is an exact repetition in another key (i.e. a harmonic real sequence) is sometimes called a *rosalia*, after an Italian popular song, *Rosalia mia cara*, which begins with this device. **2.** A type of Latin hymn (also called *prosa*,

'prose'), an important musical and literary form that flourished from the 9th century to the 16th. Sequences were sung on feast days after the alleluia at Mass in many parts of the Roman Catholic Church. A typical sequence up to the 11th century has some six to 12 pairs of lines, each pair of a different length and with a different melody. The melodies differ markedly from those of Gregorian chant, with strong cadences often approached from the note below the final and a tendency for each line to have its own individual tessitura. After AD 1000 the prose texts gave way increasingly to verse. The five sequences that remained in standard chantbooks are *Victimae paschali laudes*, *Lauda Sion*, *Veni Sancte Spiritus*, *Stabat mater dolorosa*, and *Dies irae*. Sequences were first set polyphonically in parallel *organum and two-voice *discant, and there are many polyphonic settings dating from the 15th century.

serenade (Fr.: *sérénade*; Ger.: *Serenade*, *Ständchen*; It.: *serenata*). A musical genre, the name of which derives from the word *sereno* (It., 'calm'). Serenades were originally played or sung in the evening by a lover at his lady's window, or as a greeting to an important personage, and were frequently accompanied by a guitar or other plucked instrument. In the 18th century a serenade was a piece of instrumental music of up to ten movements, scored for a small ensemble, usually with a predominance of wind instruments. There are reminiscences of the original connotations of serenade and a plucked instrument in the serenade arias of some operas. Classical instrumental serenades were scored for a variety of combinations: strings and wind, wind instruments alone, string quartet, and even double or quadruple orchestra. In the 19th century several composers wrote orchestral serenades.

serenata (It.). **1.** *'Serenade'. **2.** A large-scale, cantata-like work for performance at court or at an aristocratic home for a special occasion. A typical serenata had a pastoral, allegorical, or mythological subject which involved at least two characters; it was often divided into sections, each consisting of recitatives and arias, and was given in an elaborate setting with costumes but without dramatic action. The genre was extensively cultivated by 17th- and 18th-century Italian composers, and at the imperial court in Vienna.

serenatella (It.). Diminutive of *serenata.

serialism. A compositional technique in which the basic material is an ordered arrangement—row, set, or series—of pitches, intervals, durations, and, if required, of other musical elements. Music theorists distinguish between *twelve-note technique, in which only pitch is subject to serial principles, and serial (or 'totally serial') music, in which an attempt is made to apply serial thinking to other compositional features, e.g. rhythm, register, dynamics, and aspects of form. Serialism originated in the 12-note technique, where all 12 notes of the chromatic scale are arranged in a fixed order which is used to generate melodies and harmonies, and which normally remains binding for a whole work. Since all the elements in a series will be of equal significance, serial music is without tonality, even though examples of it emphasize certain pitches in ways that become analogous to the tonics and dominants of tonality. It was Schoenberg who, from *c*.1920, was the most important figure in the establishment and evolution of serialism as a compositional resource.

In its early form, the pitch-series can be used in a variety of ways. Even if it first occurred to the composer as a specific melodic shape, it provides a particular sequence of pitch and interval classes whose registral position can be varied at will. The whole series may be uniformly transposed onto any of the other intervals of the chromatic scale, making 11 transpositions of the principal, or prime (P), form. In addition, the series can be reversed (retrograded; R) and also inverted (I), and the inversions can be retrograded (IR), making a total of 48 possible forms for any given 12-note series. Schoenberg devised what has since become known as the 'combinatorial' principle, whereby two forms of the set would be used in combination, and those two forms would be complementary to the extent that the pitch content of the first half (or hexachord) of one 12-note set would be complemented—that is, not duplicated even to the extent of a single pitch—by the content of the first hexachord of another version of the same set.

series. The basic musical idea, usually a sequential ordering of the 12 notes of the chromatic scale, used as a starting-point in the composition of serial music. *See* SERIALISM.

serio, seria (It.). 'Serious'; *serioso*, *seriosa*, seriosamente, 'seriously'. *See also* OPERA SERIA.

serrando, serrato (It.), **serrant, serré** (Fr.). 'Pressing', 'pressed', i.e. getting quicker.

service. In the Anglican communion, a more or less elaborate and continuous setting of the canticles for Morning Prayer or Evensong, or of certain parts of the Communion Service.

The effect of the Reformation on service music was that the canticles had to be set in the vernacular, without lengthening by repetition of phrases and with one note to a syllable. The terms 'short service' and 'great service' were often used by 16th- and early 17th-century composers to distinguish between settings that followed the new regulations and those composed for festal occasions, scored for a large choir and reverting to the old length and complexity. During the 18th century almost all services were composed on the 'short' principle.

Alternatim treatment (by the *decani* and *cantoris* sides of the choir) is a frequent feature in service music, and, on the same principle, 'verse' and 'full' passages are also used, alternating a soloist accompanied by an independent organ part with full choir and organ doubling. *See also* ANTHEM.

set. A term found in mathematics and symbolic logic that was transferred to music theory in the mid-20th century to refer to discrete collections of pitch classes or durations used as the basis for 12-note or serial composition. It has also been applied in the analysis of post-tonal or atonal music, where specific units (normally of fewer than 12 elements) can be shown to be subject to such post-tonal compositional operations as transposition and inversion.

seul, seule (Fr.). 'Alone', 'solo', e.g. *violons seuls*, 'violins alone', *voix seule*, 'solo voice'.

seventh chord. A triad with a 7th added. *See* DOMINANT SEVENTH CHORD; DIMINISHED SEVENTH CHORD; SECONDARY SEVENTH CHORD.

sextet. An ensemble of six instrumentalists or singers, or music written for it. Several composers have written string sextets for two violins, two violas, and two cellos. A common combination for divertimentos in the 18th century was two horns and string quartet, and there are many wind sextets of that period for two oboes or clarinets, two horns, and two bassoons—the standard wind octet of the *Harmoniemusik, but without one of the soprano pairs.

sextuplet [sextolet]. A term for six notes that are to be performed in the time of four, either as two groups of three or as three groups of two; they are indicated by the figure '6' placed above or below the six notes (see Ex. 1).

Ex. 1

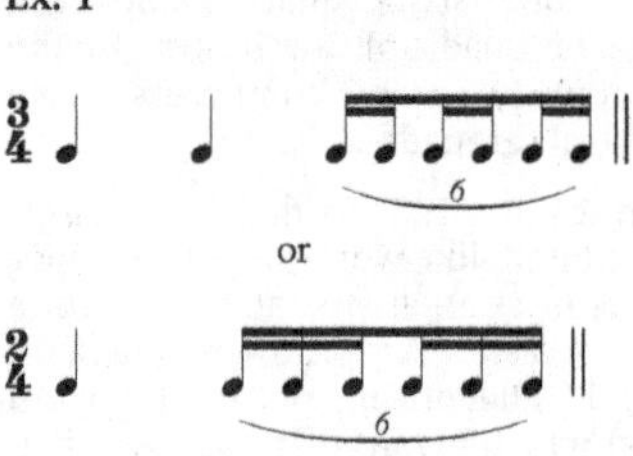

sf. Abbreviation for **sforzando* or *sforzato*; *sff*, abbreviation for *sforzatissimo*.

sfogato (It.). 'Unrestrained', i.e. in a light and easy style. A *soprano sfogato* is a light soprano voice.

sforzando, sforzato (It.). 'Forcing', 'forced', i.e. accented. In the 19th century it was used to mark an accent within the prevailing dynamic but it has now acquired the connotation of sudden loudness; it is abbreviated *sf* or *sfz*.

sfp. Abbreviation for *sforzando* followed immediately by *piano*, i.e. a strongly accented note followed by a quiet note or passage.

sfz. Abbreviation for **sforzando*.

shake. An early English name for the *trill.

shanty [chanty, sea shanty]. A British sailors' work song, with a call- and-response pattern. The 'shantyman' would improvise verses, and the working team would punctuate with invariable refrains, containing one or two accents at which combined forces would pull together. It belongs to a short period, *c.*1830–70.

shape note. A device, for singers with rudimentary musical knowledge, that indicates where the semitones are in the octave by the shape of the note-heads used. The first three notes are each a tone apart and are solmized as *fa*, *sol*, *la*; the fourth to sixth notes have the same structure and are also solmized *fa*, *sol*, *la*; but the seventh and eighth notes are separated by a semitone and indicated *mi*, *fa*. The singer knows that (ascending) *la*–*fa* is always a semitone and so is *mi*–*fa*. *Fa* notes always have a triangular head, *sol* notes a round head, *la* notes a square head, and *mi* notes are diamond-shaped. The system, also known as 'fasola', is used in the American South for church music.

sharp (Fr.: *dièse*; Ger.: *Kreuz*; It.: *diesis*). **1.** The sign (♯) that, when placed before a note, raises it in pitch by a semitone. In English terminology the verb is 'to sharpen' and the adjective 'sharpened'; in American usage the corresponding terms are 'to sharp' and 'sharped'. *See* ACCIDENTAL; for the origins of the sharp sign and its early use, *see* DURUM AND MOLLIS; NOTATION. In the 18th century, the key of 'E sharp' meant the key of E that has a major 3rd, i.e. E major. **2.** An adjective applied to vocal or instrumental performance, denoting inexact intonation on the high side.

shift. In string playing, the movement of the left hand when changing *position.

shivaree. An American corruption of *charivari.

short score [condensed score]. A reduction of a full *score to a smaller number of staves. The term is applied to that stage in the composition of an ensemble work where the composer may write out the music on a few staves, showing indications of scoring and harmonization to be written out fully later.

short service. *See* SERVICE.

si [te]. The seventh degree of the major scale in the *solmization system. In French and Italian usage it has become attached, on the fixed-*doh* principle, to the note B, in whichever scale it occurs. *See* TONIC SOL-FA.

siciliana [siciliano] (It.; Fr.: *sicilienne*). **1.** 'Sicilian'; *alla siciliana*, 'in the Sicilian style' or 'in the style of the siciliana' (see below, 2). **2.** A 17th- and 18th-century dance and aria form, probably of Sicilian origin. It was generally in ternary form (ABA), with fairly slow tempo, and in 6/8 or 12/8 metre. Many examples are in a minor key; other characteristic features include a flowing accompaniment, a gentle lyrical melody, often with a dotted rhythm, and the use of a Neapolitan 6th at cadence points. In the 18th century, the siciliana was popular as a slow movement in suites and sonatas; in operas and cantatas it was frequently used in pastoral scenes.

sighting. A 15th-century term for a technique used to facilitate the singing of parallel lines of music to the written plainchant in *faburden.

sight-reading, sight-singing. The performance of music from notation that the singer or instrumentalist has not previously seen. A number of methods have been built on sight-singing, notably the Italian *solfeggio, the English *Tonic Sol-fa, and, during the 20th century, the highly systematic method devised in Hungary by Kodály. Sight-singing plays a part in *ear-training.

signature. A sign placed at the beginning of a composition or movement, and sometimes within it, to indicate the key or a change of key (*key signature) or the metre or a change of metre (*time signature).

signature tune. Originally any popular song or dance tune which was adopted by performers as a means of identifying themselves. In the 1920s and 30s, when broadcasting, dance bands and light orchestras commonly used a signature tune.

silence (Fr.). *'Rest'.

similar motion. *See* MOTION.

simile, simili (It.). An instruction that the performer should continue with some particular effect (e.g. an accompaniment figure) or technique (e.g. a kind of bowstroke). *See also* SEGUE.

simple time. *See* TIME SIGNATURE.

simultaneity. A group of notes played at the same time. Some writers on atonal music have preferred this term to the more usual 'chord', seeking to avoid the latter's implications of harmonic function.

sin'. Abbreviation for **sino*, elided to a following vowel.

sinfonia (It.). *See* OVERTURE, 1; SYMPHONY, THE.

sinfonia concertante (It., 'concertante symphony'). *See* SYMPHONIE CONCERTANTE.

sinfonietta (Fr.: *symphoniette*). A small-scale symphony, in terms either of length or of the size of the orchestra needed to perform it.

sinfonische Dichtung (Ger.). *'Symphonic poem'.

singend (Ger.). 'Singing', i.e. in a singing style, similar to *cantabile*.

singhiozzando (It.). 'Sobbingly'.

single tonguing. *See* TONGUING.

Singspiel (Ger., 'play in song'). An opera in which relatively simple musical numbers are interspersed with spoken dialogue in German. Although the term was in use before the 1700s to denote a dramatic piece with music, it acquired its most commonly accepted meaning at the beginning of the 18th century, with the musical plays given in the Kärntnertortheater in Vienna. The rich tradition of mid-18th-century *Singspiel* in northern and central Germany followed on from this Viennese beginning, after the disappearance of Baroque opera from the German stage. From about the 1750s the genre was influenced by **opéra comique* and English *ballad opera. By the 1770s the term was also commonly used to denote any comic opera translated into German. Mozart's *Die Entführung aus dem Serail* (1782) is one of the best-known *Singspiele*.

sinistro, sinistra (It.). 'Left'; *mano sinistra*, 'left hand'. It is sometimes abbreviated *S*.

sino, sin' (It.). 'Until'; e.g. *sin'al segno*, go on 'until the sign'. *See* AL SEGNO.

sirventes, sirventois. A type of song composed by the troubadours and trouvères in which the subject matter deals with moral, political, or literary concerns. Such songs are usually satirical and are often set to pre-existing melodies.

six-four chord. *See* SECOND INVERSION; INVERSION, 1.

sixteenth-note (Amer.). *Semiquaver.

sixth, added. *See* ADDED SIXTH CHORD.

six-three chord. *See* FIRST INVERSION; INVERSION, 1.

sixty-fourth-note (Amer.). *Hemidemisemiquaver.

sketch. A record made by the composer of a composition in an unfinished state. Historically, sketches have been autograph manuscripts, but today a sketch of an electronic work might be in the form of a tape, or notation might be realized in a computer notation program, and so on.

skolion (Gk.; Ger.: *Skolie*). A drinking-song.

slancio (It.). 'Impetus', 'impulse'; *con slancio*, 'with impetus', 'with dash'.

slargando, slargandosi (It.). 'Broadening', i.e. slowing down, the same as *rallentando*.

slentando (It.). 'Slowing down', the same as *rallentando*.

slide. 1. (Fr.: *glissade*, *port de voix*; It.: *portamento*). In string playing, a method of changing position between two unadjacent notes without lifting the finger from the fingerboard. It was much used for expressive effect in the late 19th and early 20th centuries. *See* PORTAMENTO, 1. **2.** (Fr.: *coulé*, *flatté*; Ger.: *Schleifer*). An ornament common in the Baroque period, consisting of two short notes rising by step to the main note. It may be indicated by a sign or by small notes.

slur. A curved line used in musical notation to group notes for various purposes. It commonly indicates that the notes it affects are to be played or sung *legato*, or smoothly. On stringed instruments this normally implies that the notes should be taken in one bowstroke or, if this is physically impossible, that any change of bowstroke should be imperceptible. In music for wind instruments, and in vocal music, the slur implies that the affected notes should be taken in one breath. If notes within a slur have dots above or below them, they are to be played slightly detached (i.e. *mezzo-staccato*, but not as detached as *staccato*). In vocal music the slur is also used to indicate that a single syllable is to be sung to several notes. A slur over an extended group of notes may indicate the limits of a *phrase and may encompass smaller groups of slurred notes.

A curved line similar to the slur may be used to indicate a *portamento effect; the same sign between two adjacent notes of the same pitch serves as a *tie.

smorzando (It.). 'Dying away'; it is sometimes abbreviated *smorz.*

snap. *See* SCOTCH SNAP.

snello, snella, snellamente (It.). 'Nimble', 'nimbly'.

soave (It.). 'Sweet', 'soft', 'gentle'; *con soavità*, 'with gentleness'; *soavemente*, 'gently'.

sofort (Ger.). 'Immediately', i.e. **attacca*.

soft hexachord. *See* HEXACHORD; SOLMIZATION.

soggetto (It.). 'Subject', or 'theme'. In 18th-century theory, a fugue subject of a traditional nature, similar to the subjects of the earlier *ricercar.

soggetto cavato. *See* CANTUS FIRMUS.

soh. *See* SOL.

sol [soh]. The fifth degree of the scale in the *solmization system. In French and Italian usage it has become attached, on the fixed-*doh* principle, to the note G, in whichever scale it occurs. *See* TONIC SOL-FA.

sol-fa. *See* TONIC SOL-FA.

solfeggietto (It., 'little study'). A title for a short keyboard piece.

solfeggio (It.; Fr.: *solfège*). **1.** A type of vocal exercise sung either to a vowel (in which case it should properly be called a *vocalise) or to the *solmization syllables (the term is derived from 'sol-fa'). The exercise serves a dual purpose: as basic voice-training; and as practice in *sight-reading, since the student learns to recognize the intervals and notes. **2.** The term has also been applied to instruction in the rudiments of music: sight-singing, *ear-training, study of notation, and so on.

solmization. The use of syllables in association with pitches in the oral teaching of melodies. The name is derived from the most common set of such syllables known in Europe: *ut-re-mi-fa-sol-la*, frequently depicted on the so-called *Guidonian hand, a visual aid to learning solmization. By 1100 the six syllables were used not only for the six notes C–D–E–F–G–A, but also for F–G–A–B♭–C–D and for G–A–B–C–D–E, which have the same interval pattern (tone-tone-semitone-tone-tone). These three sets of six notes are known as hexachords. The hexachord on C has no B and was known as the 'natural' (*naturale*) hexachord; that on G has a B♮ and was known as 'hard' (*durum*—from the way of writing the natural B, ♮, with four corners), and that on F needed a B♭ and was known as 'soft' (*molle*—with a rounded shape, ♭). That such systems can still aid the teaching of music is demonstrated by the success of the *Tonic Sol-fa system.

solo (It.). 'Alone'; e.g. *violino solo*, 'solo violin'; the plural is *soli*.

solus tenor. A single voice part that could be substituted for both the tenor and contratenor parts in late medieval and Renaissance polyphonic music.

son, sons (Fr.). 'Sound', 'sounds', 'note', 'notes'; *son bouché, son étouffé*, 'stopped note' in horn playing; *son ouvert*, an open note on a wind instrument.

sonata. An instrumental composition. Like many terms originating *c.*1600, 'sonata' has been applied to a variety of instrumental types, with the common feature that they are all to be played. However, the Italian language had two verbs for 'play': *sonare* for bowing or blowing, *toccare* for 'touching' a keyboard. Hence, by analogy with 'cantata' for a sung piece, the Italians used 'toccata' for a piece played on a keyboard instrument and 'sonata' for a piece for strings or winds. At different times and in different places during the 17th century, 'sonata' was used synonymously with *'canzona', 'sinfonia', and *'concerto'.

Compositions called 'sonata' cover an enormous variety of pieces ranging in length from 20 to over 200 bars and including sets of variations and dances; scorings range from a single instrument to over 20. This repertory served as concert music, diversional chamber music, 'table' music, and didactic material, and for use in church. In the 17th century, if the edition contained dances unsuitable for performance in church, the sonata would be labelled 'da camera'; the description 'da chiesa' was introduced towards the end of the century.

The greater uniformity observable in sonatas *c.*1700 was to a considerable extent due to the influence of Corelli. He established the slow-fast-slow-fast order of movements in the *sonata da chiesa* ('church sonata'), which was for one or more melody instruments and continuo; the second movement was usually a fugal Allegro, and the third and fourth were binary-form, dance-like movements. The *sonata da camera* ('chamber sonata'), for the same forces, was less standardized but generally had three or more dance movements, similar to the *suite, sometimes with an introductory movement. During the early 18th century the two types merged.

In the Baroque era, the *trio sonata was the principal type, particularly for two violins and continuo. After 1700 the solo sonata, for violin, flute, oboe, or cello, became more popular. Some composers wrote sonatas for unaccompanied solo instrument. In the 1730s the term 'sonata' began to be widely used for keyboard solos, at first for the clavichord or harpsichord, later for the piano (e.g. by Scarlatti and C. P. E. Bach). By the 1750s the sonata had replaced the suite as the principal genre for multi-movement keyboard works. A peculiar product of the

Classical period was the 'accompanied sonata', for keyboard and violin, flute, or cello. Classical sonatas usually had three movements: fast–slow–fast; the first movement was in *sonata form, and occasionally a fourth movement was added. Slow movements were in simpler forms, sometimes sets of variations; final movements might be rondos or *sonata rondos. By the time of Beethoven, the sonata was a substantial form of symphonic dimensions.

By 1830 the sonata had yielded to the *character piece as the chief vehicle for expressive piano music. Significantly, the greatest 19th-century sonatas are those (e.g. by Chopin and Liszt) that break away from the traditional form to encompass the genre piece. The sonata for solo instrument and piano continued to flourish, however. The title 'sonata' was still used in the 20th century, but it no longer necessarily implied a multi-movement work or the use of sonata form.

sonata-allegro form. *See* SONATA FORM.

sonata a tre (It.). *'Trio sonata'.

sonata da camera, sonata da chiesa (It.). 'Chamber *sonata', 'church *sonata'.

sonata form. A term that refers not to the form of a whole *sonata but to the typical form of one movement of a sonata, more especially the first movement. To avoid this anomaly the terms 'first-movement form' or 'sonata-allegro form' have sometimes been substituted, but they too are inaccurate, because the form referred to is not confined either to first movements or to allegros. Sonata form is principally associated with the Classical period (*c.*1770–1820), but it was developing before that time and was used for long afterwards. It occurs most regularly in the first movement of a sonata, a multi-movement chamber work (such as a trio, quartet, or quintet), or a symphony. It is also often found in the other movements of such works, or in such single-movement pieces as an *overture, *symphonic poem, or *character piece, and it influenced many other genres including the *concerto and the *aria. Fugues, mass movements, anthems, and orchestral 'storms' were often constructed in sonata form during the height of its fashion.

Sonata form comprises a two-key tonal structure in three main sections. Section 1, the *exposition, generally presents all the thematic material of the movement, opening with one theme, or group of themes, in the tonic key. The first (or principal) theme of the first group is also known as the 'first subject'. The exposition then moves, often by means of a modulatory section called a transition or bridge passage, to a second theme or group of themes in a contrasting key. The first (or principal) theme of the second group is also known as the 'second subject'. The key of the second group is usually the dominant for movements in the major, and the relative major for movements in the minor, though other keys may be used. For example, in the 19th century it became quite common to use the mediant as the second main key area. The exposition generally closes with a codetta, a short and sometimes reiterated cadential figure in the key of the second group. A double bar, usually with repeat marks, signifies the close of the first main section.

The second section, the *development, exploits the thematic material of the exposition, though new material may be presented. These themes are often broken down into their motivic components, which are freely juxtaposed and developed. The section is tonally unstable, exploring a wide variety of keys by means of harmonic sequence and other modulatory devices. It leads most usually to the dominant chord of the principal key, in preparation for the recapitulation, the third section.

The recapitulation marks the return to the tonic key and to the thematic material of the exposition. It repeats most of the themes of the exposition in the same order, but here the second group remains in the tonic key. If there was a transition between the first and second groups it must therefore now be tonally adjusted so that the modulation of the exposition is not effected. And if the movement is in a minor key, the second theme group, formerly in the relative major, may be recapitulated either in the tonic major or in the tonic minor, with necessary modification. After all the material of the exposition has been recapitulated and a decisive cadence has been heard in the tonic key, there is sometimes a double bar indicating a repeat from the beginning of the development section. A coda may conclude the movement. It follows the cadence and double bar (if any). Codas vary in length from a few bars of cadence confirmation to a large section, with new musical ideas. The first movement of Beethoven's Piano Sonata in G major op. 14 no. 2 provides an example of the form (Table 1).

Although many sonata-form movements follow the plan outlined above, it is by no means a rigid compositional formula. Thematic and tonal elements may become separated so that, for example, a recapitulation could start with the 'right' theme in the 'wrong' key; conversely it may start with the 'wrong' theme in the 'right' key. The exposition is sometimes preceded by an introduction, which is often in a slower tempo than the rest of the movement.

TABLE 1

bar nos.	*thematic function*	*key progressions*
exposition		
1–8	First subject	G major
9–25	Transition (bridge)	G major–D major
26–32	Second group: first theme	D major
33–46	Second group: second theme	D major
47–56	Second group: third theme	D major
58–63	Codetta	D major
development		
64–73	First subject (motivic components)	G minor–V of B♭ major
74–80	Second group—first theme	B♭ major
81–98	First subject (motivic components) with new two-bar continuation	A♭ major–G minor–F minor–V of E♭ major
99–106	First subject extended	E♭ major
107–24	18 bars of dominant preparation for the return; includes motivic components of first subject	Dominant pedal
recapitulation		
125–32	First subject	G major
133–52	Transition; three inserted bars (137–9) adjust the tonality to lead to chord V of the tonic	G major–V of G major
153–86	Unaltered recapitulation of second group brought to a slightly adjusted cadence (cf. 56 and 183) (codetta omitted)	G major
187–200	Coda based on the first subject	G major

sonata rondo form. A hybrid design incorporating elements from both *sonata form and *rondo form. It may be represented by the letter-scheme ABACABA. B denotes not, as in rondo form, an episode but rather a second subject; C denotes the development or, if new material is introduced, an episode; and the final A is the coda based on the rondo theme, i.e. first subject. The scheme may be more clearly expressed as shown in Table 1.

Thus a sonata rondo is differentiated from sonata form by the additional appearance of the first subject in the tonic key after the second subject and before the development; it is differentiated from rondo form because the second subject—B—returns in the tonic key. The form was often used for the final movement of multi-movement works by Haydn, Mozart, Beethoven, and their contemporaries. Like sonata form it is not a rigid formula.

Sonata rondo form, Table 1

section	*function*	*key*
A	first subject	tonic
B	second subject	dominant or relative major
A	first subject	tonic
C	development/episode	related key or keys
A	first subject	tonic
B	second subject	tonic
A	coda	tonic

sonatina (It., dim. of 'sonata'; Fr.: *sonatine*). A short, relatively undemanding type of sonata, often for piano. In the later Classical period sonatinas were written for didactic purposes, and many are still in use as teaching material. Such works follow the general structure of the sonata, being in three or four movements, though the development sections of sonata-form movements are usually very short. In the 20th century the term was applied more loosely to lightweight (though not necessarily easy) sonata-type instrumental works, often of the less serious kind.

song. A short vocal composition. It may be for one or more voices, accompanied or unaccompanied, sacred or secular, and is usually self-contained. There are several types of song (folksong, partsong, art song) but the term is generally taken to denote a secular piece for one voice, which might be a Lied or a *mélodie*. In opera the term *'aria' or *air* is preferred for solo vocal items. *See also* AIR; AIR À BOIRE; AIR DE COUR; AYRE; BALLADE; BALLATA; BRUNETTE; CANTIGA; CHANSON; FROTTOLA; LAUDA SPIRITUALE; LIED; LUTE-SONG; MADRIGAL; MEISTERSINGER; MÉLODIE; MINNESINGER; MOTET; PARTSONG; ROMANCE; RONDEAU; TENORLIED; TROUBADOUR; TROUVÈRE; VILLANCICO; VIRELAI.

song cycle (Ger.: *Liederzyklus*). A group of songs with a common theme, usually setting a single poet. The music may have coherence of key or form and be attached to a narrative, or may more generally serve to express a unifying mood or theme. In the latter case, the German term sometimes used is *Liederkreis*, though the distinction between the two is not clear-cut. There are antecedents in various national traditions, but the song cycle came to maturity with 19th-century German *lied.

song without words (Fr.: *romance sans paroles, chanson sans paroles*; Ger.: *Lied ohne Worte*). A short, lyrical *character piece for piano; the term was invented by Mendelssohn.

sonnerie (Fr.). A signal sounded by trumpets or bells.

sonore (Fr.), **sonoro, sonora** (It.). 'Sonorous'; *sonorité* (Fr.), *sonorità* (It.), 'sonority'; *sonoramente* (It.), 'sonorously'; *onde sonore* (Fr.), 'sound wave', 'acoustic wave'.

sonority. 1. A sound defined by a combination of timbres or registers, particularly one that plays an important part in a work. **2.** The quality of tone produced by an instrumentalist.

sons bouchés (Fr.). *'Stopped notes' in horn playing.

sopra (It.). 'On', 'above'; *come sopra*, 'as above'; *mano sinistra [ms] sopra*, in keyboard playing, with the left hand above the right.

Sopran (Ger.). *'Soprano'.

sopranino (It., dim. of 'soprano'). The highest-pitched member of a family of instruments.

soprano. 1. The highest female (or artificial male) voice, with a range of roughly *b* to *c'''* (in high sopranos often to *f'''*). The word derives from the Latin *superius*, the usual term for the highest voice in 15th-century polyphonic music. There are several types of soprano, of which the commonest are the 'coloratura soprano', a light, high voice of great agility; 'lyric soprano', the most common, with a warmer tone-quality and a slightly lower range; 'dramatic soprano', with a heavier production throughout the range; and 'soprano *spinto', or 'soprano lirico spinto', basically a lyric voice that is capable of more dramatic quality and a cutting edge at climaxes. **2.** A high-pitched member of a family of instruments, with a range lower than sopranino and higher than alto.

soprano clef. A *clef, now rarely used, that places middle C on the bottom line of the staff.

sordino (It.). 'Mute'; *con sordino*, 'with the mute'.

sortie (Fr., 'exit', 'departure'). A postlude or concluding voluntary.

sospirando, sospirante, sospirevole (It.). 'Sighing', i.e. in a plaintive style.

sostenuto, sostenente (It.). 'Sustained', 'sustaining'; *andante sostenuto*, 'a sustained andante', i.e. rather slow. It is sometimes abbreviated *sost.*

sotto (It.). 'Under', 'below'; *sotto voce*, 'in a low voice', i.e. barely audible, a direction that can apply to instrumental as well as vocal performance; *mano sinistra [ms] sotto*, in keyboard playing, with the left hand below the right.

soupirant (Fr.). 'Sighing'.

sourd, sourde (Fr.). 'Muffled', 'muted'; *pédale sourde*, the soft (*una corda*) pedal.

sourdine (Fr.). 'Mute'.

soutenu (Fr.). 'Sustained'.

spacing. The arrangement of the notes of a chord, according to the requirements of the individual voices. If the upper voices are close together, the spacing is described as close position, or close harmony; if not, the arrangement is called open position, or open harmony. *See* POSITION, 2.

spasshaft (Ger.). 'Jocular'.

species counterpoint. A method (sometimes known as 'strict counterpoint') of learning the technique of 16th-century vocal counterpoint. It is usually associated with J. J. Fux's treatise *Gradus ad Parnassum* (1725). Given a *cantus firmus (a set theme in long notes), the student first learns to add one note against each note of the theme ('first species') then two against each note ('second species'), and so on, until the more complex rhythms are mastered.

spectral music. A term applied to music of several late 20th-century French composers whose works explore the acoustic properties of sound and the psychology of musical perception (of tempo, sound, and pulse).

sperdendosi (It.). 'Fading out', 'dying away'.

spezzato (It.). *See* CORI SPEZZATI.

spheres, music of the. Music thought by many medieval philosophers to be produced by the movements of the planets, either inaudible to the human ear or not involving sound at all, but nevertheless an all-pervading force in the universe. It was considered the highest form of music, itself interpreted in terms of mathematical proportion.

spianato, spianata (It.). 'Smooth', 'even'.

spiccato (It.). 'Detached'; a term used in the bowing of stringed instruments to mean **sautillé*. Before 1750 it was taken to mean simply **staccato*.

spiegando (It.). 'Unfolding', i.e. becoming louder.

Spiel, spielen (Ger.). 'Play', 'to play', 'to perform'; *spielend*, 'playing', 'playful'; *volles Spiel*, 'full organ'; *Spieler*, 'player'; *Spielfigur*, a short, playful figure or motif (mainly in early keyboard music).

Spieloper (Ger., 'opera-play'). A type of 19th-century light opera, resembling **Singspiel* in that it uses spoken dialogue.

Spinnerlied (Ger.). 'Spinner's song'; *Spinnlied*, 'spinning song'.

spinto (It., 'pushed', 'urged on'). A term applied to certain voice types, particularly *soprano and tenor, to indicate a voice that has been 'pushed' into more forceful singing.

spirito, spiritoso (It.). 'Spirit', 'spirited', i.e. at a fast tempo; *spiritosamente*, 'in a spirited manner'; *con spirito*, 'with spirit'.

spiritual. A religious folksong associated with revivalism in America from *c.*1740 to the end of the 19th century. The term is abbreviated from 'spiritual songs'. The spiritual became popular as concert music at the end of the 19th century.

Spitze (Ger.). 'Point'; *an der Spitze*, 'at the point' of the bow in string playing, 'with the toe' of the foot in organ playing.

Sprechchor (Ger., 'speech-choir'). **Sprechgesang* executed by a chorus rather than a soloist.

Sprechgesang, Sprechstimme (Ger.). 'Speech-song', 'speaking voice'. Terms denoting a vocal technique that combines elements of speaking and singing. It was introduced by Humperdinck; Schoenberg used it in several works, stipulating that the performer should give the exact pitch but leave it immediately by a fall or rise. *Sprechgesang* is often notated with x's, rather than note-heads, attached to conventional stems and flags.

Springbogen (Ger.). A kind of bow-stroke. *See* SAUTILLÉ.

springer [acute, sigh] (Fr.: *accent, aspiration, plainte*; Ger.: *Nachschlag*). An ornament used in 17th- and 18th-century music. It consists of a short auxiliary note inserted after the main note and taking part of its time-value; thus it is the opposite of an *appoggiatura, being an anticipation, rather than a delaying, of the following note. It was generally indicated with a diagonal line or with a small note (Ex. 1).

Ex. 1

squillante (It.). 'Shrill', i.e. harshly. When applied to cymbals, they should be suspended and struck with drumsticks rather than clashed together.

staccato (It.). 'Detached', i.e. the opposite of **legato*. A note to be played *staccato* is marked in notation in different ways: with a dot (the most common method), a vertical stroke, a small wedge, or a horizontal dash (implying an accent). The degree of detachment varies according to the type of instrument in question and the style and period of the music. *Staccato* dots within a slur imply a *mezzo-staccato*; a combination of a dot and a horizontal dash indicates accent and separation. *Staccatissimo* indicates extreme detachment. The term is often abbreviated *stacc.*

Stadtpfeifer (Ger., 'town piper'). A professional musician employed by German civic authorities, similar to the British *wait. *Stadtpfeifer* came into existence in the 14th century. A considerable body of **Turmmusik* ('tower music') was composed for them.

staff (pl. staves). In musical notation, a number of horizontal lines on and between which musical notes are placed. A *clef placed on the staff indicates the pitch of one line (and, by extension, of all the lines), thus defining the pitch of each note written on the staff. Notes outside the pitch range of the staff are normally given *ledger lines. Since the late Middle Ages a five-line staff has been preferred for most music. Staves may be bracketed together on the left (as in piano music) to form a 'system' (*see* SCORE). *See also* NOTATION.

Ständchen (Ger.). *'Serenade'.

stark (Ger.). 'Strong', 'loud'; *stärker*, 'stronger', 'louder'; *stärker werdend*, 'becoming louder'; *stark anblasen, stark blasend*, 'strongly blown' (in playing wind instruments).

stave. Alternative term for *staff, erroneously coined from 'staves', the plural of 'staff'.

S

Steg (Ger.). *'Bridge'.

steigern (Ger.). 'To intensify', 'to increase'; *Steigerung*, 'crescendo'.

stem. In notation, the vertical line attached to a note-head.

stendendo (It.). 'Stretching out', i.e. slowing.

stentando (It.). 'Labouring', 'holding back'; *stentato*, 'laboured'; i.e. held back with every note stressed; *stentamento*, 'laboriously', 'slowly'.

sterbend (Ger.). 'Dying away'.

steso (It.). 'Extended', 'stretched', i.e. slow.

stesso, stessa (It.). 'Same'; e.g. *lo stesso tempo, l'istesso tempo*, 'the same tempo', usually meaning that although the nominal value of the beat has changed (e.g. from a crotchet to a dotted crotchet), its duration is to remain the same.

stile antico (It., 'old style'). One of the terms frequently applied to 17th-century church music written in the style of Palestrina, with smooth, flowing polyphony and scored *a cappella* (rather than in *stile moderno*—for a few voices with continuo accompaniment). *See also* ALLA PALESTRINA.

stile concitato (It., 'agitated style'). A term used by Monteverdi in his discussion of the three main styles (*generi*) of music: *concitato, molle,* and *temperato*, which he equated with 'anger, moderation, and humility or supplication' respectively. His musical realization of this style involved using high vocal ranges and repeated semiquavers (representing Ancient Greek pyrrhic rhythms). Later Baroque composers made occasional use of this style to set passages of text describing battles or fighting.

stile lombardo (It., 'Lombardy style'). *See* SCOTCH SNAP.

stile moderno (It., 'modern style'). *See* STILE ANTICO.

stile rappresentativo (It., 'representative style'). A term for the new dramatic style of writing for the voice which was developed by members of the Florentine *Camerata as an attempt to match in emotional power the music of the Ancient Greeks. Music in this style is recitative-like and free in rhythm and phrasing, following the stresses of the text it sets, and uses such devices as frequent pauses and unusual intervals for emotional effect. *See also* MONODY, 2.

Stimme (Ger.). 'Voice', including in the sense of a vocal or instrumental part; it also means 'organ stop' and 'soundpost' (on a stringed instrument). The plural is *Stimmen*.

stimmen (Ger.). 'To tune'.

Stimmung (Ger.). **1.** 'Mood'; hence *Stimmungsbild*, a piece of music expressing a particular mood, and *Stimmungsmusik*, 'background' or 'mood' music. **2.** *'Tuning'.

stinguendo (It.). 'Extinguishing', i.e. fading out.

stirando, stirato, stiracciando, stiracchiato (It.). 'Stretching', 'stretched', i.e. expanding by means of a **ritardando*.

stochastic music (from Gk. *stokhos*, 'aim'). Originally a mathematical term, a 'stochastic process' being one whose goal can be described but whose individual details are unpredictable. In music, it refers to composition by the use of the laws of probability. By contrast with *indeterminate music, stochastic music is fully composed: chance enters only into the process of composition.

stopped notes. 1. Notes produced on stringed instruments by the application of finger pressure on the string against the fingerboard. *See* STOPPING. **2.** Notes produced on the horn by inserting the right hand in the bell, shortening the tube and thus raising the pitch, typically by a semitone.

stopping. In string playing, the placing of the fingertips of the left hand on the string (usually on the fingerboard). As the vibrating length of the string is progressively shortened, higher-pitched notes result. Double stopping is the stopping of and playing on two strings at a time. However, the term can also be applied more generally, to indicate that two notes are bowed simultaneously, whether or not they are stopped. Similarly, multiple stopping indicates the playing of more than two (and up to four) notes or strings together, either stopped or unstopped. *See also* STOPPED NOTES.

straccinato (It.). 'Stretched out', i.e. *ritardando*.

straff, straffer (Ger.). 'Strict', 'tight', 'stricter', 'tighter'; *straffen*, 'tighten' (e.g. a drum-head).

strambotto (It.). A type of strophic poem set in Renaissance Italy by composers of *frottolas and madrigals. Each verse had eight lines of 11 syllables, and the most common rhyme scheme was abababcc. Frottola composers generally set the first two lines of a *strambotto* to two musical phrases, and then repeated these for each of the following couplets; sometimes the final couplet would be set to different music.

strascinando, strascinato (It.). 'Dragging', 'dragged', i.e. played with heavily slurred notes.

straziante (It.). 'Agonizing', 'heartrending'.

street cries. The musical shouts of street vendors or pedlars; the cry of each created a different musical phrase, recognizable even at a distance when the words uttered could not be heard, thus allowing buyers to locate the goods they required. They have been used by composers from the Middle Ages to the present day, mainly in the *quodlibet.

Streich (Ger.). 'Stroke', i.e. a bowstroke; *Streichinstrumente*, 'bowed instruments'; *Streichquartett*, 'string quartet', etc.

strepitoso, strepitosamente (It.). 'Noisy', 'noisily'.

stretto (It., 'compressed'). A fugal device in which subject entries follow closely in succession, each subject overlapping with the next. *See* FUGUE.

strict counterpoint. *Counterpoint in which parts are fitted to a cantus firmus according to firm principles of part-writing as well as of consonance and dissonance.

stringendo (It.). 'Squeezing', 'pressing', i.e. getting faster.

S

string quartet. *See* QUARTET.

string quintet. *See* QUINTET.

string trio. *See* TRIO, 1.

strisciando, strisciato (It.). 'Trailing', 'trailed', i.e. smooth, slurred, or *glissando.

stromentato (It.). 'Accompanied by instruments'; *recitativo stromentato*, recitative accompanied by instruments in addition to the continuo.

strophic. In poetry, a stanzaic form in which each verse (strophe) follows the same structure, metre, and rhyme scheme. In music the term is used by extension to describe any form founded on a repeated pattern: AAAA, etc. It is most commonly found in songs, especially folksongs and art songs of a folk-like nature, in which each stanza of the poem is set to the same music.

strophic variations. In vocal music, a strophic form in which each stanza retains the same bass, while the melody or solo part is varied at each repetition of the bass pattern. The bass is not necessarily strictly identical in every repetition, but the essential outline is maintained so that the same succession of harmonies occurs in every strophe. Strophic variations were especially common in early 17th-century Italian *monody.

strumento (It.). 'Instrument'; *strumentato*, 'instrumented' or 'orchestrated'.

Stück (Ger.). 'Piece', 'composition'; *Klavierstück*, 'keyboard piece', usually 'piano piece'.

study. *See* ÉTUDE.

study score. A *miniature score, or a full score of reduced dimensions.

stürmend, stürmisch (Ger.). 'Stormy', 'passionate'.

Sturm und Drang (Ger., 'storm and stress'). A German aesthetic movement of the mid- to late 18th century. It has often been interpreted as an outcome of **Empfindsamkeit*, a heightened expressiveness or sensibility of manner. Its adherents aimed to portray violent emotions in the most dramatic way possible. It reached its climax in the literature of the 1760s and 70s of Goethe and Schiller; there are parallels in the visual arts, in representations of storms or evocations of terror. In music, the term was first applied to Haydn's symphonies, notably those of the early 1770s (mostly with numbers in the 40s), in an intense, dramatic style and in the minor mode. The *Sturm und Drang* movement also affected opera, and contained many of the seeds of *Romanticism.

style brisé (Fr., 'broken style'). The characteristic style of 17th-century lute music, in which the notes of a chord were not plucked simultaneously but arpeggiated. The style had considerable influence on late 17th- and early 18th-century composers of keyboard music, especially in France.

style galant (Fr.). *See* GALANT.

style luthé (Fr.). ***Style brisé*.**

su (It.). 'On', 'up'; e.g. *arcata in su*, 'with an up-bow'. (*See also* SUL, SULL', SULLA, SUI, SUGLI, SULLE.)

subdominant. The fourth degree of the major or minor scale. The prefix 'sub' refers to the position of the subdominant a 5th below the tonic, whereas the dominant is a 5th above the tonic.

subito (It.). 'Suddenly', 'immediately'; *attacca subito*, 'begin immediately', an indication at the end of a movement that the next should follow without a break.

subject. A structurally important theme or melodic fragment. **1.** In a *fugue, a subject is the principal theme—announced in the first part (or 'voice') to enter—on which the composition is founded. The fugal subject was derived from the 'point' and *cantus firmus of Renaissance imitative technique and is a common identifiable feature of contrapuntal structures from the Baroque period onwards. **2.** A theme in *sonata form. Thus a sonata exposition is said to have a 'first subject' and a 'second subject'. This usage appears even in the descriptions of expositions with only one theme ('monothematic'), where 'subject' refers to the entire tonic and dominant passages of the typical harmonic structure. **3.** The term is occasionally used for the sections of dance forms, the *leitmotifs of Wagner's music dramas, or the contrasting themes of *atonal music structures.

submediant. The sixth degree of the major or minor scale. The prefix 'sub' refers to the position of the submediant a 3rd below the tonic, whereas the mediant is a 3rd above the tonic.

successive counterpoint. *See* SPECIES COUNTERPOINT.

suite. An instrumental genre consisting of a succession of fairly short, congruous movements. During the Baroque period, when the suite was a principal instrumental form, each movement took on the stylized character of a particular dance; the dances were normally in the same key, were sometimes linked thematically, and were mostly in binary form. Although the term 'suite' did not appear until the mid-16th century, the form's origins lie in the pairing of dances, which dates back to the late 14th and the 15th centuries. A common pattern was for a relatively slow, duple-metre dance such as the *pavan (England, France) or the *passamezzo (Italy) to be followed by a faster, triple-metre dance such as the *galliard or *saltarello, which might use the same thematic material or at least begin with a similar melodic or rhythmic motif. During the Baroque period a typical suite would consist of an *allemande, *courante, *sarabande, and *gigue, with frequent interpolations of *minuet, *gavotte, *passepied, *bourrée, *musette, and *rigaudon. Other terms used in different countries and at different periods to describe pieces conforming to the suite principle include *ordre* (France), *sonata da *camera* (Italy), *partita or *Partie* (Italy, Germany), and *Ouvertüre* or *overture (Germany, England). The suite reached its peak in the works of Bach and Handel. In the second half of the 18th century the *sonata replaced it as the standard instrumental genre.

The instrumental suite of the late 19th and early 20th centuries had little to do with its Baroque predecessor. Traditional dance movements were supplanted by a free succession of national or folk dances, sometimes with a programmatic background, or by numbers extracted from a ballet, opera, or other dramatic work and rearranged for concert performance.

suivez (Fr.). 'Follow'. **1.** An indication at the end of a movement that the next should follow without a break, i.e. the same as **attacca*. **2.** A direction that the accompanying part or parts should follow the solo, i.e. the same as **colla parte*, *colla voce*.

sul, sull', sulla, sui, sugli, sulle (It.). 'On the'; *sul G*, 'on the G string'; *sul ponticello*, bow 'on the bridge'; *sulla tastiera*, *sul tasto*, bow 'on the fingerboard'.

sung Mass. *See* MISSA.

superius (Lat.). In early vocal music, the name given to the highest voice part in an ensemble and to the partbook that contains its music. The terms 'cantus' and 'discantus' may also be used.

supertonic. The second degree of the major or minor scale, i.e. the degree that lies one step above the tonic.

supertonic seventh chord. *See* ADDED SIXTH CHORD.

sur (Fr.). 'On'; *sur la touche*, bow 'on the fingerboard'; *sur le chevalet*, bow 'near the bridge'.

surprise cadence. *See* CADENCE.

suspended cadence. *See* CADENCE.

suspension. A form of discord arising from the holding over of a note in one chord as a momentary part of the chord which follows, it then resolving by falling a degree to a note which forms a real part of the second chord (Ex. 1). When two notes are held over in this way, it is called a double suspension.

Ex. 1

süss (Ger.). 'Sweet'.

sussurrando, sussurrante (It.). 'Whispering', 'murmuring'.

Suzuki method. A method of teaching instrumental playing named after its originator, Shin'ichi Suzuki (1898–1998), a Japanese educationist and violin teacher. He advocated starting violin training by the age of two or three, and did not teach notation until there was a grounding in playing skills and musical memory.

svegliando, svegliato (It.). 'Awakening', 'awakened', i.e. brisk, alert.

svelto (It.). 'Quick', 'smart'.

symbolism. A term for the ways in which musical elements may be connected to extra-musical phenomena: the words of a poem, a natural object, or a person or emotional state. Musical symbolism has sometimes been visual: two semibreves representing the eyes of the beloved, or black notes symbolic of death (*see* EYE MUSIC). It is also a feature of *word-painting. Numerology, key-association, individual instruments, and themes were used symbolically (*see* LEITMOTIF). Specifically, Symbolism was a late 19th- and early 20th-century literary movement, principally in France, and several French composers, including Fauré and Ravel, set Symbolist poems.

symphonic band. *See* CONCERT BAND.

symphonic poem [tone-poem]. A piece of orchestral music, usually in one movement, based on a literary, poetic, or other extra-musical idea. It originated in the mid-19th century with Liszt and, as a product of a Romantic movement which encouraged literary, pictorial, and dramatic associations in music, it developed into an important form of *programme music in the second half of the 19th century. Elements of symphonic architecture could be compressed into its single-movement form, and although the term 'tone-poem' has largely been used interchangeably with 'symphonic poem', a few composers, notably Richard Strauss and Sibelius, have preferred the former for pieces that are less 'symphonic' in design and in which there is no special emphasis on thematic or tonal contrast. The symphonic poem has its ancestry in the concert *overture of the earlier 19th century as well as in the symphony itself; it was often used for expressing *nationalism in music.

symphonic study. A term used by several composers for orchestral works akin to the *symphonic poem.

symphonie concertante (Fr., 'concertante symphony'; It.: *sinfonia concertante*). A form of concerto which flourished in the late 18th century. Of a lighthearted character, it was essentially a concerto for more than one solo instrument (between two and seven) in which the role of the orchestra was to accompany the solo parts. The *symphonie concertante* was especially popular in Paris, where the combination of soloists ranged from the usual two violins to more unusual groups. The importance in the 19th century of the star solo performer caused the decline of the *symphonie concertante* in favour of the virtuoso solo concerto.

symphony. The word 'symphony' first appeared in the late 16th century. However, it denoted nothing more specific than 'music for ensemble' (from the Greek *syn*, 'together', and *phone*, 'sounding'. 'Symphony' was thus interchangeable with *'concerto'. By the 1620s a symphony (or sinfonia) could be an instrumental piece at the beginning or the middle of a vocal work such as a motet, madrigal, or cantata—much in the manner of a *ritornello, though the sinfonia was not usually repeated throughout the piece. When public opera houses opened in Venice in the 1630s, the new operas often had a 'sinfonia' or *overture. By the end of the century these were in three movements (fast–slow–fast); the first movement tended to be constructed of short, contrasting themes with strong rhythmic shapes, underpinned with simple harmonies. It was from this form that the symphony grew.

The earliest symphonies were in three movements, the third often being in dance rhythm. In the mid-17th century, an independent minuet movement was introduced (usually after the slow movement). The main centres of symphonic composition were Mannheim (where the four-movement form was established) and Vienna, where Haydn and Mozart were the principal exponents of the Viennese Classical symphony. Richness of harmony and orchestration and a strong sense of form characterize the Viennese symphony, of which the first movement was generally in *sonata form. Beethoven transformed the symphony, in scale and weight, introducing voices in his Ninth.

During the 19th and 20th centuries, composers continued to write symphonies, but it was the more traditional who persisted with the four-movement form. The title 'symphony' could be applied to orchestral works in three, five, or six movements, with or without vocal soloists and chorus; some had a specific *programme. Many Romantic composers preferred the flexibility offered by the *symphonic poem.

syncopation. The displacement of the normal musical accent from a strong beat to a weak one. In mensural music beats fall naturally into groups of two or three with a recurring accent on the first of each group. Any irregularity, either brief or extended, that has the effect of rhythmic contradiction when introduced into this pattern may be termed syncopation. Holding notes on normally weak beats over to strong beats, using rests to displace the notes, and placing notes between beats, are among the methods used to create syncopation.

system. In musical notation, two or more staves bracketed together on the left, indicating that the music on them is to be played or sung at the same time. *See* SCORE.

T. Abbreviation for *tenor.

tablature (Fr.: *tablature*; Ger.: *Tabulatur*; It.: *intavolatura*). Musical notation for instruments, based on figures, letters, or other symbols instead of conventional staff notation. Most tablatures are tailored to the playing technique of a particular type of instrument, using one set of symbols showing pitch (which fret to stop, which key to depress, or which hole to cover) and another indicating rhythm. Grid-like tablatures for fretted strings (e.g. the lute), introduced in the late 15th century, depict the intersections of frets and sets of strings (also known as 'courses') so as to indicate where to place the fingers. From the early 14th century a combination of tablature and staff notation was used for keyboard music; the top part was notated on a five-line staff and the lower parts aligned below in letter notation, with rests indicated by the letter 's' (for Lat. *sine*, 'without'); sharps are indicated by a wavy line after the letter. The diagrammatic notation used in popular music for the guitar is a form of tablature.

table music. *See* TAFELMUSIK.

tacet (Lat.). 'Is silent'; a direction that a player remain silent; *tacet al fine*, 'remaining silent until the end'.

tactus (Lat.). A 15th- and 16th-century term for 'beat' (*see* BEAT, 1).

Tafelmusik (Ger., 'table music'; Fr.: *musique de table*). Music intended for performance at feasts. The term arose in 16th-century Germany to refer to a genre coordinate with *Kirchenmusik* and *Kammermusik*. 17th- and early 18th-century collections often included part-songs and songs with continuo as well as instrumental music.

Tagelied (Ger., 'day song'). *See* ALBA.

tail. *See* FLAG.

taille. A French term used from the 16th century to the 18th to denote the part that other languages call 'tenor'; hence *taille de violon* for the viola, *taille d'hautbois* for the tenor shawm or, from 1660, the tenor oboe, and so on.

Takt (Ger.). **1.** 'Time' or 'metre'; *Taktzeichen*, 'time signature'; 3/4 *Takt*, *Dreivierteltakt*, '3/4 time'; *im Takt*, 'in time' (i.e. *a tempo*); *taktfest*, 'in steady time'. **2.** 'Beat'; *ein Takt wie vorher zwei*, 'one beat as previously two' (i.e. one beat should be allowed as much time as two beats were previously). **3.** 'Bar'; *Taktnote* (literally 'bar-note'), *semibreve; *Taktpause*, a bar's rest; *Taktstrich*, 'bar-line'; *dreitaktig*, in three-bar phrases.

Tändelei (Ger., 'trifling'). *See* BADINAGE, BADINERIE.

tango. A dance originating in urban Argentina in the late 19th century. In duple metre, with a characteristic rhythmic figure, it consists of two sections, the second usually in the dominant or relative minor. It resembles the *habanera and is often played on the accordion, specifically the bandoneon. It became a popular society dance for couples in 1920s Paris.

tant (Fr.), **tanto** (It.). 'As much', 'so much'; *non tanto*, 'not too much', e.g. *allegro ma non tanto*, '*allegro*, but not too much so'.

Tanz, Tänze (Ger.). 'Dance', 'dances'.

tarantella (It.; Fr.: *tarentelle*). A dance that takes its name from the southern Italian seaport of Taranto. Tarantellas are in rapid 6/8 time, are often in conjunct motion, and involve *perpetuum mobile* (proceeding throughout in notes of the same value), frequently increasing in tempo throughout the piece. The *saltarello is similar.

tardo, tarda (It.). 'Slow'; *tardamente*, 'slowly'; *tardando, tardante*, 'slowing down'.

tasto (It.). **1.** A 'key' of a keyboard instrument. Hence *tasto solo* is an instruction to the keyboard player of a *continuo part to play 'a single key only', i.e. to play the written bass line without adding chords or harmonic parts. **2.** 'The fingerboard' of a stringed instrument; *sul tasto*, an instruction to bow above the fingerboard.

te. *See* SI.

tedesca (It., 'German'). In late 16th-century Italy the *tedesca* or *todesca* was a lighthearted type of villanella that mocked the accent of Germans speaking Italian. Thereafter the term *alla tedesca* can be taken to mean 'in the style of the most characteristic German dance' of the period, e.g. the allemande in the 17th century or, from *c.*1800, the ländler (or other similar dance in triple time).

Te Deum laudamus (Lat., 'We praise you, O God'). The long hymn that constitutes the supreme expression of rejoicing in the Roman Catholic, Anglican, and other Christian Churches. In the Roman rite it occurs as the climax of the service of Matins on Sundays and festivals. Vernacular versions of the hymn were made by Luther and Cranmer. There are many important settings of it from the 16th to late 20th centuries.

Teil [Theil] (Ger.). 'Part', 'portion', 'section'; *teilen (theilen)*, 'to divide'.

tema (It.). 'Theme', 'subject'; *tema con variazioni*, 'theme with variations'.

temperament. A method of tuning ('tempering') in which some concords are made slightly impure so that few or none will be unpleasantly out of tune. Such methods are necessary because the concords of tonal music (octaves, 5ths, and 3rds) do not add up to 'pure' octaves. Tuning became essential with the introduction of keyboard instruments. Voices and many other instruments can modify their notes according to context, varying the pitch slightly to keep in tune, but with keyboards all pitches are fixed. *See* EQUAL TEMPERAMENT; JUST INTONATION; MEAN-TONE TEMPERAMENT; PYTHAGOREAN INTONATION.

tempestoso, tempestosamente (It.). 'Tempestuous', 'tempestuously'.

tempo (It.). The speed at which a piece of music is performed. This is indicated in two ways: by metronome marks (e.g. ♩ = 70, meaning a tempo of 70 crotchet beats per minute); and, less precisely, by verbal instructions, conventionally (but not exclusively) in Italian (e.g. *adagio*, slow, *andante*, less slow, *allegretto*, moderately fast, *allegro*, quick, *presto*, very fast). Music before *c.*1600 rarely contains any indication of tempo, which is inferred from its notation and style. Tempo was expressed in notation by the combination of mensuration (*see* MENSURAL MUSIC, MENSURAL NOTATION), the note-values, and the fixed pulse (*tactus*; *see* BEAT, 1) assigned to a particular note-value. Later, tempo could sometimes be inferred from a work's title, or its origin in a dance form. By the 18th century, Italian terms were in common use. Some aleatory music demands a more scientifically precise (or differently defined) measurement of tempo than these traditional methods allow.

Metronome marks in 19th-century music cannot always be taken as reliable, and some are so fast as to be impracticable. Verbal directions are imprecise and their meanings and associations have changed over the years. It is not always clear whether metronome markings or verbal instructions have the composer's authority or are editorial additions.

Tempo may be subject to variation through external factors: the size and reverberation time of a hall; the differing sonorities of instruments, particularly keyboard ones; the size of an orchestra; the interpretation of a performer. The last factor accounts for the widely differing tempos encountered in different performances of the same work, all of which may be equally valid.

tempo alla breve. *See* ALLA BREVE.

tempo giusto (It.). 'The right time'; either the usual tempo for the type of music in question, or the return to a regular tempo after a passage of flexible tempo.

tempo maggiore (It.). A term equivalent to **alla breve*.

tempo ordinario (It.). **1.** At an 'ordinary speed', i.e. neither fast nor slow. **2.** Common time (4/4), with four beats in the bar (as opposed to two, as in *tempo alla breve*).

tempo primo (It.; Ger.: *Tempo wie vorher*). 'At the first tempo'; an instruction to resume the original tempo after a passage departing from it; where there has been more than one such change, 'tempo primo' refers to the first-mentioned speed.

tempo rubato. *See* RUBATO.

temps (Fr.). 'Time', usually in the sense of 'beat'; *temps fort*, the first ('strong') beat of the bar. *See* BEAT, 1.

tempus (Lat.). 'Time'. In medieval music, the term indicates the relationship between the breve and the semibreve. (*See also* PROLATION).

ten. (It.). Abbreviation for **tenuto*.

tendre, tendrement (Fr.). 'Tender', 'tenderly'.

tenebroso (It.). 'Dark', 'gloomy'.

tenendo (It.). 'Holding', sustaining'; *tenendo il canto*, 'sustaining the melody'.

teneramente (It.). 'Tenderly'.

tenor (from Lat. *tenere*, 'to hold'). **1.** The term has had various meanings in connection with plainchant, of which the most common were a melodic formula, especially a psalm tone or its termination (*see* PLAINCHANT); the final or key note of a mode; and the characteristic note of recitation in a reciting tone (also called *tuba*); *see* TONUS, 3. **2.** From the mid-13th century to the 16th, 'tenor' denoted the fundamental ('held') voice part of a polyphonic composition, usually in the form of a pre-existing *cantus firmus; the other parts were composed 'against' this (hence the term *'contratenor'), and at first were named in the order in which they were composed after the tenor (*duplum, *triplum, etc.). 'Tenor' did not imply any particular range until the 15th century, when well-known singers of tenor parts were sometimes known as 'tenoriste' or 'tenorista'. **3.** The highest male voice using normal voice production, with a range of roughly *c* (known as 'tenor C') to *b'*, or, in fine voices with good training, even high *c''* or *d*♭''. Often used for minor or comic roles in 18th-century opera, the tenor voice rose to pre-eminence in Romantic opera. A tenor can be described as one of three broad types: light, lyric, and dramatic (**spinto*). The *Heldentenor* (Ger., literally 'hero tenor'), required for Wagnerian roles such as Siegfried, is a heavy tenor with much of the quality of a baritone. *See also* COUNTERTENOR. **4.** A low-pitched member of a family of instruments, with a range lower than alto and higher than bass.

tenor clef. *See* CLEF.

Tenorlied (Ger.). The basic form of German polyphonic secular song from the 15th century to the mid-16th. 'Tenor' refers not to the voice part of the name, but to the borrowed tune, or cantus firmus, which was the only part to be underlaid with the complete text (*see* TENOR, 2). Before about 1500 this 'Tenor' was usually sung by the top voice of a three-part ensemble and accompanied by instruments, but later, when four-part writing became the norm, it moved down to the tenor voice proper and frequently received vocal accompaniment.

tenor mass. The most common type of mass based on a *cantus firmus, i.e. with the cantus firmus placed in the tenor part.

tenso. A type of troubadour or trouvère poetry cast in the form of a dialogue or debate between two or more poets with opposing views; the most common topic is love, but others include politics, religion, morality, or literature.

tento (Port., 'touch'). *See* TIENTO.

tenuto (It.). 'Held', i.e. sustained to the end of a note's full value; in opera the term may imply sustaining a note beyond that, for dramatic effect. It is sometimes abbreviated *ten.*

ternary form. A musical structure consisting of three parts or sections. It may be represented by the letter scheme ABA, the final section being a repeat of the first. Each section is usually self-contained: it closes in its own key. Hence the first 'A' section closes in the tonic, unlike *binary form, where the 'A' section modulates to and closes in a key other than the tonic (usually the dominant or relative major). In ternary form the middle section often provides a strong contrast to the outer two, both in tonality and in theme. Pieces in ternary form may be quite long, because the sections, being self-contained, will often have a formal shape of their own. For example, each of the three sections may itself be binary in structure. This is particularly true of the Classical *minuet and trio, where the ternary structure arises from the repeat of the minuet after the trio, though each section may be in either binary or ternary form.

The earliest use of ternary form dates from the Middle Ages, with examples occurring in certain monophonic song types of that period. It was rarely used in the Renaissance but came into its own during the Baroque era, especially with the development of the **da capo* aria as a standard vocal form in the late 17th and early 18th centuries. Here, after a contrasting middle section, the first section of the aria is repeated, often with elaborate embellishments.

Ternary form was also used frequently as the basic structure of many 19th-century piano works, particularly shorter ones such as the mazurka, nocturne, and *étude*. The form was also sometimes used as the basis of slow middle movements in sonatas or concertos.

tertiary harmony. The term for a harmonic system based on the interval of a 3rd, as in the major-minor tonal system, as opposed to medieval *quartal harmony.

terzina (It.). *'Triplet'.

tessitura (It., 'texture'). A term indicating the position of the notes in a composition in relation to the compass of the voice or instrument for which it was written, expressed as 'low', 'medium', and 'high'.

testa (It.). 'Head'; *voce di testa*, 'head voice'.

testo (It.). **1.** 'Text'. **2.** *'Narrator'.

tetrachord (from Gk. *tetra-*, 'four-', *chorde*, 'string'). A succession of four notes contained within the compass of a perfect 4th. In Ancient Greek theory, tetrachords with intervals in the descending order tone-tone-semitone (e.g. A–G–F–E) were joined together to form a series of eight-note *modes, which served, like the modern *scale, as the basis of melodic composition. Medieval theorists likewise adopted several ascending tetrachords, with different arrangements of tones and semitones within the perfect 4th, to act as a melodic basis (*see also* HEXACHORD). The modern diatonic scale may also be considered divisible into two tetrachords (e.g. C–D–E–F, G–A–B–C).

tetrardus. *See* MODE.

text-setting. The process of composing music for a text, and the musical expression of its words. In genres where it is especially important to convey the words clearly (e.g. operatic recitative, much liturgical music), the metre and structure of the text are often followed closely by a simple, syllabic melody with little ornamentation. In other forms, usually where the emphasis lies on the emotional expression of the words, the setting may be more florid, with large leaps, extended melismas on a single syllable, rhythmic distortion, and other devices that might obscure the communication of the text. *See also* WORD-PAINTING.

texture. The vertical build of music—the relationship between its simultaneously sounding parts—over a short period of time. If each of the combined parts is shown to have a more or less continuous linear character, all being of equal importance as horizontal lines, then the music is said to exhibit a contrapuntal texture. In a fugal texture, the parts behave as in a *fugue, imitating each other at time-intervals and pitch-intervals determined by well-established fugal practice. Texture may be conditioned by the vertical spacing of chords (density), by instrumental or vocal colour, intensity, attack, and by the aerating effect of rests. *See also* HOMOPHONY; POLYPHONY.

Theil. *See* TEIL.

thematic catalogue (Ger.: *thematisches Verzeichnis*). A catalogue which uses the quotation of musical material, usually the first few notes, or the incipit, sometimes the principal theme or themes, and occasionally (for polyphonic works) the entire texture of the opening, to provide positive identification of a musical work. One of its principal uses is in the scholarly catalogues of composers' works, the best known being those of the *BWV (Bach-Werke-Verzeichnis) for Bach, of *Deutsch for Schubert, *Hoboken for Haydn, and *Köchel for Mozart.

thematic transformation. *See* TRANSFORMATION, THEMATIC.

theme. A term most commonly used to denote the principal melodic material on which part or all of a work is based. 'Theme' usually refers to complete phrases or periods, in contrast to the terms 'idea' or 'motif', and is used of the more important melodic passages. Thus the first and second themes (or 'subjects') of a sonata-form movement may expose most of the melodic material and carry the greatest structural weight. Such a view of tonal forms is often called 'thematicism', especially when it attempts to show that apparently heterogeneous themes have one common source in a movement or work. *See also* VARIATION FORM.

theme and variations. *See* VARIATION FORM.

theory. The term is used in three main ways in music, though all three are interrelated.

The first is what is otherwise called 'rudiments', currently taught as the elements of notation, of key signatures, of time signatures, of rhythmic notation, and so on. Theory in this sense is treated as the necessary preliminary to the study of harmony, counterpoint, and form. The second is the study of writings about music from ancient times onwards. The third is an area of current musicological study that seeks to define processes and general principles in music, taking as its starting-point not the individual work or performance but the fundamental materials from which it is built.

thesis. *See* ARSIS AND THESIS.

third inversion. Only chords with four notes (e.g. the *diminished 7th and *dominant 7th chords) or more can be placed in third inversion, i.e. with the fourth note of the chord as the lowest. *See* INVERSION, 1.

thirty-second note (Amer.). *Demisemiquaver.

thoroughbass. *See* CONTINUO; FIGURED BASS.

threnody (from Gk. *threnos*, 'wailing', *oide*, 'ode'). A song of lamentation, especially on a person's death.

through-composed (Ger.: *durchkomponiert*). Any composition that does not rely on repeating sections for its formal design may be described as through-composed. However, the term is most usually applied to a song in which the music for each stanza is different.

tie [bind]. A curved line used in musical notation to join two successive notes of the same pitch, showing that they should form one sound lasting for the duration of their combined values. It is used to join notes either side of a bar-line or to make up a total note-value that is not available in single notes (e.g. five crotchets, seven quavers). A tie is also occasionally used to indicate the subtle repetition of the second note. *See also* SLUR.

tief (Ger.). 'Deep', 'low'; *tiefgespannt*, 'deep-stretched', i.e. loosely fastened (of a drum-head) to give a low-pitched sound.

tiento (Sp., 'touch'; Port.: *tento*). In Spanish and Portuguese music of the 16th century to the early 18th, an instrumental piece similar to the Italian *ricercar. The term derives from the Spanish verb *tentar*, meaning 'to try out' or 'to experiment', and denotes a kind of free study through which the performer is acquainted with playing in different modes and the technical problems associated with a particular instrument. Tientos first appeared in the 16th century; for vihuela, they were generally homophonic and of an improvisatory character, and often served as preludes to more substantial pieces. Later tientos were for keyboard.

tierce (Fr.). **1.** The interval of a 3rd. **2.** An organ stop adding the 17th, a high 3rd, to the harmonic content.

tierce de Picardie (Fr., 'Picardy 3rd'). A major 3rd in a tonic chord at the end of a composition which is otherwise in a minor key, thus converting the expected minor chord into a major one (e.g. in the key of C minor the expected closing chord C–E♭–G becomes C–E♮–G). The origin of the name is unknown. The *tierce de Picardie* was common in the 16th century and throughout the Baroque period.

time. *See* METRE; RHYTHM; TEMPO.

time signature. A sign placed at the start of a piece of music (after the clef and key signature) or during the course of it, indicating its *metre. It normally consists of two numbers, one above the other, the lower one defining the unit of measurement in relation to the semibreve, the upper one indicating the number of those units in each bar. A time signature of 3/4 therefore indicates that there are three crotchets ('quarter-notes', or notes worth a quarter of a semibreve) to the bar, one of 6/8 that there are six quavers ('eighth-notes', worth an eighth of a semibreve) to the bar. Table 1 shows the time signatures commonly found in Western mensural music since *c*.1700. Some signs (e.g. **C** and **₵**) are relics of medieval proportional notation, which had a complex system of time signatures of its own. The sign **C** now indicates 4/4 (common time); **₵** indicates 2/2 and implies a quick duple time (or **alla breve*).

'Simple' times have a binary subdivision of the unit (e.g. into two, four, eight, etc.) and 'compound' times a ternary one (e.g. into three, six, nine, etc.). The grouping together, or 'beaming', of smaller note-values within the unit in each time signature is conventionally arranged in twos or threes in accordance with these principles. Because the basic unit of measurement in compound time is always a dotted unit, which cannot be shown in the signature as a fraction of a semibreve, signatures for compound time use the next smallest unit as point of reference (e.g. two dotted crotchets to the bar has to be shown as six quavers, 6/8). Although bars under different time signatures may have the same total duration in terms of beats, there is a difference in rhythmic effect, as between, for example, a bar of 3/2 (dividing into three minims) and one of 6/4 (dividing into two dotted minims: see Table 1).

Quintuple time (subdividing into either 2 + 3 or 3 + 2, and in use since the 16th century) and other 'irregular' metres such as 7/16 and 11/8 are common in some folk musics. Composers of contemporary music, if they use time signatures at all, tend to adopt whatever symbols, conventional or

Time signature, TABLE 1

TIME \ BASIC UNIT		𝅗𝅥	♩	♪
DUPLE	SIMPLE	$\frac{2}{2}$ or ¢	$\frac{2}{4}$	$\frac{2}{8}$
	COMPOUND	$\frac{6}{4}$	$\frac{6}{8}$	$\frac{6}{16}$
TRIPLE	SIMPLE	$\frac{3}{2}$	$\frac{3}{4}$	$\frac{3}{8}$
	COMPOUND	$\frac{9}{4}$	$\frac{9}{8}$	$\frac{9}{16}$
QUADRUPLE	SIMPLE	$\frac{4}{2}$	$\frac{4}{4}$ or C	$\frac{4}{8}$
	COMPOUND	$\frac{12}{4}$	$\frac{12}{8}$	$\frac{12}{16}$

otherwise, best express the metre of their music.

tirade [coulade] (Fr.; It.: *tirata*). A Baroque ornament consisting of a quick succession, or 'run', of more than three passing notes, usually but not always consecutive, connecting two principal melody notes separated by a large interval. It was occasionally indicated by a sign (⸝⋯) but was frequently written out or improvised.

tirana (Sp.). An Andalusian dance-song usually in 6/8 time with syncopated rhythms. It was popular in Spain in the 18th century.

tirando (It.). 'Dragging'.

tirare (It.), **tirer** (Fr.). 'To draw', 'to pull out'; in string playing, down-bow; in organ playing, the pulling of a stop: *tiratutti*, a coupler on an organ or harpsichord; *tirato*, *tiré*, 'drawn'.

tiret (Fr.). A *mordent.

toccata (It., past participle of *toccare*, 'to touch'). A piece in a free and idiomatic style, usually for keyboard and often in several sections and incorporating virtuoso elements designed to show off the player's 'touch'. The term appeared in the early 16th century, but the first important collections date from the last decade of that century. 'Toccata' was also applied to fanfare-like pieces. The genre was very common in the Baroque era but was little used in the Classical period or in the early 19th century. It was revived in France by organ composers, who often concluded their massive organ symphonies with a toccata. The piano inspired a resurgence in toccata writing in the 20th century.

toccatina [toccatino] (It.). A miniature *toccata. There are many 19th-century examples.

tombeau (Fr., 'tomb', 'tombstone'). A composition written in memory of someone. Such pieces were composed in the

Baroque era, especially in France, for lute, guitar, or harpsichord.

ton. 1. A term with several meanings, of which the principal ones are as follows. (Fr.) (*a*) 'pitch'; *donner le ton*, 'to give the pitch'; (*b*) 'key', 'mode'; *ton d'ut*, 'key of C'; *ton majeur*, 'major key'; *ton d'église*, 'church mode'; (*c*) 'tone', in the sense of Gregorian tone (*see* TONUS, 3); (*d*) 'crook'; *ton de trompette*, 'trumpet crook'; *ton de rechange*, 'spare crook' (or simply 'crook'); (*e*) the interval of a whole tone, as distinct from *demiton*, 'semitone'; (*f*) 'sound', 'note'; *ton aigre*, 'shrill sound'; *ton bouché*, 'stopped note' (on a horn); *ton doux*, 'sweet tone'.

(Ger.) (*a*) 'pitch'; *den Ton angeben*, 'to give the pitch'; (*b*) 'key', 'mode'; *Tongeschlecht*, 'tone-gender' (i.e. major or minor, etc.); (*c*) 'note'; *den Ton halten*, 'to hold the note'; *Tonabstand*, 'interval'; *Tonfarbe*, 'tone-colour', i.e. timbre; *Tonfolge*, 'melody'; *Tonfülle*, 'volume of tone'; *Tonhöhe*, 'pitch', 'compass', 'register'; *Tonleiter*, 'scale'; *Tonreihe*, 'note row'; *Tonmass*, 'time', i.e. length of a beat; *Tonschlüssel*, 'keynote'; *Tonsetzer*, 'composer'; (*d*) 'sound', 'music'; *Tonkunst*, '[the art of] music'; *Tonkünstler*, 'musician'; *Tonlehre*, 'acoustics'; *Tonbühne*, 'orchestra'; *Tonbild*, 'tone-picture'; *Tonmalerei*, 'programme music'; *Tondichtung*, 'tone-poem'; *Tonmeister*, a qualified sound engineer. **2.** In German medieval and Renaissance literature, a term denoting a verse form and the specific melody associated with it. The Meistersinger wrote many new poems to existing *Töne*.

tonadilla [tonadilla escénica] (Sp., dim. of *tonada*, 'song'). A type of short, single-act comic opera that flourished in Spain from the mid-18th century to the early 19th. The *tonadilla* was originally performed in sections between the acts of a play as a kind of *intermezzo, but from the end of the 18th century it developed into a more substantial and independent piece. It consisted mostly of vocal arias. *See also* ZARZUELA.

tonal answer. *See* FUGUE.

tonality. The relationship between pitches in which one particular pitch is central; tonality controls the relative importance of all the sounds used within a work. Thus in major-minor tonality from the period *c*.1600–1900 the tonal centre, or tonic, is fixed for a passage, movement, or piece; the note a perfect 5th above is the next most important, the 5th below is the next, and so on (in C major, these notes would be the tonic C, the dominant G, the subdominant F). Before *c*.1600, it is more common to speak of modality than of tonality (*see* MODE). The tonality of a piece implies its *key. *See also* ATONALITY; BITONALITY; FUNCTIONAL HARMONY; PANTONALITY.

tonal sequence. *See* SEQUENCE, 1.

Tonart (Ger.). *'Key', in the sense of the key of C major, etc.

tonary (Lat.: *tonarium*, *tonarius*, *tonale*). A medieval chant book arranged by mode.

Tondichtung (Ger.). *'Symphonic poem'.

tone (Fr.: *ton*; Ger.: *Ton*; It.: *tono*). **1.** The quality of a musical sound; for example, a violinist may be said to have a 'powerful' or 'full-bodied' tone, a singer to have 'pure' tone. **2.** In American usage the word 'tone' is synonymous with the English 'note'. **3.** The interval of two semitones, i.e. a major 2nd (but *see* TEMPERAMENT); also known as 'whole tone'. **4.** A recitation formula in plainchant (*see* TONUS, 3).

tone-cluster. *See* CLUSTER.

tone-colour (Fr.: *timbre*; Ger.: *Klangfarbe*; It.: *timbro*). The quality of sound characteristic of a particular type of instrument or voice, as opposed to its register or pitch. Thus a violin sounds distinct from a flute even when playing exactly the same note; similarly, the tone-colour produced by a boy treble differs from that of a female soprano.

tone-poem. *See* SYMPHONIC POEM.

t

tone row. In American usage, synonym of *series.

tonguing. In the playing of woodwind and brass instruments, the interruption of the flow of wind from the lungs into the instrument by means of a motion of the tongue against the mouthpiece or reed. Tonguing is a vital means of varying articulation: a swift tongue motion and high blowing pressure result in a firm attack, while a slower tongue movement and gentler air pressure produce a *legato*, 'soft tonguing' effect. 'Double' and 'triple' tonguing, in which the motion is equivalent to the enunciation of two and three consonants respectively (e.g. T-K, D-G-D), facilitate non-*legato* playing of fast passages and rapid repetition of notes.

tonic. The first degree of the major or minor scale.

tonic accent. The effect of an *accent, produced not by emphasis but simply by a note falling on a higher pitch than those following or preceding it.

Tonic Sol-fa. A method of teaching sight-singing devised by John Curwen (1816–80) in which the degrees of the scale in any major key are given the *solmization syllables *doh, ray, me, fah, soh, lah, te, doh'* (the *doh* below the compass of the first seven degrees of the scale being marked *doh,*). The name Tonic Sol-fa emphasizes the fact that the major key note (or 'tonic') is always to be called *doh*. Curwen aimed to ensure that a note is 'heard' mentally before it is uttered. He introduced pupils first to the notes of the common chord (*doh–me–soh*), then taught the rest of the scale in stages. Chromatic degrees are named by changing the vowels of the syllables: sharpened notes use *e* (pronounced 'ee'), and flattened notes *a* (pronounced 'aw'). For the full chromatic scale in the key of F, see Ex. 1. When a tune modulates, the new key note is named *doh* ('movable *doh*'), the transition being expressed by a 'bridge note' with a double name (*see* FIXED DOH). The Tonic Sol-fa system was used extensively in the 19th century, especially in Britain, and was adopted and modified by Kodály for use in Hungary.

Tonkunst (Ger.). 'Music'; *Tonkünstler*, 'composer'.

tono. 1 (Sp.). In general, any type of Spanish song, sacred (*tono divino*) or secular (*tono humano*); more specifically in the 17th century, a short song originally for solo voice, later for two or three voices, used to introduce a play or other stage performance. **2** (It.). 'Tone', in any general sense; specifically 'whole tone' (*see* TONE, 3). **3** (It.). 'Key' or 'mode'; specifically a church mode, or the recitation formula belonging to it (*see* TONUS, 3).

Tonreihe (Ger.). 'Note row'; *see* SERIES.

tonus (Lat., from Gk. *tonos*, 'tone'). A term used in three senses in the Middle Ages. **1.** The interval of a major 2nd. **2.** *Mode. **3.** A plainchant recitation formula. For psalms there were more than a dozen, one for each of the eight modes and several others; the best-known irregular one was the **tonus peregrinus*, or 'wandering tone'.

tonus peregrinus (Lat., 'wandering tone'). A Latin psalm tone outside the system of the eight modes. Distinguished by the two reciting notes A in the first half-verse and G in the second, it was used principally for the performance of Psalm 113.

Tonic Sol-fa, Ex. 1

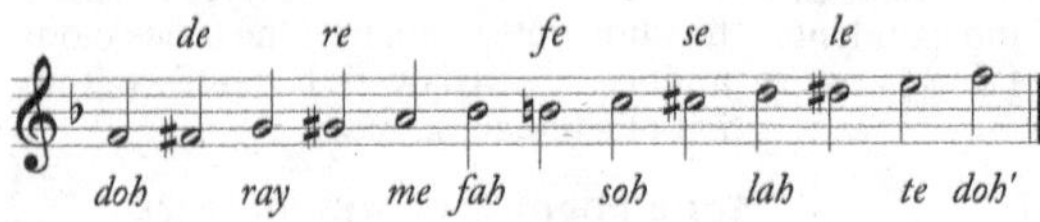

tordion [tourdion] (Fr.). A 16th-century dance in triple time; it is similar to the *galliard, but lighter and quicker, and was usually performed after a *basse danse.

tosto (It.). 'Rapid', 'at once'; *più tosto*, 'quicker' (not to be confused with *piuttosto*, 'rather'); *più che tosto*, 'as soon as'.

touch. 1. A term used to describe the amount of force needed to depress a key on a keyboard instrument, or the distance that a key may be depressed. **2.** A fanfare for trumpets and timpani (*see* TUCKET; TUSCH). **3.** A term used in English *change-ringing for a short segment of the chosen system.

touche (Fr.). **1.** A 'key' of a keyboard instrument. **2.** The 'fingerboard' of a stringed instrument. **3.** The 16th-century term for 'fret'.

tourdion. *See* TORDION.

tower music. *See* TURMMUSIK.

toye. A name given in the Elizabethan and Jacobean periods to a short, light-hearted composition for keyboard or lute.

tpt. Abbreviation for 'trumpet'.

tr. Abbreviation for 'trill', 'treble', 'transpose'.

tract. A Latin chant of the Roman Mass, usually sung before the Gospel during Lent and on other penitential days. A small group of chants for the procession to the font at the Easter vigil service were also given tract melodies. Tracts have texts comprising several psalm verses.

traduction (Fr.), **traduzione** (It.). **1.** 'Translation' (of a libretto etc.). **2.** *'Arrangement'. **3.** *'Transposition'.

tragédie lyrique. A genre of French 17th- and 18th-century opera using tragic mythological or epic subjects, characterized by declamation and naturalness of action. It reflected the *gloire* essential to Louis XIV's court entertainment and anticipated many of the rigid features of **opera seria*. The term fell into disuse in the early 19th century.

traîné (Fr.). 'Dragged'; *sans traîner*, 'without dragging'.

tranquillo (It.). 'Tranquil', 'calm'; *tranquillamente*, 'tranquilly'; *tranquillità*, *tranquillezza*, 'tranquillity'.

transcription. A term often used interchangeably with *arrangement. Transcribing, however, is copying a composition while changing layout or notation (e.g. from parts to full score), whereas arranging is changing the medium (e.g. from piano quartet to full orchestra). Transcription is carried out by ethnomusicologists to capture in staff notation a performance recorded in the field.

transformation, thematic. The process of altering a theme to change its character without losing its essential identity; another term for it is 'thematic metamorphosis'. Although the technique is found earlier, it was in the 19th century that thematic transformation was used to give unity and cohesion to multi-movement works or as an element in *programme music. Themes could be presented in different rhythms or metres, or with different orchestrations, or with slight changes in melody. The process differs from *development in that the transformed theme is likely to be treated as independently as the original. Thematic transformation is associated above all with Liszt, who used it extensively in his symphonic poems. It was a common device in opera and ballet, where it can be part of the delineation of character. Wagner's use of *leitmotif is an extension of thematic transformation.

transposition. Performance or notation of music at a pitch different from the original, effected by raising or lowering all notes by the same interval. For certain instruments (e.g. the clarinet) music is usually notated in transposition. The concept of transposition is central to theories of 12-note composition and of the set structure of post-tonal music. Messiaen codified **'modes of limited transposition'.

traquenard (Fr., 'ambush', 'trap'). A late 17th-century German dance found in orchestral suites; it is rhythmically and structurally the same as the *gavotte.

trascinando (It.). 'Dragging', i.e. holding back; *senza trascinare*, 'without dragging'.

trattenuto (It.). 'Held back', 'sustained'.

tratto (It.). 'Dragged'; usually in the negative, *non tratto*.

Trauer (Ger.). 'Mourning', 'sorrow'; *traurig*, 'mournfully'; *trauernd*, 'mourning', 'lamenting'; *Trauermarsch*, 'funeral march'; *Trauermusik*, 'funeral music'; *trauervoll*, 'sorrowful'.

Traum (Ger.). 'Dream'; *Traumbild*, 'dream picture'; *träumend*, 'dreaming'; *Träumerei*, 'reverie'; *träumerisch*, 'dreamy'; *Liebesträume*, 'dreams of love'.

traurig (Ger.). 'Mournfully'.

tre (It.). 'Three'; *a tre voci*, 'for three voices'; *tre corde*, 'three strings', an indication to remove the soft (*una corda*) pedal on the piano.

treble. 1. A high voice (particularly of a boy). In music of the 14th and 15th centuries it was the name given to the highest voice in a three-part vocal ensemble and the second highest in a four-part one; it was thus equivalent to 'superius', 'cantus', and 'discantus'. Later the voice was more usually referred to as 'soprano', except for boys' voices. **2.** A high-pitched member of a family of instruments, e.g. recorders (with a range lower than descant and higher than tenor) or viols (the highest pitched).

treble clef. The G *clef (not to be confused with the *soprano clef).

treibend (Ger.). 'Driving', i.e. hurrying.

tremando, tremante (It.). To be played or sung with *tremolo.

tremblement (Fr.). In the 17th and 18th centuries, an alternative name for the *trill; *tremblement mineur*, alternative name for *vibrato.

tremolando. *See* TREMOLO, 1.

tremolo (It., 'trembling', 'quivering'). In modern usage 'tremolo' indicates a change of intensity or repetition of a note, whereas *vibrato is a wavering or oscillation of pitch. Historically, however, many writers reverse this distinction. **1.** On stringed and other instruments, 'tremolo' indicates the fast repetition of a single note, or the alternation of two notes. It may be regular in rhythm or unmeasured, the latter sometimes being referred to as 'tremolando'. The measured repetition of a given pitch has been used to create a mood of tension and excitement in music since the early Baroque period. **2.** More specifically, tremolo is an ornament used by 17th- and 18th-century string players. The note is lightly repeated within a single bowstroke, the separations being scarcely noticeable. The sign is a wavy line above a long note, or above a series of repeated notes. **3.** In 17th-century vocal music, tremolo is an ornament consisting of a fast reiteration of one note. Confusingly, the contemporary Italian term was 'trillo', whereas 'tremolo' at the time meant a type of trill.

trepak. A Cossack dance in rapid duple time.

trg., trge. Abbreviations for 'triangle'.

triad. A chord of three notes, consisting in its most basic form of a 'root' and the notes a 3rd and a 5th above it, forming two superimposed 3rds (Ex. 1*a*). If the lower 3rd is major and the upper one minor, the triad is described as major (Ex. 1*a*); if the lower is minor and the upper major, the triad is minor (Ex. 1*b*); if both are major, the triad is augmented (Ex. 1*c*); if both are minor the triad is diminished (Ex. 1*d*). In practice, triads frequently occur in inversions (Ex. 2*a*) and in open positions (Ex. 2*b*).

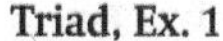

Triad, Ex. 1

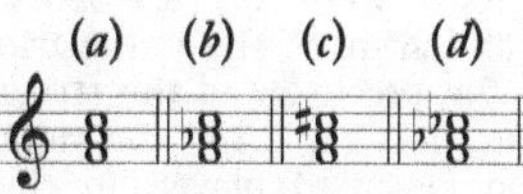

Ex. 2

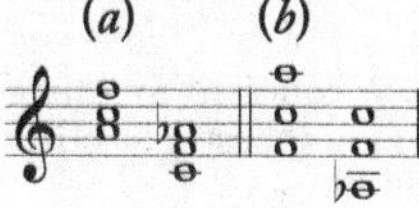

tricinium (Lat.). A composition for three voices or instruments. The term was most often used in Germany in the 16th century.

trill [shake] (Fr.: *cadence*, *tremblement*, *trille*; Ger.: *Triller*; It.: *trillo*). An ornament consisting in rapid alternation of the main (notated) pitch with a note usually a semitone or tone above it. The device is normally slurred, and applied particularly to cadences. While the effect is largely to be found in instrumental music, it has long been regarded as part of a virtuoso vocal technique.

The trill is found throughout music of the 18th century and before, particularly in early keyboard works. Its use in that context varies greatly, as indeed does the manner in which it is notated. Among the signs used are *tr*, 𝆖, and +, all appearing over the note in question. Of these signs, the first has been standard since the beginning of the 18th century. A flat, natural, or sharp sign can be placed above it, to indicate a chromatic inflection of the upper note. A wavy line may also define the extent, length, and location of the trill (see Ex. 1).

The method of performance is variable in a number of ways, and the beginning and ending of the trill have been treated differently over time. The modern trill begins on the main, or lower, note and often ends without suffix, unless specifically indicated (see Ex. 2; note that Ex. 2*d* approximates to a turn; see turn, Ex. 2*c*). The late Baroque trill, however, begins on the upper note. This may be extended into an *appoggiatura (sometimes notated 𝆖), and more complex openings are possible. Two types of ending are typical: a single note of anticipation (separated from the trill) and the turn (incorporated into the rhythm of the trill). The sign 𝆖 also indicates the turned ending. Although Baroque composers may use the extended sign (𝆖) this does not generally imply only a

Trill, Ex. 1

Ex. 2

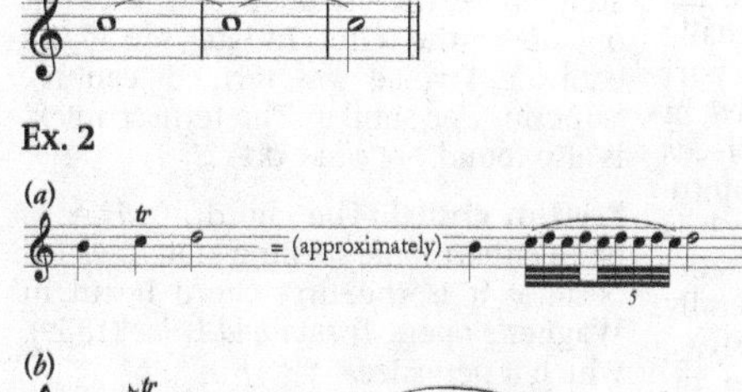

half-trill. In music of the Classical period (up to Beethoven), an upper-note start is expected. Increasingly the suffix (usually a turn) was notated in full size, or as grace notes. The present conception of the trill, starting on the main note, dates from *c.*1830.

Trinklied (Ger.). 'Drinking-song'.

trio (Ger.: *Terzett*; It.: *terzetto*). **1.** An ensemble of three singers or instrumentalists, or music written for it. The 17th- and 18th-century *trio sonata was a favourite chamber ensemble, using two treble instruments and one bass, with a keyboard or lute continuo to fill in the harmony. **2.** The central part of a *minuet or *scherzo (in a sonata, symphony, or similar work). In the 17th century it was usual, especially in France, to compose two dances to be performed in alternation: they would frequently be scored to provide contrasts, for example a minuet for strings in four or five parts would be followed by one for wind in three parts (hence the name 'trio' for this second dance). This practice led to the common 18th-century arrangement of minuet-trio-minuet (repeat of the first). In 18th- and 19th-century sonatas and symphonies the trio, which formed a part of the third movement, retained the lighter contrasting texture, in orchestral works often involving prominent woodwind. In late 19th-century orchestral works, trio sections are often in dance rhythms and styles. A trio section is normally followed by a repeat of the first part of the movement, usually modified in some way or with a coda. In some pieces the trio section may be briefly recapitulated. The central section of a march is also known as a trio, on the same principle of contrast: it, too, is generally more melodious. **3.** In organ music, a piece (or a section) to be played on manuals and pedals, each in a different registration.

trio sonata. A sonata for two melody instruments and continuo, the most important instrumental form in Baroque *chamber music. The majority were for two violins, cello, and basso continuo, but some were for two oboes, bassoon, and continuo. The string trio sonata was the precursor of the string *quartet, the viola replacing the right hand of the keyboard player. In the mid-17th century two types appeared, the *sonata da camera* and the *sonata da chiesa*. *See* SONATA.

triple concerto. A concerto for three solo instruments and orchestra or other instrumental ensemble.

triple counterpoint. *See* INVERTIBLE COUNTERPOINT.

triplet. Three notes that are to be performed in the time of two; they are indicated by the figure '3' placed above or below the three notes (see Ex. 1).

Ex. 1

triple time. *See* TIME SIGNATURE.

triple tonguing. *See* TONGUING.

triplum (Lat.). **1.** In three parts; used in medieval polyphony to describe a composition for three voices, e.g. *organum triplum*. **2.** In 13th- and 14th-century polyphony, the 'third' voice part in organum or a motet, i.e. the voice immediately above the *duplum and next but one above the tenor. In later music the equivalent voice was termed 'cantus', 'superius', or similar. The term 'triplex' is also found. *See also* PART, 1.

Tristan chord. The chord *f-b-d♯'-g♯'*, or an enharmonic spelling of it, so called because it is the first chord heard in Wagner's opera *Tristan und Isolde* (1859), which it pervades.

triste (Fr., It.). 'Sad'; *tristement*, *tristamente*, 'sadly'.

tritone (Lat.: *tritonus*). An interval of three whole tones, i.e. the augmented 4th (C–F♯) or diminished 5th (C–G♭), exactly half an octave. It acquired the nickname *diabolus in musica* ('the devil in music') because of its harmonic instability. The tritone forms part of both the diminished and the dominant 7th; it is therefore important in weakening tonality and assisting modulation, and for affirming the tonality, particularly at cadences. It has continued to be associated with evil, especially in Romantic opera.

tritus. *See* MODE.

trobairitz. A female *troubadour.

tronca (It.). 'Cut off', i.e. accented.

trop (Fr.). 'Too much'.

trope (Lat.: *tropus*, from Gk. *tropos*, 'turn (of phrase)'). A textual or musical addition (or both) to plainchant. Used by rhetoricians to denote a figure of speech, the word was also used by ancient and medieval music theorists to mean 'octave species'. The production of tropes was large, particularly from the 10th century to the 12th. Supplementary phrases were provided for three of the Proper chants of the Mass (the introit, offertory, and communion) and for the Kyrie, Gloria, Sanctus, and Agnus Dei chants from the Ordinary. Some examples of tropes for Lessons are also known, the most common being introit tropes. Other examples of tropes are the sequence (*see* SEQUENCE, 2) and organum, sometimes regarded as a sort of 'vertical troping' of plainchant.

troppo (It.). 'Too much'; *allegro ma non troppo*, 'quick but not too quick'.

troubadours (Fr.). Poet-musicians, often of noble birth, of 12th- and 13th-century Occitania (principally southern France and north-east Spain). The written legacy of the troubadours is one of the earliest substantial literatures of western Europe. To the troubadours, poetry was inextricably linked with music, since it was through performance in song, not in writing, that their compositions were communicated. Only towards the end of the tradition were any of the songs written down with musical notation. Troubadour song served as the starting-point for the songs of the *trouvères and the *Minnesinger. Its subject matter, though broad, is dominated by the idea of 'courtly' or idealized love.

trouvères (Fr.). Poet-musicians of late 12th- and 13th-century northern France, successors to the *troubadours, and linguistically defined by the use of non-standardized forms of northern French (the 'langue d'oïl'). They were principally non-literate composers and performers who invented and transmitted songs within an oral tradition. Many of their songs, however, were collected in manuscripts by professional scribes, and a few late trouvères may even have written down their own works, often with musical notation. The repertory of trouvère song thus survives reasonably intact. Like troubadours, trouvères could be of royal or noble birth, or rise up from the ranks of minstrelsy.

Although a wide range of subject matter occurs in trouvère song, the repertory is dominated by the theme of idealized love. (Other favourite topics include the Crusades, and religious belief.) Poetical genres and forms tend to be highly conventionalized. Some, including the *chanson d'amour* and **jeu-parti* (debate song), evoke the elegance, eloquence, and wit of courtly exchange. Others, such as the *chanson de toile* (weaving song) and the *pastourelle*, hint at popular traditions. Cross-reference between songs underpins the entire repertory; some songs additionally make use of *refrains—musico-literary tags of uncertain origin, many of which also occur in 13th-century *motets.

t.s. Abbreviation for *tasto solo* (*see* TASTO, 1).

tucket. A term mostly found in stage directions from the late 16th and the 17th centuries, particularly in the works of Shakespeare and his contemporaries. The word appears to be an anglicization of *toccata (though its origins may go back further), and describes a flourish of trumpets or drums. *See also* SENNET.

tuning. The process of regulating the pitch of an instrument according to a system of *temperament.

tuning-fork. A two-pronged device of tempered steel that produces a fixed pitch to which instruments may be tuned. The fork is struck so that it vibrates; holding the stem against a wooden surface causes the surface to vibrate in sympathy as a soundboard, amplifying the sound.

turca, alla. *See* ALLA TURCA.

Turkish music. *See* JANISSARY MUSIC.

Turmmusik (Ger.). 'Tower music', i.e. music played from the towers of churches, town halls, etc. by town musicians (**Stadtpfeifer*) in Germany, chiefly in the 17th century.

turn (Fr.: *doublé*; Ger.: *Doppelschlag*; It.: *gruppetto*). An ornament found chiefly in music of the 17th–19th centuries. It consists essentially of four notes encircling the main (notated) note: note above, main note, note below, and main note. Rhythmic variations are numerous and are often left to the performer's discretion, being heavily reliant on compositional context. The graphic sign is as shown in Exx. 1 and 2; in modern

Ex. 1

Ex. 2

practice (e.g. with the trill) chromatic inflections of the upper or lower note, or both, are indicated by sharp or flat signs placed above or below the turn sign as appropriate (see Ex. 2*d*).

The turn sign may be placed directly above a note, as was usual in the Baroque period (Ex. 1), or (especially from the Classical era onwards) it may be written, and the turn played, between two notes (Ex. 2). Ex. 2*c* is also suitable in music of the latter period when the sign is placed above the note. Turns are sometimes written into the score as small notes, but many 19th-century composers wrote them in full-size notation, perhaps to remove any rhythmic ambiguity. An inverted turn, indicated by ∽, ≀, or ⁓, simply reverses the direction (Ex. 3).

Ex. 3

turque (Fr., 'Turkish'). *See* JANISSARY MUSIC.

Tusch (Ger.). A 'fanfare' played on brass instruments. The term may be related etymologically to *tucket.

tutto, tutta, tutti, tutte (It.). 'All'; *tutte le corde*, 'all the strings', i.e. in piano playing, remove the *una corda* pedal. In orchestral and choral music, passages marked 'tutti' are for the whole ensemble (in contrast to those for one or more soloists, or for a small group).

twelve-note music (Eng.; Amer.: 12-note music). Music in which all 12 notes of the chromatic scale have equal importance—that is, music which is not in any key or mode and thus may be described as 'atonal'. The term has also been used for all serial music, or alternatively for serial music that follows the principles established by Schoenberg. *See* ATONALITY; SERIALISM.

twelve-note scale (Eng.; Amer.: 12-tone scale). The chromatic scale of 12 equal notes, as used in *twelve-note music. *See also* SCALE.

über (Ger.). 'Over', 'above', 'across'; *überblasen*, 'to overblow'; *Übergang, Überleitung*, 'transition', 'bridge passage'; *übergreifen*, 'to cross the hands' in piano playing; *übertragen*, to transcribe.

Übung (Ger.). *'Exercise', 'study'.

uguale (It.). 'Equal'; *ugualmente*, 'equally'.

Umfang (Ger.). *'Compass', 'range'.

Umkehrung (Ger.). 'Turning round', 'reversal', i.e. *inversion.

Umstimmung (Ger., 'tuning to another pitch'). *See* SCORDATURA.

una corda (It.). In piano playing, an instruction to depress the 'soft' pedal; it is cancelled by *tre corde* ('three strings') or *tutte le corde* ('all the strings').

unequal voices. A term given to a mixture of male and female voices; *see also* EQUAL VOICES.

unessential note. *See* ESSENTIAL NOTE.

ungebunden (Ger.). **1.** 'Free', 'unconstrained'. **2.** Of keyboard and stringed instruments, 'unfretted'.

ungerader Takt (Ger.). 'Uneven (triple) time'.

unison (Fr.: *unisson*; Ger.: *Einklang, Prime*; It.: *prima*). **1.** The simultaneous performance of the same line of music by various instruments or voices, or by a whole choir or orchestra; this may be at exactly the same pitch or in a different octave. The direction is sometimes given as *all'unisono*. **2.** The *'interval' formed between the same two notes.

uniti (It.). 'United', 'together'; it is usually used to revoke a direction such as **divisi*.

unmerklich (Ger.). 'Imperceptible'.

un peu (Fr.), **un poco** (It.). *See* POCO.

unruhig (Ger.). 'Restless'.

unter (Ger.). 'Under', 'below'; *Unterdominante*, subdominant; *Unterklavier*, lower manual; *Unterstimme*, lower or lowest voice; *Unterwerk*, choir organ.

upbeat [anacrusis] (Fr.: *anacruse*; Ger.: *Auftakt*). The 'weak' beat of the bar which anticipates the first, 'strong' beat of the following bar, or *downbeat.

upper mordent. *See* MORDENT.

upper partials. Constituents of the notes of the *harmonic series other than the main (fundamental) note, or first partial.

Urlinie. In *Schenkerian analysis, the stepwise-descending upper line in the fundamental structure (*Ursatz*) of tonal masterworks.

Ursatz. In *Schenkerian analysis, the two-voice 'fundamental structure' of tonal masterworks.

Urtext (Ger., 'original text'). A term used to describe a modern edition of music which embodies the composer's original intent with minimal editorial intervention.

ut. The first note of the scale according to the *solmization system. In the 17th century *ut* was replaced by the more singable *do* (in French and Italian usage), or *doh* (in the Tonic Sol-fa system). The French retain *ut* and the Italians use *do* to refer, on the fixed-*doh* principle, to the note C, in whichever scale it occurs. *See also* TONIC SOL-FA; HEXACHORD.

v. 1. Abbreviation for 'violin' (also found as v°, vln, or vn). **2.** Abbreviation for *voci* (It.), 'voices'.

va (It.). **1.** 'Go on', 'goes on', i.e. 'continue', 'continues', e.g. *va diminuendo*, 'go on getting quieter'. **2.** Abbreviation for 'viola' (also found as vla).

vaghezza, con (It.). 'With longing', 'with charm'.

valse (Fr.). *'Waltz'.

vamping. Improvising a simple, harmonized piano accompaniment, usually of octaves in the left hand alternating with chords in the right.

variation form. A form in which a self-contained theme is repeated and changed in some way with each successive statement. Variations may be continuous, as in *ostinato movements, or discrete, as in *strophic variations. The number and type of variations are not fixed. Many composers have grouped individual variations to create larger-scale musical forms and rhetorical patterns. Although all musical parameters can be subjected to variation processes, the repertory is dominated by a small number of types:

(*a*) cantus firmus or constant melody, in which the melody remains constant while other parameters change;

(*b*) constant bass or ostinato, in which the bass pattern remains constant (e.g. *ground bass, *passacaglia, and *chaconne);

(*c*) fixed harmony, in which the harmonic framework of the theme remains constant (e.g. variations on the **folia* and the **romanesca*);

(*d*) melodic outline, in which the melodic shape of the theme is either decorated with additional notes or replaced by a paraphrase of the original: the most common variation type in the late 18th and the 19th centuries;

(*e*) formal outline, in which the form and phrase structure of the theme are the only elements to remain constant;

(*f*) characteristic variations, in which elements of theme are reworked in different genres and types;

(*g*) fantasia variations, in which all parameters can be subjected to radical change though a narrative structure may shape the work;

(*h*) serial variations, in which the note row forms the theme for the variations.

See also CHACONNE; CHORALE VARIATIONS; DIVISIONS, 2; DOUBLE, 3; FOLIA; GROUND BASS; PASSACAGLIA; ROMANESCA; STROPHIC VARIATIONS.

variato, variata (It.). 'Varied'.

variazione, variazioni (It.). 'Variation', 'variations'. *See* VARIATION FORM.

vaudeville. 1. Two French 16th-century song types bear names that could have been corrupted to form 'vaudeville': the *val* (or *vau*) *de vire*, a popular song concerning love, drinking, and satire on topical matters, from the valley of the Vire river in Normandy; and the *voix de ville*, a courtly song that may have developed in response to the popular *vau de vire*. In the 17th and 18th centuries, vaudevilles were usually concerned with satire on political and courtly matters. **2.** In the USA the term was used in the 1880s for a variety show, similar to the much earlier British *music hall, from which it partly developed; it featured singers, dancers, comedians, and acrobats.

vc, vcl. Abbreviations for 'violoncello' (also found as vlc).

velato, velata (It.). 'Veiled', 'misty'.

veloce, velocemente (It.). 'Fast', 'quickly'; *con velocità*, 'with speed'.

Venite (Lat., 'Come'). Psalm 94 (Psalm 95 in the Hebrew), called the invitatory. In the Roman rite it is sung with a variable antiphon as the opening chant of Matins. The Anglican Church suppressed the antiphon but retained the psalm in English translation in its *Book of Common Prayer* as a fixed prelude to the morning psalms.

vent (Fr.). 'Wind'; *instruments à vent*, 'wind instruments'.

Veränderungen (Ger.). 'Variations'. A term sometimes used instead of *Variationen*.

verbunkos (from Ger. *Werbung*, 'enlistment'). A Hungarian dance, used from *c.*1780 to attract recruits into the army. It survived as a ceremonial dance and consisted of two or more sections, similar to those of the *csárdás, some in the style of a slow introduction (*lassú*), others fast and wild (*friss*). The *verbunkos* form was used by several 19th-century Hungarian composers.

verdoppeln (Ger.). 'To double'; *verdoppelt*, 'doubled'; *Verdoppelung*, 'doubling', 'duplication'.

Vergrösserung (Ger.). *'Augmentation'.

verhallend (Ger.). 'Dying away'.

verismo (It., 'realism'). A movement in Italian literature that influenced the composition of opera at the end of the 19th century and beginning of the 20th. It is characterized by the true-to-life portrayal of rural or urban poverty and often displays a strong regional character introducing songs and dances typical of the area. Mascagni's *Cavalleria rusticana* (1890) and Leoncavallo's *Pagliacci* (1892) are among the best-known operas in the tradition.

Verkleinerung, Verkürzung (Ger.). *'Diminution'.

verlierend, verlöschend (Ger.). 'Dying away', 'extinguishing'.

vermindert (Ger.). 'Diminished'.

verschwindend (Ger.). 'Disappearing', 'fading away'.

verse (Fr.: *vers*; Ger.: *Vers*; It.: *verso*; Lat.: *versus*). **1.** In poetry, a metrical line, or a group of a specific number of such lines. **2.** In plainchant, a verse of a psalm or (in responsorial forms of chant) a verse sung by a soloist, as opposed to the *respond or *response sung by the choir or congregation. The verses are usually marked V or ℣. *See* PSALMODY. A continuation of the practice of alternation can be found in the *verse anthem.

verse anthem. An *anthem in which one or more solo voices are contrasted with the full choir, as opposed to a 'full anthem' for choir without soloists. The earliest examples date from the later 16th century. The sections for soloists are oftened headed 'Verse', while those for the whole choir are headed 'Full'.

verset. A term (a diminutive of 'verse') applied in the Roman rite to a brief organ improvisation or composed piece used to replace a sung verse from a hymn, psalm, or other liturgical item, the text of which is instead recited silently by the choir. The genre reached a peak in Italy and France in the 17th century. The popularity of *messes en *noëls* in the 18th and 19th centuries ensured the survival of the 'organ mass' in France: the organist would base his versets on popular Christmas carols.

Verzierungen (Ger.). *'Ornaments'.

via (It.). 'Away'; *via sordini*, 'remove mutes'.

vibrato (It., 'shaken'; from Lat. *vibrare*). A wavering of pitch used to enrich and intensify the tone of a voice or instrument; it is practised in particular by wind players, string players, and singers. The technique is held to be an important constituent of a competent player's or singer's tone. In this form (often described as 'continuous vibrato') it has been in currency since the beginning of the 20th century, having been made popular by such players as Fritz Kreisler. In consequence, the *senza vibrato* tone has become a special effect in contemporary music. Before the 20th century vibrato was regarded as an ornament to be applied sparingly, and often discreetly, to long note-values or particularly expressive passages, or both; for many writers of vocal texts, 'vibrato' was interchangeable with *'tremolo'. Other terms used to indicate this wavering in pitch include 'ondulation' and 'close shake'.

Viertelton (Ger.). *'Quarter-tone'.

vif, vive (Fr.). 'Lively', 'fast'; *vivement*, 'briskly'.

vigoroso (It.). 'Vigorous', 'strong'.

villancico (Sp.). A variety of Spanish secular poetry current in the second half of the 15th century, generally of a pastoral or amorous nature and often set to music as a popular song. The poetic form was closely related to that of the Italian **ballata* and the French **virelai*: several stanzas (*coplas*) connected by a refrain (*estribillo*), each *copla* being divided into two sections, *mudanzas* and *vuelta*. Many three- and four-part villancicos are found in the great Spanish songbooks of the late 15th and early 16th centuries. By the late 16th century the sacred villancico had begun to predominate; such works were frequently performed in services and processions at Christmas ('villancico' has in modern times come to mean 'Christmas carol') and other festivals. The villancico developed into a large-scale composition, often with narrative or dramatic elements (sometimes including characters singing in dialect), and emphasizing contrasting sonorities including polychoral writing, solos and duets, and obbligato instrumental parts.

villanella (It.) [villanesca, canzone villanesca alla napolitana, canzone napolitana, etc.]. A three- or four-voice strophic song, setting comic or rustic texts in the Neapolitan dialect, that became popular in the mid-16th century. Musically it was characterized by its 'ungrammatical' use of consecutive 5ths, perhaps caricaturing the elegant harmony of the madrigal. The text-setting was generally syllabic, the texture mainly homophonic, and a new musical phrase was used for each line of verse, with the opening and closing lines often repeated. Its popularity spread throughout Italy and to Germany and England. From the 1570s the villanella grew more respectable, becoming virtually a small-scale madrigal. The term *'canzonetta' was often applied to such pieces, and the distinction between the two forms became less clear-cut.

villotta. A form of lighthearted song, based on popular tunes and akin to the *villanella, that originated in Venice and flourished in Italy from *c*.1520. The origins of the term lie in the north Italian dialect word *vilòte* ('peasant'). The villotta was generally for four voices, the popular or folk tune on which it was based often placed in the tenor. The texts set were usually rustic, often crude, and comic and satirical. The settings alternate chordal declamatory and more imitative writing, and sometimes have a 'fa-la' refrain.

virelai (Fr.). One of the three standard poetic forms used for 14th- and 15th-century chansons (*see also* BALLADE; RONDEAU); its precise origins are unclear but its development is linked to that of the *ballade*. The musical setting is in two clear sections (a and b). To the first is allocated the refrain (the opening and closing group of lines) and the third group of lines, which has the same structure. The second musical section, heard twice, carries the second group of lines. The resulting musical form is AbbaA (capitals indicate the refrain). Although some later 14th-century *virelais* had three stanzas, most seem to have had only one or two.

virtuoso (It., 'exceptional performer'). The term originally referred to several types of musician: performers, composers, and even theorists. By the later 18th century, however, it was generally used to dignify a singer or instrumentalist of great talent ('virtuosa' if the person was female). In the 19th century and later the term was sometimes used to describe a performer whose talent was 'merely' technical.

vite, vitement (Fr.). 'Quick', 'quickly'.

vivace (It.). 'Lively', 'brisk'; *allegro vivace*, 'faster than allegro'; *vivacetto*, 'rather lively'; *vivacissimo*, 'very lively'.

vivo, vivamente (It.). 'Lively', 'brisk'.

vl, vln. Abbreviations for 'violin'.

vla. Abbreviation for 'viola'.

vlc. Abbreviation for 'violoncello'.

vn. Abbreviation for 'violin'.

vocalise (Fr.; Ger.: *Vokalise*; It.: *vocalizzo*). A melody sung without text but to one or more vowel sounds. The term embraces vocal technical exercises (*see* SOLFEGGIO) and concert pieces.

vocal score. A *score showing all the vocal parts of a work on separate staves, with the orchestral parts reduced to a keyboard arrangement.

voce, voci (It.). 'Voice', 'voices'; *colla voce* ('with the voice') denotes that the accompanist should take the tempo from the soloist and follow him or her closely.

voce di petto, voce di testo (It.). *'Chest voice', 'head voice'.

voces aequales (Lat.). *'Equal voices'.

voci eguali (It.). *'Equal voices'.

voice exchange (Ger.: *Stimmtausch*). In polyphonic music, the alternation of phrases between two voices of equal range, a feature found frequently in 12th- and 13th-century music.

voice-leading (Amer.). *Part-writing; *see also* COUNTERPOINT. (In Schenkerian analysis, 'voice-leading' is used in preference to 'part-writing'.)

voice part. *See* PART, 1.

voilé (Fr.). 'Veiled', 'subdued'.

voix (Fr.). 'Voice'.

volante (It.). **1.** 'Flying', i.e. swift and light. **2.** In string playing, a kind of bowstroke where the bow bounces on the string to produce an effect similar to that of the *ricochet.

Volkslied (Ger.). 'Folksong'.

volkstümliches Lied (Ger.). 'Popular song' or 'folk-like song'. Lieder in a style akin to folksong, with simple accompaniment and an unembellished vocal line, were first written in Germany during the late 18th century.

volonté (Fr.). 'Will'; *à volonté*, 'at will', i.e. *ad *libitum*.

volta (It.). **1** (from *voltare*, 'to turn', 'to turn round'). A quick dance, popular in France from the 1550s; it was usually in triple time and resembled the *galliard. The name derives from one of the movements of the dance, in which the woman is lifted by her partner while turning round. It gained favour in England and Germany towards the beginning of the 17th century. It became a popular instrumental form in its own right, and English virginal and lute pieces are found with the title 'Lavolta'. *See also* WALTZ. **2.** *See* DOUBLE BAR; OUVERT AND CLOS.

volti (It.). 'Turn', 'turn over'; *volti subito*, 'turn over quickly', often found at the bottom of pages in orchestral parts. It is abbreviated *v.s.*

voluntary. A piece, written or improvised, played by the organist before, during, or after a church service. 16th- and 17th-century English composers used the term interchangeably with 'verse' or 'fancy'. In the 18th century the form became standardized as a slow introduction followed by an Allegro in concerto or fugal style.

vorbereiten (Ger.). 'Prepare'; the term is used in organ music, often in the form *bereite vor*, 'prepare for', followed by a particular stop.

vorgetragen (Ger.). 'Brought out', i.e. prominent.

Vorhalt (Ger.). **1.** A *suspension (*vorbereiteter Vorhalt*). **2.** An *appoggiatura (*freier Vorhalt*).

Vorschlag (Ger.). An *appoggiatura; *kurzer Vorschlag*, 'short appoggiatura'; *langer Vorschlag*, 'long appoggiatura'.

Vorspiel (Ger.). *'Prelude'.

Vortrag (Ger.). 'Performance', 'execution', or 'recital'; *Vortragsstück*, a virtuoso showpiece; *Vortragzeichen*, expression marks; *vortragen*, 'to perform', or 'to bring into prominence', 'to emphasize'.

vorwärts (Ger.). 'Forward'; *vorwärts gehen*, 'progress', 'move on', i.e. faster.

Vorzeichnung (Ger.). 'Signature'; sometimes time signature and key signature are specified as *Taktvorzeichnung* and *Tonartvorzeichnung* respectively.

vox principalis, vox organalis (Lat.). In *organum, respectively the 'principal voice' (i.e. the pre-existing part used as a basis for polyphony) and the composed second voice.

v.s. Abbreviation for *volti subito*, 'turn over quickly'.

vuoto, vuota (It.). 'Empty'; *corda vuota*, 'open string'.

wachsend (Ger.). 'Growing', 'increasing', i.e. *crescendo.*

wait [wayte]. Originally, a watchman; later, a civic minstrel. In the 13th and 14th centuries watchmen sounded the hours and used a type of shawm, also known as a wait- or wayte-pipe. In the 15th and 16th centuries civic minstrels were also called waits (they were equivalent to the German **Stadtpfeifer*). Many were good musicians who could play a variety of 'outdoor', loud-toned (*haut*) instruments (shawm, slide trumpet, sackbut, etc.); later they also sang and used quieter instruments (recorder, cornett, viol). They attended civic functions and ceremonial occasions. The term 'wait' survived well into the 19th century to describe street musicians who performed Christmas songs and music. *See also* MINSTREL.

walking bass. A type of bass line, often found in Baroque compositions, which moves continuously and with purposeful regularity, setting off the more sustained melodic writing above.

waltz (Fr.: *valse*; Ger.: *Walzer*). A dance in 3/4 time which became popular in the last quarter of the 18th century; it gradually replaced the stately and artificial minuet. Its origins remain obscure but, with its heavy accent on the first beat of the bar, it must have been influenced by the Austrian *ländler. Classical and Romantic composers exploited the waltz in every possible way: there are numerous examples for piano, and the genre appeared in operas, operettas, and ballets. The waltz encouraged the emergence of specialist composers of dance music, particularly in Vienna, where its greatest exponent was the younger Johann Strauss. In its classical form, the Viennese waltz featured a slight anticipation of the second beat of the bar known as the *Atempause* (literally 'breathing-space'), which gives a distinctive lilt to the playing. The French waltz returned the emphasis to the first beat, while the 'English' or 'Boston' waltz went back to a more even emphasis on all three beats.

Walze (Ger.). A term used in the 18th century for conventional musical figures such as the *Alberti bass.

Walzer (Ger.). *'Waltz'.

Wärme, mit (Ger.). 'With warmth', 'passionately'.

wehmütig (Ger.). 'Sorrowful', 'melancholic'.

weich (Ger.). 'Soft', 'delicate', 'tender'.

Weihnachtslied (Ger.). 'Christmas song', i.e. *carol.

Weinlied (Ger.). 'Drinking-song'.

wenig (Ger.). 'Little', 'slightly'; *ein wenig*, 'a little'; *weniger*, 'less'.

whole note (Amer.). *Semibreve.

whole tone. An *interval of two semitones.

whole-tone scale (Ger.: *Ganztonleiter*). A scale of six whole tones. *See* SCALE.

Wiegenlied (Ger.). 'Cradle-song', 'lullaby'; *see* BERCEUSE.

wind quintet. An ensemble of five wind instrumentalists, or music written for it. It normally consists of flute, oboe, clarinet, bassoon, and horn.

Wirbel (Ger.). 'Drumroll'.

wolf note. 1. A perfect 5th that is noticeably out of tune with the others in a given *temperament, so that it 'howls'; *see also* COMMA. **2.** An unstable note found on some stringed instruments, usually at the main wood resonance frequency.

WoO. Abbreviation for *Werk ohne Opuszahl* (Ger.), 'work without opus number'. The term is common in references to Beethoven's music, since a number of his works were not published in his lifetime. *See* OPUS.

word-painting. The musical depiction of the text of a vocal work. Strictly speaking, 'word-painting' implies the focus on a single term—'love', 'death', 'joy', 'sorrow'—which stands out from a context that is musically portrayed in much less specific, decorative fashion, as in many 16th-century *madrigals. During the Renaissance and the Baroque period the sense in which music might imitate not only nature but also human thought and behaviour led to the establishment of certain patterns, like slow descending lines suggesting lament; these patterns came to be used for the purely instrumental evocation of certain emotional states.

word-setting. *See* TEXT-SETTING.

working out. The development section of a movement in *sonata form.

work song. A song performed usually by a group during and in time to the actions of work. A heavily rhythmic nature, an open form, and a call-and-response structure are typical. *See also* SHANTY.

world music. Used initially by ethnomusicologists to refer to the diverse local musics of the world, 'world music' has also become a term for any commercially available music of non-Western origin, and for musics of ethnic minorities; it is also applied to contemporary fusions or collaborations with local 'traditional' or 'roots' musics and Western pop and rock musics.

Wotquenne. Abbreviation for the standard *thematic catalogue of the works of C. P. E. Bach drawn up by the Belgian bibliographer Alfred Wotquenne (1867–1939). Bach's works are often referred to by Wotquenne number, usually further abbreviated to WQ.

WQ. Abbreviation for *Wotquenne.

würdig (Ger.). 'Stately', 'dignified'.

wütend (Ger.). 'Raging', 'furious'; also *wütig*.

xácara (Sp., Port.). *See* JÁCARA.

X

yodel (Ger.: *Jodel*). A type of singing characterized by frequent alternation between low and high (including falsetto) registers, using vowel sounds rather than words. It is associated particularly with the Alpine areas of Austria and Switzerland, where solo and ensemble compositions are performed by virtuosos.

Zahlzeit (Ger.). 'Beat' (in the sense of 'beats in a bar'); *see* BEAT, 1.

zart (Ger.) 'Tender', 'delicate'; *zärtlich*, 'tenderly'.

zarzuela. Traditional Spanish opera. For over 300 years the term has been applied indiscriminately to Baroque semi-operas, three-act Romantic operas, short comic pieces, full-blown Viennese-style operettas, and musicals, written in Spain, Cuba, and elsewhere in the Spanish-speaking world. In most cases, spoken dialogue is an indispensable feature. The name probably came from the royal hunting-lodge, situated near Madrid in countryside thick with brambles (*zarzas*). The courtly Baroque zarzuela, a mixture of sophisticated verse drama, allegorical opera, popular song, and dance, remained in fashion for over 100 years until it was finally displaced by Italian opera. The zarzuela reappeared after 1850 in Madrid with the rise of Spanish nationalism. A distinctively national operatic style was created from the fusion of the traditional *tonadilla* and the old, aristocratic drama. Soon *género grande* ('large style' zarzuelas in three acts) gave way to *género chico* ('small style', one-act farces, often with social or political satire and containing less music). Over 10,000 zarzuelas were written in the hundred years after 1850. In the 20th century the zarzuela evolved with popular taste, though the mixture of spoken play and operatic music in roughly equal proportions remained.

Zeitmass (Ger.). *'Tempo'; *im ersten Zeitmass*, 'in tempo primo'.

ziemlich (Ger.). 'Rather'; e.g. *ziemlich schnell*, 'rather fast'.

zingarese, alla. *See* ALLA ZINGARESE.

zitternd (Ger.). 'Trembling', i.e. *tremolando*; *see* TREMOLO, 1.

zögernd (Ger.). 'Delaying', 'lingering', i.e. **rallentando*.

zoppa, alla. *See* ALLA ZOPPA.

zurückgehend (Ger.). 'Returning', i.e. resuming the original tempo; *zurückhaltend*, 'holding back', i.e. **rallentando*.

Zusammenschlag (Ger., 'together-stroke'). *Acciaccatura.

Zwischenspiel (Ger.). 'Interlude' or 'entr'acte'. Besides its use in connection with music for the stage, the term can denote the instrumental interludes between the stanzas of a vocal piece or the solo portions between the tutti sections of a concerto. It is also applied to episodes in fugue or rondo form, and to the organ interludes between stanzas of a congregational hymn.

zyklisch (Ger.). 'Cyclic'; *see* CYCLIC FORM.

OXFORD

Oxford Quick Reference

A Dictionary of Marketing
Charles Doyle

Covers traditional marketing techniques and theories alongside the latest concepts in over 2,000 clear and authoritative entries.

'Flick to any page [for] a lecture's worth of well thought through information'

Dan Germain, Head of Creative, innocent ltd

A Dictionary of Media and Communication
Daniel Chandler and Rod Munday

Provides over 2,200 authoritative entries on terms used in media and communication, from concepts and theories to technical terms, across subject areas that include advertising, digital culture, journalism, new media, radio studies, and telecommunications.

'a wonderful volume that is much more than a simple dictionary'

Professor Joshua Meyrowitz, University of New Hampshire

A Dictionary of Film Studies
Annette Kuhn and Guy Westwell

Features terms covering all aspects of film studies in 500 detailed entries, from theory and history to technical terms and practices.

A Dictionary of Journalism
Tony Harcup

Covers terminology relating to the practice, business, and technology of journalism, as well as its concepts and theories, organizations and institutions, publications, and key events.